Lecture Notes in Computer Science 5053

Commenced Publication in 1973
Founding and Former Series Editors:
Gerhard Goos, Juris Hartmanis, and Jan van Leeuwen

René Meier   Sotirios Terzis (Eds.)

Distributed Applications and Interoperable Systems

8th IFIP WG 6.1 International Conference, DAIS 2008
Oslo, Norway, June 4-6, 2008
Proceedings

 Springer

Volume Editors

René Meier
Trinity College Dublin
School of Computer Science and Statistics
Dublin 2, Ireland
E-mail: rene.meier@cs.tcd.ie

Sotirios Terzis
University of Strathclyde
Department of Computer and Information Science
Livingstone Tower, 26 Richmond Street, Glasgow, G1 1XH, UK
E-mail: Sotirios.Terzis@cis.strath.ac.uk

Library of Congress Control Number: 2008927527

CR Subject Classification (1998): D.2, C.2.4, I.2.11, D.4, H.4

LNCS Sublibrary: SL 3 – Information Systems and Application, incl. Internet/Web
and HCI

ISSN	0302-9743
ISBN-10	3-540-68639-8 Springer Berlin Heidelberg New York
ISBN-13	978-3-540-68639-2 Springer Berlin Heidelberg New York

Typesetting: Camera-ready by author, data conversion by Scientific Publishing Services, Chennai, India
Printed on acid-free paper   SPIN: 12275939   06/3180   5 4 3 2 1 0

Preface

This volume contains the proceedings of DAIS 2008, the 8th IFIP International Conference on Distributed Applications and Interoperable Systems. The conference was held in Oslo, Norway during June 4–6, 2008 as part of the DisCoTec (Distributed Object Techniques) federated conference, in conjunction with the 10th International Conference on Coordination Models and Languages (COORDINATION) and the 10th IFIP International Conference on Formal Methods for Open Object-Based Distributed Systems (FMOODS). The conference was sponsored by IFIP (International Federation for Information Processing) and was organized by the IFIP Working Group 6.1.

Distributed applications and interoperable systems have become an integral part of everyday living and hence part of the socio-economic ecosystem of our human environment. With such pervasive distribution of software systems across a multitude of heterogeneous environments and user domains, distributed applications must support seamless provision of services, as well as service evolution and adaptability to ensure long-term sustainability. This support must go beyond the provision of individual services in isolation, towards systems in which such services can interoperate and be integrated into the everyday environment catering for the changing needs of their users.

The conference papers aimed to address the following questions:

– How can our distributed applications integrate into global environments?
– How do we ensure the seamless provision of services in these global environments?
– How do we make our interoperable systems adaptable and evolvable in the face of widespread changes to their environments?
– How can distributed applications and interoperable systems capitalize and exploit future trends and the changing user demographic?

The conference program comprised research contributions addressing service orientation issues; quality of service (QoS) management and composition in service-oriented architectures; dependability and reliability issues for Web services, distributed real-time embedded issues, component-based systems and distributed applications; analysis and management of peer-to-peer overlays; the challenges of pervasive computing systems; dynamic adaptation in smart environments, peer-to-peer systems and Web services; model-driven design, development and instrumentation; protocols and interactions for components, Web services and gossip-based systems. This year, the technical program of DAIS drew from 66 submissions, accepting for presentation 19 research papers and 5 work-in-progress papers. All submitted papers were reviewed by at least three reviewers, coordinated by our International Program Committee. The conference program also included three keynote addresses, in conjunction with the other two DisCoTec conferences, from Alexander L. Wolf, Professor at the Department of Computing, Imperial College London, titled "New Uses of Simulation in Distributed Systems Engineering," Matt Welsh, Associate Professor of Computer Science at the School of Engineering and Applied Sciences, Harvard University, titled "Fiji: A Platform for Data-Intensive Sensor Network Applications," and Andrew Myers, Associate Professor at the Department of Computer Science, Cornell University, titled "Guiding Distributed Systems Synthesis with Language-Based Security Policies."

We would like to take this opportunity to thank the numerous people whose work made this conference possible. We wish to express our deepest gratitude to the authors of submitted papers, to all Program Committee members and external reviewers for their participation in the paper review process, to Hartmut König for publicity, to the DAIS Steering Committee for their advice, to the University of Oslo for hosting DisCoTec, and to Frank Eliassen and Einar Broch Johnsen for acting as the General Chairs of DisCoTec.

June 2008   René Meier
                                                                      Sotirios Terzis

Conference Committees and Organization

Executive Committee

Conference Chairs	Frank Eliassen (University of Oslo, Norway)
	Einar Broch Johnsen (University of Oslo, Norway)
Program Chairs	René Meier (Trinity College Dublin, Ireland)
	Sotirios Terzis (University of Strathclyde, UK)
Publicity Chair	Hartmut König (BTU Cottbus, Germany)

Steering Committee

Frank Eliassen	University of Oslo, Norway
Kurt Geihs	University of Kassel, Germany
Jadwiga Indulska	University of Queensland, Australia
Hartmut König	BTU Cottbus, Germany
Lea Kutvonen	University of Helsinki, Finland
Alberto Montresor	University of Trento, Italy
Elie Najm	TELECOM ParisTech, France
Kerry Raymond	Queensland University of Technology, Australia

Sponsoring Institutions

IFIP WG 6.1

Program Committee

N. Alonistioti	University of Athens, Greece
D. Bakken	Washington State University, USA
Y. Berbers	Katholieke Universiteit Leuven, Belgium
A. Beresford	University of Cambridge, UK
A. Beugnard	TELECOM Bretagne, France
G. Blair	Lancaster University, UK
A. Casimiro	University of Lisbon, Portugal
I. Demeure	TELECOM ParisTech, France
S. Dobson	University College Dublin, Ireland
D. Donsez	Université Joseph Fourier, France
N. Dulay	Imperial College London, UK
F. Eliassen	University of Oslo, Norway
P. Felber	Université de Neuchâtel, Switzerland

K. Geihs	University of Kassel, Germany
N. Georgantas	INRIA, France
R. Grønmo	SINTEF ICT, Norway
D. Hagimont	INP Toulouse, France
S. Hallsteinsen	SINTEF ICT, Norway
P. Herrmann	NTNU Trondheim, Norway
J. Indulska	University of Queensland, Australia
R. Kapitza	University of Erlangen-Nuremberg, Germany
H. König	BTU Cottbus, Germany
R. Kroeger	University of Applied Sciences, Wiesbaden, Germany
L. Kutvonen	University of Helsinki, Finland
W. Lamersdorf	University of Hamburg, Germany
M. Lawley	Queensland University of Technology, Australia
P. Linington	University of Kent, UK
C. Linnhoff-Popien	University of Munich, Germany
K. Lund	Norwegian Defence Research Establishment (FFI), Norway
R. Meier	Trinity College Dublin, Ireland
A. Montresor	University of Trento, Italy
E. Najm	TELECOM ParisTech, France
N. Narasimhan	Motorola Labs, USA
R. Oliveira	Universidade do Minho, Portugal
P. Pietzuch	Imperial College London, UK
A. Puder	San Francisco State University, USA
K. Raymond	Queensland University of Technology, Australia
D. Schmidt	Vanderbilt University, USA
T. Senivongse	Chulalongkorn University, Thailand
K. Sere	Åbo Akademi University, Finland
E. Tanter	University of Chile, Chile
S. Terzis	University of Strathclyde, UK

Additional Referees

D. Bade	F. Fuchs	M. Schiely
U. Bareth	H. Gjermundrod	M. Schmid
S. Bleul	P. Grace	A. Sousa
G. Brataas	X. Grehant	G. Treu
L. Braubach	I. Hamid	M. Wagner
J. Buisson	M. Ullah Khan	T. Weise
F. Campos	W. Maiden	D. Weiss
R. Cunningham	P.H. Meland	L. Wienhofen
I. Dionysiou	A. Opitz	R. Wishart
V.S. Wold Eide	L. Petre	S. Zaplata
R.I. Ferguson	A. Pokahr	
J. Fox	R. Rouvoy	

Table of Contents

Peer-to-Peer Overlays

Adaptation

Model-Driven Development

Components, Protocols and Interactions

Perasive Computing

iSOAMM: An Independent SOA Maturity Model

Christoph Rathfelder and Henning Groenda

FZI Research Center for Information Technology, Software Engineering
Haid-und-Neu-Straße 10-14, 76131 Karlsruhe, Germany
{rathfelder,groenda}@fzi.de

Abstract. The implementation of an enterprise-wide Service Oriented Architecture (SOA) is a complex task. In most cases, evolutional approaches are used to handle this complexity. Maturity models are a possibility to plan and control such an evolution as they allow evaluating the current maturity and identifying current shortcomings. In order to support an SOA implementation, maturity models should also support in the selection of the most adequate maturity level and the deduction of a roadmap to this level. Existing SOA maturity models provide only weak assistance with the selection of an adequate maturity level. Most of them are developed by vendors of SOA products and often used to promote their products. In this paper, we introduce our independent SOA Maturity Model (iSOAMM), which is independent of the used technologies and products. In addition to the impacts on IT systems, it reflects the implications on organizational structures and governance. Furthermore, the iSOAMM lists the challenges, benefits and risks associated with each maturity level. This enables enterprises to select the most adequate maturity level for them, which is not necessarily the highest one.

1 Introduction

The use of an SOA promises organizations to adapt their software more rapidly to changing business needs. A successful implementation of an SOA is not limited to IT systems and requires changes throughout the whole enterprise [1, 2]. In order to handle this complexity, it is appropriate to implement an enterprise-wide SOA step by step using evolutional approches [3]. These approaches can also aid enterprises upgrading an already implemented SOA.

Maturity models are a possibility to support the planning and controlling of such evolutional approaches. They can be used to assess the maturity and assist in improving the maturity as they provide the possibility to deduce a roadmap to a successful SOA implementation. The selection of the most adequate maturity level is an important part of developing a roadmap as the highest maturity level is not always the most suitable one for each enterprise. The benefits promised by a level have to be weighed against the costs to reach and maintain that level.

In order to ease the level selection, an SOA maturity model should exhibit levels, which are oriented at the capability of an SOA to support business processes. Additionally, it should also point out the benefits and costs that are associated with each maturity level. An SOA maturity model should furthermore be independent of the used technologies and products, as existing SOA implementations are based on a variety of technologies (e.g., CORBA, J2EE) [4, 5] and enterprises avoid to be dependent on a certain SOA vendor or product [6, 4]. Different case studies [7, 6] show that the success

R. Meier and S. Terzis (Eds.): DAIS 2008, LNCS 5053, pp. 1–15, 2008.

of an enterprise-wide SOA implementation is often affected by organizational structures and IT governance. Therefore, an SOA maturity model should also consider the necessary alterations within these domains.

Existing SOA maturity models were in most cases developed by SOA vendors (e.g., IBM, BEA, HP, or Oracle) and cannot deny a dependency on the respective products. Additionally, the vendors take the desire to reach the highest maturity level for granted. Therefore, they often neglect supporting an enterprise in the selection of the most *appropriate* maturity level.

The contribution of this paper is the 1) product and technology independent SOA Maturity Model (iSOAMM), which 2) considers technical as well as organizational aspects. 3) It eases the selection of the most adequate maturity level by pointing out the challenges, benefits, and risks associated with each level. This distinguishes the iSOAMM from other SOA maturity models. The maturity levels are aligned with the SOA's capabilities to support business processes. This means that an SOA with higher maturity possesses more features, which are useful within business processes.

The development of the iSOAMM is based on a sound literature review as well as the experiences we have gained within different SOA projects. One example of a large SOA project we are currently involved in is the "Karlsruher Integriertes Informations-Management" (KIM) [8]. Its aim is the implementation of a university-wide SOA which supports students as well as staff. In addition, we have taken several published SOA case studies (e.g., Deutsche Post [6,4,5], Credit Suisse [4,5], ABB [7], and Sparkassen Informatik [9]) into account. Furthermore, we evaluated a variety of articles, which document best practices, success factors, and experiences related to SOA implementations, as well as publications, which present new research results and open research questions. In order to validate the iSOAMM we evaluated the case studies and rated the maturity of documented SOA implementation.

This paper is structured as follows: Section 2 gives an overview of related work. Section 3 describes the different viewpoints that are used to define the maturity levels. Section 4 presents the requirements, which have to be satisfied for each maturity level. Section 5 points out the challenges, benefits, and risks associated with each maturity level. Section 6 presents the validation of the iSOAMM. Section 7 concludes the paper and provides an outlook to future work.

2   Related Work

Regarding the maturity of enterprise architectures the US Department of Commerce (DoC) has developed the Architecture Capability Maturity Model (ACMM) [10]. It differentiates nine evaluation categories. This granularity enables to identify areas that are more ahead or behind than others and eases the planning of the next steps to reach a higher overall maturity. The different categories of the ACMM reflect that it is insufficient to analyze the architecture of a software system only, as the maturity is also heavily influenced by the organizational structure of an enterprise. The ACMM is a general architecture maturity model. However, the ACMM does not consider the particularities of an SOA, such as dynamic adaptation through loose coupling of services, the consequences of higher business alignment, or reuse of services.

The most well-known maturity model for SOA is the New SOA Maturity Model (NSOAMM) [11] developed by Sonic Software, AmberPoint, BearingPoint, and Systinet. The NSOAMM is limited to WS-based SOA implementations. It does not consider areas like security, monitoring, and management of services. Especially in this model, a particularly high product dependency of the model is obvious. Furthermore, it neglects areas like organizational structure and governance.

The Oracle Maturity Model (OMM) [12] is divided into five maturity levels. Each level is split into eight categories, which cover the software architecture and infrastructure as well as governance, development, and enterprise structure. Additionally, a list of Key Indicators (KI) for each maturity level sorted by the categories is available in [13]. The OMM stipulates the use of WS-technology to implement an SOA. Furthermore, the support of user integration or automated business-to-business (B2B)-processes is not part of this model.

The Service Integration Maturity Model (SIMM) [14] was developed by IBM in 2005. It consists of seven maturity levels, whereas only the last four maturity levels consider services [15]. Comparable to the OMM, the SIMM is split into seven independent categories but the KI are not publicly available. IBM has externalized the SIMM to the Open Group at the beginning of 2007. The Open Group plans to enhance it and publish it as the Open Group Service Integration Maturity Model (OSIMM) [15]. Hence, this will lead to a publication of the KI in the near future.

Based on the SIMM and the NSOAMM, Meier defined the Combined SOA Maturity Model (CSOAMM) [16]. It is a scientific model, which is a common denominator of these two models enabling a comparison of the evaluation results. With this target in mind, he considers only the different maturity levels and neglects the more detailed subdivision into categories given by the SIMM. Additionally, all the non-technical indicators regarded in the SIMM are not taken into account.

3   Evaluation Viewpoints

As already mentioned, it is not sufficient to limit the evaluation of an SOA's maturity solely to technology-dependent criteria. The iSOAMM uses the following 5 viewpoints which regard technological as well organizational aspects. Overall, they cover the same domains as the SIMM, the OMM, and the ACMM.

1. **Service Architecture:** This viewpoint regards architectural layers of an SOA as well as services, their roles within business processes, and the interaction between them. The architecture can vary from providing an integration layer only to direct support of business processes with orchestrated services, user interaction, and B2B-cooperation.

2. **Infrastructure:** The loose coupling of services facilitated by an SOA supports a rapid adaptation to new business requirements. However, this high adaptability requires a stable infrastructure [6, 4]. It is therefore necessary to examine the infrastructure separate from the services, their composition, and their interaction. The SOA infrastructure mainly provides a common communication layer to all services [5, 4], which can be extended by additional components and layers (e.g., monitoring or security enforcement) [17, 4].

3. **Enterprise Structure:** SOA affects IT systems as well as business processes [2]. Changes which affect organizational structure and responsibilities of the different divisions are therefore required [7, 18, 5]. This viewpoint regards the different divisions of the company, which are affected by the SOA, as well as their responsibilities and duties.

4. **Service Development:** The design and implementation of services is a crucial aspect in the implementation of an SOA. As Cox and Kreger emphasize in [19], the development process of services needs to be adjusted and it is therefore regarded as a separate viewpoint. In general, an increase in maturity leads to a higher rate of automation within the development process [9, 6].

5. **Governance:** The successful implementation and usage of an SOA has to come along with an adaptation of the whole enterprise [1]. This viewpoint considers changes, rules, and guidelines that are relevant for the whole enterprise and are not limited to *Enterprise Structure* and *Service Development*. The topic of SOA governance is so large, that we can only present the main KI of this viewpoint for each maturity level.

4   iSOAMM Maturity Levels

After the introduction of the evaluation viewpoints, this section describes the five different maturity levels (*Trial SOA*, *Integrative SOA*, *Administered SOA*, *Cooperative SOA*, and *On Demand SOA*) and their Key Indicators (KI). In defiance of the iSOAMM's indepenence, the examples within the description of the maturity levels use web service (WS) standards as illustration since many implemented SOAs are based upon WS [20].

Note that each maturity level constitutes an enhancement of the previous level and hence bases on changes and features already introduced at lower levels. However, KI of lower levels can also be overruled, for example if the structure of an enterprise changes and organizational units are dissolved and replaced by others. Figure 1 gives an overview of iSOAMM and its subdivision into maturity levels and evaluation viewpoints. The different maturity levels are described in detail in the following subsections.

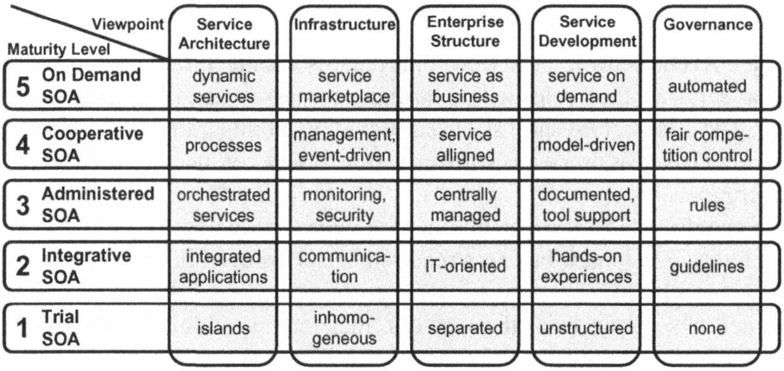

Viewpoint / Maturity Level	Service Architecture	Infrastructure	Enterprise Structure	Service Development	Governance
5 On Demand SOA	dynamic services	service marketplace	service as business	service on demand	automated
4 Cooperative SOA	processes	management, event-driven	service alligned	model-driven	fair competition control
3 Administered SOA	orchestrated services	monitoring, security	centrally managed	documented, tool support	rules
2 Integrative SOA	integrated applications	communication	IT-oriented	hands-on experiences	guidelines
1 Trial SOA	islands	inhomogeneous	separated	unstructured	none

Fig. 1. Maturity Levels

4.1   Level 1: Trial SOA

This level of maturity can be attested to small, mostly independent SOA projects. Within these projects, an enterprise gains first experiences with services. There is no common technology or fixed set of standards that is used within all projects.

Service Architecture. The point-to-point interfaces between legacy applications, which link a pair of applications, are substituted by services that can be used by more than one application. Due to the lack of standardization, it is possible that different services use incompatible technologies and standards. So this level is a collection of miscellaneous service islands rather than a real service architecture.

Infrastructure. Due to the independency of the small SOA projects, it is likely that different communication systems and standards are chosen. This inhomogeneous infrastructure often leads to incompatible service islands.

Enterprise Structure. The enterprise structure is characterized by a strict separation into independent business departments. Each department has its own application landscape which is developed and maintained by a separate IT section. Cooperation across business unit borders is very rare.

Service Development. The development of services is unstructured and done independently for each SOA project. In most cases, the purpose is to gain experience and develop best practices and guidelines for the implementation of an enterprise-wide SOA.

Governance. Early SOA projects are mainly initiated by IT departments, which are responsible for the integration of diverse applications. SOA is therefore often regarded as a pure IT project, which only marginally affects other business units. This is usually accompanied by a lack of support of SOA projects by the top management of the enterprise.

4.2   Level 2: Integrative SOA

The experience gained in SOA projects at the previous level or drawn from best practice reports is used to select an adequate infrastructural basis for the enterprise. The target of SOAs at this maturity level is mainly the integration of systems in the IT landscape and the realization of Enterprise Application Integration (EAI) [21].

Service Architecture. The different standards and technologies used in the previous maturity level are substituted by a common Service Bus (SB) [4]. The implementation of standardized service interfaces leads to a common high level Application Programming Interface (API), which can be used by frontend applications to access different backend systems [9].

Infrastructure. The common infrastructure represents the backbone of an SOA. Hence, the requirements in terms of scalability, reliability, availability, and performance that are imposed on the SB are very high [4]. Depending on the needs of an enterprise, a SB is built upon quite different technologies and standards. For example, Credit Suisse uses CORBA within their SB [4], Sparkassen Informatik uses WS technology [9], and the SB of Deutsche Post is based on J2EE technology [5]. The SB additionally provides logical addressing of services. This allows changing the physical location of a service.

Enterprise Structure. The cooperation between different business units increases in comparison to the previous maturity level. The major alteration is the introduction of an SOA team. It is an independent group of IT experts, which is the contact point for all business units regarding SOA-related questions. The team members are responsible for the design of the SB and for consulting and training personnel concerning the implementation and integration of services. For example, all enterprises regarded in [5] have established such a central SOA team.

Service Development. Service developers are supported by a knowledge-base that includes lessons learned, best practices and guidelines. Thanks to the regulation of the used standards and technology, a better tool support (a service stub generator or a test environment for example) is provided and not every development team has to find the most appropriate toolset on its own.

Governance. A consistent change management and versioning becomes necessary since provided services can be consumed by several applications or services. Therefore, enterprise-wide guidelines have to be defined, that standardize the handling of change requests and the rollout of altered services [6]. Especially in the initial stage of an SOA of maturity level two, the integration of services into the SB is more complex than using different proprietary interfaces, because of a lack of experience. Therefore, an enterprise-wide compensation payment system has to be instantiated that balances these extra costs [4].

4.3   Level 3: Administered SOA

The third maturity level is characterized by orchestrated services. The IT-system oriented integration services described in the previous levels are orchestrated to implement services with a higher alignment of service's functionality to business processes. Figure2 sketches the *Service Architecture* and *Infrastructure* of an SOA on level 3.

Service Architecture. The existence of an orchestration layer distinguishes the *Service Architecture* between maturity level two and three, and allows a higher degree of business alignment. Orchestrations are generally implemented in a process-oriented way

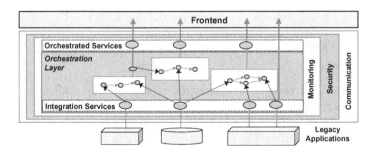

Fig. 2. iSOAMM: Maturity Level 3

and represent the business logic that was formerly hardcoded into the frontend applications [22]. Orchestrated services represent the composition of IT-oriented functionality and realize business-oriented functionality. For example, the "Web Services Business Process Execution Language" (WSBPEL) [23] is one of the most well-known programming languages to implement WS orchestrations. Supplementary to the introduction of orchestrated services, a standardization of business relevant data types (*customer* or *product* for example) is necessary. This minimizes the need for data transformations within orchestrations and thereby eases the reuse of integration services that work on this data.

Infrastructure. The orchestration's implementations are process descriptions and not native executable code. These languages need a runtime environment, the orchestration engine, which is one of the mandatory extensions of the infrastructure. The SB has to be enriched with additional functionality [17]. The communication infrastructure has to be flanked with a monitoring and a security infrastructure. This extension can for example also be found in the "Web Services Architecture Stack" [24] proposed by the W3C. The monitoring infrastructure enables the observation of performance and availability of the services. It is sufficient to monitor the messages, respectively the service invocations and the corresponding responses. A more detailed monitoring including the internal states of a service is not mandatory at this maturity level. Comparable to the monitoring, the security infrastructure of this maturity level operates only on message and service granularity. This enables the definition and enforcement of access rights for services, whereas the actual data of a service call is not part of the security policies. Furthermore, a secure message exchange between service provider and the service consumer is possible.

Enterprise Structure. Regarding the functionality and the data that is provided by services they can be split up into different service domains, e.g. accounting, customer master data, customer relationship etc. [6]. Each department is responsible for a certain domain and the included services. Besides the development of mainly orchestrated services each department is responsible for the operation of the services. Service operation is often assigned to an own IT unit or a common IT department. The SOA team is adapted to reflect the higher business alignment. On level two, it mainly consists of IT experts whereas on this level it is an interdisciplinary team that includes IT experts as well as business experts of different business units [7]. This team is also responsible for defining common data standards and the splitting of services into service domains.

Service Development. The knowledge and tool repository, which supports service developers, is enhanced and the share of automated development steps is increased [6]. The degree of automation can be risen by using Model-Driven Software Development (MDSD) for the development of orchestrated services. The use of MDSD is much easier for orchestrated services than integration services, as the first ones use only standardized services and feature a common implementation language.

Governance. An enterprise-wide policy has to be established that the service orientation paradigm has to be applied throughout the IT landscape. However, reasonable exceptions can still be allowed by the SOA team. The use of services by other parties induces costs for the operation at the service provider instead of the consumer. Hence, the compensation payment system has to be adapted so service providers are not punished for providing reusable services. The reuse factor of services can vary to a big extent, as the case study of Credit Suisse in [4] shows for example that in spite of an overall reuse factor of 1.6 some services are reused up to 12 times. Part of the governance of this level also is the establishment of enterprise-wide rules, guidelines, and policies which regulate security concerns.

4.4 Level 4: Cooperative SOA

This maturity level is characterized by Service Level Agreements (SLA), which have to be concluded between service consumer and provider. An SLA warrants a specified service quality if the consumer uses the service in conformance to a specified usage profile. An additional architecture layer closes the gap between services and business processes [25]. Corresponding to [11], it has to be distinguished between B2B-processes, which are mainly full automated, and internal processes, which involve human interaction. The *Service Architecture* and the *Infrastructure* of an SOA at this level are sketched in Figure 3.

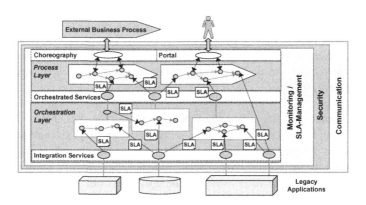

Fig. 3. iSOAMM: Maturity Level 4

Service Architecture. As mentioned above, the service architecture can have two different characteristics (B2B-processes and human interaction), even both at the same time. In order to support B2B-scenarios this layer supports the choreography of processes. In contrast to an orchestration, choreography is a cooperation between processes [26]. The integration of human users is necessary to support most internal processes, thus they can not be implemented as orchestrations, which allow solely a composition of services. The common way is to use a portal that presents the tasks to the users, which are assigned within the process. One example for such an user integration is the "WSBPEL Extension for People" (BPEL4People) [27]. The availability of business rules is an additional property of the process layer. The business rules allow a reconfiguration of processes without a redeployment [28]. Secondary, as presented in [29], events play a decisive role within real-world business processes. Therefore, the communication between services is extended to support events in addition to direct service invocations by other services.

Infrastructure. First of all, the communication infrastructure has to be adapted in order to support the event-based communication whereas the possibility of active service invocations is still available. One example is the "Event Bus Infrastructure" [4] developed by Credit Suisse. The introduction of the process layer puts new requirements on the infrastructure. It has to provide a rule system. Additionally, components are necessary, which either allow the integration of user actions into a process - mainly by a portal - or the choreography of processes. Similar to orchestrations, processes require a runtime environment. These process engines are mainly orchestration engines that provide the additionally needed functionality of choreography and user integration. Generally, business experts rather than IT experts design processes. Therefore, descriptions of services that are located within the repository have to include a semantic description. An example of a UDDI-based repository that allows the integration of semantic descriptions is presented in [30]. At this maturity level, SLAs are concluded during the development of an orchestration or a process and changed rather seldom. An automation of this task is therefore not yet mandatory. Nevertheless, a more detailed monitoring of the services is essential, especially the internal states of orchestrations and processes have to be monitored [31]. An example of such a monitoring infrastructure for WSBPEL orchestrations is presented in [32]. The security infrastructure has to be extended. As shown in [33], it is insufficient to define access policies on services or even interface level. In fact, it is necessary to take the data into account, which is included in the service call.

Enterprise Structure. The subdivision of the enterprise into several departments, which correspond to the service domains, is refined into smaller units. Bieberstein et al [1] propose a service alignment down to the granularity of teams that are responsible and specialized for only one service. Thus, the establishment of new business functionality is not solely a composition of services. It is rather a new interdisciplinary staffed combination of teams within the enterprise. Nevertheless, a separate IT department, which operates and maintains the infrastructure, is still necessary.

Service Development. The development process has to consider the potentials of business rules and events. The development is based on the MDSD and uses graphical models to design processes and orchestrations, which are transformed into interpretable code. The use of graphical models simplifies the development so that it is easier for business experts. Furthermore, the integration into the security infrastructure is an important extension of the development process. The SLAs include quality parameters, which are guaranteed by the provider. It is therefore essential to consider the quality of service (QoS) within the development process. This means the development process has to be extended with activities to predict or at least estimate the QoS in relation to the QoS guaranteed by the included services [31]. The SLAs include a charge, which has to be paid to use the service [34]. This allows the optimization of costs regarding the quality, which is guaranteed to the consumer [31].

Governance. At least from this maturity level on, all new IT systems have to be implemented in a service-oriented manner. Furthermore, it is mandatory that all legacy applications are extended with service interfaces and integrated into the SOA. The compensation payment system is replaced by SLAs because they define fees for the usage of the service. The teams can balance the additional expenses that are induced by the service development and the service operation on their own. Nevertheless, enterprise-wide rules and a regulating instance exercising fair competition control is necessary in order to prevent unfair enrichment through monopoly positions on crucial services. Key process indicators and metrics have to be defined, which enable monitoring of the enterprise-wide SOA adoption and the business processes. Especially the business process monitoring can use the already present monitoring infrastructure.

4.5   Level 5: On Demand SOA

At the previous level, services were published including their available quality levels. Such a request triggers the provider to check if he can offer the demanded quality level. The provider in turn often has to conclude new SLAs with his own service providers. In addition to the long term contracts on level four, it is possible to negotiate SLAs on a short-term basis. This can even be as short as a single service invocation. Because of these short-term SLAs, an automation of the SLA negotiation is necessary [35].

Service Architecture. Since services are selected automatically, a service and data ontology is needed [31]. The static binding of the services is replaced with a dynamic binding using the semantic description of the required functionality. This description in combination with the ontology enables the selection of suitable services. Furthermore, policies have to be defined that control the choice of the most adequate service. By using semantic service matching, it is possible that there is a mismatch between the data formats used in the process and the ones that are used by integrated services. A data ontology enables an automated transformation of different data formats.

Infrastructure. A trading platform, which is called marketplace [36] in the following, is required to support the automated search and provisioning of services. It can provide a variety of different purchasing models. Two examples are public sale of services [36] and the selection out of several offers [34]. The introduction of automated service selection leads to further changes in the infrastructure because components for automatic SLA negotiation and service selection become necessary. One framework that allows such negotiations and additionally the monitoring of SLAs is described in [35]. In order to enable an optimized service selection at runtime, a detailed monitoring of the orchestrations and processes is needed [31].

Enterprise Structure. There are only minor changes to the enterprise structure in comparison to level four. The provisioning of services is now the primary goal of the enterprise and the management has to ensure the agility to adapt to changes in customer requests.

Service Development. In contrary to maturity level four, services are not choosen at design-time. In fact, they are selected during runtime and therefore service selection regarding the costs and the quality is more flexible. This shift of the optimization from design-time to runtime has some serious implications. Rules and policies, which control the service selection during runtime, have to be defined within the design phase. The service development evolves from a combination of services into a composition of functionality. Orchestrations and processes contain the semantic specification of services that can be used to automatically query service repositories or the marketplace for compatible services.

Governance. The business process monitoring evolves into Business Process Management, which allows the control and optimization of business processes. Due to the dynamic conclusion of SLAs, the monitoring of the compliance with the rules, which have been introduced with maturity level four, has to be automated

5 Challenges, Benefits, and Risks

This section presents the benefits that are promised by tackling the challenges of each maturity level. Additionally, the risks that are associated with the ascent from one level to the next are listed. This eases a comparison and evaluation of the most adequate maturity level because the benefits can be weighted up against the challenges and risks.

5.1 Level 1: Trial SOA

The challenge is comprised of the introduction of the service paradigm involving the way of thinking and often the use of new technologies. Particularly in this first maturity level, the development costs associated with the development of a service are slightly higher than the costs of point-to-point interfaces.

A major benefit for the enterprise is to gain experience in adopting SOA in their environment. Especially the lessons learned in the use of the technology and standards are valuable when striving for the next maturity level.

The risks involved in adopting the SOA approach at this maturity level are relatively low as only small and delimited projects are affected.

5.2 Level 2: Integrative SOA

The selection or rather implementation of the SB is difficult because many aspects like availability, performance, and especially scalability have to be considered [4]. Secondary, the developers have to be trained in the technologies and standards provided by the SB.

The availability of a high-level API that offers standardized access to the services is the main gain of an SOA on this maturity level [9]. Such an API eases the service reuse within new application and leads to an reduction of development costs [4]. Furthermore, the knowledge-base and extensive tool support can speed up the development time.

The SB is a central component within the enterprises IT landscape. As shown in [4], the scalability of the SB represents a large risk to the success of the SOA and with it to the success of the whole enterprise. The regulation of new common standards and technologies is an additional risk as such introductions often do not find wide acceptance amongst the developers [37].

5.3   Level 3: Administered SOA

The extensions of the infrastructure that are enjoined for this maturity level produce obviously high one-time effort. The introduction of an appropriate monitoring and security infrastructure is challenging as future requirements have to be anticipated. Secondary, a development method for orchestrated services has to be implemented.

The service orchestrations allow a stronger alignment of IT and business. They can be changed quickly according to new or changed business needs and the time-to-market is reduced [4, 25]. The implementation of new frontend applications is easier due to the higher business alignment and therefore faster in general. Redundant effort is decreased through the exchange of experiences and the increased reuse potential of services enabled by the standardized data types. Additionally, establishment of the orchestration layer is comparable to the separation of business logic from the data layer and the user interface, which is generally considered an advantage.

The step from level two to level three requires the instantiation of the interdisciplinary SOA team and the reorganization of business departments. The acceptance of these changes presents a non-negligible risk for the SOA implementation. Services can be reused within several orchestrations and applications, therefore a failure of this single service can affect a lot of different services and applications.

5.4   Level 4: Cooperative SOA

An SLA management has to be introduced. Employees have to be trained in handling SLAs on the technical and on the business side. Furthermore, the integration of user interaction lead to substantial enhancements of the infrastructure. The application of business rules in orchestrations requires an anticipation of changes in designing of business processes. Another challenge is the reorganization of the departments into teams as this needs a lot of support by many stakeholders throughout the whole enterprise.

The process layer promises better business support by integrating human interactions. The choreography enables the realization of complex B2B-processes. The business rules allow a faster reaction to changes in the process specification and a seamless transition at runtime. The use of SLAs enables the inclusion of extra-functional quality properties and hence the consideration of costs in relation to quality properties like performance [31]. Additionally, the fine-grained security model allows a rollout of services even in vital areas of the enterprise. Last but not least, the service selection is eased by the fact that semantic searches in the service repository are possible. The decisive role that events play in business processes can now directly be mapped to the IT processes.

The risk for IT-related changes like introducing the process layer as well as a business rules engine is comparable low. The structural reorganization of the enterprise depends to a big extent on the support of all employees and also requires the sensitivity if all are willing to take the risk. In total, SOA becomes an essential factor for success or failure in achieving the business objectives of an enterprise.

5.5   Level 5: On Demand SOA

This maturity level induces large challenges. First, a change in the way of thinking is necessary. The on demand negotiation substitutes the offering of services with preassigned QoS. This means the costumer can make demands, which the provider endeavors to realize. Secondly, mainly all activities related to the operation of the SOA have to be automated in order to enable the dynamic service selection and binding. This is not only a technical challenge, because the staff member carrying out these tasks manually before are affected.

This maturity level promises an even faster adaptability and higher flexibility than the previous levels [38]. A higher customer orientation is possible due to the on demand provisioning of services. Especially in combination with an underlying virtualized computing infrastructure, the proposed resource efficiency can be optimized [38].

If the new on demand paradigm is not put into practice by the employees, the promised benefits can not be reached. Furthermore, the full automation can be misinterpreted as a loss of control by the managers leading to a disaffirmation of SOA.

6   Validation

In order to validate the iSOAMM, we rated several SOAs based on the information provided in the case studies. For the sake of brevity, we only present the results and omit evaluation details. The SOA of Sparkassen Informatik [9] is one example that is ranked on level two. The KIM project was also ranked on level two when it started in 2004 and reached level three last year. The SOA of Deutsche Post [6, 4] is also ranked on iSOAMM level three. Currently, there are no level four SOAs known to the authors. That is not unexpected as SLA management and QoS assurance are still two large research challenges that are not fully mastered [39]. Level five is more or less a vision only, although a lot of research is done on topics linked to this level. For example, the European Union funds research projects which address these aspects of an SOA within the ICT domain of the 7th Framework Programme.

7   Conclusion and Outlook

This paper introduces the iSOAMM and its five maturity levels. The maturity levels were explored from five different viewpoints to highlight changes in IT systems, procedure, and the organizational structure of an enterprise. In addition, the challenges, benefits, and risks associated with each level were pointed out which enables enterprises to select the most adequate maturity level for them. In order to validate the iSOAMM, the implemented SOAs referenced in this article were ranked according to the maturity levels, as far as the corresponding documentation allowed it.

The iSOAMM enables enterprises to identify rewarding areas for further SOA adoption and to develop a roadmap for an SOA introduction. Due to the independency of the iSOAMM, they are free to choose the most adequate technologies, standards, and products. The iSOAMM consolidates current knowledge about the introduction and implementation of an SOA. It also merges the experience gained in SOA projects in industry with latest research results.

As a next step, we plan a further validation of the iSOAMM. For example, we aim to evaluate more enterprises using our model. We also plan to compare the KI of the iSOAMM to the ones of the OSIMM, as soon as they are publicly available. In the long run, the refinement of KI of the levels four and, in particular, five is planned. As these levels cover current research fields, new scientific knowledge and practical experience may lead to adaptations in the KIs.

References

1. Bieberstein, N., Bose, S., Walker, L., Lynch, A.: Impact of service-oriented architecture on enterprise systems, organizational structures, and individuals. IBM Systems Journal 44(4), 691–708 (2005)
2. Cherbakov, L., Galambos, G., Harishankar, R., Kalyana, S., Rackham, G.: Impact of service orientation at the business level. IBM Systems Journal 44(4), 653–668 (2005)
3. Heffner, R., Fulton, L., Stone, J.: Key SOA Success Factors: A Starter Kit For SOA. Forrester Research (2006)
4. Krafzig, D., Banke, K., Slama, D.: Enterprise SOA. reprint. edn. Prentice Hall PTR, Englewood Cliffs (2006)
5. Legner, C., Heutschi, R.: SOA Adoption in Practice - Findings from Early SOA Implementations. In: Proc. of European Conference on Information Systems (ECIS 2007) (2007)
6. Helbig, J.: SOA Serie: Teil 1-5. CIO (2007),
   `http://www.cio.de/schwerpunkt/d/Deutsche-Post-Brief.html`
7. Gizanis, D., Heutschi, R., Solberg, T.: Global Order Management Services Support Businesses at ABB (2005),
   `http://www.alexandria.unisg.ch/Publikationen/23667`
8. Freudenstein, P., Liu, L., Majer, F., Maurer, A., Momm, C., Ried, D., Juling, W.: Architektur für ein universitätsweit integriertes Informations- und Dienstmanagement. In: INFORMATIK 2006 - Informatik für Menschen (Band 1), pp. 50–54 (2006)
9. Zimmermann, O., Milinski, S., Craes, M., Oellermann, F.: Second generation web services-oriented architecture in production in the finance industry. In: OOPSLA 2004 (2004)
10. Department of Commerce (Introduction - IT Architecture Capability Maturity Model),
    `http://ocio.os.doc.gov/groups/public/@doc/@os/@ocio/@oitpp/`
    `documents/content/prod01_002340.pdf`
11. Bachman, J., Ng, D., Kline, S., Horst, E.: A New Service-Oriented Architecture (SOA) Maturity Model. whitepaper (2006), `http://www.sonicsoftware.com/soamm`
12. Trops, B.: SOA Maturity Modell, oder der Weg zu einer Service Orientierten Architektur. Java Forum Stuttgart (2006),
    `http://www.jfs2006.de/jfs/2006/folien/B7_Trops_ORACLE.pdf`
13. ORACLE (SOA Maturity Cheat Sheet), `http://www.oracle.com/technologies/`
    `soa/docs/oracle-soa-maturity-modelcheat-sheet.pdf`
14. Arsanjani, A., Holley, K.: Increase flexibility with the Service Integration Maturity Model (SIMM) (2005), `http://www.ibm.com/developerworks/webservices/`
    `library/ws-soa-simm/`
15. The Open Group, OSIMM Working group: Launch Presentation and WG Updates 1.0 (2007),
    `http://www.opengroup.org/projects/osimm/`
16. Meier, F.: Service Oriented Architecture Maturity Models - A guide to SOA adoption. Master's thesis, University of Skövde, School of Humanities and Informatics (2006)

17. Papazoglou, M.P.: Extending the Service-Oriented Architecture. Business integration journal, 18–21 (2005)
18. Baer, T.: SOA: BUILDING THE ROADMAP. zapthink white paper (2007)
19. Cox, D.E., Kreger, H.: Management of the service-oriented-architecture life cycle. IBM Systems Journal 44(4), 709–726 (2005)
20. Austvold, E., Carter, K.: Service-Oriented Architectures: Survey Findings on Deployment and Plans for the Future. AMR Research, Inc., Research Report (2005)
21. Linthicum, D.S.: Next generation application integration, 3rd printing edn. Addison-Wesley, Reading
22. Wong-Bushby, I., Egan, R., Isaacson, C.: A Case Study in SOA and Re-architecture at Company ABC. In: Proc. of the HICSS 2006 (2006)
23. OASIS: Web Services Business Process Execution Language (WSBPEL) (2007)
24. Booth, D., Haas, H., McCabe, F., Newcomer, E., Champion, M., Ferris, C., Orchard, D.: Web Services Architecture. W3C Working Group Note (2004)
25. Zimmermann, O., Doubrovski, V., Grundler, J., Hogg, K.: Service-oriented architecture and business process choreography in an order management scenario: rationale, concepts, lessons learned. In: Proc. of OOPSLA 2005 (2005)
26. Peltz, C.: Web Service Orchestration and Choreography: A look at WSCI and BPEL4WS. WebServices Journal (2003)
27. Agrawal, A., Amend, M., Das, M., Ford, M., Keller, C., Kloppmann, M., König, D., Leymann, F., Müller, R., Pfau, G., Plösser, K., Rangaswamy, R., Rickayzen, A., Rowley, M., Schmidt, P., Trickovic, I., Yiu, A., Zeller, M.: WS-BPEL Extension for People (BPEL4People) (2007), https://www.sdn.sap.com/irj/sdn/bpel4people
28. Charfi, A., Mezini, M.: Hybrid web service composition: business processes meet business rules. In: Proceedings of ICSOC 2004 (2004)
29. Schulte, R.W.: The Growing Role of Events in Enterprise Applications. Gartner Research (2003), http://www.gartner.com/DisplayDocument?doc_cd=116129
30. Paoli, H., Schmidt, A., Lockemann, P.C.: User-Driven Semantic Wiki-based Business Service Description. In: Proceedings of I-Semantics 2007 (2007)
31. Zeng, L., Benatallah, B., Ngu, A., Dumas, M., Kalagnanam, J., Chang, H.: QoS-aware middleware for Web services composition. IEEE Trans. on Softw. Eng. 30(5) (2004)
32. Momm, C., Mayerl, C., Rathfelder, C., Abeck, S.: A Manageability Infrastructure for the Monitoring of Web Service. In: 14th Annual Workshop of HP SUA (2007)
33. Emig, C., Brandt, F., Kreuzer, S., Abeck, S.: Identity as a Service - Towards a Service-Oriented Identity Management Architecture. In: Pras, A., van Sinderen, M. (eds.) EUNICE 2007. LNCS, vol. 4606, pp. 1–8. Springer, Heidelberg (2007)
34. Tosic, V., Patel, K., Pagurek, B.: WSOL - Web Service Offerings Language. In: Bressan, S., Chaudhri, A.B., Li Lee, M., Yu, J.X., Lacroix, Z. (eds.) CAiSE 2002 and VLDB 2002. LNCS, vol. 2590, pp. 57–67. Springer, Heidelberg (2003)
35. Dan, A., Davis, D., Kearney, R., Keller, A., King, R., Kuebler, D., Ludwig, H., Polan, M., Spreitzer, M., Youssef, A.: Web services on demand: WSLA-driven automated management. IBM Systems Journal 43(1), 136–158 (2004)
36. Lamparter, S., Schnizler, B.: Trading services in ontology-driven markets. In: Biham, E., Youssef, A.M. (eds.) SAC 2006. LNCS, vol. 4356, Springer, Heidelberg (2007)
37. Haft, M., Humm, B., Siedersleben, J.: The Architect's Dilemma - Will Reference Architectures Help?. In: Quality of Software Architectures and Software Quality, pp. 106–122 (2005)
38. Crawford, C.H., Bate, G.P., Cherbakov, L., Holley, K., Tsocanos, C.: Toward an on demand service-oriented architecture. IBM Systems Journal 44(1), 81–107 (2005)
39. Papazoglou, M.P., Heuvel, W.J.: Service oriented architectures: approaches, technologies and research issues. The VLDB Journal 16(3), 389–415 (2007)

Describing Component Collaboration
Using Goal Sequences

Cyril Carrez[1], Jacqueline Floch[2], and Richard Sanders[2]

[1] NTNU,
Department of Telematics,
7431 Trondheim, Norway
carrez@item.ntnu.no
[2] SINTEF ICT,
7465 Trondheim, Norway
{jacqueline.floch,richard.sanders}@sintef.no

Abstract. Services are normally not performed by a single component, but result from the collaboration of several distributed components. Their precise specification and validation require complex models, where the *intention* of the service is easily lost in the detail. This paper exploits the concept of *service goals* that was earlier introduced to simplify service modeling. It describes the semantics of service goals, how to specify and how to use them. We show that so-called *goal sequences* can provide a designer-friendly, high-level description of the intention of the service, while maintaining simplicity, reusability and flexibility when composing from elementary services. By way of examples, we illustrate the difference between goal sequences and behavior descriptions. Finally we discuss issues related to the validation of goal sequences and their use at design time and runtime, for example in connection with service discovery.

Keywords: Goal sequences, collaborative components, high-level service specification.

1 Introduction

Ensuring interoperability in distributed systems has been a software engineering topic for decades. Recently the ICT community has rallied around the principles of a service oriented architecture (SOA) in order to address this challenge, see e.g. [1]. Within contemporary SOA, the composition approach called *choreography* is concerned with collaborative business processes involving multiple autonomous services, where different participants can assume different roles with different relationships. However, so far only informal specifications of service choreography have been suggested [2]. At the same time, semantic web services seek to characterize what a service can provide by offering means of expressing interfaces using Web Services Description Language (WSDL) [3]. Although WSDL aims at providing a formal definition of the interface to a service, it is restricted to a static description of operations and associated messages.

R. Meier and S. Terzis (Eds.): DAIS 2008, LNCS 5053, pp. 16–29, 2008.
© IFIP International Federation for Information Processing 2008

We have previously suggested the concept of a *service goal* to characterize the possible achievements of a service, and have shown how service goals can simplify service modeling in UML2 [4]. This article refines the semantics of service goals, which is one result of the EU IST project SIMS[1]. We have also suggested *goal sequences* as a means of expressing the intensions of a composite service [5], i.e. the intention of a choreography. In this article we argue for the merits of goal sequences by means of simple examples, and contribute with advances on how to model them. However, while goal sequences provide a designer-friendly overview, they do not specify everything. In this article we discuss in particular the difference between goal sequences and behavior.

SOA is increasingly gaining acceptance, influencing the way people understand and define services. However, there is a fundamental limitation of SOA as it is currently understood. In SOA, services are provided by a service provider to a service consumer. A service provider is normally a "passive object" in the sense that it never takes any initiatives towards a service user. *Collaborative services* on the other hand entail collaborations between several autonomous entities that may behave in a proactive manner and may take initiatives towards each other. This is typical for telecom services, but also for a large class of services such as attentive services, context aware services, notification services and ambient intelligence. In this paper we consider collaborative services, where multiple components interact to perform a composite service. This generalization allows for a wider class of services.

The structure of this position paper is as follows: in section 2 we present service goals and their semantics, showing how composite services are modeled from elementary services using UML2 collaborations, and how goals characterize so-called semantic interfaces. Section 3 presents goal sequences as an intuitive way of modeling the intention of composite services, similar to choreographies. In section 4 we discuss issues related to validation and composition at design time and at runtime. We also discuss related work, and finally conclude by drawing some perspectives.

2   Semantics of Service Goals

As proposed by Sanders et al. [4], services are modeled by UML2 collaborations [6]. We distinguish between *composite* and *elementary* collaborations, as shown in Fig. 1. Elementary collaborations specify partial service behaviors. They define a collaboration between exactly two parts, called *semantic interfaces*, as well as the service goals of the collaboration. Semantic interfaces specify interface behavior, while service goals (or *goals* for short) specify the desired outcome of that behavior; both are discussed in this section. Composite collaborations, on the other hand, specify the service roles implemented by components[2] that take part in the service. Composite collaborations are in fact composed of UML2 *collaboration uses*, where each collaboration use is typed by an elementary collaboration. A service role can be bound to a number of semantic

---

[1]   Semantic Interfaces for Mobile Services; see http://www.ist-sims.org

[2]   We distinguish between the specification of a service, and its implementation. With that distinction in mind, we speak of service roles when specifying the service (at design time), while we speak of components when we execute the service implementation (at runtime). Service roles are depicted by an octagon in the composite collaboration.

interfaces, which thus type its ports. For example, Fig. 1a specifies a service where a *Traveler* interacts with a *Hotel* and a *Plane* in order to plan a travel. The interactions are typed by the elementary collaborations *ReserveHotel* and *ReservePlane*.

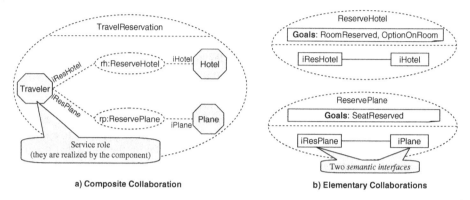

Fig. 1. Travel service modeled using collaborations and collaboration uses

2.1   Service Goals and Elementary Collaborations

The elementary collaborations of Fig. 1b identify the goals reachable by each of them. Service goals do not define the behavior of an application, but rather the desired outcome of a behavior: they describe its *intention*. For example, concerning *ReserveHotel*, two goals can be achieved: *RoomReserved* or *OptionOnRoom*. Both are desirable outcomes of this micro-service. However, this does not mean that those goals must or will be achieved during an interaction between the *Traveler* and *Hotel*: possibly the hotel has no rooms left, meaning neither goal can be achieved.

Service goals were first proposed by Sanders [5, 7]. While Sanders described service goals using OCL expressions, we describe the goals using ontologies [8]. Ontologies allow us to describe the semantics of the goals (for instance "establish a multimedia call"), allowing flexible reasoning on goals and user-friendly descriptions.

We also differ from Sanders in the number of goals an elementary collaboration can achieve. Specifically we do not consider partial or sub-goals to describe a partial achievement in the collaboration. Several goals can be specified, but only one can be achieved during the execution of the elementary collaboration at runtime. This restriction was motivated by the desire to have a simple and intuitive specification when service goals are used during composition of a service (see section 3).

2.2   Service Goals and Semantic Interfaces

While a goal characterizes the desired outcome of a behavior, the behavior itself is described by a semantic interface [9]. A semantic interface describes the visible behavior of a service role at a connection endpoint. Goals are attached to that behavior, allowing one to specify how a semantic interface can achieve a goal in a collaboration. Semantic interfaces type the ports of the service role, and are used to validate the composite service: when two service roles interact through ports, compatibility checks can be applied on complementary semantic interfaces to ensure a consistent interaction [10, 11].

Semantic interfaces are specified using UML state machines, with message passing semantics. Triggers and effects specify respectively a reception or a sending of a signal, thus specifying how to interact with the semantic interface[3]. We use a stereotype <<goal>> state to specify that the interaction has achieved a particular goal at this point. This way, goals represent "progress" in the behavior, and thus are a characterization of liveness. For example, Fig. 2 shows the state machine of the semantic interface *iHotel* of the elementary collaboration *ReserveHotel* presented in Fig. 1. One can ask for available rooms at specific dates, and either reserve the room and thus achieve the goal *RoomReserved*[4], or take an option on that room and achieve the goal *OptionOnRoom*. A <<goal>> state has exactly one outgoing transition, stereotyped <<transitionGoal>>: this transition is instantaneous. Goal states are represented by a dashed state symbol in Fig. 2.

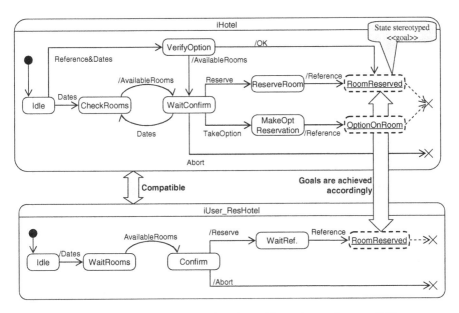

Fig. 2. Two compatible semantic interfaces, illustrating goal compatibility

We draw attention to two important issues regarding the goals and how they relate to the behavior of a semantic interface. First of all, different behaviors can lead to the same goal: for instance to achieve the goal *RoomReserved*, it is possible to ask for available dates and reserve the room as the *iUser_ResHotel* does, or give the reference of an option on a room that was made earlier, and reserve the room if the option is still valid, shown in the upper part of the state machine of *iHotel*. Secondly,

---

[3] Parameters of signals are not taken into account.
[4] Payment of the room is performed by another elementary collaboration, as shown in section 3. For sake of simplicity, it is not included here.

some behavior can still occur at the semantic interface after a goal has been reached, e.g. clean-up messages (for instance closing a session). Hence achieving a goal does not mean terminating a behavior.

The power of semantic interfaces lies in their use during composition. When two service roles interact, the connected semantic interfaces must be compatible, as we defined it in [11]: their interaction does not lead to unspecified message reception, deadlock, or improper termination, and their interaction is live. Concerning deadlock, we restrict ourselves to avoiding deadlocks between two semantic interfaces by ensuring that one of them will always be able to take action. By improper termination, we mean that both semantic interfaces should terminate accordingly. Finally, by live interaction, we mean they are capable of reaching a common goal. The compatibility relation is illustrated in Fig. 2, with the semantic interface *iUser_ResHotel* shown at the bottom. This semantic interface cannot make any option on a room, but is still goal compatible with *iHotel* as they can achieve the goal *RoomReserved*.

As a final point, all the entities we presented so far are elements of reuse: elementary collaborations, semantic interfaces and service roles can be reused in other composite collaborations, hence taking part in services they were not designed for in the first place. This reusability is illustrated through the examples of the article.

3 Goal Sequences

So far we have shown how service goals describe the intention of partial service behaviors, and how they are related to elementary collaborations and semantic interfaces. When it comes to the service, service goals are composed in order to specify the intention of the whole service. This composition is specified by what we call *goal sequences*. Goal sequences were first introduced by Sanders [5]; in this article we propose a precise semantics allowing one to exploit them for validation purposes.

A goal sequence is a high-level specification which describes a desirable behavior, namely how goals depend on each other in terms of pre-conditions. As shown in section 4, they are used to verify that a composition of service roles is live (i.e. something useful may be achieved), or during service discovery. We distinguish between *Collaboration goal sequences* and *Role goal sequences*. The difference is that the former applies to composite collaborations and refers to goals of the elementary collaborations, while the latter applies to the service roles, and refers to the goals of its semantic interfaces. The principles presented in this section apply to both kinds of goal sequences; we will only discuss in length about collaboration goal sequences (here denoted goal sequences for short).

A goal sequence describes dependencies between the goals of the elementary collaborations that are used in a particular composite collaboration. They describe the *intention* of the composite service: that something useful can be achieved, and how it should be achieved (i.e. how the different elementary collaboration goals should be sequenced). We suggest that goal sequences are specified using UML Activity diagrams, where an activity represents a collaboration use[5] of the composite

---

[5] Recall that a collaboration use is typed by an elementary collaboration. Hence the goals of the collaboration use are the goals of the corresponding elementary collaboration. This way, an elementary collaboration can be used in many places in a composite collaboration.

collaboration[6], and outgoing arrows represent the goals achieved by that collaboration use. Activity diagrams are very helpful for goal sequences, as several collaborations may execute in parallel. Moreover, activity diagrams are in line with the semantics of goal sequences: each activity represents a goal to be achieved. Sanders proposed interaction overview diagrams for goal sequences [4, 7]; however such diagrams currently lack tool support. We investigated using state diagrams in [11], which have more tool support, but they tend to get cluttered up when expressing parallel behavior in orthogonal states.

Fig. 3 shows the goal sequence for the *TravelReservation* presented in Fig. 1a. The two collaboration uses are represented by the two activities *rh* and *rp*. The goal sequence specifies the intention of the service, which is to reserve a room and a seat in a plane (goals *RoomReserved* and *SeatReserved*). We have deliberately chosen to drop the goal *OptionOnRoom*, as *TravelReservation* does not propose such an intention (in fact, *TravelReservation* is reusing *ReserveHotel* which may have been specified in another service). We define that it does not matter in which order the goals are achieved, as long as both of them can be achieved before the termination of the composite service. Note that this describes the intention of the service, and does not mean that each execution will actually achieve those goals: possibly the plane or the hotel is full. This example shows the primary advantage of goal sequences: it is easy to show the intention of the service. We believe that goal sequences are quite intuitive, and maintain simplicity during composition.

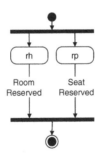

Fig. 3. Goal sequence for the composite collaboration *TravelReservation*

Fig. 3 shows one typical pattern for goal sequences, namely two goals that can be achieved in parallel. Fig. 4 shows patterns needed to specify different kinds of preconditions. The first one, on the upper left corner, shows the principle of goal sequences. In this pattern, two goals *g1* and *g2* are sequenced; the semantics is that the achievement of *g1* is a pre-condition for the achievement of *g2*. We say that *g1* *enables* *g2*. As we shall see in section 4, this does not mean that *g1* enables the collaboration *C2*, as the behavior of *C2* may start before or without *g1* being achieved. Boolean expressions AND and OR can also be specified in pre-conditions, as shown at the bottom of the figure.

---

[6] For role goal sequences, activities represent semantic interfaces.

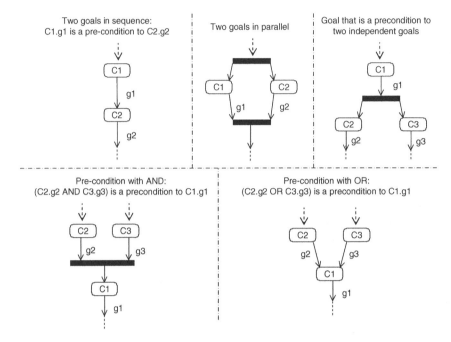

Fig. 4. Patterns for collaboration goal sequences

Goal sequences are very useful and intuitive when it comes to the design of collaborative services, i.e. when several participants can take initiative. For instance, Fig. 5 specifies a payment functionality when reserving a room to the hotel. As shown on the left of the figure, three service roles take part in the service: in addition to the *User* and the *Hotel*, there is also a *Bank*. Several collaboration uses demonstrate the composition of micro-services, most of them can be reused in different services: *Pay* and *ConfirmPayment* can be used in any service where money is involved. The goal sequence is shown in Fig. 5b: the room has first to be reserved, and then the user pays the bank, which in turn pays the hotel. Confirmation of payment and booking ends the service. Note, again, that the order of those two goals is of no importance.

Fig. 5 also shows the difference between the (collaboration) goal sequence and the role goal sequence: Fig. 5c is the role goal sequence for the *Bank*, which specifies how the service role should sequence the goals. We see the role goal sequence is in fact a subset of the collaboration goal sequence in Fig. 5b. Role goal sequences should not need to be specified by hand, but rather be derived automatically from the collaboration goal sequence.

A role goal sequence sets constraints on the behavior of a service role: the service role should sequence the goals of its semantic interfaces in the proper order. For instance, the *Bank* should be paid before it pays the booking of the room, which in turn should happen before it confirms payment to the *User*. Such constraints are one of the uses of goal sequences we discuss in the next section. However, role goal sequences do not specify precisely how to compose semantic interfaces: even though some goals should be sequenced, the service role could nonetheless interact in parallel on the associated semantic interfaces (see section 4.2).

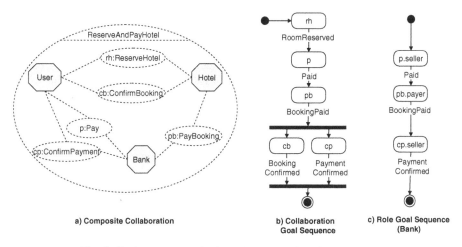

a) Composite Collaboration

b) Collaboration
Goal Sequence

c) Role Goal Sequence
(Bank)

Fig. 5. Goal sequence and role goal sequence in a three-party service

4   Discussion

This section discusses several remaining open issues. We show how resolving them will enable validation of interoperability between components in a flexible manner. We first discuss the validation of goal sequences at design time, and how they can be used at runtime. We show that although they can be useful for service discovery, goal sequences are not sufficient to ensure safe composition.

4.1   Validation of Goal Sequences at Design Time and Runtime

Goal sequences can be used to verify if a composition is live, meaning that the interconnected service roles are able to achieve something useful together. To ensure that the intention of the service is achievable, validation using tools can be performed; preferably this is done at design time, but if necessary it can be done at run time. The validation will ensure the correctness of a composition of service roles.

At design time, service roles can be validated against their semantic interfaces and the goal sequences. Projection and refinement mechanisms can be used in order to verify that the service role is compatible with the semantic interfaces [10, 11]. It should also be possible to check if the service role satisfies the pre-conditions on goals imposed by the role goal sequence, i.e. it sequences the goals of its semantic interfaces in the proper order.

Once service roles have been validated against service specifications (i.e. the collaborations, semantic interfaces and goal sequence), components that implement these roles can be developed[7] and deployed along with descriptors that describe their behavioral properties: semantic interfaces and role goal sequences.

At runtime, the descriptors can be used to validate a dynamic composition. Semantic interfaces can be used to check that two interconnected components are goal

---

[7] Components also implement some functionality related to their execution environment (e.g. underlying middleware for component registration, etc).

compatible, implying that they can achieve a goal together, for instance that a *User* and a *Hotel* can achieve the *OptionOnRoom* goal. The same principle applies to goal sequences: if components cannot sequence their goals correctly, then there is no use in starting a service session. E.g. if a particular *Hotel* requires payment before confirming a booking, then it is of no interest to a *User* that behaves according to the *ReserveAndPayHotel* service. However, several questions arise concerning such validation: given the role goal sequences of each component, is it possible to validate component collaborations on the fly in an efficient manner, i.e. so the validation can be performed by the device? Is it possible to automatically derive a collaboration goal sequence? If so, what will be the semantics of that goal sequence, i.e. the intention of the resulting service? Should it be presented to the user? If so, how?

4.2   Goal Sequences and Safe Composition

While the previous section focused on the use of goal sequences to ensure a composition of service roles does something useful, we also need to take into account safety properties during composition. A component interacts through its semantic interfaces; some of them will be active when the component starts, while others will become active as a result of its own or external initiatives. A safe composition should make sure that if a component receives a signal on one of its semantic interfaces, it is actually ready to receive such a signal.

Unfortunately, goal sequences fall short in that area; it turns out that they only provide support for loose composition. As illustrated in Fig. 6, goal sequences do not specify how elementary collaborations are composed (i.e. in sequence or in parallel for instance). In this example, the *Boss* first asks his/her *Secretary* to plan a travel for him/her. The *Secretary* will reserve the *Hotel* and the *Plane*, and give the *Boss* a confirmation. The goal sequence shows that the elementary collaboration *PlanTravel* should not achieve its goal before the end, while in fact *PlanTravel* initiates the whole service.

In addition goal sequences are not well suited for detecting deadlocks. In the *ReserveAndPayHotel* (Fig. 5a), one should make sure that the three components will not be in deadlock, i.e. each one waiting for the other in a circular manner. However, as goal sequences do not describe temporal dependencies between behaviors, it is not possible to detect deadlocks using goal sequences alone. One should not aim at simply detecting the deadlock when it happens, but rather at detecting possible deadlocks *before* starting the service, i.e. detecting *deadlock-free configurations* of components.

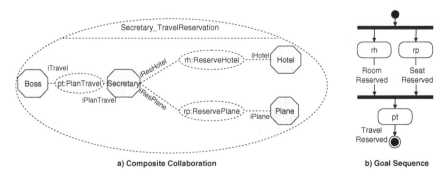

Fig. 6. Goal sequences and order of execution of elementary collaborations

4.3   Goal Sequences in Service Discovery at Runtime

Goals and Goal sequences can be exploited in service discovery at runtime. For instance a *Caller* may need to discover a *Callee* that is capable of using *Video*, and does not want to interact with a component that can only communicate via SMS.

At runtime, when a user starts a service, he/she will start some component on his/her device. This component will be involved in some service, which means it wants to discover compatible components in order to interact with them to provide some useful functionality to the user. This entails discovering components that have compatible semantic interfaces, and a compatible role goal sequence.

The discovery of compatible components can result in numerous configurations, as shown in Fig. 7. In this example, the *Traveler* wants to discover components that are compatible with its semantic interfaces and role goal sequence. Several configurations of components might be discovered, as shown on the left. Possibly some service providers have heard of this service, and developed a *TravelAgency* that performs the reservations, or the *Hotel* and the *Plane* may interact with each other to order a taxi; in all the cases, the goal sequences need to be compared and the resulting composition needs to be validated.

Without such validation, seemingly compatible but useless components might be discovered. Using goal sequences, we restrict the discovery to components that can potentially achieve the behavior intended by the user when he/she started the service. Moreover, we can take advantage of ontologies to first filter components that achieve the most appropriate goals.

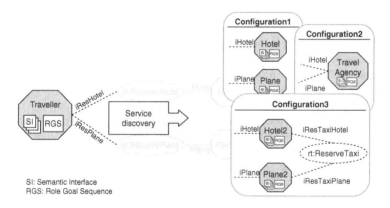

Fig. 7. Discovery of compatible components

5   Related Work

The understanding that services entail collaboration among several distributed autonomous components is not new. This was recognized since the early days of telecommunications, but is also typical for many new services such as attentive services, context aware services, notification services and ambient intelligence. In terms of modeling of collaborations, various dialects of interaction diagrams existed prior to the first standardization of the ITU-T MSC language in 1994 [12]. However, interactions alone do not really cover structural aspects nor provide flexible binding of interfaces to roles in the way now made possible using UML2 collaborations. While interaction diagrams provide a cross-cutting view of a service, they are often too detailed to be easily understood. Our approach abstracts the cross-cutting view on the service using collaborations and goal sequences, and describes the detailed behavior of interfaces using state machines.

In model driven development one strongly argues for developing abstract models that can be refined and transformed into implementation specific models [13]. Model driven approaches to service engineering are still in their infancy. Most of the UML-based approaches developed for service modeling focus on consumer-provider services. For example, Kramler et al. [14] propose to use UML2 collaborations for modeling web service collaboration protocols, and activity and interaction diagrams for more detailed specification. In the same way, Kraemer and Herrmann [15] specify reactive systems with UML2 collaborations for structural properties, and UML2 activities for behavioral aspects. However, the authors are more focused on design time, while we take advantage of service goals to discover useful compositions at runtime. Similarly Ermagan and Krüger [16] consider services to be collaborations between roles. They introduce a UML2 profile for the specification of service-oriented architectures. However they do not seem to exploit the capability of composition of collaborations (i.e. using UML2 collaboration uses). The definition of a UML Profile for services is an ongoing activity at the OMG. The responses submitted to the OMG RFP (request for proposal) "UML Profile and Metamodel for Services (UPMS) RFP" [17] indicate that UML2 collaborations will gain importance in the future modeling of services. At the time of writing the submitted responses to UMPS are under discussion, and we are contributing to this work. A mechanism for expressing goals is one such contribution.

Goals have been extensively used in the engineering domain to capture, analyze, validate and document the properties a system should have [18, 19]. Similarly goals are proposed in service modeling to represent the properties desired by the user [20, 21]. While the term goal is a concept related to the user, capability is used in relation with the service and represents what the service does. In their conceptual service framework Quartel et al. [20] suggest that the definition of the user goal should provide a high-level description of the service, this to facilitate the discovery of services. They propose an abstraction level at which a service is modeled as a single interaction, that somehow matches an elementary collaboration in our work.

To the best of our knowledge, no one has used goal sequences before to represent the overall functionality of services and the dependencies between elementary collaborative behaviors. Goals associated to components and represented in the state machines are similar to progress labels introduced by Holzmann [22] and can be exploited to validate the liveness properties of interacting state machines. Related to our work and also building upon on [4], Castejón and Bræk extend the concept of goal sequences allowing a precise specification of services solely using collaborations and goal sequences (but not state machines) [23]. Their aim is to develop abstract service models that can be used for early detection of errors, such as implied scenarios. Their approach focuses on service composition at design time. Differently we consider discovery and composition at runtime and therefore need more simple service representations.

In the web service domain, intensive research work aims at the automation of service discovery and composition. Current web technologies operate at a syntactic level and therefore require human interaction. The Web Service Modeling Ontology (WSMO) is a result of that research effort [21, 24]. WSMO provides a formal language for semantically describing all relevant aspects of Web services. It defines the concepts of capability and goal that respectively relate to the Web service and the user. Capabilities include the semantic description of a variety of properties such as non-functional properties (e.g. financial or security aspects), pre- and post-conditions and interface behaviors. As a complementary concept, a goal includes the requested capability that the user expects from a service. Although detailed service descriptions are needed for precise discovery, unlike our goals WSMO does not provide any abstract description of services that would facilitate a quick initial discovery of potential, relevant services. The detailed interface behaviors, called choreographies in WSMO, are described using UML state machines in our work.

We have intentionally avoided replication between UML models and ontology artifacts. We do not define the semantics of each message using ontologies, but this could be done in the same way as for goals. Beyond discovery, WSMO also aims at facilitating service composition. It is not clear how this objective can be achieved as no support for describing temporal dependencies between composed services is provided. WSMO defines the concept of orchestration to describe how a service makes use of other services. This concept restricts to the hierarchical composition of services. WSMO does not provide support for more complex compositions such as collaborative composition. Collaborative composition is called choreography in Erl [1] and in the WS-CDL standard [2]. This use of the term choreography differs from WSMO where choreography is restricted to the definition of interface behaviors.

6   Conclusion and Perspectives

Systems modeling in high-level graphical design languages such as UML and access to advanced tools for validation, simulation and code generation has been available within certain engineering areas for quite some time, the telecoms domain being one that matured early in this respect, defining formal languages [12, 25]. It is therefore somewhat surprising that service engineering is still largely implementation-oriented without any clear separation between service logic and implementation detail. This is a paradox since service-orientation essentially means to focus on service specification and to hide the details of component design and implementation, allowing different realizations of the same service.

In this paper we argue for the benefits of characterizing partial service behaviors with goals, and of modeling them with elementary collaborations in UML2. A mechanism for expressing goals is currently being input to the upcoming UML profile and metamodel for services (UPMS).

Focusing on goals enables service engineers to design and analyze service composition at a high level; we argue for the merits of goal sequences as an intuitive description of the intention of service choreographies. We have discussed how goal sequences can benefit service discovery, while they fall short of being sufficient for comprehensive validation and automated composition. Solutions for dynamic composition and runtime validation require further work. However, there is much to be gained both at design time and for service discovery at runtime by abstracting away unnecessary implementation details.

Acknowledgements. Our work is supported by the EU IST 6th framework program.

References

1. Erl, T.: Service-Oriented Architecture - Concepts, Technology, and Design, 6th edn. Prentice Hall, Englewood Cliffs (2006)
2. W3C. Web Services Choreography Description Language (WSCDL) Version 1.0 - W3C Candidate Recommendation - 9 November 2005 (2005)
3. W3C. Web Services Description Language (WSDL) Version 2.0 - W3C Recommendation - 26 June 2007 (2007)
4. Sanders, R., Castejón, H., Kraemer, F., Bræk, R.: Using UML 2.0 Collaborations for Compositional Service Specification. In: Briand, L.C., Williams, C. (eds.) MoDELS 2005. LNCS, vol. 3713, Springer, Heidelberg (2005)
5. Sanders, R., Bræk, R.: Modeling Peer-to-peer Service Goals in UML. In: Proc. of the 2nd Intl. Conf. on Software Engineering and Formal Methods (SEFM 2004), IEEE Computer Society Press, Los Alamitos (2004)
6. Object Management Group: Unified Modeling Language: Superstructure version 2.1.1, formal/2007-02-05 (2007), http://www.omg.org/cgi-bin/doc?formal/07-02-05
7. Sanders, R.: Collaborations, Semantic Interfaces and Service Goals: a way forward for Service Engineering. Doctoral theses at NTNU 2007:68. NTNU (2007)
8. SIMS: Deliverable D3.4 Techniques for Ontology-Driven Semantic Interface Artefacts, final version (2007), http://www.ist-sims.org/
9. Sanders, R., Bræk, R., Bochmann, G., Amyot., D.: Service Discovery and Component Reuse with Semantic Interfaces. In: Prinz, A., Reed, R., Reed, J. (eds.) SDL 2005. LNCS, vol. 3530, pp. 85–102. Springer, Heidelberg (2005)
10. Floch, J.: Towards Plug-and-Play Services: Design and Validation using Roles. PhD Thesis 2003:47. NTNU (2003)
11. SIMS: Deliverable D2.1 Languages and Method Guidelines, first version (2007), http://www.ist-sims.org/
12. ITU-T Recommendation Z.120: Message Sequence Charts (MSC) (2004)
13. Mellor, S., Clark, A., Futagami, T.: Special Issue on Model-Driven Development. IEEE Software 20(5) (2003)
14. Kramler, G., Kapsammer, E., Retschitzegger, W., Kappel, G.: Towards Using UML 2 for Modelling Web Service Collaboration Protocols. In: Proceedings of the First International Conference on Interoperability of Enterprise Software and Applications. Springer, London (2005)
15. Kraemer, F.A., Herrmann, P.: Service Specification by Composition of Collaborations – An Example. In: Proc. of the 2nd Intl. Workshop on Service Composition (Sercomp), IEEE Computer Society, Los Alamitos (2006)
16. Ermagan, V., Krüger, I.H.: A UML2 Profile for Service Modeling. In: Proceedings of the 10th Intl. Conf. of Model Driven Engineering Languages and Systems (2007)

17. OMG. UML Profile and Metamodel for Services (UPMS) RFP - soa/06-09-09, `http://www.omg.org/cgi-bin/doc?soa/2006-9-9`

18. Lamsweerde, A.: Goal-oriented requirements engineering: A guided tour. In: Proceedings of the 5th IEEE International Symposium on Requirements Engineering (2001)

19. Yu, E.: Towards modelling and reasoning support for early phase requirements engineering. In: Proceedings of the 3rd IEEE Intl. Symposium on Requirements Engineering (1997)

20. Quartel, D.A.C., Stehen, M.W.A., Pokraev, S., van Sinderen, M.J.: COSMO: A conceptual framework for service modelling and refinement. Information Systems Frontiers 9(2-3) (2007)

21. Roman, D., et al.: Web Service Modeling Ontology. Journal of Applied Ontology 1 (2005) (IOS Press)

22. Holzmann, G.J.: Design and Validation of Computer Protocols. Prentice Hall, Englewood Cliffs (1991)

23. Castejón, H.N., Bræk, R.: A Collaboration-based Approach to Service Specification and Detection of Implied Scenarios. In: ICSE's 5th Workshop on Scenarios and State Machines: Models, Algorithms and Tools (SCESM 2006) (2006)

24. Web Service Modeling Ontology (WSMO). D2v1.3. WSMO Final Draft 21 (October 2006)

25. ITU-T Recommendation Z.100: Specification and Description Language (SDL) (2002)

Adaptive and Fault-Tolerant
Service Composition in Peer-to-Peer Systems

Vivian Prinz[1], Florian Fuchs[2], Peter Ruppel[2], Christoph Gerdes[3],
and Alan Southall[3]

[1] Group of Applied Informatics - Cooperative Systems, Institute for Informatics,
Technische Universität München, Germany
[2] Mobile and Distributed Systems Group, Institute for Informatics,
Ludwig-Maximilians-Universität München, Germany
[3] Siemens AG, Corporate Technology, Information and Communications,
Intelligent Autonomous Systems

Abstract. Service-orientation enables dynamic interoperation of distributed services and facilitates seamless service provision or runtime creation of new applications. This dynamic service composition is particularly powerful in peer-to-peer (P2P) systems which offer scalability through self-management and autonomy. However, P2P service composition is nontrivial due to permanent peer churn and lack of central control. Existing approaches reduce composite service initialization to an NP-hard path finding problem. Thus, peer failure adaptation is costly and runtime consideration of peer logons or load changes is not practicable. This paper introduces logical peer groups for service composition. They enable runtime composite service reconfiguration including the migration of services to other peers. A prototype implementation is presented and the algorithms are evaluated through both formal and empirical analysis. The evaluation shows that the approach results in significant reduction of computational complexity, improves fault-tolerance and enables adaptation of logons and load changes which has not been possible so far.

Keywords: Adaptive, reconfigurable, self-managing, quality of service-aware applications, autonomic applications and systems, peer-to-peer computing, service composition, service-oriented applications.

1   Introduction

In recent years the composition of services has been one of the major enablers for many IT companies. Different companies automate order and payment procedures. Portals, online maps or logistic applications offer information aggregated from different providers. In [1], composability is even called the *reason to be* for services because it allows them to be used for multiple purposes. In general, services can be composed statically or dynamically. They are either selected and put together once during composite service implementation, or selected and put together at runtime, i.e. on demand. The latter approach enables runtime integration of intermediate services and permits, for example, the adaptation of

R. Meier and S. Terzis (Eds.): DAIS 2008, LNCS 5053, pp. 30–43, 2008.

current service usage context or the dynamic creation of new services out of existing ones. In large-scale networks, single services are furthermore offered by different providers. Dynamic service composition facilitates the selection of subservice providers with respect to parameters like availability, performance, load, monetary costs or quality of service (QoS). In this paper, we will call these parameters execution properties. Finally, subservices of a composite service can be exchanged during runtime. Consider a composite service comprising three subservices: one is an RSS reader that delivers text messages to a second subservice that translates the text into another language. The third subservice converts the translated text into speech the user can listen to. The user might want to hear the latest news using a PDA while driving a car. If, for example, the text-to-speech subservice gets overloaded meanwhile, the composite service can switch to a better performing entity which also offers a text-to-speech service.

Our focus is this dynamic service composition in P2P systems. Service providers as well as users are regarded as peers of a fully decentralized distributed system. That is, we assume that the network is not able to, or shall not, provide a central controlling component but is self-managed. Thus composite services can be provided without broker infrastructure and associated administration costs. Moreover, there is no central component that can become a bottleneck or even fail – essential when considering the evolution of distributed systems towards large-scale networks and accompanied scalability requirements. However, inter-peer service composition is nontrivial due to dynamic peer arrivals and departures (churn) implying high failure probabilities and the required decentralization.

Regarding related work, a lot of research has been done on optimized service selection and execution, for example in the fields of load balancing and context-aware computing. Concerning service composition, many central approaches exist, for example for grid environments or web services. Also for P2P systems some solutions have been proposed: *PCOM* [2], *A Scalable QoS-Aware Service Aggregation Model for Peer-to-Peer Computing Grids* [3] and *SpiderNet* [4] [5]. These approaches solve composite service initialization by regarding all possible service paths between all service providing peers. They show that the corresponding class of computational problems is NP-hard. This is basically due to the multitude of possible paths that have to be computed using distributed graph or tree algorithms. In addition, these paths have to be compared considering multiple constraints like QoS parameters. The only system that realizes fault-tolerant P2P service composition is *SpiderNet*. It utilizes a Distributed Hash Table (DHT) for decentralized information management and allows dynamic composition and proactive error detection for stateless services. Failures are compensated by migrating the composite service, i.e. the service path selected before, to a backup path. Backup paths are computed during initialization as well and are monitored at runtime using messages along the paths. However, migrating the whole service path on a single subservice failure is costly. None of the existing approaches is able to adapt peer arrivals or variations of execution properties because this requires expensive runtime re-initialization.

In this paper we describe a concept that supports adaptive and fault-tolerant dynamic service composition. Peer churn and changes of execution properties are detected at all times and may cause the migration of single services to other peers. The solution is realized by interacting and self-organizing peer groups and the underlying algorithms are based on nothing but local peer decisions. The remainder of this paper is structured as follows: Section 2 introduces our concept and explains the associated algorithms. Section 3 describes the prototype implementation of the system. Section 4 provides a formal analysis of the algorithms' computational complexity as well as an empirical evaluation of our approach. Section 5 concludes the paper and suggests future work.

2 Service Composition Based on Interaction Between Logical Service Groups

In this section, we describe our concept for adaptive and fault-tolerant service composition in P2P systems. Thereby, we assume the possibility to store, modify, delete and search for information within the P2P network. Example solutions for this discovery functionality are Pastry [6], Chord [7], CAN [8], Tapestry [10] or Freenet [11]. We refer to information as *resources* and to distributed storage as *resource publishing*. Furthermore, we assume that the P2P network is realized using DHTs and thus enables the implementation of a publish-subscribe mechanism. Publish-subscribe mechanisms are, for example, proclaimed in [12,13]. They enable single peers to subscribe to a certain kind of resource. Hence, they are notified, if a resource of that type is published, modified or deleted.

2.1 Basic Idea: Logical Service Groups

As explained in Section 1, existing solutions for service composition in P2P systems are very static. Service and backup paths are computed only once during initial service composition and cannot be adapted at runtime because their recomputation is too costly. The idea for a more dynamic service composition solution is not to analyze all possible paths between the peers, but to regard all peers providing a dedicated subservice as a group. Such a *Logical Service Group (LSG)* is defined as the set of available peers that locally provide a dedicated subservice. During subservice execution, one peer of the LSG executes the subservice and n other group members monitor its *heartbeat*. The monitoring peers are called *watchdogs*. Heartbeats are continuous messages being sent to the watchdogs. They enable the watchdogs to detect if the executing peer has failed. Figure 1 illustrates the members of a LSG and their roles. All peers providing a subservice are group members and one of them is executing the subservice. The group is part of a composite service comprising 4 subservices. Data to process, for example RSS feeds, are forwarded between the groups. In general, every peer can be a subservice providing peer in multiple groups. It might be able to execute different subservices of a composite service and LSGs are a logical construct.

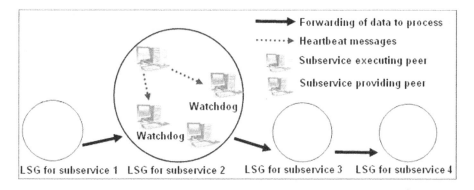

Fig. 1. Service composition based on LSGs

The formation of a LSG is carried out as follows: On a subservice request, the requesting peer publishes a *SubtaskResource*. This resource specifies the subservice to be executed including information about the composite service it is part of. Above others, it contains input parameters of the subservice and requirements concerning peers' execution properties. Every peer that participates in the group-based execution of subservices subscribes to SubtaskResources it can perform. As soon as a peer is notified about a corresponding subservice request, it publishes a *CandidateResource*. The CandidateResource names it as a candidate for the subservices it can provide. Furthermore, it describes its current execution properties. The group formation is carried out by an initial coordinator. It collects information about all peers providing the subservice by searching appropriate CandidateResources. Afterwards, it compares these information and assigns the role of the executing peer to the best performing peer. The selection criterion is given by the requirements specified in the SubtaskResource. Likewise, it assigns the following n highest ranked peers the role of the watchdogs.

The best performing peer then takes over the subservice execution and the group coordinator role. Because this peer is being monitored, fault-tolerant service execution is guaranteed and the group coordinator is always existent. During subservice execution, the state of the subservice is periodically saved within the *ServiceStateResource*. In case the executing peer fails, the best performing watchdog continues service execution. Thereby, it obtains the current subservice state from the ServiceStateResource. Moreover, the watchdogs are completed by adding another peer. Consequently, failure adaptation takes place with no need to search for a qualified peer first. Besides by peer failure, a subservice take-over can also be initiated if a better performing peer becomes available. This is when the group coordinator comes into operation. As soon as a candidate peer logs on to the network, it is notified about the existing subservice request due to its subscription to the SubtaskResources. It publishes its CandidateResource. By subscribing to these CandidateResources, the coordinator knows if a new CandidateResource is published. It integrates the new candidate into the current peer ratings. Apart from that, other peers' execution properties can get better or the properties of the executing peer can get worse because of dynamic load changes for example. To handle this, the peers of the group keep their execution properties in the CandidateResources up-to-date. If these resources are modified, the group coordinator is also notified. Thus it is able to recognize if an existing group member should take over subservice execution. In all three cases, the coordinator triggers appropriate role take-overs within the group if necessary.

2.2   Initial Service Composition

An environment that supports service composition has to provide two components – a design component and a runtime environment. Our research focus is the latter. We assume applications with graphical user interfaces exist that support the generation of valid specifications of composite services and their requirements and that translate them into a composite service description the runtime environment can interpret. Given such a composite service request, the runtime environment has to perform the initial service composition. That means it has to select an executing peer for each requested subservice and the selected peers have to know each other to be able to forward data between the subservices.

Regarding the LSG approach, the requesting peer first publishes the SubtaskResource for the preceding subservice in the service chain. In the example given in Section 1 the PDA publishes the one of the text-to-speech service. The subservices and their order are read out of the interpretable composite service description. Afterwards, the requesting peer carries out the formation of the first LSG. As soon as the executing peer of the new LSG is identified, it publishes the SubtaskResource of its preceding LSG, in our example for the translation, and again performs its formation. The procedure is continued until the LSG of the last subservice has been formed.

During these step-by-step LSG formations, the interpretable composite service description is recorded in every newly published SubtaskResource so that peers know which group to form next. Additionaly, every newly selected group coordinator stores the structure of its LSG within a *ServiceGroupResource* and publishes it. The identifiers of these resources are passed stepwise within the SubtaskResources, too. Thus, all executing peers are able to subscribe to the ServiceGroupResource of their successive LSG. The subscriptions facilitate the permanent addressability of a LSG, which becomes relevant during service execution. The same way, the identifier of a resource containing the state of the entire composite service is passed. If a group's executing peer changes, the new one knows if the composite service is still in the initial service composition phase – it must only send heartbeats – or if subservice execution has to be continued. As soon as all LSGs have been formed, the initial service composition is complete. Figure 2 shows the core algorithm of our initial service composition approach. ICD represents the interpretable composite service description. SR, SGR, CR and $CSSR$ stand for SubtaskResources, ServiceGroupResources, CandidateResources and the state resource of the composite service.

An important advantage of our initial service composition approach is that the load for the service group formations is distributed amongst different peers.

INITIAL-SERVICEGROUP-COORDINATION()
   ▷ Peer p_{t-1} forms logical service group for SR_t
1 Determine $ICD \in SR_{t-1}$
2 Determine $SR_t \in ICD$
   ▷ Additional information passed using SR_t
3 Set published SGR-Ids, $CSSR$-Id and the service requesting peer's id/port in SR_t
4 Set ICD as attribute of SR_t
5 Publish SR_t
6 Search next subservice's CRs $c_{t1}, \ldots, c_{tk}$
7 Determine selection criteria $\in SR_t$
8 Sort $c_{t1}, \ldots, c_{tk}$
   ▷ Ranking is forwarded within SGR
9 Create SGR_t
10 Set candidates according to their ranking in SGR_t
11 Determine best performing peer's id/port $\in CR_{best}$
12 Inform best performing peer to continue group coordination passing SGR_t

SERVICEGROUP-COORDINATION(SGR_t)
   ▷ Peer p_t continues group coordination
1 Subscribe to own logical service group's CRs
2 Publish SGR_t
   ▷ Service providing peers know SR_t due to subscription
3 Determine $CSSR - Id \in SR_t$
4 Subscribe to $CSSR$
5 Determine best performing peers' ids/ports $\in SGR_t$
6 Tell them their roles
   ▷ Subscription to SGR for addressability
7 if $SGR_{t-1} - Id \in SR_t$
8   then Subscribe to SGR_{t-1}
   ▷ Form preceding logical service group if existent
9 Determine $ICD \in SR_t$
10 if $SR_{t+1} \in ICD$
11   then INITIAL-SERVICEGROUP-COORDINATION()
12   else Determine id/port of service requesting peer $\in SR_t$
13   Tell it successful initial composition passing SGR_t

Fig. 2. Pseudocode notation of the initial service composition algorithm

These peers are best performing peers of their service groups at least in terms of their subservice's requirements. Moreover, the initial service group formations are executed fault-tolerantly. If the requesting peer fails, the composite service is not required anymore. All further initial coordinators are executing peers of their own service group. If they fail, a member of their LSG continues their role. Hence, initial service composition is performed fault-tolerantly.

Enhancements. Our approach includes further processes carried out during initial service composition: If a peer is selected for a dedicated subservice, it is taken into account that its execution properties change and that it might not be able to execute other subservices it could provide. In addition, single subservices of a composite service can be marked optional. This way, one can determine that a composite service is executed even though no peer is available that provides that subservice and fulfills its requirements. In our example, the translation might be helpful for the user but not necessary to get the RSS feeds' messages. Initial service composition is also successful if single optional subservices are not available. Finally, we described linear service chains to simplify matters. Our concept also allows nonlinear subservice arrangements through nestings in the (XML-based) interpretable composite service description and appropriate conceptual extensions. However, a detailed explanation of these mechanisms would go beyond the scope of this paper and is not needed to depict the core features decisive to realize adaptive and fault-tolerant service composition.

2.3 Composite Service Execution

Besides the initial service composition a runtime environment supporting composite services in P2P systems is responsible for the stable and fault-tolerant execution of the subservices and for the data exchange between them. To start composite service execution in our approach, the executing peer last determined informs the requesting peer about the successful initial service composition. Thereby it passes its ServiceGroupResource identifier which the requesting peer then subscribes to. Afterwards, the requesting peer modifies the state of the composite service so that it is now declaring its execution and triggers a ring message indicating subservice instantiation. Every executing peer reads its succeeding executing peer out of the associated ServiceGroupResource to be able to forward that message. As soon as the requesting peer receives the ring message again, the composite service has been successfully instantiated.

During execution, peers may fail, their execution properties may change or better performing peers may arrive. To adapt the resulting subservice take-overs, the coordinator of every LSG saves the current structure of the group within the ServiceGroupResource, i.e. who is the executing peer and which peers are in the role of the watchdogs. On a subservice take-over, the new coordinator updates these information. As a consequence, the preceding executing peer is notified due to its subscription to that ServiceGroupResource. It reads the new processing peer out of the modified ServiceGroupResource and updates the data link. Every new executing peer first subscribes to that resource. Afterwards, it fetches the current subservice execution state using the ServiceStateResource and continues service processing. Thereby, adequate rollback mechanisms have to be established to guarantee that no intermediate results get lost and no calculations that were already saved in the current subservice state are repeated (see Section 3).

Enhancements. Our approach also integrates the adaptation of failures of entire LSGs. They are monitored using detection messages along the ring of executing peers. A LSG fails as soon as the last peer that was able to perform the subservice can not fulfill the service requirements any longer or leaves the network. The preceding executing peer establishes a connection to the next but one LSG. Therefore, all ServiceGroupResources are stepwise forwarded during initial service composition. If the subservice was optional, the execution of the composite service can be continued without adverse effects. Otherwise, the preceding executing peer triggers a ring-message that indicates that the composite service has to be aborted. If no necessary group failed, the completion of a composite service is signalled by the requesting peer or by an executing peer that finalized service execution. Figure 3 shows the pseudocode notation of the algorithms applied during entire, exception-free composite service execution.

```
ON-COMPOSITION-FINISHED-RECEIVED(SGR_last)
   ▷ Requesting peer receives "INITIAL
     SERVICE COMPOSITION COMPLETE"-message
1  Subscribe to SGR_last
2  Set CSSR state to executing
3  Modify CSSR
4  POST-RINGMESSAGE("START PROCESSING")

ON-START-SERVICE-PROCESSING-RECEIVED()
   ▷ Peer p_t receives
     "START PROCESSING"-message
1  Publish SSR
2  Start service execution
3  POST-RINGMESSAGE("START PROCESSING")

POST-RINGMESSAGE(Message)
   ▷ Peer p_t forwards ring message
1  if SGR_{t-1} - Id ∈ SR_t
   ▷ Knows SGR_{t-1} due to subscription:
2     then Determine executing peer's id/port ∈ SGR_{t-1}
3     else Determine requesting peer's id/port ∈ SR_t
4        Send Message to (id, port)

STOP-COMPOSITE-SERVICE-PROCESSING()
   ▷ Peer triggers completion of the composite service
1  Set CSSR state to finished
2  Modify CSSR
3  POST-RINGMESSAGE("STOP PROCESSING")
```

Fig. 3. Pseudocode notation of the composite service execution algorithm

3   Implementation

To show the applicability of our concept, we have implemented the *Service Composition Framework (SCF)*. Because the project comprises 73 java classes and more than 10000 lines of code, we only describe selected elements in this section.

3.1   The Service Composition Framework

For the implementation of the SCF we utilized the *Siemens Resource Management Framework (RMF)* [9]. The RMF realizes basic features of a P2P network. Above others, it provides the two functionalities our concept relies on: a fully decentralized discovery and a publish-subscribe mechanism. Thus the SCF is based upon the RMF. The SCF itself provides an interface for developers. Every service that implements this interface can be executed as a subservice of a composite service. The interface could be kept quite simple. A subservice has to implement four methods that are used by the SCF to control its execution. One that executes the service on passing parameters, a second that stops it, a third that enforces a checkpoint of the current subservice state and a fourth that returns the state. Every result is passed to the framework using a given method. The framework then performs the result's faultless forwarding in case a successive subservice exists. That is, it repeats the forwarding if a results' receipt is not acknowledged and does not enforce a checkpoint until successful transmission. If the local peer fails and a result has not been forwarded, the related input is processed again. Of course it can not be assumed that every subservice generates elementary results but may, for example, work on continuous data streams. In cases like this, developers have to forward their results themselves. Therefore, another interface is provided. It declares a method through which the SCF passes the identifier and the port of the successive executing peer both during initial service composition and on executing peer changes.

By starting a dedicated class of the SCF, a host joins the RMF-network and subscribes to SubtaskResources it can perform. The new peer is then able to participate in composite service execution. To this end, the SCF implements the roles of watchdogs, of executing peers and of (initial) coordinators and allows to request a composite service. Also, it provides different simple comparator classes like a CPU-comparator. Requesting peers refer to them when specifying required execution properties within the (XML-based) composite service description. Coordinators use them accordingly for peer comparisons. Comparator classes can consider an arbitrary number of attributes and may prioritize them differently.

3.2   Test Environment and Example Services

To test the implemented mechanisms we developed a diversified test environment. The environment starts a variable number of peers and triggers a composite service request. During initial service composition, it checks whether all LSGs have been formed, whether the best performing peers send heartbeats and whether the determined number of watchdogs is active. When the execution phase sets off, it tests if all groups have started execution. Additionally, the environment integrates tests that stepwise change the execution properties of the group members in such a way that a subservice take-over has to take place. Furthermore, we have implemented tests that force peer failures in all LSGs. All these further tests are executed during initial service composition as well as during execution phase. They check whether the new best performing peer resumed the role of the executing peer and sends heartbeats and whether the determined number of watchdogs is active again. In addition, they test if the new peer knows its successor and if its predecessor was notified about the change. During execution, the resume of the subservice's execution is checked as well. Finally, the environment waits for finalization of the composite service and verifies if all results have been forwarded completely and not redundantly.

For test purposes and to visualise the framework's possible fields of application, we have implemented different simple services, i.e. performing certain calculations, and the mentioned example subservices – an RSS reader, a translator and a text-to-speech subservice. All composite example applications were successfully executed using the test environment. Even if executing peers change frequently, all results are forwarded and processed correctly. The system changes the executing peers as soon as their execution characteristics degrade, better performing peers become available or peers fail. The initial service composition and the execution of composite services are performed correctly and fault-tolerantly and all subservices are always executed by the best performing peers.

4   Evaluation

Having shown the applicability of our concept, we now focus on the efficiency of the integrated mechanisms. Therefore, this section provides both an analytical evaluation of the presented service composition approach and an experimental evaluation to substantiate the formal results.

4.1   Formal Analysis

The analytical evaluation investigates the computational complexity of the proposed approach. It aims to quantify the amount of computational resources needed in relation to the problem instance specified by the number of peers, services and so on. The complexity result will subsequently be compared with the complexity of the corresponding *SpiderNet* algorithms (see Section 1).

The use of computational resources is modelled as cost. As our algorithms are not tailored towards a particular DHT implementation, but only assume a DHT with publish-subscribe functionality, we base the cost model on primitive DHT operations. This way, the analytical results are independent from the characteristics of a particular DHT implementation. We distinguish three cost types for DHT operations: $c_{publish}$ is the cost required for making a piece of information available in the DHT for retrieval; c_{search} is the cost incurred when discovering and retrieving a dedicated piece of information; c_{send} is the cost for directly sending a message to a particular peer. We will quantify the DHT operation calls performed in our algorithms as well as those executed in *SpiderNet* to determine cost functions. To simplify these functions, we make the following two assumptions: The number of candidate peers is the same for each subservice and the number of watchdogs is the same for each LSG. So we will use three different variables: n denotes the number of subservices in the composite service, k is the number of candidate peers for each subservice (which is equivalent to the size of the LSG), and w denotes the number of watchdogs for each LSG.

Initial Service Composition. With respect to the previously introduced cost model and variables, the initial service composition algorithm (see Section 2.2) has the following cost function:

$$T_{initial}(n, k, w) = (kn + 5n + 1)c_{publish} + (n + wn + kn + 1)c_{send} + nc_{search}.$$

One can argue that choosing two watchdogs for each LSG ($w = 2$) results in sufficiently low probability for overall failure. Then $T_{initial}(n, k, w)$ can be written as $T_{initial}(n, k) = O(kn)$. Thus, the complexity of the initial service composition algorithm is linear in the total number of candidates for the composite service.

Composite Service Execution. We distinguish between the exception-free execution and monitoring of the composite service and the handling of different exceptions. The exact cost function for the execution and monitoring algorithm (see Section 2.3) has to include the total duration D of the composite service execution. This is because it influences the number of ring messages and heartbeat messages (interval I_{ring} and interval $I_{heartbeat}$) used for failure detection:

$$T_{exec}(n, w) = (n+2)c_{publish}+(D/I_{ring}(n+1)+D/I_{heartbeat}wn+wn+2n+2)c_{send}.$$

The intervals for heartbeat and ring messages are QoS parameters to be chosen, for example, according to real-time requirements of a composite service. With neglection of D, I_{ring} and $I_{heartbeat}$ and with $w = 2$ the cost function can be written as $T_{exec}(n) = O(n)$. The complexity of composite service execution and monitoring is linear in the number of subservices of the composite service.

Handling exceptions during execution triggers different further steps (see Section 2.3). When execution properties of a peer change or a new peer becomes available, adaptation incurs the following cost:

$$T_{adapt}(w) = 5c_{publish} + (2w + 2)c_{send} + c_{search}.$$

If we again assume $w = 2$, this adaptation requires only constant cost: $T_{adapt} = O(1)$. Handling the failure of a service executing peer has the following cost, which are again constant:

$$T_{failure} = 4c_{publish} + c_{send} + c_{search}, \quad T_{failure} = O(1).$$

Comparison to SpiderNet. The previously obtained complexity results are now compared to the complexities of the corresponding *SpiderNet* algorithms

[4]. We chose *SpiderNet* because it is the only existing approach realizing fault-tolerant service composition in P2P systems.

It can be shown that *SpiderNet*, which is also DHT-based, produces cost $T_{initial}^{S}(n,k) = O(k^{2}(n-1))$ during initial service composition. This is in contrast to $T_{initial}(n,k) = O(kn)$ in our approach. For example, assume a scenario where the composite service is composed of 5 subservices and there are 10 candidate peers for each subservice. Then *SpiderNet* is in the order of 400 calls to primitive DHT operations, while our approach only requires 50 calls.

Analyzing the *SpiderNet* algorithms for service execution yields the cost function $T_{execution}^{S}(n) = O(n)$. This is in the same order as our approach ($T_{execution}(n) = O(n)$). However, adaptation to failures requires more resources than our approach. This is because *SpiderNet* does not use watchdogs, but monitors multiple backup paths. As a result, exception handling requires to change not a single subservice but the whole service path and more monitoring messages are required in order to achieve the same level of fault-tolerance.

In conclusion, analyzing the complexities of the proposed algorithms showed that the introduction of LSGs results in significant reduction of complexity during initial service composition. Furthermore, the use of watchdogs for detecting failures results in higher fault-tolerance without increasing complexity. These are additional achievements to the newly introduced ability to adapt performance variations and peer arrivals.

4.2   Empirical Analysis

In this section we describe the results of our empirical analysis and evaluate if the results confirm our formal findings. To this end, we have carried out over 8700 measurements of our approach's core procedures with the aid of the SCF.

Initial Service Composition. In Section 4.1 we concluded that the complexity of the initial service composition algorithm is linear in the total number of candidates for the composite service. To verify this, we have measured the duration of initial service composition for two, six and ten candidates per LSG with up to twelve subservices. We raised the number of subservices stepwise recording 100 measurements each time which results in 3600 measurements. Figure 4 (a) charts initial service composition duration for a varying total number of candidates of the composite service (kn). It can be seen that it makes a difference if the total number of 20 candidates arises from 2 subservices with 10 candidates each or from 10 subservices with 2 candidates which is due to the stepwise group formations. Thus the graphs grow linear, which verifies our formal findings.

Composite Service Execution. The computational complexity of exception-free composite service execution depends on the duration of the composite service. Hence, we focus on the complexity of mechanisms realizing adaptive and fault-tolerant execution here.

We have formally shown that adaptation requires only constant cost when peers' execution properties change or new peers become available. Figure 4 (b)

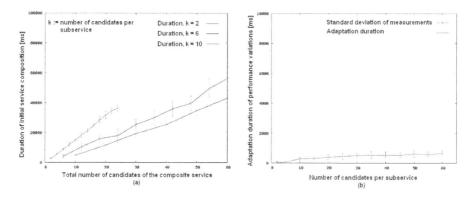

Fig. 4. Experimental results for initial service composition (a) and adaptation of changes of execution properties (b)

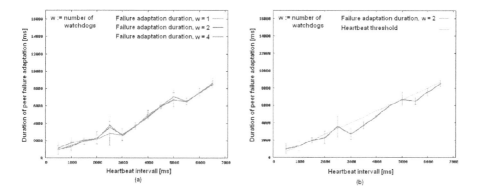

Fig. 5. Experimental results concerning peer failure adaptation

illustrates the duration measurements for this adaptation based on 1200 measurements taken for LSGs with up to 60 members. During formal evaluation, we neglected the costs for integrating a candidate into the current peer ranking because they depend on the subservice's selection criteria. Regarding the experimental results one can see that duration for adaptation behaves almost constant. The slight raise is caused by the growing number of peers to be compared with the candidate. Thus, our formal results have been confirmed.

Concerning the handling of failures of service executing peers, we arrived at the conclusion that this again requires constant cost. Figure 5 charts our results retained from 3900 measurements of failure adaptation duration using varying heartbeat intervals. Figure 5 (a) shows that the number of watchdogs does not influence the adaptation duration. In figure 5 (b) we contrast the duration for failure adaptation with the current heartbeat threshold. This threshold is directly derived from the heartbeat interval. It represents the time the watchdogs shall wait for the next heartbeat of the executing peer, whereby a little time interval is added to compensate delays in message passing. It becomes apparent that average adaptation duration is partially even below the current threshold. In this context one has to be aware that an executing peer can fail shortly before sending its next heartbeat. Hence, the next heartbeat is overdue soon. Nevertheless, one can state that the average adaptation duration is even below the current heartbeat threshold constant which is in agreement with our formal results, too.

5   Conclusion

We have presented an approach for adaptive and fault-tolerant dynamic service composition in P2P systems. Composite services are provided by interacting and self-organizing peer groups. Within these groups, watchdog peers monitor sub-service executing peers and coordinators detect peer arrivals and variations of peers' execution properties. If necessary, they cause the migration of subservices to other peers. The underlying algorithms are fully decentralized, i.e. they are only based on local peer decisions. The concept has been implemented and formally and empirically evaluated. Amongst others, we were able to show that the introduction of service groups results in significant reduction of computational complexity. The use of watchdogs for detecting failures results in higher fault-tolerance without increasing complexity. Moreover, all data are transferred and processed correctly during composite service execution even if single subservices are often migrated. Our approach is the first one that enables the adaptation of peer arrivals and changes of their execution properties.

A future field of interest is the consideration of deviation from service requirements if no peer is able to fulfill them. Another topic is the integration of a further selection level. One can think of the composition of services that integrate advertisement into content like audio or video and services that provide that kind of media content. Thus, users might pay less for the content. Now it can be left open which advertisement service to integrate. The decision is made during runtime and can depend on information about the user's end device or the user's profile. Users provide these information due to cheaper content. This way, advertisers can be offered a dedicated target group. Because service composition is P2P-based, advertisers can furthermore be arbitrary users that publish the existence of the advertisement service – for example a student giving classes in math to pupils living in his neighbourhood. Our concept therefore has to integrate a further selection level: before selecting a peer for service execution it must be determined which service of a specified kind, i.e. which kind of advertisement service, to integrate.

References

1. Singh, M., Huhns, M.: Service-Oriented Computing. John Wiley & Sons Inc., Chichester (2005)
2. Becker, C., Handte, M., Schiele, G., Rothermel, K.: PCOM - A Component System for Pervasive Computing. In: Proceedings of the 2nd IEEE International Conference on Pervasive Computing and Communications (PerCom 2004), IEEE Press, Orlando, USA (2004)

3. Gu, X., Nahrstedt, K.: A Scalable QoS-Aware Service Aggregation Model for Peer-to-Peer Computing Grids. In: Proceedings of IEEE International Symposium on High Performance Distributed Computing (HPDC 2002), IEEE Press, Edinburgh, Scotland (2002)

4. Gu, X., Nahrstedt, K., Yu, B.: SpiderNet: An Integrated Peer-to-Peer Service Composition Framework. Technical report, Department of Computer Science. University of Illinois at Urbana-Champaign (2003)

5. Gu, X.: A Quality-Aware Service Composition Middleware. PhD thesis, Department of Computer Science. University of Illinois at Urbana-Champaign (2004)

6. Rowstron, A., Druschel, P.: Pastry: Scalable, decentralized object location and routing for large-scale peer-to-peer systems. In: Guerraoui, R. (ed.) Middleware 2001. LNCS, vol. 2218, pp. 329–350. Springer, Heidelberg (2001)

7. Stoica, I., Morris, R., Karger, D.R., Kaashoek, M.F., Liben-Nowell, D., Dabek, F., Balakrishnan, H.: Chord: A Scalable Peer-to-peer Lookup Service for Internet Applications. IEEE/ACM Trans. Netw. 11, 17–32 (2003)

8. Ratnasamy, S., Francis, P., Handley, M., Karp, R., Schenker, S.: A Scalable Content-Addressable Network. In: Applications, Technologies, Architectures,and Protocols for Computer Communication, ACM Press, San Diego (2001)

9. Rusitschka, S., Southall, A.: The Resource Management Framework: A System for Managing Metadata in Decentralized Networks Using Peer-to-Peer Technology. In: Moro, G., Koubarakis, M. (eds.) AP2PC 2002. LNCS (LNAI), vol. 2530, pp. 144–149. Springer, Heidelberg (2003)

10. Zhao, B., Kubiatowicz, J., Joseph, A.: Tapestry: An infrastructure for fault-tolerant wide-area location and routing. Technical report, Computer Science Division, U. C. Berkeley (2001)

11. Clarke, I., Sandberg, O., Wiley, B., Hong, T.W.: Freenet: A Distributed Anonymous Information Storage and Retrieval System. In: Federrath, H. (ed.) Designing Privacy Enhancing Technologies. LNCS, vol. 2009, pp. 46–66. Springer, Heidelberg (2001)

12. Terpstra, W., Behnel, S., Fiege, L., Zeidler, A., Buchmann, A.P.: A peer-to-peer approach to content-based publish/subscribe. In: Proceedings of the 2nd international workshop on Distributed event-based systems, ACM Press, San Diego (2003)

13. Castro, M., Druschel, P., Kermarrec, A.-M., Rowstron, A.: Scribe: A large-scale and decentralized publish-subscribe infrastructure. In: Crowcroft, J., Hofmann, M. (eds.) NGC 2001. LNCS, vol. 2233, pp. 30–43. Springer, Heidelberg (2001)

Decentralised QoS-Management in Service Oriented Architectures

Markus Schmid and Reinhold Kroeger

Wiesbaden University of Applied Sciences
Distributed Systems Lab
Kurt-Schumacher-Ring 18, D-65197 Wiesbaden, Germany
{schmid,kroeger}@informatik.fh-wiesbaden.de

Abstract. Traditional hierarchical Service Level Management (SLM) frameworks fail to cope with the challenges imposed by the runtime dynamics of Service Oriented Architectures (SOA). This paper introduces a decentralised management approach that successfully uses emerging self-management techniques to realise a flexible SLM system and presents an architecture that implements this approach. The architecture consists of a modular self-manager framework that provides the basis for component-level and workflow-level management. It provides sensor and effector modules to monitor and manage different classes of applications. Integration with existing SOA components is based on the Service Component Architecture (SCA). The presented framework has been prototypically implemented and is currently evaluated in terms of efficiency and scalability.

1 Motivation

Traditionally, *Service Level Management* (SLM) is the discipline concerned with monitoring and management of processes and applications according to agreed-upon *Quality of Service* (QoS) criteria. In service provisioning relationships, provider and customer agree on QoS criteria and failure penalties in formal contracts, called *Service Level Agreements* (SLAs). SLAs contain *SLA Parameters* that define QoS aspects to consider and *Service Level Objectives* (SLOs) to be met regarding these parameters.

At runtime the agreed-on SLOs are monitored by a dedicated SLM architecture. Based on this monitoring information administrators and operators take care of necessary system reconfigurations. In current installations, a SLM architecture is often integrated with large-scale enterprise management systems, e.g. *HP OpenView, IBM Tivoli* or *CA Unicenter*. These systems started as management frameworks, and today consist of a number of more or less closely integrated components. The frameworks originate from the network management area and therefore implement a centralised, relatively static, and strictly hierarchical management approach.

However, looking at SLM on the application-level, emerging Service Oriented Architectures tremendously increase the overall complexity of enterprise applications, both in terms of the number of components involved and in the overall

R. Meier and S. Terzis (Eds.): DAIS 2008, LNCS 5053, pp. 44–57, 2008.
© IFIP International Federation for Information Processing 2008

runtime dynamics of the resulting system. In addition, the current trend towards virtualisation of computing resources adds another layer with dynamic bindings and thus aggravates the matching of application level failures to physical resources in large-scale systems.

In this paper, we present a decentralised and adaptive SLM architecture for dynamic SOA-based applications. The architecture employs self-management techniques to realise SLM for individual services. The structure of the management system automatically adapts to the SOA's business architecture.

The paper is structured as follows: section 2 describes the characteristics of emerging SOAs and presents commonly used implementation technologies. In section 3 we discuss challenges for SLM in SOA environments and give a short introduction to currently emerging self-management approaches. Our decentralised SLM architecture, which in parts relies on self-management, is presented in section 4. This section also gives a description of implementation details. Related work is discussed in section 5. The paper closes with a conclusion and a description of future work.

2   Service Oriented Architectures

Traditionally, *multi-tier architectures* are used to implement large-scale enterprise applications. They provide a clear separation of presentation, business logic and data storage, which alleviates the impact of a change in one of these tiers regarding the rest of the application. Multi-tier architectures are often based on standard middleware, e.g. J2EE or CORBA, with relatively static component bindings. Benefit of a multi-tier architecture is the stability of the interfaces between components in different tiers. A drawback however is the inability to perform quick reorganisations as business needs change – the rather static design of a multi-tier application results in an inability to quickly follow changes in the overall organisational structure of an enterprise. For that reason a more flexible and dynamic enterprise software architecture has evolved in recent years:

Independent and loosely coupled services define the building blocks of a *Service Oriented Architecture*. All services in a SOA environment are accessible in a standardised way, as they inter-operate based on a formal interface definition which is independent of the underlying computing platform and programming language. Services are dynamically composed into business workflows to form applications. This breakup into workflows and (shared) services however makes the concept of strictly separated applications dispensable.

At runtime, workflow descriptions are interpreted by a *workflow management system (WfMS)* that invokes the participating services. A major design goal for SOA is to bring the architecture of enterprise IT applications in line with the enterprises' organisational structure. Thus, while services are considered as static entities, SOA workflows may be adapted to business needs and thus can change on a regular basis. In todays B2B scenarios SOA workflows can even span across administrative boundaries of organisations. From an IT management perspective this complicates the enforcement of quality-of-service parameters.

Looking at the technical realisation of a SOA we distinguish several abstraction layers within the architecture (see fig. 1). At the lowest layer are the operational systems, networked hardware resources, operating systems and so forth. These resources are utilised by enterprise components, which themselves provide service interfaces. The second layer, called service layer, which we can also find in traditional multi-tier enterprise applications, is the typical domain of existing hierarchical SLM-approaches for applications. On top of the service layer we find the workflow orchestration layer, which dynamically involves the underlying services. Service interfaces hide all implementation details from the workflows in this layer. Workflows do also provide a service interface to the outside world and thus may themselves be accessed by other workflows in the same way like basic services. This allows to design complex, nested workflows.

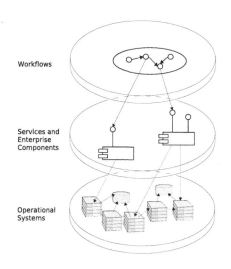

Workflows

Services and
Enterprise
Components

Operational
Systems

Fig. 1. Technical layering of a SOA

Today, common technologies for implementing a SOA environment are Web Services based on the Web Services Description Language (WSDL) for the description of service interfaces, SOAP as communication protocol, and the Business Process Execution Language (BPEL) [1] for the description of business processes and workflows. BPEL is an XML-based notation that defines a number of so-called BPEL activities. Activities represent single steps of a workflow, e.g. synchronous or asynchronous service invocations, variable assignment and evaluation, case differentiations, loops, etc. BPEL activities are divided into basic activities that include service invocations and other straight-forward operations, and complex activities which wrap a number of basic activities (e.g. loops). Regarding SLM on the workflow layer, BPEL activities are of special interest, as they reflect the progress of the real-world business activities. In terms of QoS observation, complex BPEL activities can be expressed as a combination of basic activities. QoS characteristics of these activities currently can be monitored, but a reconfiguration of services (accessed through BPEL activities) according to SLA requirements is difficult in dynamic environments (see[2]).

The *Service Component Architecture* (SCA) [3] is a specification that allows to create a standardised view on services, workflows and their static interdependencies within a SOA. As such SCA complements workflow modelling languages, like e.g. BPEL, which concentrate on runtime aspects of component interactions. SCA Revision 1.0 has been specified by the *Open SOA Collaboration*[1], an industry

---

[1] See http://www.osoa.org for details.

consortium that consists of a number of IT companies with SOA activities (e.g. IBM, Sun, Oracle, SAP, and BEA). Further standardisation of SCA in the meantime has been transferred to OASIS.

SCA models services and workflows as *SCA Components*. These components comprise any number of interfaces, named *SCA Services*, and dependencies (*SCA References*) to other SCA services. A dependency between two components is named *SCA Binding*. In addition SCA components can specify a number of static *SCA properties* to be accessed during runtime.

SCA components and their bindings can be grouped into an *SCA composite*, which hides its inner structure from the outside and thus can be handled the same way as a plain SCA component. This allows to create recursive structures of SCA composites within a SOA. Services and references of SCA composites are specified by propagation of component interfaces or references.

Figure 2 depicts the graphical notation of an SCA composite ABC, which comprises three SCA components. The composite offers a service a', which is propagated from the contained SCA component A. A also holds a Property P_1. In addition, the composite defines bindings between the components A, B and C and propagates the reference d of C to the outside.

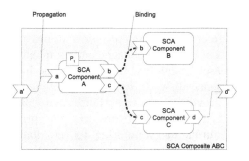

Fig. 2. Example SCA composite comprising three SCA components [3]

In order to support administrative tasks, SCA defines the concept of *SCA Domains*. Common policies can be applied to all domain entities. Currently SCA assumes that within one SCA domain components and composites of just a single vendor are deployed. This allows vendors to implement proprietary binding protocols. Currently SCA composites cannot spread across domain boundaries, however inter-domain communication between components is possible.

To date, SCA defines a number of different mappings for component implementation (*SCA implementation bindings*): there are Java and C++-bindings, but also bindings for BPEL, Enterprise JavaBeans (EJB), Java Messaging Service (JMS) and Spring. The component structure, bindings and services are detailed in an XML-based *Service Component Description Language* (SCDL) descriptor which is interpreted by an SCA runtime in order to instantiate the defined implementation bindings.

3 Necessity for Self-management

For several reasons a strictly hierarchical and centralised approach is not applicable for establishing SLM within a SOA:

(1) Because of the flexible, dynamic and compositional structure of a SOA, traditional static management structures cannot adapt fast enough to the system dynamics.

(2) SOA environments implement large scale processes. Traditional centralised management approaches with semi-automatic problem solving strategies do not scale sufficiently to meet SOA demands.

(3) A SOA may well spread across enterprise boundaries and therefore also across management domains.

(4) SLAs may be defined on different abstraction layers (e.g., for parts of workflows, or single services). Conflict resolution strategies must take organisational boundaries into account.

An SLM architecture for SOA has to consider the complexity of a SOA environment while it has to cope with permanent changes in composition and cooperation.

Recently, *self-management* approaches have become popular, because they aim at reduced management complexity (for the human administrator) and increased scalability. In addition, the introduction of self-managing system components allows to establish a decentralised management architecture and thus to provide increased stability on a global level.

Self-management projects the principles of autonomic computing to the domain of IT-management. [5] gives a compact overview of current challenges in the self-management domain. Self-management summarises approaches for autonomic reconfiguration, error recovery and optimisation of system behaviour of hard- and software components. [4] describes relevant attributes of self-managed systems as *Self-X Properties*. In contrast to traditional management architectures, where

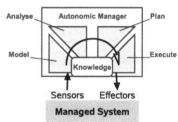

Fig. 3. Structure of an autonomic manager, as defined by [4]

a human administrator controls the system, self-managed systems are controlled by algorithms that – within certain constraints – operate autonomously.

Figure 3 depicts the principle structure of an autonomic manager. The manager is loosely coupled with a managed system through well-defined sensor and effector interfaces. Sensors are used to retrieve information about the current state of the system, effectors are used to dynamically reconfigure the system with the aim to drive it to a desired state. A manager may for example change a systems' strategy in terms of CPU and memory allocation, or may trigger the reinitialisation of a certain sub-module.

In a self-management setting, the autonomic manager and the managed system form a unit: the self-managed system. Such a system can again offer high-level sensors and effectors to the outside world, thus reducing the globally visible complexity of the system. As a result, a self-managed architecture can consist of several layers of control loops with increasing levels of abstraction.

Self-management alone however does not provide sufficient adaptability to global business goals. For that reason we suggest to apply self-management techniques only to SLM on the service layer of a SOA environment and to align the overall management architecture to the structure of the SOA's business processes.

4   Decentralised Management Approach

4.1   General Approach

A flexible SLM architecture for SOA environments has to meet the challenges described in section 3. Our SLM approach for SOA applications aims at providing scalability and flexibility through its decentralised structure, which uses self-management mechanisms for management automation at the service-layer. The SLM architecture automatically aligns with the structure of the business processes defined, as each SOA business component (that is all corresponding workflows and services) is associated with a *Manager* component, which is responsible for monitoring the components' behaviour with regard to its previously defined QoS requirements. Each manager component offers an interface for communicating QoS requirements.

Our approach realises a logically layered SLM management architecture, as managers associated to workflow components communicate with the managers of the participating services in order to enforce the QoS requirements that have been defined for a workflow. QoS requirements are represented as SLAs, which can be specified for workflows or individual services. Each manager gets assigned one or more individual SLOs, in the following termed *iSLOs*. The approach uses WSLA [6], an XML-based specification for SLA description as a formal notation for SLAs.

In the following, the underlying common architecture for service and workflow managers is presented. Afterwards, we describe the functionality offered by managers for services and managers for workflows. Last, we present the integration of our architecture with SCA-based SOA components.

4.2   Generic Manager Architecture

In compliance with the IBM reference architecture in [4], we have developed a modular self-manager framework that provides a customisable basis for the managers on the service and the workflow layers.

The core manager framework supports three different kinds of extension modules (see fig. 4 for details): `event modules`, `action modules`, and `control modules`. `Event modules` possess their own threads and thus are able to react actively to changes within the environment, e.g. by creating internal messages. `Action modules` are passive; they act – triggered by internal messages – by analysing application-specific sensors, or performing management tasks. Sensors can be realised using either `event modules` (push model) or `action` `modules` (pull model). Application-specific actuators are realised through `action modules`.

`Control modules` form the "brain" of the self-manager as they contain the management knowledge and implement control algorithms. `Control modules` act periodically or are triggered by incoming messages. Management decisions are communicated to other modules using the internal messaging capabilities.

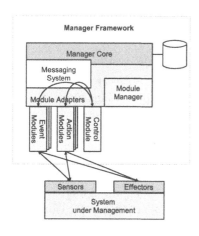

At startup the manager core starts a `module manager` component, which then instantiates the configured extension modules and controls their lifecycle. Each instantiated extension module is in one of the states `DOWN`, `UP`, or `ERROR`, the module manager regularly checks the state of the modules and is able to stop and reinstantiate modules that are in the `ERROR` state. Dependencies on the availability of other modules are also handled by the module manager (e.g. relevant event and action modules are to be started usually before the corresponding control module). Module configuration is remotely accessible through a management interface, which in principle allows runtime reconfiguration and reinstantiation of manager modules.

Fig. 4. Modular architecture of the underlying management framework

Managers on the service and workflow layers are designed to integrate into an SCA-based SOA as SCA components (see fig. 5). Each manager consists of the core manager described above, a number of extension modules, and an SCA adapter that

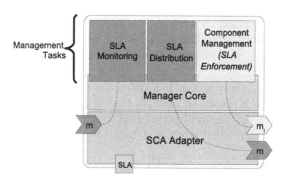

Fig. 5. Overall architecture of a manager component

provides SCA-compliant connectivity to other components, e.g. by offering a management interface m that is used for communicating QoS requirements.

Depending on the position of the manager in the architecture, its functionality is enhanced with one or more task-specific extension modules, namely for (A) SLA distribution, (B) SLA monitoring and escalation, and (C) SLA enforcement.

In the following we discuss the assignment of these management tasks to service and workflow managers.

4.3   Service Managers

For service managers, SLA monitoring (B) is performed with the help of appropriate event and action modules. Usually SOA services are realised based on enterprise software stacks that also provide standardised monitoring and management interfaces (e.g. [7,8,9]).

Several `action` and `event` modules have been implemented, that allow a powerful interaction with management interfaces, typically available in the domain of business-critical applications:

- A *Web Services Distributed Management (WSDM)* [10] module handles generic Web Services management invocations, implementing the *Management of Web Services (MOWS)* part of WSDM.
- The *Web-based Enterprise Management (WBEM)/Common Information Model (CIM)* [11] module allows the self-manager to act as a CIM client.
- A *Java Management Extensions (JMX)* [12] module allows to control any JMX-instrumented application.
- An *Application Response Measurement (ARM)* [13] module can retrieve performance-related information (e.g. response times) from ARM-instrumented applications.
- Command-execution supports the execution of shell scripts and other locally available executables.

Due to the modular architecture of the framework additional modules can be implemented without much effort.

SLA monitoring and escalation is performed by each manager in a separate SLA parameter-specific control module. A manager permanently monitors whether the iSLOs defined for the service are met, and – in case of a violation – notifies the requesting party (the manager, which communicated the SLA).

SLA enforcement (C) is solely performed by managers on the service layer. In order to fulfil the iSLOs that have been agreed on, a manager uses self-management techniques to reconfigure its managed service. Reconfiguration makes use of application specific interfaces (symbolically depicted as m_i in fig. 5) and may comprise dynamic resizing of application clusters, reallocation of resources, migration of virtual machines, or other highly component-specific tasks. Therefore, it is impossible to specify a generic SLA enforcement module, however managers typically implement a specialised controller module for the management algorithm and can possibly utilise existing action and event modules.

In order to customise a manager for controlling a software component that provides a service, a service vendor has to select appropriate event and action modules for monitoring and control of the service. As an example, one would probably choose the JMX module to control a Java-based service implementation. Performance monitoring of a service that runs on an IBM WebSphere application server can be achieved using the ARM event module as WebSphere offers an ARM-compliant performane monitoring interface. In addition, the control algorithm that is used for SLA enforcement has to be customised for the management of the software component, i.e. to reflect the possible reconfigurations offered by the software components' JMX interface.

In [14] we give an example for the customisation of a service manager component by describing an example SLA enforcement mechanism for a dynamically resized Cluster of JBoss application servers that uses a predecessor of the presented management framework: The approach minimises the resource consumption of the JBoss servers while still granting a maximum response time for the requests served. For this management scenario a state machine acts as self-management controller for the cluster, the communication with the JBoss cluster is realised based on ARM and CIM/WBEM modules.

4.4   Workflow Managers

SLA distribution (A) is a task primarily assigned to managers that are responsible for workflow components. SLAs that are assigned to a workflow need to be adequately distributed to the services that are involved in executing the workflows' steps. The distribution of the SLA comprehends an SLA parameter-specific fragmentation of the original SLA into iSLOs for the individual services and can e.g. take historical data into account. Afterwards, the iSLOs are communicated to the managers of the participating services via the SCA adapter.

SLA distribution has to take into account, that services offered by external providers are typically accessed with a fixed SLA (that has been previously negotiated by the parties), which cannot be manipulated by the SLM system. Such an SLA is treated as constant in the fragmentation process. In addition, also fully unmanaged services can be invoked by a workflow. Such services introduce a certain degree of uncertainty regarding the overall QoS behaviour of the workflow. Unmanaged services initially are assigned a random iSLO which is later adjusted according to monitoring information.

Fig. 6 gives an example for the process of SLA fragmentation and distribution. We discuss the fragmentation exemplarily for an SLO t_{max} that limits the maximum response time of the workflow. Fig. 6, part a) depicts the graphical representation of a workflow that invokes four different services, C1 - C4. After the request to C1 has returned, C2 and C3 are executed in parallel in a loop. Afterwards the service C4 is invoked.

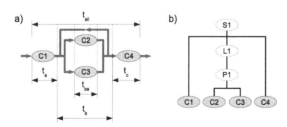

Fig. 6. SLA fragmentation example

Fig. 6, part b) shows the overall structure of the workflow, which is used to fragment the global SLO into iSLOs for the participating services. Initially, t_{all} is composed of three components t_a, t_b and t_c, where t_a describes C1 and t_c describes C4. $t_b = n * t_{ba}$ represents the loop execution time, being n the number of iterations and t_{ba} the maximum execution time of C2/C3. Ideally, t_a, t_{ba}, t_b, and n are estimated from historical data, which allows to proportionally fragment the SLO into iSLOs for C1 - C4. If no historical data is available, the proportions for the fragmentation have to be selected randomly and need to be readjusted later.

As for managers on the service layer, SLA monitoring and escalation (B) is executed by each manager on the workflow layer in a separate control module. In order to increase the overall system stability, a workflow manager only sends a notification in case the SLA for the workflow is violated, but does generally not forward notifications from individual participating services. In case a workflow manager receives a notification from a participating service, SLA distribution is triggered again to perform a restructuring of the existing SLA fragmentation, aiming at relaxing the iSLO of the component that sent the notification.

For workflow managers SLA monitoring is implemented generically for each supported SLA parameter. Workflow managers internally monitor workflow progress and calculate SLA parameters like workflow response times and throughput from this data.

4.5   SCA Integration

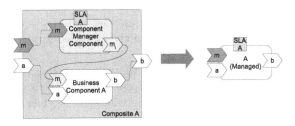

Fig. 7. Managed SCA Composite

In order to integrate managers transparently with existing business components, we make use of the SCA composition feature. Figure 7 depicts the association between a business component and a manager: Manager and business component are grouped into a single SCA composite, which propagates both the interface of the business component and the managers' management interface to the outside world. In addition, existing references to other components are also propagated by the SCA composite. We assume that workflow components are realised using the SCA BPEL implementation binding as the manager component at runtime needs to access structural workflow information; services may use any SCA binding available. The major advantage of the composition of business component and manager into a *managed SCA composite* is, that the existence of the management component remains transparent for management-unaware services that reference the business component. A drawback is an increase in the response time of requests sent to the managed SCA composite, that is in parts caused by the transport protocol used (e.g. one additional Web Service call between composite and service) but also depends on the overhead of the SCA runtime. We performed measurements for a worst case scenario that consists of an empty service implementation, which provides an interface with two double parameters. On an Intel Pentium M, 1.6 GHz (Apache Tuscany SCA Runtime, Apache Tomcat 5.5 AS) we measured a mean response time of 3.02 ms per invocation for the pure service implementation and 8.75 ms for a composite that references this service. This response time contains an overhead of $\tilde{2}$ ms for SCA processing. In a real world SOA setting these calls however typically take much longer as services perform complex business tasks while the SCA processing overhead remains constant.

In a SOA, services are typically accessed by multiple workflows at a time. The presented management architecture is able to cope with several concurrent SLAs, by using a QoS-Proxy mechanism as depicted in fig. 8. Here a management proxy component offers several service queues, one for each SLA to be met. The proxy references the business interface of the managed service and propagates this interface

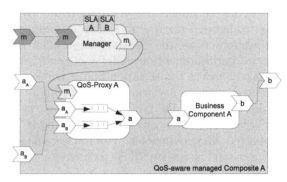

Fig. 8. Managed SCA composite with QoS proxy component

multiple times, thus offering the same service in different qualities. External services reference one of the QoS proxys' interfaces instead of the managed service itself.

The manager however can implement a number of different strategies for SLA enforcement, e.g. priority-based enforcement, or approaches known from the networking area such as weighted fair queueing or bandwidth management.

4.6   Prototypical Implementation

The presented self-management framework has been prototypically implemented in Java. Internal communication is based on a lightweight, process-local *Java Message Service (JMS)* implementation. The integration with SCA is based on the Apache Tuscany SCA project runtime. The SLA distribution functionality is based on the BPEL parser of the Apache ODE BPEL engine.

In our lab the architecture has been applied to example scenarios for SLA enforcement that have been implemented based on Apache Tomcat and JBoss as underlying Middleware. In this context, we used Apache Axis2 and JBoss for Web Service provisioning. JBoss and Tomcat were equipped with fine-grained performance monitoring sensors using the ARM API (see [9] for details). We implemented an actuator module to start and stop server instances on different hosts. In addition, we designed a rule-based control module that uses the ARM performance monitoring data in combination with the actuator module to increase or reduce the size of the managed server cluster according to the average response time measured. The control module was able to keep the service response times within a predefined range under different load conditions.

The global stability of the SLM framework depends on constant response times of the participating services. In cases where we observe a high standard deviation from the average response time, workflow managers tend to unnecessarily recalculate iSLOs. However this can be minimised by defining appropriate thresholds for workflow managers or alternatively by adding a predefined safety margin to the iSLOs assigned to individual services. In addition we observed that it is essential that service managers pause after executing a reconfiguration in order to allow the changes to take effect. In the example above, the start of a new server instance took about 40s – the manager had to take this into account in order not to trigger the start of additional instances in the meantime.

5 Related Work

Many architectures for SLM-enforcement do exist for multi-tier environments [15,16,17] or single enterprise components [18,19]. Some of these architectures already employ controllers that are able to manage certain aspects of the system without human interaction (self-management, autonomic management). To give an example, [19] uses a feedback-control approach for autonomic optimisation of Apache Web server response times. In contrast to our architecture these approaches mainly focus on the service layer, i.e., they are not capable of dealing with changing SOA workflows.

[20] discusses the topic of QoS enforcement in Web Services environments and points out current challenges in this area. A management architecture that itself is organised as a SOA is discussed in [21]. The authors describe their SOA-based management approach as a novel way to integrate different management applications but do not provide automatic alignment with changes in the business architecture.[22] presents a method for analysing the effects of service-local SLAs on global business processes. The approach gives hints for future investments (in terms of resources) to improve the overall QoS. It could therefore complement our work as it assists long-term management decisions on business restructuring.

In [23] the authors present WSQoSX, an SLM architecture for SOA environments. WSQoSX consists of a number of management components that control the lifecycle of SOA components, e.g. service discovery, selection, and workflow assembly. The architecture focuses on QoS-dependent service binding, i.e. the management system evaluates workflows and selects participating services based on their response time to fulfil predefined SLOs. When compared to our SLM architecture for SOA management, WSQoSX focuses on scenarios where different services with equivalent functionality are available and does not deal with the possibility of QoS-improvement for individual services. Thus WSQoSX focuses on B2B scenarios where multiple providers offer standardised services to choose from, whereas our approach focuses on SLM in inner-enterprise scenarios. In contrast to our approach, WSQoSX is realised as a number of centralised services, which may eventually lead to scalability issues.

6 Summary and Conclusions

We presented a decentralised management approach for SOA environments that uses emerging self-management techniques to realise a flexible SLM system. The

SLM architecture consists of a modular self-manager framework that provides the basis for component-level and workflow-level managers. The framework provides a number of sensor and effector modules to monitor and manage different classes of enterprise components. The seamless integration with existing SOA components is based on the Service Component Architecture (SCA).

The underlying manager framework has also been used in a different context: we designed an autonomic management framework for virtual machines [24], which is going to be integrated with the work presented in this paper. We are also working on basing our inter-manager SLA communication on WS-Agreement (see [25]). In addition, future work concentrates on exploiting the potential for system-wide optimisations, which are made possible by the homogeneous view on all applications of an enterprise that is provided by a SOA. We currently work on enhancing the existing architecture with self-organisation aspects for service managers. We aim to minimise global service resource usage by establishing a P2P-based trading mechanism for iSLO parts. A first approach that uses auction and bazaar protocols for transferring iSLO shares between participating components of a workflow has already been described in [26].

References

1. Organization for the Advancement of Structured Information Standards (OASIS): Web Services Business Process Execution Language Version 2.0 - OASIS Standard (April 2007) (Last visited 10/12/2007),
   `http://docs.oasis-open.org/wsbpel/2.0/OS/wsbpel-v2.0-OS.pdf`
2. Rud, D., Schmietendorf, A., Dumke, R.: Performance Modeling of WS-BPEL-Based Web Service Compositions. In: IEEE Services Computing Workshop (2006)
3. Open SOA Collaboration: SCA Service Component Architecture – Assembly Model Specification Version 1.0 (March 2007) (Last visited 10/12/2007), `http://www.osoa.org/display/Main/Service+Component+Architecture+Specifications`
4. Kephart, J.O., Chess, D.M.: The Vision of Autonomic Computing. Computer 36(1), 41–50 (2003)
5. Herrmann, K., Muehl, G., Geihs, K.: Self-Management: The Solution to Complexity or Just Another Problem?. IEEE Distributed Systems Online 6(1) (2005)
6. Keller, A., Ludwig, H.: The WSLA Framework: Specifying and Monitoring Service Level Agreements for Web Services. Journal of Network and Systems Management 11(1), 57–81 (2003)
7. Schaefer, J.: An Approach for Fine-Grained Web Service Performance Monitoring. In: Eliassen, F., Montresor, A. (eds.) DAIS 2006. LNCS, vol. 4025, Springer, Heidelberg (2006)
8. IBM: IBM Systems Software Information Center: Application instrumentation (Last visited August 2007), `http://publib.boulder.ibm.com/infocenter/eserver/v1r2/index.jsp?topic=/ewlminfo/eicaaappinstrument.htm`
9. Schmid, M., Thoss, M., Termin, T., Kroeger, R.: A Generic Application-Oriented Performance Instrumentation for Multi-Tier Environments. In: IM 2007 - IFIP/IEEE Int. Symp. on Integrated Network Management, IEEE, Los Alamitos (2007)
10. OASIS: Web Services Distributed Management: Management of Web Services 1.0 (2005), `http://docs.oasisopen.org/wsdm/2004/12/wsdm-mows-1.0.pdf`

11. Distributed Management Task Force, Inc.: Common Information Model Specification 2.2 (1999), http://www.dmtf.org/standards/documents/CIM/DSP0004.pdf
12. Sun Microsystems: Java Management Extensions Instrumentation and Agent Specification, V1.2 (2002),
    http://jcp.org/aboutJava/community-process/final/jsr003/index3.html
13. The OpenGroup: Application Response Measurement (ARM) Issue 4.0, V2 - C Binding (2004), http://www.opengroup.org/management/arm/
14. Debusmann, M., Schmid, M., Kroeger, R.: Model-Driven Self-Management of Legacy Applications. In: Kutvonen, L., Alonistioti, N. (eds.) DAIS 2005. LNCS, vol. 3543, pp. 56–67. Springer, Heidelberg (2005)
15. Menasce, D.A., Barbara, D., Dodge, R.: Preserving QoS of e-commerce sites through self-tuning: A performance model approach. In: Proceedings of the 3rd ACM Conference on Electronic Commerce, pp. 224–234. ACM Press, New York (2001)
16. Urgaonkar, B., Shenoy, P., Chandra, A., Goyal, P.: Dynamic provisioning of multi-tier internet applications. In: Proceedings of the 2nd International Conference on Autonomic Computing (ICAC 2005) (June 2005)
17. Ranjan, S., Rolia, J., Fu, H., Knightly, E.: QoS-driven server migration for internet data centers. In: Proceedings of the 10th International Workshop on Quality of Service (IWQoS 2002), May 2002, pp. 3–12 (2002)
18. Diao, Y., Eskesen, F., Froehlich, S., Hellerstein, J.L., Spainhower, L.F., Surendra, M.: Generic Online Optimization of Multiple configuration Parameters With Application to a Database Server. In: Brunner, M., Keller, A. (eds.) DSOM 2003. LNCS, vol. 2867, Springer, Heidelberg (2003)
19. Diao, Y., Gandhi, N., Hellerstein, J.L., Parekh, S., Tilbury, D.M.: Using MIMO Feedback Control to Enforce Policies for Interrelated Metrics With Application to the Apache Web Server. In: Proceedings of Network Operations and Management 2002 (NOMS), pp. 219–234 (2002)
20. Ludwig, H.: Web services QoS: external SLAs and internal policies or: how do we deliver what we promise?. In: Proceedings of Fourth International Conference on Web Information Systems Engineering Workshops, 2003 (2003)
21. Mayerl, C., Vogel, T., Abeck, S.: SOA-based integration of IT service management applications. In: Web Services, 2005. ICWS 2005. Proceedings. 2005 IEEE International Conference on (2005)
22. Moura, A., Sauv, J., Jornada, J., Radziuk, E.: A Quantitative Approach to IT Investment Allocation to Improve Business Results. In: Seventh IEEE International Workshop on Policies for Distributed Systems and Networks (POLICY 2006) (2006)
23. Berbner, R., Grollius, T., Repp, N., Heckmann, O., Ortner, E., Steinmetz, R.: An approach for the Management of Service-oriented Architecture (SoA) based Application Systems. In: Enterprise Modelling and Information Systems Architectures, Proceedings, 2005, October 2005, pp. 208–221 (2005)
24. Marinescu, D., Kroeger, R.: Towards a Framework for the Autonomic Management of Virtualization-Based Environments. In: Erstes GI/ITG KuVS Fachgespraech Virtualisierung, Paderborn (February 2008)
25. Andrieux, A., Czajkowski, K., Dan, A., Keahey, K., Ludwig, H., Nakata, T., Pruyne, J., Rofrano, J., Tuecke, S., Xu., M.: Web Services Agreement Specification (WS-Agreement). Open Grid Forum GWD-R (Proposed Recommendation) (2007)
26. Schmid, M.: Ein Ansatz fuer das Service Level Management in dynamischen Architekturen. In: Braun, T., Carle, G., Stiller, B. (eds.) KiVS 2007 - Kommunikation in Verteilten Systemen, March 2007, pp. 255–266. VDE Verlag (2007) (in German)

QoS-Based Service Provision Schemes and Plan Durability in Service Composition

Koramit Pichanaharee and Twittie Senivongse

Department of Computer Engineering, Faculty of Engineering, Chulalongkorn University
Phyathai Road, Pathumwan, Bangkok 10330 Thailand
koramit.p@gmail.com, twittie.s@chula.ac.th

Abstract. In service composition, quality of service is a major criterion for selecting services to collaborate in a process flow to satisfy a certain quality goal. This paper presents an approach for service composition which considers QoS-based service provision schemes and variability of the QoS when planning. The QoS of a service can be stated in terms of complex service provision schemes, e.g. its service cost is offered at different rates for different classes of processing time, or its partnership with another service gives a special class of QoS when they operate in the same plan. We also address that it is desirable for service planning to result in a plan that is durable and reusable since change in the plan, e.g. by deviation of the actual QoS, would incur overheads. Our planning approach takes into account these dynamic situations and is demonstrated by using the Estimation of Distribution Algorithm.

Keywords: Service Composition, QoS, Estimation of Distribution Algorithm.

1 Introduction

Service composition is a process that selects software units, called services, and composes them into a workflow that represents a business process [1]. The workflow can be viewed as a composite service since it provides an aggregated function and can be used further in composition of other services or business processes. A service composition problem can be considered a planning problem. That is, given a flow of abstract services (AS) for a particular business domain as a goal, composition will create a plan that satisfies such a goal by assigning a service instance (SI) in place of each abstract service. A flow for a travel planner, for example, may consist of three abstract services, i.e. tourist information, transportation, and accommodation services. A service instance will be selected for each abstract service to make a concrete plan.

Quality of service (QoS) has been considered widely in the composition problem. Service instances that collectively give the optimal quality or meet the quality defined by the user will be the solution to planning. Several publications [2-5] give slightly different QoS definitions but the most common QoS attributes include cost, time, availability, reliability, reputation, and security of services. A number of research efforts have proposed ways to compose services based on QoS attributes by using

R. Meier and S. Terzis (Eds.): DAIS 2008, LNCS 5053, pp. 58–71, 2008.

several optimisation methods and techniques, e.g. integer programming, linear programming, genetic algorithm. We are interested in using QoS attributes to determine the solution plan, but also discuss the following issues:

1. The QoS of service instances may vary when the instances are used in different operational environments, and therefore different users may have different experiences when using the same service instance. To have an accurate view of the actual QoS, each user will maintain his/her own experiences in using particular service instances, i.e. how much the actual QoS deviates from what was published by service providers. Such information should be fed into future planning which involves those service instances.

2. In certain cases, an organisation that formulates a composition plan to represent a business process would expect the plan to last and can be reused at least for some time. A travel planning organisation, for example, would use the plan which consists of particular instances of tourist information, transportation, and accommodation services to arrange trips for its customers. If the actual QoS of these instances is quite stable compared to what was published at planning time, the organisation can reuse the plan in serving its customers. Deviation of the QoS of each service instance can affect the overall QoS of the flow and hence will call for a new plan to be composed. Such replanning incurs overheads and is not desirable if it happens frequently. We address this issue as plan durability.

3. Instead of publishing service quality in terms of individual QoS attributes, service providers can state the QoS in terms of complex service provision schemes to realise various classes of service provision. For example, a service instance may offer different classes of service time which vary by the cost charged to the user, or the availability of the service instance may vary by the time of use. A service provider may also work in partnership with another provider to provide a special class of service, e.g. they give a discount in cost or offer less service time if their instances operate together in a plan. Partnership nevertheless can affect plan durability. When two service instances are coupled, a QoS deviation at one instance could affect its partner and lead to change at both instances; the plan becomes less durable as a single deviation may incur change to a large extent of the plan.

In this paper, we propose an extended QoS model and a planning approach that will result in composition plans that address the three situations above. QoS-based service provision schemes will be taken into account when service instances are selected for the plans. Our QoS model captures common quality attributes, i.e. cost, time, reliability, and availability, and enhances with durability quality via self-rating and partnership-coupling metrics. Self-rating refers to the rating an individual user gives to a particular service instance based on his/her own experience in its QoS. Partnership coupling refers to the degree of coupling between service instances which is present in the plan via partnership schemes. We see that considering the durability issue at planning time will result in a plan that lasts longer and thus help reduce the chance of frequent replanning. We use the Estimation of Distribution Algorithm (EDA) [6], which is a technique of the Genetic Algorithm (GA) [7], as the planning algorithm. To search for a planning solution, the EDA generates population by a probabilistic model which is derived from the knowledge obtained from the past generations of population. We are interested in this characteristic of the EDA because such knowledge should facilitate the creation of a new population during a solution search process, and should additionally contribute to replanning when a new plan is needed. A simulation of service instances QoS and EDA-based planning will be conducted.

Our approach can be used for both offline and runtime planning. A concrete plan is composed with regard to a given abstract flow, service provision schemes, and the durability issue. The plan should last until there is a requirement for a new plan, e.g. when there are new service instances or new updates on the QoS of existing instances. If runtime monitoring of the flow is supported, planning can also be triggered when there are service outages or serious deviations of the QOS. This work assumes that all service instances that are bound to a plan are compatible in terms of interface signatures and semantics. Service providers will publish the QoS of service instances in a public registry, e.g. UDDI for Web services, or provide other means for users to have access to QoS attributes.

The paper is organised as follows. Section 2 presents related work and Section 3 discusses our approach to QoS-based service provision schemes and variability of the QoS. We present the extended QoS model in Section 4 and describe how EDA is used in planning in Section 5. Simulation results from running the EDA are shown in Section 6 and the paper concludes with a discussion and future work in Section 7.

2   Related Work

Research works in QoS-based service planning tackle this problem by using different optimisation techniques to find composition plans based on slightly different QoS models. One of the major efforts in this area is the work in [2] which proposes a QoS model that captures execution price, execution duration, reputation, successful execution rate, and availability. By using integer programming, its QoS-aware composition maximises the QoS of composite services while taking into account the constraints of the users. Its supporting execution environment also considers runtime changes in the QoS of the service instances. The QoS model in [8] is used as a fitness function for composing a plan by GA. The QoS attributes include time, cost, reliability, and availability, and the plan will be penalised if it violates user QoS constraints. In [9], time, cost, and reliability are of concern in the QoS model and a distance function-based multi-objective evolutionary algorithm is used to find an optimised composition. A QoS reference vector is proposed in [10] to model price, time, reliability, trust (i.e. subjective rating), and security. The work evaluates service quality against cost of service selection by comparing a global exhaustive search and the integer programming approach. The work in [11] introduces a model-driven methodology for building QoS-optimised composite services and uses UML profile for QoS to model QoS requirements. The overall QoS of a plan is determined based on the multiple criteria decision making approach and patterns of control flow. Price, execution time, user rating, and encryption level are the QoS attributes of concern.

The paper [12] proposes a broker that supports planning and execution of any composite services with multiple QoS classes. Since a particular plan can be reused and executed repetitively as a flow, the QoS can be guaranteed on a per-flow rather than a per-request basis, and different QoS levels can be negotiated with respect to the volume of execution requests. Time, cost, and availability are included in the QoS model, and linear programming is used as the planning algorithm. The work in [13] presents a semantics-based planning approach in which data semantics, functional semantics, QoS (i.e. time, cost, reliability, availability, domain-specific QoS metrics), and constraints of service instances are considered. Ontology-based service dependencies such as business/technological constraints and partnership between services are addressed, and integer linear programming is used as the planning algorithm.

Regarding the works above, we see that EDA is only an alternative planning algorithm with a means to utilise prior knowledge when finding a solution plan and thus we do not aim to compare its performance with the algorithms in other approaches. Nevertheless, we share with them the common QoS attributes, but the reputation attribute is captured by a self-rating metric which is derived from a user's own experiences in the delivered QoS rather than from other users' subjective opinions. None of the related works address QoS-based service provision schemes and plan durability at planning time.

3   QoS-Based Service Provision Schemes and QoS Variability

In this section, we present our view on QoS-based service provision schemes and variability of the QoS towards plan durability. The following contribute to the extended QoS model and EDA-based planning in Sections 4 and 5.

3.1   QoS-Based Service Provision Schemes

Service providers can state the QoS in terms of complex service provision schemes to realise various classes of service provision. We give three examples here:

Multi-level QoS. A particular QoS attribute value may be published at different rates. Table 1 shows an example of multi-level availability of a service instance based on time of day. Multi-level QoS can be modelled in other ways, e.g. availability rates by classes of users, or by both time and classes of users. The scheme relating to cost, time, and reliability can be formulated in a similar manner.

Table 1. Example of multi-level availability

Service Instance A	
Time of Day	Availability
06:01 – 18:00	Base availability
18:01 – 00:00	+3 %
00:01 – 06:00	+5 %

Multi-level QoS affects service instance selection for abstract services. With the scheme in Table 1, a single service instance A effectively 'spawned' into three logical service instances; each of them is in service during particular time of day and with a particular availability rate. The planning algorithm considers them as three candidates for the abstract service.

QoS Interdependency. This service provision scheme forms a relation between different kinds of QoS attributes of a particular service instance. In Table 2, a service instance offers different classes of processing time based on service cost charged to the user. This QoS interdependency can be modelled in other ways, e.g. offering classes of discount for different levels of increased processing time. The scheme relating to availability and reliability can be formulated in a similar manner.

Table 2. Example of cost-processing time dependency

Service Instance A	
Cost	Processing Time
Base cost	Base processing time
+3%	-5%
+5%	-8%

Similarly to multi-level QoS, QoS interdependency affects the number of service instances that is associated with an abstract service. With the scheme in Table 2, a single service instance A is viewed as three logical instances; each of them offers service at the designated cost and processing time.

Partnership. Partnership refers to an agreement between service instances to offer a special class of service to attract users. The partnered instances may belong to the same service provider or different providers. A partnership scheme thus models dependencies between QoS attributes of the partnered instances. Table 3 shows a partnership scheme between service providers A, B, and C. The scheme offers a 10% discount in cost when the following instances of A, B, and C altogether participate in a particular plan: (1) any instance offered by A (2) any instance of abstract service X offered by B and (3) instance x1 of abstract service X or instance y1 of abstract service Y offered by C.

Partnership nevertheless can affect plan durability. When any two service instances are partners, it is likely that a QoS deviation in one instance could affect its partner. For example, when the instance y1 fails or has a QoS deviation and is replaced by another instance of a service provider D, the discount in Table 3 will no longer apply. The planning algorithm may choose to replace also the instances of A and B in order to benefit from the partnership scheme that D has with other service providers. In this view, partnership leads to coupling between service instances and the plan becomes less durable as a single deviation may incur change to a larger extent of the plan.

Table 3. Example of partnership

10% discount in cost when these instances collaborate	
Service Provider	Constraint on Instances
A	Any instance
B	Any instance of abstract service X
C	Instance x1 of abstract service X, or instance y1 of abstract service Y

3.2 QoS Variability

The QoS of a service instance may be affected not only by communication networks but also by the service instance itself. Since each service instance is built and tested independently in certain environment, the QoS behaviour may vary when it is used in different operational environment. Therefore different users may have different experiences in using the same service instance. We address QoS variability through user self-rating, which is given to service instances, and a supporting planning architecture.

Self-rating. Instead of using users' subjective opinions to determine the confidence in the overall quality of service provision, we aim for a self-rating approach which is more objective and respects users' personal experiences in service usage. Self-rating follows the idea of [14] such that service rating is based on deviation of the delivered QoS from the published QoS; the rating score is increased if the QoS fluctuates in a good way, and decreased otherwise. However, the score by [14] is computed at the service side and based on users' invocations from different network environments. The score is therefore biased from a particular user's viewpoint. We propose a self-rating metric (P) which reflects QoS fluctuations of a service instance experienced by a particular user:

$$Rating_s(P) = \frac{N}{E} \tag{1}$$

where N is the reward score given when the delivered QoS deviates in a good way, and E is the penalty score given otherwise. Rating runs between $(0, 1]$, and when it reaches 1, it stops responding to any more rewards. For an initial rating given to any service instance that is first known to the user, we adopt the mid-value 0.5 rather than an external rating score (e.g. published rating or other users' rating). This is because we prefer the user to truly rate service behaviour from personal experiences and not to be biased by the score determined under different operational settings. This initial score, in other words, is a representation of an initial N (e.g. 10) divided by an initial E (e.g. 20). When a user invokes any service instance, delivered QoS will be measured in order to update rating according to the user's own rating rules. We allow for personal rating rules since different users may be sensitive to QoS deviation in different manners and may opt for different reward-penalty schemes. Table 4 shows rating rules for time and availability defined by a user. The time rating rules are based on the distance of the delivered QoS from the published QoS under an acceptable fluctuation range $(\pm f)$. The availability rating rules penalise the service instance if it is not accessible at the time the invocation is made and retried. Given a scenario that a service instance is known to a user for the first time, the user sees the rating score 0.5 (i.e. 10/20). Suppose when the user invokes the service instance, it does not respond at first but a retry succeeds, and the delivered time of this invocation falls under the third rule of time rating rules. Hence the score of the service instance in this scenario will be $(10+1)/(20+1) = 11/21 = 0.524$. The values N = 11 and E = 21 become the new base values for this service instance for the next rating computation. While the user experiences the quality of the service instance through repeated invocations, the rating score is refined and becomes more accurate.

Table 4. Example of personal rating rules for time and availability

Time		Availability	
Event	Action	Event	Action
• $T_s$delivered > $T_s$published + f	+1 to E	• Not available first time	+1 to E
• $T_s$published + f ≤ $T_s$delivered ≤ $T_s$published – f	+0.25 to N	• Not available next time	+2 to E
• $T_s$delivered < $T_s$published – f	+1 to N		

This QoS-based self-rating contributes to plan durability. If all service instances in a plan are quite stable or do not fluctuate much in a bad way (i.e. good rating), the plan becomes durable and can be reused. On the contrary, if any service instance behaves much badly (i.e. low rating), the QoS of the whole plan may be affected and replanning becomes necessary.

Planning Architecture. To support QoS-based service provision schemes and QoS variability, we assume each user has a planning architecture as in Fig. 1.

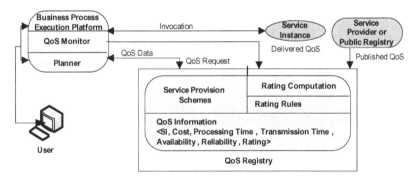

Fig. 1. Client-side planning architecture

The QoS registry stores QoS information of all service instances which are relevant to his/her business domain; discovery of these instances can be performed manually or automatically prior to composition. Cost, time, availability, and reliability information is retrieved from a public service registry or directly from service providers, and can be refreshed periodically or before planning. In contrast, rating information is initialised to 0.5 and gets updated only by rating rules. Note that each of the logical instances (e.g. each of the three logical instances of A according to Table 1) has its QoS information stored separately but they all share the same rating score. With the QoS information, plans are created by the planner and executed on the business process execution platform. During execution, delivered QoS is monitored by the QoS monitor and fed to the QoS registry where rating is then computed for service instances. Such knowledge of the QoS and personal experiences regarding particular service instances can help the planner to replan existing abstract flows for the user when necessary and to compose plans for new abstract flows that involve those service instances.

4 Extended QoS Model

Our QoS model comprises five quality attributes: time (i.e. processing time + transmission time), cost, availability, reliability, and rating. The definitions of the first four can be found in [2] while rating refers to the proposed self-rating in Section 3.2. Since a composition can be viewed as an aggregation of control flow constructs, the overall QoS of the flow is based on the QoS concerning each construct. We adopt a set of QoS metrics for common control flow constructs (i.e. sequence, switch, fork, and loop) of [8] and extend it with self-rating metrics (shown in boldface type) as in Table 5.

Table 5. Metrics for control flow construct-QoS pairs

QoS	Sequence	Switch	Fork	Loop
Time (T)	$\sum_{i=1}^{m} T(t_i)$	$\sum_{i=1}^{n} p_{ai} * T(t_i)$	$Max\{T(t_i)_{i \in \{1...p\}}\}$	$k * T(t)$
Cost (C)	$\sum_{i=1}^{m} C(t_i)$	$\sum_{i=1}^{n} p_{ai} * C(t_i)$	$\sum_{i=1}^{p} C(t_i)$	$k * C(t)$
Availability (A)	$\prod_{i=1}^{m} A(t_i)$	$\sum_{i=1}^{n} p_{ai} * A(t_i)$	$\prod_{i=1}^{p} A(t_i)$	$A(t)^k$
Reliability (R)	$\prod_{i=1}^{m} R(t_i)$	$\sum_{i=1}^{n} p_{ai} * R(t_i)$	$\prod_{i=1}^{p} R(t_i)$	$R(t)^k$
Rating (P)	$\prod_{i=1}^{m} P(t_i)$	$\sum_{i=1}^{n} p_{ai} * P(t_i)$	$\prod_{i=1}^{p} P(t_i)$	$P(t)^k$

The metrics are recursively defined on compound nodes of the flow. For a Sequence construct of tasks $\{t_1,..., t_m\}$, the time and cost metrics are additive, while availability, reliability, and rating are multiplicative. Each of the Cases 1,..., n of the Switch construct is annotated with the probability to be chosen (p_{ai}); probabilities are initialised by the user and can be updated later considering the information obtained by monitoring flow execution. The functions for the Fork construct are essentially the same as those for the Sequence construct, except for the time attribute where this is the maximum time of the parallel tasks $\{t_1,..., t_p\}$. Finally, the Loop construct with k iterations of task t is equivalent to the Sequence construct of k copies of t.

5 Planning Algorithm

Planning a composite service is a constraint optimisation problem that needs to

1. Meet user QoS constraints. For example, an abstract service must not have service cost above a given limit, or the overall cost of the plan is constrained. The former is called a local constraint and the latter a global constraint.
2. Optimise a function of some QoS attributes. For example, the user may want to minimise service time while keeping cost below the limit.

This section describes how EDA is applied to find QoS-optimised solution plans.

5.1 Planning with EDA

Like other evolutionary computation techniques, EDA follows the process in Fig. 2(a) to find a solution to an optimisation problem.

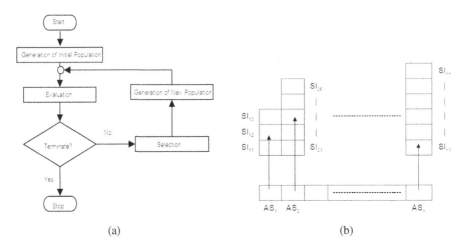

(a)   (b)

Fig. 2. EDA (a) Evolutionary computation process (b) Chromosome encoding (similar to encoding in GA [8])

The algorithm starts with a generation of a fixed-size initial population, which consists of a number of randomised encoded solutions called chromosomes. The initial population is allowed to evolve under specified selection rules to a state that satisfies user constraints and optimises a particular fitness function. Each chromosome will be evaluated against the constraints and its fitness is computed. If any chromosome satisfies the constraints, the algorithm may stop and the chromosome becomes the solution. Otherwise the algorithm continues to find a more optimised solution until a certain number of generations have been processed. To generate a new generation of population, some best-fitted chromosomes from the previous generation are selected for the new generation, and additional chromosomes are generated until the population size is reached. Then the algorithm repeats.

An EDA chromosome is encoded in a bit string of a fixed length. Sub-bit strings represent service instances (SI) that are mapped to abstract services (AS). In Fig. 2(b), AS_1 has three SIs and therefore is encoded with two bits, whereas AS_2 has five SIs and is encoded with three bits. Suppose SI_{12} is selected for AS_1, its sub-bit string is *10*, and if SI_{25} is selected for AS_2, its sub-bit string is *101*. A chromosome is then a sequence of sub-bit strings representing all selected service instances for the abstract flow.

Each chromosome g in a generation has its fitness computed by using the following fitness function (to be minimised); the function is similar to the one proposed in [8] except for *Rating(g)* and $D_p(g)$ components (shown in boldface type) that we augment to represent self-rating and partnership coupling respectively:

$$F(g) = \frac{w_1 Cost(g) + w_2 Time(g)}{w_3 Availability(g) + w_4 Reliability(g) + \boldsymbol{w_5 Rating(g)}} + w_6 D(g) + \boldsymbol{w_7 D_p(g)} \qquad (2)$$

- $Cost(g)$, $Time(g)$, $Availability(g)$, $Reliability(g)$, and $Rating(g)$ are the QoS values computed for the chromosome g using the metrics in Table 5.
- $D(g)$ is the distance of the chromosome g from constraints satisfaction, i.e. $F(g)$ penalises the chromosome that does not meet the user's constraints and drives the evolution towards constraints satisfaction. It is defined by

$$D(g) = \sum_{i=1}^{n} cl_i(g) * y_i$$

where $cl_i(g)$, $i = 1,\dots, n$, is g's distance from i^{th} constraint, and

$$y_i = 0 \quad \text{when} \quad cl_i(g) \leq 0 \quad \text{(positive or no distance)}$$
$$y_i = 1 \quad \text{when} \quad cl_i(g) > 0 \quad \text{(negative distance)}$$

- $D_p(g)$ is the degree of partnership coupling, i.e. $F(g)$ penalises the chromosome in which associated service instances are part of partnership schemes. It is defined by

$$D_p(g) = \frac{S_p}{n}$$

where S_p is the number of service instances involved in partnership schemes, and n is the total number of service instances in g.
- w_i indicates the weight (i.e. importance) the user gives to each component of $F(g)$.

When a satisfactory solution is not yet found, there are several strategies for EDA to generate a new generation of population. We use the one called Probabilistic Building Increasing Learning (PBIL) to generate chromosomes for the new generation by using Generator Function (GF). A GF contains probabilities p_i, i.e. $\{p_1, \dots, p_n\}$, where p_i is the probability that the ith bit of an n-bit chromosome is 0. For a given population with m chromosomes, p_i is the proportion of the number of 0 bits found in the ith bit position to the total number of bits in the ith bit position (i.e. m). For example, given a population with four chromosomes $\{010, 100, 111, 101\}$, the GF contains $p_1 = 0.25$, $p_2 = 0.5$, and $p_3 = 0.5$. To generate a new generation of population, each new chromosome in the new population would have 0 (zero) assigned to its 1st, 2nd, and 3rd bit with the probabilities 0.25, 0.5, and 0.5 respectively. In this manner, GF reflects knowledge from the past which guides how to generate good chromosomes. This knowledge would be refined as the population evolves from one generation to the next.

5.2 Durable Planning

In the fitness function above, rating and partnership coupling components contribute to durability of the generated plan. Since rating concerns QoS fluctuation while partnership coupling signifies a potential that a single service change may affect the plan to a larger extent, putting weights on them will indicate to EDA to find an optimised plan with good rating and low partnership coupling. That is, when it is less likely for the plan to require change, the plan is durable and can be reused.

At execution time, service instances, and hence the business process flow, may suffer from performance degradation and cannot deliver service quality as planned. The flow should be prepared to survive in unstable operational environment by considering performance deviation at planning time. We can simulate the situation by injecting QoS deviation to service instances and letting the EDA process makes a plan out of those instances (see Section 6.2).

6   Experimental Studies

We conducted a couple of simulations to study the behaviour of EDA-based planning with respect to QoS-based service provision schemes and plan durability. Note that service provision schemes took part in the experiments by constraining the QoS of candidate service instances. The first study focused on the use of GF from previous planning in building a new composition plan when published QoS of service instances was updated. The second study focused on durable planning. In each study, the population size was 200, the maximum number of generations to run EDA is 50, and the experiment was repeated for 50 times to obtain average results. The simulation program was written in Java with J2SDK 1.6. Experiments were run on a 1.8 GHz Intel Pentium^{TM}, 1 GB of RAM, and Ubuntu Linux version 7.04.

6.1   Use of GF

This study focused on the use of GF from previous planning in building a new composition plan when the published QoS of service instances was updated by service providers. This will demonstrate how GF benefits a search for a new solution plan. Suppose a user constraint was that the fitness value of the plan had to be below 9,600. The QoS of service instances was updated 4 times after the instances were first published. To simulate each update, we degraded all QoS values of the instances 0-5% at random. For example, if a service instance, with 1,500-millisecond service time, was randomised to degrade 1%, its service time would be updated to 1,515 milliseconds. At each update, EDA generated a new plan. There were 10 abstract services and each of them had 111 candidate service instances.

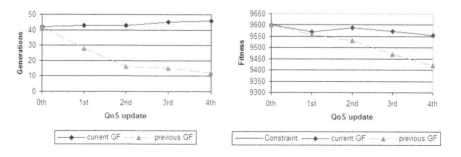

Fig. 3. Composition with GF

We compare between a composition that does not use GF from previous planning (i.e. it uses GF in current planning only) and the one that does. In Fig. 3, the left graph shows that, when GF from previous planning involves in the creation of chromosomes in the new planning after a QoS update, convergence time decreases. This means it takes less time (i.e. less number of generations) to find an optimised solution plan. This is because GF from previous planning is the knowledge that guides the characteristics of good solutions. It can be seen that, for example, the $1^{st} - 50^{th}$ generations of the planning on the 1st QoS update are effectively the $51^{st} - 100^{th}$ generations of the initial 0th planning. The right graph shows that, under a user constraint on the fitness value of the plan (i.e. below 9,600), composition that uses GF from previous planning gives better solutions. As GF is passed along, each composition gives a more optimised solution plan.

6.2 Plan Durability

Usually service QoS that is published by service providers is considered during planning. We expect that early (i.e. planning-time) consideration about the possibility of QoS deviation from what was published should result in solution plans that are more durable at execution time. This study focused on composition of plans that can survive unstable execution environment. Given a flow of 20 abstract services and a user constraint such that the fitness value of the plan had to be under 9,600, two groups of 100 plans were generated. For the first group, published QoS was considered during planning; this represented composition with ideal service instances with no QoS deviation. The second group comprised the concrete plans from the first group but with degraded QoS; this represented composition with an expectation of service QoS deviation. The service instances of each plan within the second group had all their QoS values degraded by 1-5% randomly.

After two groups of 100 concrete plans were obtained, we simulated their execution under unstable environment. Each service instance in any of these plans was randomised with a 40% chance to have its QoS degraded at run time. For the service instance that was to degrade, its QoS was degraded by 1-10% randomly. Then the fitness values of the plans in these two groups were computed to determine a percentage of survival, i.e. how many of the plans in each group still met the user constraint (with an acceptable 5% deviation) in unstable runtime environment.

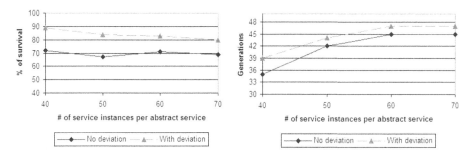

Fig. 4. Effects of plan durability

We experimented with various number of service instances per abstract service; this reflected the variation in size of solution search space. In Fig. 4, the left graph shows that the plans in the second group (i.e. those created with consideration about QoS deviation) can survive runtime degradation better than those in the first group (i.e. those created with no QoS deviation). This observation is true regardless of the size of solution search space. Nevertheless, the right graph indicates that it takes longer time (i.e. more number of generations) for EDA to find an optimised plan when the possibility of QoS deviation is considered during planning.

7 Discussion and Conclusion

In this paper, we discuss various schemes of QoS-based service provision and address a plan durability issue concerning QoS deviation and service relations. Self-rating and partnership coupling are introduced as part of the extended QoS model for service instances and workflows. A client-side planning architecture is also proposed. Using EDA as the planning algorithm, our experiments show that GF can benefit planning since knowledge of good solutions is utilised in finding a QoS-optimised plan. Considering the possibility of QoS deviation early at planning time will also result in more durable plans which can survive performance degradation at execution time.

On plan durability, our approach does not aim to make very durable plans so as to replace runtime replanning. Replanning capability is necessary when new services are offered or there are service outages or severe QoS degradation during flow execution. In commercial scenarios today, it is common practice that service providers publish their service instances QoS with a possible reduced QoS rate as a safety buffer. This safety buffer is taken into consideration at run time to determine QoS violation. Our work is aligned with this compromised QoS approach but takes the QoS safety buffer into consideration at planning time. By planning with degraded service instances in mind, we obtain the solutions that are more durable at run time. Our approach thus reduces the chance that a solution will need runtime replanning. It is also worth noting that our approach assumes the published QoS information is accurate. If service providers understate their service QoS only to boost their ratings, they put their service instances at the risk of not being selected to the plans from the beginning.

On performance of EDA, we rely on the performance result of the GA-based algorithm compared to that of the integer programming approach as reported in [8]. GA takes less time to find a solution and its timing performance is almost constant when the solution search space grows (i.e. when the number of service instances per abstract service increases). Thus it is preferred for the case of widely used abstract services, such as hotel booking and ecommerce services, which have a large number of candidate service instances. By using EDA, we also observe that the solutions generated in each generation can be very much similar to those in the previous generation because of knowledge in GF. That is, GF can lead EDA to fall easily into local optima. We will find a way to detect the situation and adjust GF. Nevertheless, we expect that knowledge in GF would be useful for runtime replanning, either in making a whole new plan or replacing specific part of the plan. We will explore more about the influence of GF over replanning.

References

1. Barry, D.K.: Web Services and Service-Oriented Architecture. Morgan Kaufmann, San Francisco (2003)
2. Zeng, L., Benatallah, B., Ngu, A.H.H., Dumas, M., Kalagnanam, J., Chang, H.: QoS-Aware Middleware for Web Services Composition. IEEE Transactions on Software Engineering 30(5), 311–327 (2004)
3. Cardoso, J., Sheth, A., Miller, J., Arnold, J., Kochut, K.: Quality of Service for Workflows and Web Service Processes. Journal of Web Semantics 1(3), 281–308 (2004)
4. Menasce, D.A.: QoS Issues in Web Services. IEEE Internet Computing 6(6), 72–75 (2002)
5. Mani, M., Nagarajan, A.: Understanding Quality of Service for Web Services, http://www-128.ibm.com/developerworks/library/ws-quality.html
6. Goldberg, D.E.: The Design of Innovation Lessons from and for Competent Genetic Algorithms. Kluwer Academic Publishers, Dordrecht (2002)
7. Goldberg, D.E.: Genetic Algorithms in Search, Optimization and Machine Learning. Addison-Wesley, Reading (1989)
8. Canfora, G., Di Penta, M., Esposito, R., Villani, M.L.: An Approach for QoS-Aware Service Composition Based on Genetic Algorithms. In: Proceedings of Genetic and Evolutionary Computation Conference (GECCO 2005), Washington DC, USA, June 2005, pp. 1069–1075 (2005)
9. Chang, W.C., Wu, C.H., Chang, C.: Optimizing Dynamic Web Service Component Composition by Using Evolutionary Algorithms. In: Proceedings of 2005 IEEE/WIC/ACM International Conference on Web Intelligence September 2005, pp. 708–711 (2005)
10. Wu, B.Y., Chi, C.H., Xu, S.: Service Selection Model Based on QoS Reference Vector. In: Proceedings of 2007 IEEE Congress on Services (SERVICES 2007), Salt Lake City, Utah, July 2007, pp. 270–277 (2007)
11. Grønmo, R., Jaeger, M.C.: Model-Driven Methodology for Building QoS-Optimised Web Service Compositions. In: Kutvonen, L., Alonistioti, N. (eds.) DAIS 2005. LNCS, vol. 3543, Springer, Heidelberg (2005)
12. Cardellini, V., Casalicchio, E., Grassi, V., Lo Presti, F.: Flow-Based Service Selection for Web Service Composition Supporting Multiple QoS Classes. In: Proceedings of 2007 IEEE International Conference on Web Services (ICWS 2007), Salt Lake City, Utah, July 2007, pp. 743–750 (2007)
13. Aggarwal, R., Verma, K., Miller, J., Milner, W.: Constraint-Driven Web Service Composition in METEOR-S. In: Proceedings of IEEE International Conference on Services Computing (SCC 2004), Shanghai, China, September 2004, pp. 23–30 (2004)
14. Mourad, O., Athman, B.: Efficient Access to Web Services. IEEE Internet Computing, 34–44, March-April (2004)

Towards Middleware for Fault-Tolerance in Distributed Real-Time and Embedded Systems

Jaiganesh Balasubramanian[1], Aniruddha Gokhale[1], Douglas C. Schmidt[1],
and Nanbor Wang[2]

[1] Department of Electrical Engineering and Computer Science,
Vanderbilt University, Nashville, TN 37203, USA
[2] Tech-X Corporation, Boulder, CO, USA

Abstract. Distributed real-time and embedded (DRE) systems often
require support for multiple simultaneous quality of service (QoS) properties, such as real-timeliness and fault tolerance, that operate within
resource constrained environments. These resource constraints motivate
the need for a lightweight middleware infrastructure, while the need for
simultaneous QoS properties require the middleware to provide fault
tolerance capabilities that respect time-critical needs of DRE systems.
Conventional middleware solutions, such as Fault-tolerant CORBA (FT-
CORBA) and Continuous Availability API for J2EE, have limited utility
for DRE systems because they are heavyweight (e.g., the complexity of
their feature-rich fault tolerance capabilities consumes excessive runtime
resources), yet incomplete (e.g., they lack mechanisms that enable fault
tolerance while maintaining real-time predictability).

This paper provides three contributions to the development and standardization of lightweight real-time and fault-tolerant middleware for
DRE systems. First, we discuss the challenges in realizing real-time fault-
tolerant solutions for DRE systems using contemporary middleware.
Second, we describe recent progress towards standardizing a CORBA
lightweight fault-tolerance specification for DRE systems. Third, we
present the architecture of FLARe, which is a prototype based on the
OMG real-time fault-tolerant CORBA middleware standardization efforts that is lightweight (e.g., leverages only those server- and client-side
mechanisms required for real-time systems) and predictable (e.g., provides fault-tolerant mechanisms that respect time-critical performance
needs of DRE systems).

1 Introduction

Emerging trends and challenges. Distributed object computing (DOC) middleware, such as CORBA and Real-time CORBA (RT-CORBA), is used to
support the development and deployment of many distributed real-time and
embedded (DRE) systems, such as shipboard computing systems and intelligence, surveillance, and reconnaissance systems. Such systems often operate
in resource-constrained environments and consist of soft real-time applications
whose availability and timeliness requirements must be satisfied simultaneously.

R. Meier and S. Terzis (Eds.): DAIS 2008, LNCS 5053, pp. 72–85, 2008.

For example, target tracking systems should provide timely response for analyzing sensor readings even when hardware and software failures occur.

Prior research on providing quality of service (QoS) using DOC middleware has addressed the timeliness [20] and availability [16, 19] requirements of DRE systems. Moreover, several standards have defined interfaces and provide services and strategies to enhance the timeliness and fault-tolerance capabilities of DRE systems. For example, RT-CORBA [14] and Distributed Real-time Java [7] provide capabilities to ensure predictable end-to-end behavior for remote object method invocations. Similarly, Fault-Tolerant CORBA (FT-CORBA) [13] and Continuous Availability API for J2EE [23] provide services and strategies to enhance the dependability of DRE applications.

Despite promising prior work on providing timeliness and fault-tolerance capabilities for DRE systems, key problems remain unsolved. Existing approaches provide solutions that address only one QoS dimension (e.g., timeliness) at a time. As such, these approaches do not simultaneously satisfy multiple QoS requirements, such as timeliness *and* availability. For example, fault-tolerance solutions are often not designed to honor timeliness while recovering from failures, whereas real-time solutions often do not recover from failures while ensuring predictable end-to-end behavior for remote object method invocations.

Moreover, *ad hoc* solutions—where availability and timeliness capabilities are obtained by simply adopting a combination of one or more solutions (e.g., FT-CORBA and RT-CORBA) described above—are brittle and hard to maintain and upgrade. Likewise, many DRE systems run in dynamic operating environments where workloads and resource availabilities fluctuate, which affect availability and timeliness requirements of applications. DRE systems therefore need middleware that (1) integrates real-time and fault-tolerance by design, rather than in an *ad hoc* manner, (2) is lightweight so that it is suitable for resource-constrained deployments, and (3) is adaptive so that availability and timeliness properties can be tuned dynamically at runtime to maintain soft real-time and fault-tolerant performance.

Solution approach → Lightweight Real-time Fault-tolerant Middleware. To address these unresolved challenges with prior work, this paper describes FLARe (*F*ault-tolerant *L*ightweight *A*daptive *Re*al-time (FLARe)), which is a CORBA-based middleware characterized by the following contributions:

• *Lightweight middleware architecture*, that integrates fault-tolerance and real-time solutions by design, instead of via an *ad hoc* combination of the complete FT-CORBA and RT-CORBA specifications. FLARe supports the provisioning of fault-tolerance functionality based on application time requirements, *e.g.*, to make failure recovery faster and more predictable for critical (as opposed to non-critical) applications.

• *Resource-aware adaptive fault-tolerance*, where the middleware supports flexible fault-tolerant system configurations (rather than inflexible configuration prevalent in conventional FT solutions) whose behavior depends on resource availability and utilization levels. When resource availability fluctuates due to failures, FLARe allocates the most suitable resources amongst the available resources for critical applications to increase the probability of meeting deadlines after failure recovery.

FLARe's design is based on the Object Management Group (OMG)'s standardization efforts to define a *Lightweight Fault-tolerance for Distributed Real-time Systems* (Lw-FT-RT-CORBA) [15] specification for CORBA-based DRE systems. In addition to summarizing these efforts, this paper focuses on the novel techniques that FLARe uses to provide fast, predictable, and resource-aware failure recovery for DRE systems. FLARe is developed atop the TAO (www.dre.vanderbilt.edu/TAO) RT-CORBA object request broker (ORB).

2   Objectives of the Lw-FT-RT-CORBA Effort

The goal of Lw-FT-RT-CORBA is to provide middleware mechanisms that simultaneously support availability and timeliness QoS for DRE systems. This section first describes the system and fault model of DRE systems that Lw-FT-RT-CORBA is intended to support. We then describe the key challenges of simultaneously providing availability and fault-tolerance capabilities for DRE systems and explain why the FT-CORBA [13] standard is inadequate for DRE systems. Finally, we summarize how FLARe achieves the objectives of Lw-FT-RT-CORBA to resolve these challenges effectively.

2.1   System and Fault Model

This paper focuses on request/response-based DRE systems, where clients invoke remote operations on servers and where client timeliness and availability requirements must be satisfied. Many real-time services (*e.g.*, sensor data acquisition and processing) are inherently stateless. For example, in target tracking systems the coordinate calculator that receives images from an image forwarding base station and calculates coordinates of surveillance images can be designed to process each image independently to avoid maintaining state between each invocation. Such systems need to provide real-time performance to clients, even in the presence of failures and load fluctuations. The goal of Lw-FT-RT-CORBA is to support soft real-time and fault-tolerant QoS properties for these applications.

Replication style. ACTIVE and PASSIVE replication are two approaches for building fault-tolerant distributed systems [16]. In ACTIVE replication, client requests are multicast and executed at all replicas to maintain strong consistency and provide fast failure recovery. ACTIVE replication, however, can incur excessive overhead for DRE systems composed of (1) stateless applications, such as the coordinate calculator systems which do not maintain state from prior sampling period's request processing as the processing in the current sampling period is independent from previous sampling periods, and (2) soft real-time applications that can tolerate occasional deadline misses. Prior research [4,18] has shown that PASSIVE replication and its variants are more effective for DRE systems because of its low execution overhead, and hence our focus is on how Lw-FT-RT-CORBA can effectively support real-time and fault-tolerant requirements of applications using PASSIVE replication.

System and fault model. The clients and servers (*e.g.*, the image forwarding base station and coordinate calculator services in the target tracking example) are implemented as RT-CORBA objects. The processors and the processes hosted by the processors are designed using a *fail-stop* model, where (1) each processor or a process halts in response to a failure rather than produce erroneous results and (2) a processor's or process' halted state can be detected by a failure detector. These types of faults may occur due to aging or acute damage. Considering unpredictable behavior of processes or processors is beyond the scope of this paper. We assume that networks provide bounded communication latencies and do not fail. This assumption is reasonable for many DRE systems, such as avionics mission computing and shipboard computing environments, where nodes are connected by highly redundant high-speed networks.

2.2   Resource-Aware Fault Recovery Challenges for Lw-RT-FT CORBA

In the context of the system and fault model described in Section 2.1, the following are key unresolved failure recovery challenges for using PASSIVE replication effectively in CORBA-based DRE systems.

• **Challenge 1: Providing efficient and predictable system/failure management.** As described in Section 1 and Section 2.1, DRE systems operate in dynamic operating environments, where new applications are deployed in response to changing workloads and failures. This dynamic deployment causes (1) increased resource utilization in certain processors and (2) load imbalance amongst the processors in the system. Middleware that is designed to provide failure recovery and management in a timely manner needs mechanisms that can react to changing load conditions and failures. Such dynamic environment changes must be communicated to the fault-tolerant middleware quickly and predictably so that failure management decisions, such as failover target selection, can be adapted and updated at runtime.

• **Challenge 2: Providing adaptive failover target selection.** When a CORBA application fails due to a processor/process failure, the respective client-side ORB receives a CORBA COMM_FAILURE exception [13]. Fault-tolerant ORBs therefore need to mask clients from those exceptions and transparently redirect clients to appropriately chosen backups. After a failover, the CPU utilization of the processors hosting the failover targets increase and the response times of the clients depend on the utilization levels of those processors.

If the failover targets are chosen statically—and without the knowledge of current system resource availability—client failovers could cause system resource overload, where different processor failures cause all the clients to failover to the same processor. A well-known approach for maintaining deadlines of application tasks in a processor is to ensure that its utilization remains below its schedulable utilization bound [10]. If resource overloads occur, however, this could cause increased utilization that exceeds the schedulable bound in those processors, thereby causing applications to miss deadlines. Failover targets must therefore be chosen based on system's resource availability, as well as replica's resource requirements, so that application timeliness requirements are not compromised.

• **Challenge 3: Providing transparent and predictable failure recovery.** One way to provide appropriate failure recovery is to decide on a failover target after receiving the CORBA COMM_FAILURE exception. This approach increases the time clients need to failover to an appropriate backup, however, and thus affects application deadlines. Failover target information must therefore be available at the client-side fault-tolerant middleware ahead of the failure time, so that the clients can failover to appropriate backups quickly and predictably.

2.3   Limitations of FT-CORBA for DRE Systems

To support PASSIVE replication, the FT-CORBA [13] specification collects CORBA objects into *replication groups*. Replica addresses are grouped by a standard mechanism called an *interoperable object group reference* (IOGR), which comprises a sequence of CORBA *interoperable object references* (IORs), each of which points to a server replica IOR. FT-CORBA clients invoke operations using IOGRs as if they were making invocations using IORs.

If a server object fails in the IOGR model the client-side ORB catches the exception, and cycles through the IORs in the IOGR to handle the request at a different replica. This approach ensures faster client failover and provides clients with a transparent abstraction as though the service was provided by a single server. If no IORs in the IOGR list are valid (*e.g.*, if no replicas are live) an exception is propagated to the client application so it can start a recovery process to find a new set of server object addresses.

Although the IOGR provides a standardized, transparent mechanism for client-side failover if a server replica fails, the overall architecture has the following shortcomings:

• **No seamless integration with RT-CORBA.** Not all RT-CORBA ORBs support the FT-CORBA IOGR feature. Even if it is supported, there are no guidelines on how the FT-CORBA services will work with RT-CORBA features, such as *thread pool with lanes* and *banded connections*. Without these features higher priority applications cannot be provided with fault-tolerance capabilities in a timely manner due to lack of support for for prioritizing failure detections and notifications.

• **Fixed and load-unaware replica selection.** FT-CORBA's mechanism of selecting the next IOR from a sequence provides fast failover. The default FT-CORBA replica selection policy, however, does not consider each server's resource utilization, which may affect client response times after failover. For example, due to dynamic task arrivals and changing system utilization levels, a replica that was a suitable failover target at deployment time may be a poor choice at runtime.

These shortcoming of FT-CORBA for DRE systems described above motivate the need for—and approach taken by—the Lw-FT-RT-CORBA standardization effort.

2.4 Salient Features of Lw-FT-RT-CORBA

To overcome the limitations of FT-CORBA for DRE systems, Lw-FT-RT-CORBA requires the integration of real-time and fault-tolerance capabilities into a DRE system by design. Lw-FT-RT-CORBA combines the following capabilities: (1) *FT-enabled middleware*, which provides fault-tolerance capabilities that does not require any real-time features, *e.g.*, a client-side interceptor can catch failure exceptions irrespective of the priority of the server process that has failed, (2) *FT-enabled real-time middleware*, which provides fault-tolerance capabilities that requires real-time features, *e.g.*, a failure detector needs to differentiate between the reporting of the failure of a higher priority object from that of a lower priority object so that fault recovery can be prioritized, and (3) *middleware-independent fault-tolerance mechanisms*, which support adaptive fault-tolerance, *e.g.*, fault-tolerant decision making, such as failover target selection, can be made using algorithms that are independent of the supported middleware.

The Lw-FT-RT-CORBA approach is different than the FT-CORBA approach, which provisions all fault-tolerance capabilities using FT-enabled middleware. For example, in FT-CORBA fault recovery is provided by (1) a *fault detector*, which is a CORBA component that detects CORBA object failures, (2) a *fault notifier*, which is a CORBA component that notifies CORBA object failures, and (3) a *client-side interceptor*, which is a CORBA component that detects client-side failure exceptions to redirect clients to the next profile in the server IOGRs. As described in Section 2.3, however, these capabilities do not function properly due to the non-adaptive, resource-unaware recovery mechanisms in FT-CORBA. To address these limitations, Lw-FT-RT-CORBA uses a micro-kernel approach that provisions fault-tolerance functionality via the combination of capabilities described above that collaborate to provide real-time fault-tolerance capabilities for DRE systems.

3 The Design of FLARe

This section describes the design of FLARe and shows how it addresses the resource-aware fault recovery challenges described in Section 2.2. FLARe is designed to address the requirements of Lw-FT-RT-CORBA *i.e.*, provide both availability and timeliness capabilities for DRE systems. Figure 1 shows the key components of FLARe's architecture, which includes protocols, mechanisms, and services for supporting fault-tolerance capabilities using PASSIVE replication for DRE systems.

The novel aspects of FLARe's design include the combination of (1) *client-side FT-enabled middleware components*, which transparently provide client redirection and request reinvocation, (2) *server-side FT-enabled real-time middleware*

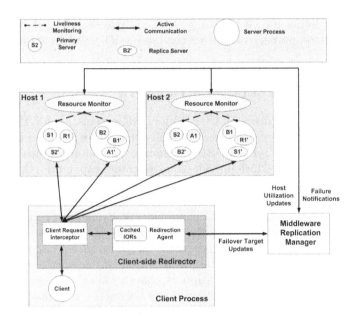

Fig. 1. FLARe Middleware Architecture

components, which monitor replica and process failures along with system parameters, such as CPU utilization, and help provide resource-aware and priority-aware
tunable fault-tolerance, and (3) *infrastructure-specific middleware-independent
mechanisms*, which use interfaces for replica registration and specifying application QoS requirements to support fine-grained tuning of fault-tolerance policies to
ensure timely performance of DRE applications.

The interactions between the FLARe components combine real-time and fault-
tolerance features, and hence provide an open platform for evaluating key issues
in real-time fault-tolerance capabilities for DRE systems. Moreover, while describing the interactions between these different components, we also elaborate
on the design choices we made and patterns used to implement various entities
of FLARe's architecture. FLARe's pattern-based design enhances its flexibility
and portability, without impeding the primary objectives of fault tolerance and
real-time.

3.1   Providing Efficient and Predictable System/Failure Management

DRE systems often operate in dynamic operating environments, where processor utillizations fluctuate due to dynamic application deployments and failures.
Changes in the system (*e.g.*, increase in CPU load) must therefore be conveyed
to the fault-tolerant middleware quickly so appropriate actions can be taken.

Problem. In FT-CORBA, liveness checking is typically accomplished via an
is_alive message from a *fault detector* component to all the CORBA objects

it monitors. However, as described in [15], the failures and recovery occur at the granularity level of a process and its address space. Liveness checking of individual objects for failure detection can therefore introduce unwanted and substantial overhead that adversely impacts real-time requirements. Moreover, introducing messaging for liveness check introduces additional system overhead.

Moreover, multiple objects and processes could fail simultaneously in DRE systems. Since the objects differ by their priority, failure and recovery management of those objects must also be prioritized. What is needed therefore is a resource monitoring infrastructure that is (1) decentralized, so that processor-specific local monitors can monitor the liveness of processes and their hosted objects, and (2) scalable and predictable, so that the failure as well as utilization reports are communicated with the fault-tolerant middleware according to the priority of the applications monitored.

Solution → Predictable and scalable resource monitors. As shown in Figure 1, FLARe employs a pair of FT-enabled real-time middleware components namely *middleware replication manager* and *resource monitor* to provide a decentralized, and predictable failure and system management for DRE systems. The middleware replication manager is composed of several sub-components, including a (1) *failure manager*, (2) *system manager*, (3) *resource manager*, and (4) *fault-tolerance manager*.

The failure manager receives failure notifications and works with the system manager to start new replicas if the replication degree of replica is below an acceptable threshold. The system manager receives system runtime information (such as CPU utilizations at different processors) and works with the resource manager to tune fault-tolerance decisions (*e.g.*, failover targets) dyhamically. The fault-tolerance manager works with the client-side and server-side middleware to notify the fault-tolerance decisions made by the resource manager.

FLARe runs a *resource monitor* on each processor to track the CPU utilization and liveness of the processes hosted by the processor. On Linux platforms, for example, the resource monitor uses the `/proc/stat` file to estimate the CPU utilization in each sampling period. This file records the number of "jiffies" (a default duration of 10ms in Linux) when the CPU is in user, nice, system, and idle modes. At the end of each sampling period, the resource monitor reads the counters and estimates the CPU utilization as the fraction of time when the CPU is not idle.

To perform liveness checking of processes in a processor, FLARe uses the *Acceptor/Connector* [21] pattern that decouples connection establishment and service initialization in a distributed system from the processing performed once the service is initialized. Since the server process and resource monitor run on the same host, the connection uses local connection mechanisms, such as a POSIX local socket (also known as a UNIX domain socket) or Windows named pipes.

For example, on Linux each application process opens a passive (*i.e.*, Acceptor role) POSIX local socket, and registers the port number with the resource monitor. The resource monitor connects to (*i.e.*, Connector role) and performs a blocking read on the socket. If an application process crashes, the socket and the opened port will be invalidated. The resource monitor then receives an invalid read error on the socket, which indicates the failure of the process.

Resource monitors generate periodic and event-driven notifications regarding failures and system utilization. FLARe's replication manager (the system and failure manager sub-components) must handle these periodic requests from all hosts it manages. The replication manager must therefore allocate appropriate resources to serve these requests concurrently and these events may be treated at different levels of priorities, depending on the criticality of the process and processor being monitored.

Addressing the challenges outlined above requires an approach that can handle incoming requests concurrently with negligible overhead stemming from context switching and data copying activities. The client-side (resource monitors) defines the priority at which the requests will be executed at the system and failure managers. FLARe therefore uses RT-CORBA's CLIENT_PROPAGATED priority model, which allows clients to dictate the CPU priority using which the server executes the client request.

To allow the system and failure managers to serve the requests arriving at different priorities, FLARe uses the RT-CORBA *thread pool with lanes* feature, which partitions the available number of threads across different priorities, so that each server can simultaneously serve multiple client requests arriving at multiple priorities. The number of threads is configured at deployment time depending on the number of resource monitors deployed in the system. By selecting real-time features, such as *thread pool with lanes*, and integrating them with fault-tolerance features, such as process liveness checking, FLARe provides prioritized failure management for applications using the combination of the FT-enabled real-time middleware components.

3.2   Providing Adaptive Failover Target Selection

For every replica in the system, failover targets should be determined based on updated information about the processor utilizations and failures, so that clients do not failover to replicas that (1) *are overloaded*, which can cause potential deadline misses, and (2) *have already failed*, which can potentially increases failure recovery time.

Problem. Fault-tolerant middleware needs to make per-replica failover target decisions based on algorithms [12, 2]. DRE systems, however, often have a wide variety of applications with different characteristics and priorities. Hence, a single decision making algorithm will not suffice for the needs of all applications. What is needed, therefore, is middleware that can support real-time fault-tolerant decision making based on various algorithms specialized for the needs of different applications.

Solution → Adaptive resource manager. As described in Section 3.1, the middleware replication manager has a subcomponent *resource manager* that works with the *system manager* to tune fault-tolerance configurations of the system in response to changing system configurations. FLARe's resource manager makes run-time, resource-aware decisions about the fault-tolerance configurations so that the clients can access the services in a fault-tolerant and timely manner. Example fault-tolerance configurations include per-replica failover targets, per-replica physical mapping onto processors, and per-replica weaker consistency optimizations. Research has been done in each of these decision-making dimension (*e.g.*, failover target selection) and many algorithms have been proposed [12,25,1].

To allow the resource manager to make decisions using a wide variety of algorithms, FLARe uses the *Strategy* pattern [5] to factor out similarities among algorithmic alternatives. For each decision-making dimension, the resource manager can be configured at deployment time with an algorithm strategy that is customized for application-specific availability and timeliness requirements.

The capability to plug-in many different decision-making algorithms allows FLARe to cater to the needs of a wide variery of applications. FLARe provides a failover target selection algorithm that determines a list of failover targets ordered by the predicted CPU utilization of the processors if a failover occurs (the processor with the lowest predicted CPU utilization is the first in the list). The algorithm and the subsequent performance within the context of FLARe is described in [2]. Moreover, as described in Section 3.1, the system manager receives information about the processor utilizations in a prioritized manner. Hence, the resource manager can provide predictable fault-tolerance by working on tuning the fault-tolerance configurations of higher priority objects rather than lower priority objects, whenever there are changes in resource availability and utilizations.

3.3   Providing Transparent and Predictable Failure Recovery

Client-side middleware in DRE systems must transparently handle failure exceptions caught as a result of process and processor failures and redirect clients to appropriate failover targets in a predictable and faster manner.

Problem. The per-replica failover target information computed by FLARe's resource manager is used by the client-side middleware to redirect clients after receiving a failure exception. The latency and timeliness properties of applications can be negatively affected, however, by invoking a remote method on the resource manager to obtain the failover target address after receiving a failure. What is needed therefore are mechanisms that can proactively update the failover targets on the client side.

Solution → Client-side redirectors. FLARe provides fast failover with predictable latencies by proactively updating the failover targets on the client side. It therefore employs a *client-side redirector* in each client process to handle failures transparently to each client object. The client-side redirector comprises a *client request interceptor* for each client object and a *redirection agent* in each client process.

Interceptors are software components that can increase the flexibility of client and server applications by modifying their behavior with little or no change to existing application software [21]. FLARe redirection agent uses a CORBA *client request interceptor* [3] at system initialization time to handle CORBA COMM_FAILURE exceptions that are raised in response to server or service failures. CORBA in turn relies on the underlying network transport protocol's (*e.g.,* TCP) connection timeout mechanisms to detect server failures. Since TAO supports client/server communications using many different protocols, its failure detection mechanism can be configured to use advanced fault-tolerance protocols, such as SCTP [22].

After catching a failure exception the client request interceptor attempts to redirect the clients to the appropriate failover target, rather than propagating that exception to the client application. As mentioned in the solution to challenge 2 above, the resource manager maintains information about the failover targets for each replica. One way to update the client request interceptor with these failover target decisions would be to establish remote communications between the resource manager and the client request interceptor. As discussed in [3], however, portable interceptors are not remote objects and do not have their own thread of control. No external service or object can thus invoke a remote operation on the client request interceptor (which is a CORBA-based portable interceptor) and the client request interceptor cannot periodically invoke a remote operation on an external object or service.

Moreover, such a remote invocation will increase failover or failure recovery latency. If an appropriate failover target information is available at the client request interceptor even before the failure happens, then client redirection will be predictable, fast, and timely, *i.e.,* failover latency will only depend on the time taken for the clients to receive the COMM_FAILURE exception after a server failure. FLARe's redirection agent is a CORBA object that runs in its own thread within the client process to allow FLARe's resource manager to send object failover information to the client request interceptor.

FLARe's redirection agent communicates with FLARe's resource manager so it is updated with the failover information proactively, *i.e.,* before failures occur. Since it is conceivable that multiple clients may invoke the same server, the resource manager uses real-time publish-subscribe communication to scalably and efficiently disseminate the failover targets to all the concerned redirection agents. After catching an exception, the client request interceptor contacts the redirection agent to obtain the failover object address, and redirects the client to that server object. By proactively selecting failover target updates, FLARe can provide timely and predictable failover.

4   Related Work

Our work on FLARe can be compared with related research along the following dimensions:

Real-time fault-tolerant systems. Delta-4/XPA [18] provided real-time fault-tolerant solutions to distributed systems by using the semi-active replication model. MEAD [17] and its proactive recovery strategy for distributed CORBA applications can minimize the recovery time for DRE systems. The Time-triggered Message-triggered Objects (TMO) project [9] considers replication schemes such as the primary-shadow TMO replication (PSTR) scheme, for which recovery time bounds can be quantitatively established, and real-time fault tolerance guarantees can be provided to applications. DARX [11] provides adaptive fault-tolerance for multi-agent software platforms by dynamically changing replication styles in response to changing resource availabilities and application performance.

FLARe builds upon and extends this prior work by focusing on a combination of server-side, client-side, and infrastructure-specific middleware components. These together address an important challenge of using PASSIVE replication in fault-tolerant real-time systems: maintaining soft real-time performance after failure recovery.

Scheduling algorithms. Fundamental ideas and challenges in combining real-time and fault tolerance are described in [24], where imprecise computations are used to provide degraded QoS to applications operating in the presence of failures. [6] proposes adaptive fault tolerance mechanisms to choose a suitable redundancy strategy for dynamically arriving aperiodic tasks based on system resource availability. The Realize middleware [8] provides dynamic scheduling techniques that observes the execution times, slack, and resource requirements of applications to dynamically schedule tasks that are recovering from failure, and make sure that non-faulty tasks do not get affected by the recovering tasks.

FLARe differs from these approaches in providing fault tolerance capabilities to soft real-time applications. Rather than ensuring hard deadlines are met in the presence of failures, FLARe focuses on minimizing the impact of failure recovery on client response times and system resource utilization, and also provides timely client failover to appropriate failover targets.

5   Concluding Remarks

The FLARe middleware described in this paper provides both timeliness and availability to distributed real-time and embedded (DRE) systems. FLARe focuses on passive replication to meet the needs of resource-constrained environments. FLARe identifies and provisions those fault-tolerance functionalities, which if not designed properly could also affect the timeliness properties of the applications. To design and implement those functionalities, FLARe overcomes limitations of current middleware approaches, by providing a proactive, adaptive, and resource-aware fault-tolerance solution for clients.

The lessons we learned developing and applying FLARe thus far include:

• Common CORBA features, such as portable interceptors, and POSIX features, such as local sockets, can be leveraged to provide fault tolerance capabilities to soft real-time systems without modifying the implementation of standard-compliant RT-CORBA ORBs. Moreover, well-known architectural and design patterns can be carefully chosen to design key components of a fault-tolerant middleware, so that the fault-tolerance functionalities can be provided in an effective and timely manner.

• FLARe currently does not support stateful applications, so its resource manager uses a failover target selection algorithm that selects failover targets without considering the consistency levels of the replicas. Supporting stateful applications in DRE systems not only requires timely failover, but also supporting different client consistency requirements, such as weak or strong consistency models. This is part of our future work.

• FLARe is designed for environments where the networks provide bounded communication latencies and have no single point of failure. Certain DRE systems, however, run in environments where networks fail, which can cause resource contention in the remaining links. Our future work is therefore focusing on integrating FLARe with network QoS mechanisms, such as DiffServ and Bandwidth Brokers so that critical communications can use network QoS mechanisms to meet critical QoS requirements.

FLARe is open-source software that can be downloaded from `www.dre.vanderbilt.edu/~jai/FLARe`

References

1. Assayad, I., Girault, A., Kalla, H.: A bi-criteria scheduling heuristic for distributed embedded systems under reliability and real-time constraints. In: DSN 2004, Florence, Italy, p. 347 (2004)
2. Balasubramanian, J., Tambe, S., Gokhale, A., Lu, C., Gill, C., Schmidt, D.C.: FLARe: A Fault-tolerant Lightweight Adaptive Real-time Middleware for Distributed Real-time and Embedded Systems. Technical Report ISIS-07-812, Institute for Software Integrated Systems, Vanderbilt University, Nashville, TN (May 2007)
3. Bennani, T., Blain, L., Courtes, L., Fabre, J.-C., Killijian, M.-O., Marsden, E., Taiani, F.: Implementing Simple Replication Protocols using CORBA Portable Interceptors and Java Serialization. In: DSN 2004, Florence, Italy, pp. 549–554 (2004)
4. Déplanche, A.M., Théaudi'ere, P.Y., Trinquet, Y.: Implementing a semi-active replication strategy in chorus/classix, a distributed real-time executive. In: SRDS 1999: Proceedings of the 18th IEEE Symposium on Reliable Distributed Systems, Washington, DC, USA, p. 90. IEEE Computer Society, Los Alamitos (1999)
5. Gamma, E., Helm, R., Johnson, R., Vlissides, J.: Design Patterns: Elements of Reusable Object-Oriented Software. Addison-Wesley, Reading (1995)
6. Gonzalez, O., Shrikumar, H., Stankovic, J.A., Ramamritham, K.: Adaptive fault tolerance and graceful degradation under dynamic hard real-time scheduling. In: RTSS 1997, San Francisco, CA, USA, p. 79 (1997)
7. Douglas Jensen, E.: Distributed Real-time Specification for Java (2000), `java.sun.com/aboutJava/communityprocess/jsr/jsr_050_drt.html`
8. Kalogeraki, V., Melliar-Smith, P.M., Moser, L.E.: Dynamic Scheduling of Distributed Method Invocations. In: 21st IEEE Real-time Systems Symposium, Orlando. IEEE, Los Alamitos (2000)
9. Kim, K.H., Subbaraman, C.: The pstr/sns scheme for real-time fault tolerance via active object replication and network surveillance. IEEE Trans. on Know. and Data Engg. 12(2) (2000)

10. Lehoczky, J., Sha, L., Ding, Y.: The Rate Monotonic Scheduling Algorithm: Exact Characterization and Average Case Behavior. In: RTSS 1989, pp. 166–171 (1989)
11. Marin, O., Bertier, M., Sens, P.: Darx: A framework for the fault tolerant support of agent software. In: ISSRE 2003: Proceedings of the 14th International Symposium on Software Reliability Engineering, Washington, DC, USA, p. 406. IEEE Computer Society, Los Alamitos (2003)
12. Van Moorsel, A.P.A.: The 'qos query service' for improved quality-of-service decision making in corba. In: SRDS 1999, Lausanne, Switzerland, p. 274 (1999)
13. Object Management Group. Fault Tolerant CORBA, Chapter 23, CORBA v3.0.3, OMG Document formal/04-03-10 edition (March 2004)
14. Object Management Group. Real-time CORBA Specification v1.2 (static), OMG Document formal/05-01-04 edition (November 2005)
15. Object Management Group. Lightweight Real-Time Fault Tolerant CORBA DRAFT RFP, OMG Document realtime/06-06-06 edition (June 2006)
16. Felber, P., Narasimhan, P.: Experiences, Approaches and Challenges in building Fault-tolerant CORBA Systems. Transactions of Computers 54(5), 497–511 (2004)
17. Pertet, S., Narasimhan, P.: Proactive recovery in distributed corba applications. In: DSN 2004, Florence, Italy, p. 357 (2004)
18. Powell, D.: Distributed fault tolerance: Lessons from delta-4. IEEE Micro. 14(1), 36–47 (1994)
19. Prez-Sorrosal, F., Patino-Martinez, M., Jimenez-Peris, R., Vuckovic, J.: Highly available long running transactions and activities for j2ee applications. In: ICDCS 2006: Proceedings of the 26th IEEE International Conference on Distributed Computing Systems, Washington, DC, USA, p. 2. IEEE Computer Society, Los Alamitos (2006)
20. Ravindran, B., Curley, E., Anderson, J.S., Jensen, E.D.: On best-effort real-time assurances for recovering from distributable thread failures in distributed real-time systems. In: ISORC 2007: Proceedings of the 10th IEEE International Symposium on Object and Component-Oriented Real-Time Distributed Computing, Washington, DC, USA, pp. 344–353. IEEE Computer Society, Los Alamitos (2007)
21. Schmidt, D.C., Stal, M., Rohnert, H., Buschmann, F.: Pattern- Oriented Software Architecture: Patterns for Concurrent and Networked Objects, vol. 2. Wiley & Sons, New York (2000)
22. Stewart, R., Xie, Q.: Stream Control Transmission Protocol (SCTP) A Reference Guide. Addison-Wesley, Reading (2001)
23. Sun Microsystems. Java Specification Request, JSR 117, J2EE APIs for Continuous Availability, JSR 117 edition (April 2001)
24. Wang, F., Ramamritham, K., Stankovic, J.A.: Determining redun- dancy levels for fault tolerant real-time systems. IEEE Transactions on Computers 44(2), 292–301 (1995)
25. Cai, Z., Kumar, V., Cooper, B.F., Eisenhauer, G., Schwan, K., Strom, R.E.: Utility-Driven Proactive Management of Availability in Enterprise-Scale Information Flows. Proceedings of ACM/Usenix/IFIP Middleware, 382–403 (2006)

Using Object Replication for Building a Dependable Version Control System

Rüdiger Kapitza[1], Peter Baumann[1], and Hans P. Reiser[2]

[1] Dept. of Comp. Sciences 4, University of Erlangen-Nürnberg, Germany
rrkapitz@cs.fau.de
[2] LaSIGE, University of Lisboa, Portugal
hans@di.fc.ul.pt

Abstract. Object-oriented technologies are frequently used to design and implement distributed applications. Object replication is a well-established approach to increase the dependability for such applications. Generic replication infrastructures often fail to meet non-standard application-specific requirements such as support for client-side computing. Our F*T*flex replication infrastructure combines the fragmented object model with semantic annotations in order to customize and optimize replication mechanisms, and thus provides a more flexible replication infrastructure.

This paper presents DiGit, a replicated version control system based on the architecture of Git. DiGit is implemented with the help of the F*T*flex infrastructure for object replication. The contributions of this paper are twofold. First, the paper evaluates the fitness of our replication framework for a specific, complex application. We identify two advantages of the replication infrastructure: the ability to provide client-side code as a conceptually integral part of a remote service, and support for an optimized protocol for remote interaction. As a second contribution, the paper presents a powerful replicated version control system and shows the lessons learned from using object replication in such a system.

Keywords: Object Replication, Version Control System.

1 Introduction

Object-oriented technologies are frequently used to design and implement distributed applications. Such applications are faced with failures of various kinds. For example, nodes may crash or may even suffer from malicious intrusions, and communication between nodes may temporarily break down. Object replication is a well-established approach for coping with such kinds of failures. Many distributed object infrastructures provide support for object replication, either as an integral part or as an external add-on.

Generic object replication infrastructures frequently have some limitations. Being generic implies that the infrastructure implementation has to be suitable for many different kinds of applications. It is a hard challenge for a middleware to provide a range of configuration variants that include an ideal solution for every application, and make an automated selection of the best variant. Fragmented objects [14,11,19] are a technology that provides means for flexible adjustment to individual needs by the generation of custom code. This code substitutes the static stub and skeleton

R. Meier and S. Terzis (Eds.): DAIS 2008, LNCS 5053, pp. 86–99, 2008.

that is commonly used in distributed object middleware. The FT*flex* replication infrastructure [20] combines the fragmented object model with semantic annotations in order to customize and optimize replication mechanisms. In this paper, we use a specific complex application—a distributed version control system—to assess the replication mechanisms provided by that replication infrastructure.

Version control systems, such as Concurrent Versions System (CVS) [3] and Subversion (SVN) [17], are commonly used for software development. Most systems use a central server for storing all data and history information. This server may fail due to hardware or software problems. If developers use a third-party service (as it is the case for many open-source projects that use, for example, the SourceForge service), there is also the risk of intentional shut-down of that service. Replicating a repository on multiple hosts, potentially located in independent administrative domains, helps to maintain system functionality in spite of such failures. Usually, the repositories of large projects are mirrored using tools like rsync or FTP. This approach reduces the risk of data loss in case of failures and provides scalability for read-only access. However, manual intervention is necessary to determine the last valid state of the repository and to set up the a new primary repository to recover from a failure of the main site. During this time a coordinated exchange of development progress is hard to achieve.

In this paper, we present the design of DiGit, a replicated version control system based on the architecture of Git [4], which is the system that the Linux kernel project currently uses for version management. DiGit provides fault-tolerant replication mechanisms for a global repository in combination with decentralized client-side repositories. DiGit uses the FT*flex* object replication infrastructure and thus its implementation is based on the concept of fragmented objects. The replication infrastructure uses semantic information on operations to tailor the provided mechanisms. In essence, this paper makes two important contributions. First, it evaluates the fitness of the adaptable FT*flex* replication framework for a specific, real-world application. Second, it presents an architecture for a powerful replicated version control system that is able to transparently tolerate a limited number of faults without service unavailability and shows the lessons learned from using object replication in such a system.

This paper is structured as follows. First, we survey related work. In Section 3, we briefly describe the generic FT*flex* infrastructure. Section 4 presents the design of our DiGit distributed version control system. Then we outline evaluation results. In Section 6, we discuss the lessons learned from our implementation. Section 7 concludes.

2 Related Work

Object replication is supported in many distributed middleware systems. A prominent example for such support is the Fault-Tolerant CORBA (FT-CORBA) standard [16]. This standard is implemented in existing systems in various ways, for example using an interception approach in the Eternal system [15], an integration approach in Orbix+Isis [12], or a service approach in OGS [6]. The FT-CORBA standard is an example of a complex standard for fault-tolerant middleware infrastructures targeted at heterogeneous systems. Even after maturing for more than a decade, many deficiencies can still be identified [7]. An important observation is that replication cannot easily be added to object-oriented applications in a transparent way. In this paper, we discuss some slightly different limitations of existing object-replication frameworks: The main challenges that arise from replicating a version control system are the local manipulation of files at the client side and efficient protocols for the transfer of large data (e.g., client operations on the repository).

The issue of customizing (and thus optimizing) remote communication for simple, non-replicated distributed objects has previously been investigated in various projects. Usual solutions provide a framework [18] or, as in Kurmann and Stricker [1], completely redesign the communication stack and the ORB. Such extensions to object middleware systems are incompatible with extensions for fault-tolerant replication. For example, efficient communication needs to be integrated into state transfer, and all client operations that modify the object state must be applied consistently to all replicas.

Fragmented objects have previously been used to construct flexible distributed systems. Replication with fragmented objects has previously been used in Globe [2]. Unlike the version control system that we propose in this paper, Globe does not consider client-side computing or custom communication protocols.

While traditional version control systems such as CVS and SVN use a central repository server, a decentralized approach has gained popularity in systems such as Arch [8], Darcs [5], Monotone [10], and Git [4]. These systems focus on a decentralized development model, in which each developer can have their own local repository. This approach makes off-line work under local revision control possible. Local changes can later be re-integrated into a central main branch, usually maintained by a head developer. The head developer may also allow authorized users to write directly to the central repository, thus allowing to mimic a centralized development model as well. If the central repository becomes unavailable, only local repository operations are possible, and interaction between developers is not possible. In DiGit, we also support developer-side local repositories, but the key advantage of our system is that it aims at increasing the availability of the central repository by fault-tolerant replication.

The Pastwatch [22] version control system is similar to our approach in the sense that it replicates a repository on multiple hosts, while providing a functionality similar to CVS. However, Pastwatch uses optimistic replication on a peer-to-peer-infrastructure and does not make strong guarantees about data consistency. Conflicting modifications by multiple developers are handled by creating branches that require manual conflict resolution. DiGit, on the other hand, uses a general-purpose replication infrastructure (FT*flex*) and provides strong consistency guarantees on the replicated repository.

3   Replication Infrastructure Based on Fragmented Objects

The FT*flex* object replication infrastructure [20] uses the fragmented-object model [14,11,19] provided by the Aspectix middleware to integrate replication mechanisms into distributed applications. From an abstract point of view, a fragmented object is defined by its identity, interface, functionality, and state. The implementation of these items is not bound to a specific location, but instead can be distributed arbitrarily over multiple fragments, located on multiple hosts. The FT*flex* infrastructure supplies a code generation tool that creates object-specific fragment code for client access and for replica consistency management. The replication of an application remains fully transparent to clients. Semantic annotations at the interface level allow the developer to customize the provision of fault tolerance.

3.1   Replication with Fragmented Objects in FT*flex*

For realizing a replicated service, FT*flex* uses the fragmented object infrastructure of Aspectix to load service-specific fragment code at the client side and at replica locations, without requiring internal middleware modifications (see [9] for details). Fig. 1 shows a fragmented object that implements a fault-tolerant service; this object is internally composed of replica fragments and access fragments.

The development process of a replicated service in FT*flex* consists of defining the global object interface in CORBA IDL, implementing the functional parts of the service, and creating the fragment code. The creation of fragment code is done automatically by tools; these tools can make use of semantic annotations provided by the developer, as we will describe in Section 3.2. The annotations enable creating a customized layer between the client and the core framework and also between the framework and the replica implementation.

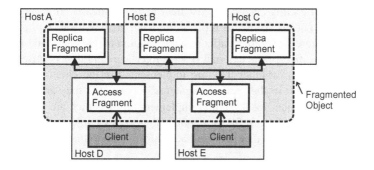

Fig. 1. A replicated service realized as a fragmented object

The generated fragment code handles most replication-relevant issues. It implements marshalling and unmarshalling, similar to an ordinary stub. Furthermore, it handles communication of clients with an available member of the replica group, ensuring at-most-once call semantics even in case of fail-over handling. With an active replication strategy, all client requests are distributed to the replicas using totally ordered group communication. In addition, each replica fragment contains semantic information about methods that has been extracted from the annotations. This information is used to improve the performance of request executions.

The Aspectix middleware uses CORBA IORs to reference fragmented objects via an APX profile. This profile contains a unique object ID, a specification of the initial fragment type to load and contact information of other fragments. The initial fragment type can be specified in a language-independent way; a code-loading service [13] is used for obtaining the corresponding code for the local platform. The contact data in the APX profile contains information about the replica group.

3.2   Semantic Information and Code Generation

Similar to a traditional CORBA IDL compiler for stubs and skeletons, FT*flex* can generate client-side and replica-side fragments using IDL interface information. In addition, our architecture allows the developer to express semantic knowledge in order to improve and customize the replication mechanisms. Currently, FT*flex* supports several annotations on a per-method basis: annotations can be provided to specify if an object operation interacts with the replica and modifies its state, if it is a read-only operation, if it is parallelizable with other methods, or if it is a method that can be computed locally at the client side without interacting with the replica group.

The current prototype of the code-generation tool is based on IDL*flex* [21]. IDL*flex* parses CORBA IDL, evaluates an XML-based mapping specification, and uses this specification to create arbitrary output code. The tool supports semantic annotations in IDL files, expressed as `#pragma annotate` statements. A custom mapping specification defines how to evaluate these statements and defines the corresponding code-generation process.

If a method is marked as read-only, the communication with the replica group will be handled differently (using unicast instead of multicast). Information about parallelizability is passed from the replica fragment to the local application-level scheduler. Furthermore, annotations affecting the location of code have an influence on whether methods are part of the external service interface (and thus part of the client-side fragment interface), whether they are implemented in the client-side fragments only (but may be absent in the replica fragments), or whether they are implemented in replica fragments. Client-local method implementations (which are still part of the abstract service interface) are useful for methods that, for example, validate client data in a state-independent way or that provide static information to the client.

4   Replicated Decentralized Version Control

This section presents the design and implementation of DiGit, a reliable distributed version control system. DiGit uses FT*flex* for replicating a central repository service, and thus evaluates the FT*flex* infrastructure using a complex real-world application.

4.1   Background

A version control system records the development history and enables collaboration of multiple developers by supporting distributed and concurrent work on a source-code tree. To take part in the development, a developer checks out the sources, modifies them, and finally commits her changes. If the repository is provided via a central service (e.g., CVS), the unavailability of this service prevents coordinated development progress.

Our DiGit implementation aims at offering high availability of a virtual central repository. By virtual we mean that the repository is, in fact, replicated over multiple physical hosts, but for clients it appears as a single central repository. Our prototype re-implements the Git system that was originally invented by Linus Torvalds. Git has a lean storage model that can be implemented in a straightforward way; it is proven to work well in large-scale projects such as the Linux kernel. Git already offers decentralized revision control of software. However, this support primarily targets the local availability of a repository and the possibility to later re-integrate local changes to a remote main repository. A public main repository, such as used in the case of the Linux project, still represents a single point of failure. Once down, no further check-outs and check-ins are possible. Thus, a centralized, prompt exchange of development progress is stopped. In addition, Git provides no out-of-the-box support for mirroring or replication of the repository on order to achieve scalability and fault tolerance. In the context of the Linux project this is solved by considerable big hardware efforts (see http://www.kernel.org) and replication via FTP or rsync. For this reason, the main goals of our reimplementation are to achieve fault tolerance and high availability without requiring external mechanisms or manual intervention.

Next, the basic concepts of Git and its storage format are explained. Then, the architecture and the API of our replicated Git repository are described. Our prototype implementation provides a command-line tool for repository management, but we will not focus in this tool.

4.2   Basic Concepts of Git

The storage model of Git is composed of four basic object types that are stored as ordinary files on disk. Each object has a header that identifies the type and the size of the object. The files are named after the SHA1 hash calculated over the content. Any modification to a file will result in a mismatch between the file content hash and the file name, and these modifications can easily be detected.

The four basic object types are Blob, Tree, Commit, and Tag. A *Blob* represents a file that is under version control. A Blob does not reference any other object. A *Tree* object contains of a list of names that reference Blob and Tree objects, together with meta data for each list entry, such as access time and permissions. A Tree object thus is similar to a directory. Third, a *Commit* object uniquely identifies a certain version of a branch. A Commit object consists of a changelog message, the names of the modified Tree objects, and the name of the direct ancestor Commit objects if there are any. A *Tag* object offers the additional support to uniquely identify and secure certain source code versions by a name and an optional certificate.

Fig. 2 illustrates the basic storage model of Git. The example shows the use of the three main object types, Blob, Tree, and Commit. Three files are represented by Blobs. There is one Tree object that represents the project directory and one Commit object that describes the initial version.

If a developer commits changes to the repository, all modified files have a different hash value than before and thus result in new Blobs. This leads to changes in the corresponding Tree objects, which results in different hash sums of the Trees and thus in the generation of new Tree objects. The Commit object documents the dependencies between the former version of the project and the new one. Fig. 3 shows three check-in

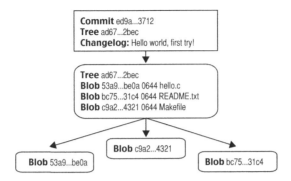

Fig. 2. Example of the basic Git storage model

operations on a repository with two files: the first operation creates the initial version, the second revision only modifies one file, and the third update changes all files.

This structure enables easy branching and merging of different development lines. The only things that are necessary are to store the modified files and to insert a new Commit object that references the joint branches.

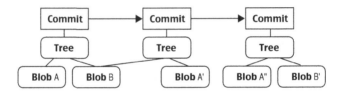

Fig. 3. Commit operation in Git

The Git storage model can be implemented in a straightforward way, and it prevents the undiscovered modification of files due to the rigorous usage of hashes. The drawback of the storage model is the redundancy it introduces. Versions that differ only slightly result in completely new Blob objects. This leads to an enormous waste of storage. Common version control systems like CVS or SVN usually store only the difference between two successive versions of files. To achieve a similar behaviour, Git supports custom archives, named *pack files*. A pack file is a collection of objects, individually compressed, with delta compression applied. These pack files are used to reduce the repository size by archiving older revisions and to enable an efficient network transfer for data-intensive repository operations, such as the initial checkout of a project.

4.3 Design of the DiGit Version Control System

Git uses a distributed development model that requires every developer to have their own local repository. The same basic model is used in our replicated variant. The goal of DiGit is to provide the same functionality as Git for the local repository operations,

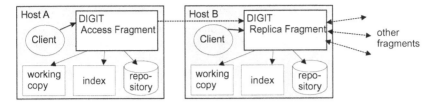

Fig. 4. A DiGit service is composed of access fragments and repository fragments, and both manage a working copy, an index, and the repository

and in addition support a replicated global repository that remains available in spite of the failure of some replicas.

DiGit is implemented as a fragmented object, as illustrated by Fig. 4. The object interface of the DiGit service offers an interface that includes methods to operate on the local as well as on the global repository. A single fragment handles both kinds of repositories. Operations on the local repository are executed locally, while operations on the replicated repository require communication with the group of replicas.

A client-side fragment may either work as a smart stub to access a remote group of replica fragments, or it may be part of the replica group itself. A local repository and a local replica of the global repository share the same storage. This means that a data object that is stored in both needs only a single entry in the storage under its hash. Furthermore the hash is registered in a shared index file for fast access.

The local repository can be synchronized to the global repository in the same way as a local Git repository is synchronized to a remote server. A developer does not operate directly on the global repository. Instead a copy of the global repository, called a clone, is created in the local repository, and all local modifications are first committed to a local branch of that clone. A `pull()` operation transfers updates from the global repository to the local clone, and these updates can then be merged to the local development branch. Conversely, `push()` applies changes in the local branch to the global repository.

Most of the DiGit operations operate on the local working copy, the index, or the local repository. These operations are implemented in a client-side fragment in a way that closely resembles the original Git implementation. The operations for cloning, pushing, and pulling repository data are the key operations that access the global repository. The main challenge that the DiGit implementation addresses is to make these operations work reliably and efficiently on a group of repository replicas.

4.4 DiGit Operations on a Local Repository

The DiGit methods for local revision management are annotated via the *local* keyword (see interface definition in Fig. 5). This tells the FT*flex* framework that the operations are implemented in the client-side fragment instead of at a remote server fragment.

At this point, we assume that the client-local repository is already populated by data from the global repository (how this is achieved is explained in the following section). A developer can `checkout()` a certain source version from the local repository into

```
#pragma annotate(local)
void checkout(in string ref) raises (NonExistingBranch, NonExistingObject);

#pragma annotate(local)
string add(in string filePath);

#pragma annotate(local)
string refresh(in string filePath);

#pragma annotate(local)
string commit(in string ref) raises (NonExistingObject);

#pragma annotate(local)
boolean merge(in string ref) raises (NonExistingBranch);

#pragma annotate(local)
void branch(in string name) raises (NonExistingBranch);
```

Fig. 5. Basic operations to manage the local repository

a local working directory, and can add() new files to the repository. The commit() operation creates a new version in the local repository, and the merge() operations updates the local working copy with data from the repository. If a certain source version should be used for subsequent independent development, the developer can use the branch() operation a new development branch.

Identical to Git, the data of files is internally stored in an index file. An add() operation automatically adds the content of the file at addition time to the index. The index content defines the updates that will be made to the local repository by the commit() operation. The refresh() operation updates the index data with the file data in the local working copy. With the explicit refresh() operation, a developer has the option to collect distinct changes for the next commit while keep on developing.

4.5 DiGit Operations on a Distributed Repository

The part of the DiGit interface relevant for operations on the distributed global repository is shown in Fig. 6. Several of the operations, such as the initial check-out of a repository and the update of large source trees, are data intensive. Such data intensive operations are a great challenge for replication infrastructures based on distributed object middleware. Many infrastructures provide only a plain remote invocation mechanism without dedicated support for efficient bulk data transfer.

The fragmented object model provides an alternative solution, as a service developer has the freedom of choice to use arbitrary object-internal communication. DiGit uses this approach to make a clear separation between control messages and file transfer, wherever it is possible. Control messages and state-modifying messages are handled by the implemented framework as standard method invocations, whereas data is transferred via an adapted custom protocol taken from the original Git implementation.

First of all, a decentralized Git service has to be initialized and started. This is achieved by creating an initial replica on some host, and this replica has an associated

```
#pragma annotate(local)
boolean clone(in string path);

#pragma annotate(local)
boolean pull();

#pragma annotate(local)
BranchArray push();

BranchArray pushPack(in ByteArray pack, in BranchArray old, in BranchArray new);

#pragma annotate(readonly,private)
StringArray getRepositoryServers();

#pragma annotate(private)
void addRepositoryServer(in string address);
```

Fig. 6. Operations to manage and synchronize the local with the global repository

IOR for a fragmented object. All service replicas provide not only a complete copy of the repository, but also run a TCP server for bulk data transfer. This server is started during the creation of a replica. As soon as an initial service replica has been successfully started, any client can use the repository service by binding to its IOR.

After binding to the repository service, the client has to populate the local repository using the sources of the replicated global repository. Only after this step, a developer can use the set of methods for local repository management described before. The clone() method populates the local repository with a copy of the global repository. The client-side access fragment selects one of the service replicas and requests a transfer of the current repository state. The TCP server of the contacted replica provides this state as a pack file. The client-side fragment uses the pack file to populate the local clone of the repository.

As the client-side IOR that contains contact addresses may partially be out of date, the replica group provides a getRepositoryServers() method that returns all data server addresses. This method is annotated as *private* and *read-only* method, which means that it is not visible on the outer interface of the DiGit services, and that it is invoked at only a single replica, instead of being distributed to all replicas.

After the repository of the access fragment has been initialized, it can be updated by calling pull(). The pull() method is also implemented as a custom local operation. It requests the current state of the repository from one of the replicas using the TCP server for bulk transfer. The bulk transfer implements an interactive process with the replica. First, the replica returns meta data about all branches and their current head versions (the last commits). The access fragment compares this information with the entries of the global part of the repository and then determines the missing commit objects. Finally, all modified objects are sent to the client as a pack file.

A developer commits local changes into the replicated global repository by calling the push() method. This local method communicates with the bulk transfer server of a replica to determine whether there is a conflict with the global repository. If the global state has been modified since the last comparison, the return values signals a conflict, which has to be resolved before the changes can be committed to the global repository. Otherwise, the method generates a pack file that describes the updates to be made to the central repository. The pack file is then passed to the pushPack() method, which consistently modifies the state in the replicas. This global state modification is executed with the generic replication methods that the FTflex replication infrastructure provides. This implies that the update is consistently distributed to all replicas using totally ordered group communication.

Setting up a new replica requires a state transfer. The generic way for creating additional replicas in FTflex is first to bind to the IOR of the replicated service (thus instantiating a local access fragment), and then to upgrade the local fragment to a full replica. In DiGit, a local access fragment generally has a clone of the central repository. Thus, there is no need for a full state transfer from existing replicas to the new replicas. However, the local clone of the global replicated repository could be outdated, as there might have been commits to global repository since the last invocation of pull(). An extended state transfer implementation accounts for this fact and minimizes the transfer costs. The new replica submits revision information about its local copy of the global repository to all state providing nodes. Next, the replicas use this information to generate a pack file that is transferred to the joining replica. After this operation, the new replica adds the address of its data server via addRepositoryServer() to the set of state-providing replica servers.

5   Evaluation

This section evaluates the basic operations of our prototype and compares a DiGit repository with three replicas with the original non-replicated implementation of Git version 1.5.3.7. All measurements have been made in a 100 MBit/s switched Ethernet network on a homogeneous set of PCs with a AMD Athlon 2.0 GHz CPU and 1 GB RAM, using Linux kernel 2.6.17 and SUN Java SDK 1.5.0_09. The tests used a small project repository hosting 600 files with a history of 504 revisions and a size of 87 MB. For Git we used ssh as underlying remote protocol. We focused on operations with remote interaction. Tab. 1 summaries the results.

First we evaluated the time to initialize a client and clone the repository from a remote site or a remote global repository in case of DiGit. For DiGit this operation is independent from the number of replicas as clone represents a read-only operation and only one replica is accessed. Albeit using a similar protocol and performing almost identical operations Git is 6 times faster. The reason for this large performance gap lies in fact that the native Git implementation is highly optimized and makes heavy use of memory mapped files and uses faster compression routines to build the pack files, while our DiGit prototype does not yet use such techniques.

Next we measured the time to set up a new replica from an up-to-date client node. This operation is important if a replica crashed or was intentionally shut down and needs to be replaced. It took 793 ms on average to integrate a initialized client node.

This leads to the last two experiments. We updated the global/remote repository via push. The update consisted of 100 locally committed revisions. This time Git was twice as fast as DiGit. The reasons are similar to the first measurement, but in addition the

Table 1. Measurements DiGit vs. Git

	Initialize client fragment / Clone	*Become a replica*	*Push (100 revisions)*	*Pull (up to date)*
DiGit	90843 ms	793 ms	20866 ms	15 ms
Git	14613 ms		10271 ms	1665 ms

pushed revisions have to be distributed to all replicas via the group communication framework when using DiGit. The last measurement pulled the latest revisions from the remote/global repository. In the context of the measurement the local repository include already the current version so we measured only the request. This time DiGit performed much better than Git. The reason is that DiGit had an open connection from the client to the server, whereas for Git the connection process took most of the time.

6 Lessons Learned

We discuss the following three questions in order to analyse our replication strategy for the version control application:

- Is object replication suitable for providing a dependable version control system?
- What are the potential benefits from the fragmented object model?
- What are the potential benefits from semantic annotations?

In general, it is not easy to describe a version control system as a service object with an adequate interface, because there is an inherent lack of distribution transparency. Usually, the interface of a remote service is the basic contract for the interaction of a client with a remote service.

In the context of a version control system, however, the service functionality is not limited to the remote server, but also includes the protocol for applying modifications to client-local file. A typical object-oriented implementation would only specify the interface of the remote service, and let the client implement all the parts that are necessary at the client side. The fragmented object model makes a huge difference here, as client-side functionality can be implemented as a fragment of the version control service. This fragment is conceptionally part of the service itself, and it can be loaded automatically at the client, using a dynamic loading service if it is not available locally.

A second requirement is the need for efficient bulk data transfer for data-intensive operations. If the repository is implemented as an object-oriented service, this requirement is also hard to fulfil with standard replication infrastructures for objects. However, the concept of fragmented objects can again provide a large benefit: A local fragment at the client side can implement custom optimized communication protocols between client-side fragments and repository fragments.

The dynamic loading of fragments at the client side is, of course, faced with security considerations. These can be addressed by using digital signatures for code that is loaded automatically.

Finally, annotations are an important aspect to improve throughput. The DiGit implementation uses annotations mainly to specify that code shall be local to the client.

This is not only used for code that handles the local repository and working copy, but also for implementing custom mechanism for bulk transfer of data. For interaction between fragments, our prototype uses private methods, which are not visible to clients, but available for internal use in client-side fragments. The read-only annotation speeds up the method that queries the up-to-date replica list.

7 Conclusions

This paper presented the design of DiGit, a replicated version control system based Git. Our system provides a consistent, dependable central repository even in failure situation by using efficient object replication technology. Our approach differs from most current distributed version control systems, which typically use a single central repository, in combination with decentralized local repositories that allow the tracking of changes during times in which the central repository is not available. Our approach replicates the central repository in order to make it more available. DiGit can be combined with local repositories, which are still useful, for example, for clients with no network connectivity at all and for local development.

A useful future extension of DiGit could allow developers to replicate their local repositories as separate branches in the global repository. This way, snapshots of their work could be accessed by other developers and their work would be preserved if their local machine crashed. Furthermore, additional evaluation could focus on WAN scenarios and performance in failure situations.

The replication of DiGit has been realized with support from our FT*flex* replication infrastructure. This infrastructure uses fragmented objects and annotations-based code generation in order to provide a high degree of customizability. The DiGit system benefits from this architecture in a way that would not have been possible in a traditional object replication infrastructure. First, the fragments allow loading repository-specific code automatically at the client side for manipulating the client-local repository. Conceptionally, this code is still part of the remote central repository. Second, the annotations allow optimizing the performance of the replication strategies.

References

1. Kurmann, C., Stricker, T.M.: Zero-copy for CORBA - efficient communication for distributed object middleware. In: 12th IEEE Int. Symp. on High Performance Distributed Computing, pp. 4–13. IEEE Computer Society, Los Alamitos (2003)
2. Bakker, A., Amade, E., Ballintijn, G., Kuz, I., Verkaik, P., van der Wijk, I., van Steen, M., Tanenbaum, A.S.: The globe distribution network. In: Proc. of the USENIX Annual Conference, pp. 141–152 (2000)
3. Bar, M., Fogel, K.: Open Source Development with CVS, 3rd edn. Paraglyph (2003)
4. Baudis, P.: Git - fast version control system, http://git.or.cz
5. Darcs, http://abridgegame.org/darcs
6. Felber, P.: The CORBA Object Group Service: A Service Approach to Object Groups in CORBA. PhD thesis, EPLF, Switzerland, Number 1867 (1998)
7. Felber, P., Narasimhan, P.: Experiences, strategies, and challenges in building fault-tolerant CORBA systems. IEEE Trans. Comput. 53(5), 497–511 (2004)

8. GNU arch, `http://www.gnu.org/software/gnu-arch`
9. Hauck, F.J., Kapitza, R., Reiser, H.P., Schmied, A.I.: A flexible and extensible object middleware: CORBA and beyond. In: Proc. of the Fifth Int. Workshop on Software Engineering and Middleware. ACM Digital Library (2005)
10. Hoare, G., Smith, N., Scherger, D.: Monotone - A distributed version control system, document version 0.35 (2006)
11. Homburg, P., van Doorn, L., van Steen, M., Tanenbaum, A.S., de Jonge, W.: An object model for flexible distributed systems. In: Proc. of the 1st Annual ASCI Conference, pp. 69–78 (1995)
12. IONA and Isis. An introduction to Orbix+Isis. IONA Technologies Ltd. And Isis Distributed Systems, Inc. (1994)
13. Kapitza, R., Schmidt, H., Bartlang, U., Hauck, F.J.: A generic infrastructure for decentralised dynamic loading of platform-specific code. In: Indulska, J., Raymond, K. (eds.) DAIS 2007. LNCS, vol. 4531, Springer, Heidelberg (2007)
14. Makpangou, M., Gourhant, Y., Narzul, J.-P.L., Shapiro, M.: Fragmented objects for distributed abstractions. In: Casavant, T.L., Singhal, M. (eds.) Readings in distributed computing systems, pp. 170–186. IEEE Computer Society Press, Los Alamitos (1994)
15. Moser, L.E., Melliar-Smith, P.M., Narasimhan, P.: Consistent object replication in the eternal system. Theor. Pract. Object Syst. 4(2), 81–92 (1998)
16. Object Management Group (OMG). Common object request broker architecture: Core specification, version 3.0.2. OMG document formal/02-12-02 (2002)
17. Pilato, C.M., Collins-Sussman, B., Fitzpatrick, B.W.: Version Control with Subversion, 1st edn. O'Reilly Media, Sebastopol (2004)
18. Pyarali, I., Harrison, T.H., Schmidt, D.C.: Design and performance of an object-oriented framework for high-speed electronic medical imaging. Computing Systems 9(4), 331–375 (1996)
19. Reiser, H.P., Hauck, F.J., Kapitza, R., Schmied, A.I.: Integrating fragmented objects into a CORBA environment. In: Proc. of the Net.ObjectDays, pp. 264–272 (2003)
20. Reiser, H.P., Kapitza, R., Domaschka, J., Hauck, F.J.: Fault-tolerant replication based on fragmented objects. In: Eliassen, F., Montresor, A. (eds.) DAIS 2006. LNCS, vol. 4025, pp. 256–271. Springer, Heidelberg (2006)
21. Reiser, H.P., Steckermeier, M., Hauck, F.J.: IDLflex: a flexible and generic compiler for CORBA IDL. In: Proc. of the Net.Object Days, pp. 151–160 (2001)
22. Yip, A., Chen, B., Morris, R.: Pastwatch: a distributed version control system. In: Proc. of the USENIX/ACM 3rd NSDI (2006)

Recovery Mechanisms for Semantic Web Services

Kevin Wiesner, Roman Vaculín, Martin Kollingbaum, and Katia Sycara*

The Robotics Institute, Carnegie Mellon University
{kwiesner,rvaculin,mkolling,katia}@cs.cmu.edu

Abstract. Web service-based applications are widely used, which has inevitably led to the need for proper mechanisms for the web service paradigm that can provide sustainable and reliable execution flows. In this paper we revise recovery techniques in OWL-S and show how semantic annotations may ensure seamless web service provision in a sophisticated way, such as, exploiting the ontology-based description of processes in order to dynamically find alternative services as substitutes for failed services. We also discuss the consequences of these semantic-enabled approaches and point out required changes for integration in OWL-S.

Keywords: Semantic Web, Web Services, Recovery, OWL-S.

1 Introduction

The web services (WS) paradigm is widely used and many enterprises deploy their business processes as web services. Typically, web service-based processes tend to operate in rapidly changing environments where two main concerns need to be addressed. First, the business process has to fulfill the goals for which it was designed. Second, the process must respond to changes in its operating environment by adapting to them in order to guarantee long-term sustainability. These two concerns are orthogonal. Current WS and business process standards focus on the first issue. Constructs for control and data flow specifications are typically based on some form of process algebra and thus, allow an easy design of structured processes that are particularly suitable for stable environments. Exception and recovery mechanisms are used to deal with unusual situations and changes. Current web service recovery mechanisms are highly inflexible. BPEL [1], for instance, uses compensation handlers with explicitly defined compensation actions (i.e., service calls). This provides only one solution for recovery at a particular time. Other possible solutions that might exist are not taken into account. Since the environment is changing constantly, the availability and reachability of services may vary over time. With conventional approaches to recovery and exception handling, it is not possible to adapt to such changes.

* This research was supported in part by Darpa contract FA865006C7606, by AFOSR FA9550-07-1-0039, and by funding from France Telecom.

R. Meier and S. Terzis (Eds.): DAIS 2008, LNCS 5053, pp. 100–105, 2008.
© IFIP International Federation for Information Processing 2008

A compensation containing a non-reachable service, for example, results in an inconsistent state of the system in the case of a failure, even though other services could be used as compensation for the failed process.

These shortcomings reveal a need for stronger and more flexible recovery mechanisms that allow a process to adapt while simultaneously respecting the design of the original process. Semantic Web Services (SWS) appear to be ideal for achieving this. The SWS standards introduce means for providing service specifications with rich semantic annotations that facilitate flexible dynamic discovery, invocation and composition of services. This paper focuses on how techniques such as dynamic discovery and composition can be exploited in the context of recovery and process adaptation. For example, SWS can take advantage of the dynamic discovery of either equivalent services (as a replacement) or other appropriate services, that may help to recover from a failure (e.g. for compensation), instead of relying on explicitly specified recovery solutions. In our previous work [2] OWL-S was extended with exception handling and basic recovery mechanisms. This paper revises recovery techniques introduced previously, and further presents new semantic-enabled mechanisms. We propose *ReplaceByEquivalent* and *Advanced Back & Forward Recovery* actions, which try to dynamically discover alternatives for erroneous tasks. Next, the *Automatic Compensation* technique exploits the semantic information to undo finished processes.

This paper is organized as follows: in Sect. 2 the existing exception handling and recovery in OWL-S is presented, followed by the introduction of new semantic-enabled mechanisms in Sect. 3. Next, these approaches and their consequences are discussed in Sect. 4 and related work is summarized in Sect. 5. In Sect. 6 we conclude and give an outlook on future work.

2   OWL-S and Recovery

OWL-S [3] is a description language for Semantic Web Services, based on OWL [4], that defines services through three kinds of information: the Service Profile describes what the service does in terms of its capabilities and is used for discovering and selecting suitable providers; the Process Model specifies how clients can interact with the service by defining the requester-provider interaction protocol; the Grounding links the Process Model to the specific execution infrastructure. For exception handling and recovery, the Process Model is of particular importance. Its elementary unit is an atomic process, which represents one indivisible operation. Processes are specified by means of their inputs, outputs, preconditions, and effects (IOPEs). Atomic processes can be combined into composite processes by using control constructs (e.g. sequence, split, etc.). All processes and control constructs must be strictly nested in order to ensure that every process or control construct has a defined parent.

To support basic fault handling and recovery, the OWL-S Process Model was extended in [2]. In addition to the IOPEs, every process can define fault handlers, standard event handlers, constraint violation handlers (CV-handlers), and compensation (FECCs). *Fault handlers* are used to respond to standard failures in the form of an exception event during the execution. The *CV-handlers* augment the basic fault handling by allowing a designer to define what situations during execution are supposed to trigger an erroneous state and how to recover from it. This is achieved by combining event expressions known from event algebras for specifying arbitrary event patterns [5] in the condition part of a CV-Handler, and *recovery actions* in the action part of a CV-Handler. The event conditions defined in CV-handlers are treated as hard constraints that lead to an abnormal execution state. In contrast, *event handlers* are used to express soft constraints. If the event condition of an event handler is met, its actions are processed without changing the execution state. In the *compensation* block, actions which are supposed to undo the effects of a process in case of a failure can be specified.

The following *recovery actions* were introduced in [2] to enable essential recovery in OWL-S:

Compensation: For every process, compensation can be defined. The actions specified in the compensation are used to undo the effects of the previously performed process. Compensation can be triggered either by *Compensate*, which invokes the compensation of the corresponding process, or by *CompensateProcess*, which enables to perform compensation for another process.

Retry: *Retry* simply restarts the same process again (which is especially useful for communication failures). It can be used in fault and CV-handlers to restore a normal execution flow after a failure has occurred. It either retries to execute the corresponding process n-times, or until the specified time expires (*timeout*).

Replace: Two replace operations are provided to replace a process by an alternative one which is supposed to achieve the same goal: *ReplaceBy* simply replaces the *failed* process with an alternative one explicitly specified in the process model. In contrast, *ReplaceProcessBy* replaces any *arbitrary* process with another one, which makes it possible to change the overall workflow.

Skip: The *Skip* action can be used in all FECC handlers to skip a process that has become dispensable as long as it has not been started yet.

Terminate: All running activities are stopped and performed tasks on the same level are undone. Subsequently, the same is done for parent levels. Termination is realized in two ways. *HardTerminate* terminates all running process without allowing compensation, whereas *SoftTerminate* compensates finished processes before terminating.

3   Semantic-Enabled Recovery

In this section, new recovery actions enabled by computer-interpretable descriptions of services are introduced in order to enhance and improve our existing mechanisms [2]. The following operations distinguish themselves in providing a flexible and adaptable way to recover from failures. We achieve this by exploiting mainly existing semantic annotations in OWL-S. The actions either replace or roll back the process with the help of dynamically discovered services.

ReplaceByEquivalent: The described *Replace* action recovers through a replacement, either specified in advance or selected by a human agent. We defined a more flexible operation, *ReplaceByEquivalent*, which dynamically adapts to the current situation, by using the information about the service capabilities. The OWL-S Process Model specifies inputs, outputs, preconditions, and effects, which we utilize to find an alternative service with the help of existing algorithms for automatic web service discovery (matchmaking) [6]. Since the replacement service is not selected in advance but discovered during run-time, the chances of a successful recovery and completion of the overall process are substantially increased.

Advanced Back & Forward Recovery: A possible operation for recovery is the *Back & Forward Recovery (BFR)*. After a failure, first a rollback is performed for all finished processes on the same level (of the process hierarchy) where the failure occured (*Back* phase). If the parent is non-vital for the overall outcome, the execution can continue in spite of the failure (*Forward* phase). If the parent is vital, the *Back* phase is repeated until the parent is non-vital, so that eventually *Forward* can be performed. In the worst case, i.e. when all tasks are vital, a complete rollback is performed. However, OWL-S does not support such an operation currently, since all processes are considered to be vital. A parameter indicating whether a process is *Vital/Non-Vital* can be easily added, and so recovery can be neglected for non-vital processes. Independently, we introduced a variation of the *BFR* operation, *Advanced Back & Forward Recovery (ABFR)*. The basic *BFR* goes back in the process hierarchy until a non-vital parent is found. The advanced variation of this makes use of the *ReplaceByEquivalent* in such a way that for each parent that is vital an alternative service is searched for. If an appropriate service exists, it is executed as a replacement and normal execution is resumed. If no replacement is found, *ABFR* continues just as the original approach and goes one step higher in the hierarchy. The following pseudo code demonstrates the ABFR algorithm:

> **if** $hasParent(process) = false$ **then**
>> $abortExecution$
>
> **else**
>> $compensateSiblings$
>> **if** $parentOf(process) \neq vital$ **then**
>>> $continueExecution$
>>
>> **else**
>>> $successfulReplaced \Leftarrow ReplaceByEquivalent(process)$
>>> **if** $successfulReplaced \neq true$ **then**
>>>> $ABFR(parentOf(process))$

Automatic Compensation: The definition of the Process in OWL-S contains information about the effects of a service. This can be exploited to discover an automatic compensation. If a service with the effects ε need to be compensated and no compensation has been specified, it is searched for a service with the effects ε^{-1} which undoes all changes. In particular, we assume that a service without effects does not need to be compensated. This simplifies the recovery.

4   Discussion

Although replacing an erroneous service with a dynamically discovered alternative by using an operation like *ReplaceByEquivalent* can significantly increase the robustness of workflows, it also adds some degree of non-determinism to it. Unbeknownst to the user, malicious services could be executed. In contrast, searching for an alternative only in a local, controlled environment (e.g. within a company's intranet) would not really exploit the potential of such recovery operations; consequently, a central pool with trusted services is a possible solution. The same applies for ABFR as well. Furthermore, the latter poses another problem. ABFR might go back several steps in the hierarchy before finding a replacement, which would lead to a substantial change of the original service. In this case, the user may perform a largely different service than he wanted or the process designer intended him to run. This, however, can be bypassed by specifying tasks as *replaceable/non-replaceable*. As a result, the process designer is able to ensure that some core processes cannot be replaced. This also facilitates a way to specify recovery operations in a more general way. Instead of specifying recovery actions for each process separately, the expressivity of FECC handlers can be exploited. A CV-handler might associate the *ReplaceByEquivalent* with an event expression like $ServiceInvocationException \wedge replaceable$, so that each service that cannot be invoked is automatically replaced.

5   Related Work

The approach introduced in [7], is based on *long-lived transactions* (LLTs). A LLT can be broken up into several sub-transactions, which are then executed as an atomic unit and can be compared to traditional transactions. Only complete executions are accepted, so some sub-transactions have to be undone in the case of failures. This is solved by providing a compensation for each of them and executing those in the reverse order. E.g. WS-BPEL [1] exploits this method for its error handling. In [8], Greenfield et al. discuss this approach in detail.

Intended especially for distributed transactions, several mechanisms for *Web service transactions* have evolved, as Business Transaction Protocol (BTP), WS-Tx[1]. These approaches provide protocols enabling a two-phase commit as in traditional transactions, but also leaving applications in full control of single steps. A failure in a sub-transaction does not inevitably lead to an abortion of the actual transaction. In [9], Papazoglou gives an extensive overview. Curbera et al. [10] suggest a combination of WS-BPEL and WS-Tx. The incorporation of both is discussed in [11].

Workflow transaction approaches (such as in [12]) primarily focus on ensuring a consistent state from a business point of view, i.e. achieving the business goal. In case of a failure, the execution returns to the most recent consistent state and tries to continue the execution in order to complete the workflow.

---

[1] WS-Tx (WS-Transaction) includes WS-Coordination, WS-AtomicTransaction, and WS-BusinessActivity.

6   Conclusions and Future Work

In this paper we revised current recovery techniques in OWL-S and presented new mechanisms enabled by the semantic layer. We introduced a new kind of recovery actions that exploit the semantic annotation of SWS to facilitate dynamic discovery of alternative or auxiliary web services. We proposed that semantic web services can be a key technology in achieving reliable and adaptable service executions. We are curently working on the implementation of semantic-enabled recovery actions mechanisms in the OWL-S Virtual Machine [13]. We plan to extend the process specification to support features like *(non)-vital* as well as *(non)-replaceable*. Additionally, we will investigate further possibilities of semantic-enabled recovery actions.

References

1. Alves, A., et al.: Web Services Business Process Execution Language Version 2.0 (April 2007),
   http://docs.oasis-open.org/wsbpel/2.0/OS/wsbpel-v2.0-OS.html
2. Vaculín, R., Wiesner, K., Sycara, K.: Exception handling and recovery of semantic web services. In: The Fourth International Conference on Networking and Services, IEEE Computer Society, Los Alamitos (2008)
3. The OWL Services Coaltion: Semantic Markup for Web Services (OWL-S),
   http://www.daml.org/services/owl-s/1.1/
4. Bechhofer, S., van Harmelen, F., Hendler, J., Horrocks, I., McGuinness, D., Patel-Schneider, P., Stein, L., et al.: OWL Web Ontology Language Reference. W3C Recommendation (February 2004), http://www.w3.org/TR/owl-ref/
5. Vaculín, R., Sycara, K.: Specifying and Monitoring Composite Events for Semantic Web Services. In: The 5th IEEE European Conference on Web Services, IEEE Computer Society, Los Alamitos (2007)
6. Sycara, K., Paolucci, M., Ankolekar, A., Srinivasan, N.: Automated discovery, interaction and composition of Semantic Web services. Web Semantics: Science, Services and Agents on the World Wide Web 1(1), 27–46 (2003)
7. Garcia-Molina, H., Salem, K.: Sagas. SIGMOD Rec. 16(3), 249–259 (1987)
8. Greenfield, P., Fekete, A., Jang, J., Kuo, D.: Compensation is Not Enough. In: Proceedings of the 7th International Enterprise Distributed Object Computing Conference (EDOC) (2003)
9. Papazoglou, M.: Web Services and Business Transactions. World Wide Web 6(1), 49–91 (2003)
10. Curbera, F., Khalaf, R., Mukhi, N., Tai, S., Weerawarana, S.: The Next Step in Web Services. Communications of the ACM 46(10), 29–34 (2003)
11. Sauter, P., Melzer, I.: A Comparison of WS-BusinessActivity and BPEL4WS Long-Running Transaction. In: Kommunikation in Verteilten Systemen (KiVS), ser. Informatik Aktuell, pp. 115–125. Springer, Heidelberg (2005)
12. Eder, J., Liebhart, W.: Workflow recovery. In: Proceedings of the First IFCIS International Conference on Cooperative Information Systems, pp. 124–134 (1996)
13. Paolucci, M., Ankolekar, A., Srinivasan, N., Sycara, K.P.: The DAML-S virtual machine. In: Fensel, D., Sycara, K.P., Mylopoulos, J. (eds.) ISWC 2003. LNCS, vol. 2870, pp. 290–305. Springer, Heidelberg (2003)

A Multi-stage Approach for Reliable Dynamic Reconfigurations of Component-Based Systems[*]

Pierre-Charles David[1], Marc Léger[2], Hervé Grall[1],
Thomas Ledoux[1], and Thierry Coupaye[2]

[1] OBASCO Group, EMN / INRIA, Lina
École des Mines de Nantes
4 rue Alfred Kastler
F-44307 Nantes CEDEX 3
[2] France Télécom, Recherche & Développement
28, chemin du vieux chêne
F-38243 Meylan

Abstract. In this paper we present an end-to-end solution to define and execute reliable dynamic reconfigurations of open component-based systems while guaranteeing their continuity of service. It uses a multi-stage approach in order to deal with the different kinds of possible errors in the most appropriate way; in particular, the goal is to detect errors as early as possible to minimize their impact on the target system. Reconfigurations are expressed in a restricted, domain-specific language in order to allow different levels of static and dynamic validation, thus detecting errors before executing the reconfiguration where possible. For errors that can not be detected early (including software and hardware faults), a runtime environment provides transactional semantics to the reconfigurations.

1 Introduction

Complex software systems must be modified/maintained during their lifetime, for example to fix bugs or include new functionalities. It is often not practical – or even possible – to stop the system in order to perform these changes. Instead, the changes must be applied dynamically to keep the running system available.

There are two conflicting forces that make evolution especially challenging. On the one hand, the evolutions that will be applied to a system cannot be precisely anticipated at the time it is initially built and deployed. This means the system must be kept open and flexible to accommodate future needs. On the other hand, modifying production systems that are often business-critical is very risky, and we need to ensure that these changes will cause the minimum possible disruption, even though we do not know ahead of time the actual changes that will be made. In short, we need a way to provide *reliable dynamic reconfigurations*.

[*] This work is partially funded by the Selfware RNTL project (http://sardes. inrialpes.fr/selfware) and the Selfman IST project (http://www.ist-selfman. org/).

R. Meier and S. Terzis (Eds.): DAIS 2008, LNCS 5053, pp. 106–111, 2008.

By *reliable* we mean: *(i)* reducing as much as possible the occurrence of errors (fault prevention), *(ii)* when errors that could not be prevented actually happen, minimize the damage they cause to the system (fault tolerance).

This paper introduces a modular validation chain to support *reliable* dynamic reconfigurations on top of general-purpose component models like Fractal [1]. The chain is based on a decomposition of the life-cycle of individual reconfigurations in multiple stages, from their definition to their actual execution on the target system. As reconfiguration scripts go through these successive stages, different techniques are used to "weed out" incorrect reconfigurations and handle errors that could not be prevented. The different stages of the validation chain complement each other to offer strong reliability guarantees. At the same time, the chain stays modular and can be customized to support different tradeoffs between performance and guarantees depending on the domain.

In the rest of this paper, we first present the overall architecture of our approach (Sect. 2), detailing the different kinds of errors our validation chain handles thanks to its multi-stage architecture. Sections 3 to 5 then give more details on each successive stage of the chain. We conclude (Sect. 6) with an overview of the current status of these different modules and of the future work.

2   Overview of the Validation Chain

The goal of the proposed validation chain is to ensure the reliability of the dynamic reconfigurations of software architectures (e.g. component replacement, reconnection of component bindings). It relies on the use of a dynamic component model that supports unanticipated reconfigurations, typically thanks to reflective features. In our case we use Fractal [1] for its flexibility and extensibility.

The main idea behind our proposal is to handle the different kinds of errors at different points in the life-cycle of a reconfiguration. Accordingly, the validation chain is organized with three main stages as illustrated in figure 1, each stage corresponding to a different step in the life-cycle of the scripts that describe the reconfigurations to be executed. At each stage, if an error is detected, the reconfiguration is immediately rejected. Hence the whole chain acts as a sequence of increasingly specific sieves that scripts must pass through, from basic sanity checks to a full-blown managed execution of the reconfigurations as transactions.

Loading. First, the specification of a reconfiguration is loaded into the validation chain, in the form of a *reconfiguration script*. Such a script can be executed many times in its lifetime, with different target architectures, but it is loaded only once. For example, a generic component replacement script can be reused with different parameters each time a component must be updated to a new version. At this time, the possible target architecture are only specified by the architecture model, which defines some rules that the architectures under consideration satisfy. With these informations, the possible validations include various levels of *static analyses* filtering out reconfiguration scripts that could cause errors when applied to a concrete architecture.

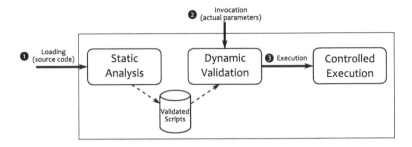

Fig. 1. The validation chain's architecture

Invocation. After loading, a user may want to actually execute the reconfiguration on a particular target architecture. Some additional validations can now be performed: this stage filters out scripts that are incompatible with the given target architecture.

Execution. Finally, the reconfiguration is executed on the target architecture. If the previous steps have been precise enough, most erroneous reconfigurations have already been rejected at this point. However, some kinds of errors are either impossible to predict (e.g. hardware faults) or too costly to detect. To handle these errors, the execution stage uses a runtime environment providing transactional properties to reconfigurations in the Fractal model. Although it can actually handle all the errors detected by earlier stages, this choice may make the architecture not available during a too long time.

The different stages of the validation chain work together providing an integrated whole. At the same time, the chain stays modular, and some of the stages can be disabled or replaced. As the different analysis techniques have different costs, the validation chain can be customized depending on the target architectures: critical systems will require more complex static analyses in the earlier stages, and may even include a test run on a replica system whereas the cost of these steps may be redhibitory in other contexts. The rest of the paper gives more details on each of the successive chain stages.

3   Static Analysis with Respect to the Architecture Model

The first stage in the validation chain loads the source code of the reconfiguration script into the chain. Its goal is to verify the validity of the reconfiguration with respect to the underlying architecture model. The component model defines some rules to be satisfied by the architectures under consideration. At this point, the actual architectures to which the script will be applied are unknown.

The reconfiguration scripts are written in a domain-specific language named FScript [2] that we have defined for this purpose. This language not only allows reconfigurations to be easily expressed, but also ensures some safety properties: for instance, any well-formed script terminates.

When a script is well-formed, a semantic analysis introduces an axiomatic definition of the script execution. This analysis is parameterized by a selection of the rules of the architecture model: this allows us to easily support variants, at the infrastructure or application levels, like different architectural styles. Note that some rules can be discarded because they are too costly to analyze. The analysis defines Hoare's correctness formulas $\{P\}S\{Q\}$ where S is the script and P and Q are properties describing the architecture to be reconfigured (expressed in first-order logic). Such a formula means that any architecture satisfying the precondition P will satisfy the postcondition Q after the completion of the script S. The aim of the semantic analysis is to determine a precondition P that does not lead to an error state where the architecture violates some invariant rules under consideration: only the architectures that satisfy the precondition P will be reconfigured by the script. Therefore, if the precondition P is *false*, it means that the script is not useful according to the analysis and should be rejected. Otherwise, the script is considered as potentially valid, and passed to the next stage of the validation chain along with the computed precondition. Note that the semantic analysis can be more or less precise: the precondition P is sufficient to ensure the absence of errors with respect to the selected rules, but not necessary.

4   Validation with Respect to the Target Architecture

The second stage in the validation chain is triggered each time the user requests the invocation of a reconfiguration script by giving a target architecture and actual parameters. This stage performs additional validations thanks to this information, but without actually modifying the target architecture.

At this point, the script has already passed the first stage of the chain, and has a pre-condition associated to it. The first step is thus a simple *compatibility check*, which consists in evaluating the pre-condition on the target architecture and the actual parameters. This can be done easily, and only requires to introspect the target architecture, without modifications.

If the compatibility check has succeeded, an optional second step can be included, which consists in a *simulation* of the script's execution. This step uses a virtual implementation of the target architecture, on which the reconfiguration script is executed using the script interpreter. The virtual architecture is initialized with the initial state of the target system, but implements "copy-on-write" semantics: operations are applied to the virtual copy, and do not modify the actual target system. If any of the component model invariant rules of the architectural model are violated during the simulation, the invocation is rejected.

One advantage of the simulation is that it can be more precise (and thus can catch more errors) that the static analyses, which may be restricted by a selection of the invariant rules to be preserved. Also, by instrumenting the virtual architecture to be reconfigured, it can generate the exact trace of the reconfiguration performed by the script, which can be "replayed" with very little overhead to reproduce its effect on the actual target system [3]. The only drawback is that this step can increase the latency of the reconfiguration.

5   Execution of Reconfigurations as Transactions

The final stage of the chain is the actual application of the reconfiguration script on the target architecture. Depending on how the previous stage was configured, it uses either a compiled form of the script, or the specialized trace of reconfiguration operations that was generated during the simulation.

Because the overall objective of the validation chain is to guarantee the reliability of the reconfiguration, this step must either apply the complete reconfiguration script without errors, or, in case of errors, restore the system to the last consistent state before the execution of the script by rollbacking the failed reconfiguration: it must be fault tolerant. The failures that happen during the actual execution of the reconfiguration include software failures (e.g. violation of the architecture model) that were not detected earlier, and some errors that are fundamentally impossible to predict (e.g. hardware crashes). In all cases, the resulting architecture must be in a consistent state according to the definition of the underlying architecture model.

These objectives call for the use of transaction management techniques, as they closely match the standard ACID properties (Atomicity, Consistency, Isolation, Durability) of transactions in distributed computing [4]. In order to execute reconfiguration scripts inside global transactions with automatic demarcation, we use an extended version of the Fractal component model [5], which provides transactional semantics for Fractal architectures. Therefore, reconfigurations can benefit from ACID properties to support concurrency, recovery, and to guarantee system consistency.

6   Conclusion and Future Work

The objective of this work is to make runtime reconfigurations of open software architectures reliable while maximizing their availability. We specially target reflexive component-based architectures for their suitable adaptability property, as exemplified by the use of the Fractal model in our current implementation. Our solution relies on a multi-stage validation chain with two main dependability methods: fault prevention and fault tolerance. Fault prevention notably includes the use of static analysis on a dedicated reconfiguration language in order to detect invalid reconfigurations with respect to the architecture model, and an additional simulation stage on the target architecture. Fault-tolerance is ensured by a transactional runtime for the actual execution of reconfigurations.

Although several component models support open dynamic reconfigurations, they do no take into account the reliability of reconfigurations. On the contrary, most work on reliability and validation for component-based architectures deal with Architecture Description Languages [6,7] only include static validations and do not support unanticipated reconfigurations. Recent component models, like FORMAware [8] and Plastik [9], rely on reflexive architectures to allow unanticipated reconfigurations while supporting some kinds of guarantees checked at runtime. Our work differs in that we provide a multi-stage architecture that integrates different complementary validation techniques in a consistent whole. Depending on the domain requirements, the focus of the validation chain can be put on the static validation, the controlled execution, or both, for instance for critical systems.

Currently the overall architecture of the validation chain is in place, and the whole system is usable although some of the individual stages are not yet complete: the simulation and execution of reconfiguration programs is fully functional, including transactional guarantees. Our current focus is on the earlier steps, and in particular the definition and implementation of the static analysis of reconfiguration scripts, which requires a formal definition of both the FScript language and the Fractal model. Once we have a fully implemented validation chain for Fractal, we plan to extend it to support other component models.

References

1. Bruneton, E., Coupaye, T., Leclercq, M., Quéma, V., Stefani, J.B.: The Fractal Component Model and its Support in Java. Software Practice and Experience, special issue on Experiences with Auto-adaptive and Reconfigurable Systems 36(11-12), 1257–1284 (2006)
2. David, P.C., Ledoux, T.: Safe dynamic reconfigurations of Fractal architectures with FScript. In: Thomas, D. (ed.) ECOOP 2006. LNCS, vol. 4067, Springer, Heidelberg (2006)
3. Polakovic, J., Mazaré, S., Stefani, J.B., David, P.C.: Experience with implementing safe reconfigurations in component-based embedded systems. In: Schmidt, H.W., Crnković, I., Heineman, G.T., Stafford, J.A. (eds.) CBSE 2007. LNCS, vol. 4608, Springer, Heidelberg (2007)
4. Traiger, I.L., Gray, J., Galtieri, C.A., Lindsay, B.G.: Transactions and consistency in distributed database systems. ACM Trans. Database Syst. 7(3), 323–342 (1982)
5. Léger, M., Ledoux, T., Coupaye, T.: Reliable dynamic reconfigurations in the Fractal component model. In: Proceedings of the 6th workshop on Adaptive and reflective middleware (ARM 2007), p. 6. ACM, New York (2007)
6. Allen, R.J.: A Formal Approach to Software Architecture. PhD thesis, Carnegie Mellon University Technical Report Number: CMU-CS-97-144 (May 1997)
7. Medvidovic, N., Oreizy, P., Robbins, J.E., Taylor, R.N.: Using object-oriented typing to support architectural design in the C2 style. In: Proceedings of the ACM SIGSOFT 1996 Fourth Symposium on the Foundations of Software Engineering, San Francisco, CA, USA, ACM SIGSOFT, October 1996, pp. 24–32 (1996)
8. Moreira, R.S., Blair, G.S., Carrapatoso, E.: Supporting adaptable distributed systems with FORMAware. In: ICDCSW 2004: Proceedings of the 24th International Conference on Distributed Computing Systems Workshops, Washington, DC, USA, pp. 320–325. IEEE Computer Society Press, Los Alamitos (2004)
9. Batista, T., Joolia, A., Coulson, G.: Managing dynamic reconfiguration in component-based systems. In: Morrison, R., Oquendo, F. (eds.) EWSA 2005. LNCS, vol. 3527, Springer, Heidelberg (2005)

Virtual Overlays: An Approach to the Management of Competing or Collaborating Overlay Structures

Paul M. Okanda[1], Sebastian Steinhauer[2], and Gordon Blair[1]

[1] Next Generation Middleware Group, Computing Department,
InfoLab21, Lancaster University, Lancaster, LA1 4WA, UK
{okanda,gordon}@comp.lancs.ac.uk
[2] Business User Imagineering, SAP Labs, LLC,
Palo Alto, CA, USA
sebastian.steinhauer@sap.com

Abstract. Overlay networks are a technique whereby application developers create virtual customized networks on top of physical networks. Recent implementations of peer-to-peer applications such as file sharing and VoIP have increasingly meant that overlay networks have almost become ubiquitous. As a result, future overlay networks will increasingly coexist on the same node. A number of middleware frameworks such as GRIDKIT [1], P2 [2] and ODIN-S [3] currently offer support for the co-existence of multiple overlay networks. However, co-existing overlay networks interfere with each other's performance either through competition for resources or the lack of collaboration between them. This paper introduces an approach called virtual overlays which manages competition and collaboration between co-existing overlay networks in a way that is expressive, flexible, configurable and dynamically adaptable.

Keywords: Overlay Network, Virtual Overlay, Middleware.

1 Introduction

An overlay network can be seen as an application level network layer or partial network stack which represents a virtual network. This virtual network is realized as a composition of nodes and logical links abstracting from an underlying existing network. The main motivation behind overlay networks is the provision of more tailored application services to support applications in different domains e.g. multimedia file sharing, peer-to-peer networks etc. Overlay networks have gained widespread utilization in recent years as a way through which services offered by the underlying physical network can be tailored to better support the requirements of applications. Applications such as multimedia file sharing and Virtual Private Networks (VPNs) have proven that overlay networks provide a powerful and efficient solution for specific problems, e.g. security and content distribution.

The success of current overlay networks e.g. Chord [5], SCRIBE [6] and Pastry [7] has meant that future trends will result in nodes that run different distributed applications hosting multiple overlays at a time. This is bound to introduce competition for

R. Meier and S. Terzis (Eds.): DAIS 2008, LNCS 5053, pp. 112–125, 2008.
© IFIP International Federation for Information Processing 2008

local resources such as CPU time, memory consumption and network resources such as bandwidth. There is therefore a need for a framework that resolves competition for local and network resources, manages collaboration between two or more overlay networks and, creates a higher level of abstraction that provides developers with better control over the management of resource conflicts and collaboration between overlay networks.

We propose the use of *virtual overlays* as a means through which the strengths of multiple overlapping overlay networks can be combined to not only efficiently resolve conflicts between overlay networks but also manage competition between them and support their collaboration in a flexible, adaptive and configurable way.

2 Background on Overlays

2.1 Definition of Network Overlays

An overlay network can be defined as an application level network layer or partial network stack which represents a virtual network. This virtual network is realized as a composition of nodes and logical links that are an abstraction from an underlying existing network. The main motivation behind the implementation of overlays is to provide more application-specific or tailored network services which are not provided by the underlying network. The advantages of overlay networks are pointed out in Aberer et al. [4] thus:

> "In principle, distributed application services could also use directly the physical networking layer for managing their resources, but using an overlay network has the advantage of supporting application specific identifiers and semantic routing, and offers the possibility to provide additional, generic services for supporting network maintenance, authentication, trust, etc., all of which would be very hard to integrate into and support at the networking layer."

This general idea of overlay networks is well known and has been shown to work well. Transmitting information by sending telegraphs on top of a circuit switched network can be seen as a historic example. Dial-up connections between computers and bulletin board systems are an example that is close to the type of overlay that is the subject of this research paper. Modern overlay networks are a critical part of distributed applications. For instance peer-to-peer applications use overlay technologies to create virtual networks as an abstraction from heterogeneous underlying networks, Virtual Private Networks (VPNs) add authentication and encryption to messages sent through them, which often cannot be provided by the underlying networks while peer-to-peer applications are ubiquitous and are used broadly.

Current software systems that utilize overlay technologies, e.g. Chord [5], SCRIBE [6], or Pastry [7], usually implement a specific well known and well defined overlay routing mechanism and a corresponding topology. These virtual networks act like classic, message based, networks on top of underlying networks. They can be used in a stacked manner, but they keep their basic topology. Hence if an overlay network layer is designed as a ring network it maintains this structure when stacked with other overlay networks.

2.2 Why Virtual Overlays?

Current overlay networks have been shown to provide software engineers with high levels of abstraction at the cost of fine grained control on the message transmission. The wide adoption of overlay technologies results in co-existing implementations executing in nodes, e.g. the deployment of a VPN and a peer-to-peer file sharing application on a single computer. The new concept presented in this paper aims to provide an approach for controlling and orchestrating multiple coexistent overlay networks. In order to address the requirement mentioned in the introduction, virtual overlays provide a technology that can be used to a) resolve resource conflicts, e.g. competition for memory between an application specific implementation of a multicast overlay network and an unreliable transmission overlay network, b) manage collaboration between coexisting overlay networks e.g. between an overlay providing reliable transmission and an overlay providing multicast without forcing developers to give up the advantages of application-specific overlays and, c) provide a higher-level abstraction that gives developers the ability to configure the behaviour of overlays at a fine grained level, i.e. on a per message basis. This fine-grained per-message manipulation of behaviour implies that an overlay's behaviour is not only dependent on its static forwarding mechanism but also on the message which is passed. This also implies that technologies which are usually used on a packet level within the ISO/OSI layers can be used to orchestrate overlay networks.

As will be seen in the next section, the focus of the design and implementation of the proof-of-concept system is on the manipulation of message routing in overlay networks at a finer level of granularity and in a more flexible way, without having a significant negative impact on understandability or system performance.

3   Design and Implementation of the Virtual Overlay

In this section, we describe our design of a virtual overlay by presenting a background on GRIDKIT and demonstrating how the design is realized on top of the GRIDKIT middleware framework. Crucially, the goal is to provide an approach that manages competition and collaboration between multiple overlay structures.

3.1 Background on GRIDKIT

GRIDKIT is a middleware solution whose aim is to provide support for the development of complex distributed systems. It can be used to develop a range of approaches some of which are service-oriented. In order to provide an array of interaction types, GRIDKIT provides different plug-able overlays at different levels of abstraction. The set of services provided by the GRIDKIT middleware for grid environments consists of service bindings, resource discovery, resource management and security. All of these can be combined with the communication layer realized by the GRIDKIT Overlay Framework [1]. GRIDKIT addresses the common challenges of middleware systems by providing developers with the possibility to interconnect overlays in different ways. In their paper 'GRIDKIT: Pluggable Overlay Networks for Grid Computing', Grace et al. [1] summarize the main goal of the GRIDKIT framework as follows:

> "The goal of our research in this area is to develop ways of building fully customizable, extensible, and evolvable overlays by factoring out generic techniques and protocols (e.g., large-scale neighbor discovery, and network capability discovery techniques), and enabling these to be composed, extended and dynamically reconfigured under the auspices of a well - defined [component frameworks]."

As described above, overlay networks can be used to create functionality on top of underlying networks. In GRIDKIT, the developer is given the freedom to combine different overlay networks or even components of different overlay networks to create custom overlay networks. These custom overlay networks are created by interconnecting OpenCOMJ [1] components and component frameworks (CFs). This provides software developers with the tools to create custom interaction types based on pre-existing building blocks. This approach gives software architects more flexibility during the design of their applications [9], [1]. As described above, every overlay consists of OpenCOMJ components [1]. As shown in Figure 1 below, an overlay has to control its topology and provide its forwarding technique. Since the topology management and the forwarding are based on shared information, a third component is used to provide state information.

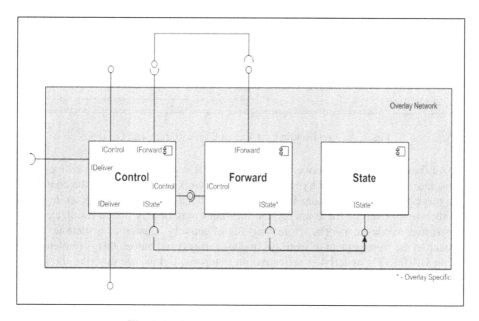

Fig. 1. An Architecture for a GRIDKIT Overlay

Each overlay layer needs to be connected to an IDeliver interface and provides an IDeliver interface. This interface is used in the GRIDKIT framework to pass messages between layers of stacked overlays. An integer value is used to identify the overlay class that a message is passed to. The IDeliver interface is used to pass messages upwards through the overlay stack. Each overlay also provides and consumes at least one IForward interface. In contrast to IDeliver, the IForward interface is used to pass messages downwards through the overlay stack. High level control functionality is accessed using the IControl interface as it can be used to join and leave overlay networks.

3.2 Extensions on GRIDKIT to Support Virtual Overlays

The system is implemented as part of GRIDKIT which features support for the co-existence of overlay networks.

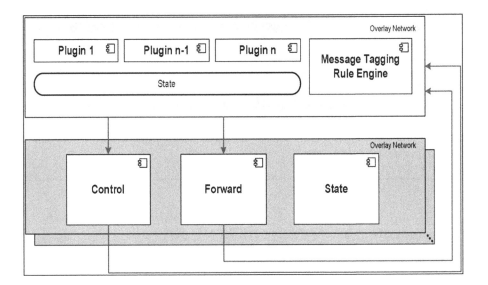

Fig. 2. An Architecture for a Virtual Overlay built on an Overlay

As shown in Figure 2 above, a virtual overlay component intercepts all messages sent, received or forwarded by native overlay networks. Depending on the content of the messages and the functions implemented by the plugins and the rule set deployed by the virtual overlay, these intercepted messages may or may not be re-injected into the native overlay networks. Note that this effectively equates to a meta-level approach to the management of overlays (meta-overlays) and indeed this is implemented using GRIDKIT's underlying reflective mechanisms. Below, we describe the fundamental constituents of the virtual overlay.

Message Tagging and Rule Engine. The general concept of tagging messages was inspired by IP Filters [12] and Conoboy et al.'s [11] work on the rule language and its influence on packets being processed by the packet filter. All messages are tagged by all applicable rules; the process of tagging does not alter the message itself but adds a flag to the message for each applied rule. After adding all applicable flags to the message, a set of filters is used to alter the message according to the flags the message was tagged with. To ensure consistency with the idea of an interchangeable rule engines, the central requirement for a rule engine in the context of this project is its full compliance to JSR 94 [13]. This specification defines the general interfaces a rule engine needs to implement without specifying a rule definition language or a specific technology for the rule engine. Since the main differences for rule engines in this context are the technology and the language used to define the rules, the number of candidates for the virtual overlay's implementation was fairly limited. The following criteria were used during the decision making process: complexity, license, rule language, community, and documentation. Amongst the rule engines evaluated were Jess [14], JBoss Rules [15] and Hammurapi Rules [16]. Although the Hammurapi Rules development community is relatively small, its lightweight implementation made it the best choice for a prototype system.

Plugins. The intercepted messages are tagged according to a rule set and based on the tagging of each message, control plugins manipulate the message. Finally the message is injected into or sent via a native overlay. Each plugin checks whether a message contains specific tags and if the message does, it performs some action, otherwise the plugin executes its default action.

Crucially, the virtual overlay does not only intercept messages within the existing overlays but is in itself an overlay which can be stacked on top of existing overlays. It can receive messages from other overlays and send messages using the default set of overlay interfaces. In order to offer support for the orchestration of overlays, the system's overlay components implement an interception and injection interface.

Figure 3 below illustrates a plugin that checks whether a message contains specific tags. If the message does, it performs some action, otherwise the plugin executes its default action.

```
public class DropPlugin
        extends GenericPlugin
        implements IPlugin, IConnections, ILifeCycle, IUnknown, IMetaInterface{

        public DropPlugin(IUnknown runtime) {
                super(runtime);
        }

        @Override
        public MessageDecorator processMessage(MessageDecorator message) {
                if (    (message!=null)  &&
                                (message.Tags.contains(DROP.getInstance())) &&
                                (!(message.Tags.contains(PASS.getInstance()))))

                        ) {
                        message = null;
                }

                return super.processMessage(message);
        }

}
```

Fig. 3. Java Source Code for a Sample Filter Plugin

The method `processMessage` checks if a message was passed to it, and it was it checks for the tag DROP and the absence of the tag PASS. If a DROP tag is found and not a PASS tag the message is set to null. If a PASS tag is found or no DROP tag is found the message is not manipulated. In either case, the message or null is passed to the next plugin by calling the parent method `processMessage`. This ensures that the entire chain of plugins is processed and the default action is carried out. Cases which require to process all messages can be imagined hence it is required that the messages are passed down the chain even if they are null. The inherited class `GenericPlugin` also implements the entire OpenCOMJ functionality. The development of a plugin only requires overloading the `processMessage` function - if a behavior different from just passing the message is required.

The tagging engine in this prototype was developed as a façade around the rule engine to tag messages. In order to show that the tagging of messages with a following processing of the messages based on their tags is an efficient way of manipulating messages on middleware level a small rule set was defined. Figure 4 below shows how a rule can be created by implementing the infer method in a class inheriting from Rule.

```
public class TagDROP extends Rule {

    public void infer(MessageDecorator msg){
        String PATTERN = Arrays.toString("DEBUG".getBytes());

        if (Arrays.toString(msg.RawData).indexOf(PATTERN)>-1){
            msg.Tags.add(DROP.getInstance());
        }
    }
}
```

Fig. 4. A sample rule for Hammurapi Rules

The next section details a set of experiments that were developed over the GRID-KIT overlay framework.

4   Experimental Evaluation

This section details an experimental evaluation of the implementation of the design discussed in section 3.2 above. To facilitate the experiments, two representative and existing overlay networks are used to prove the concept of the described system; Tree Building Control Protocol (TBCP) [8] and Chord [5]. TBCP is used to span a balanced application level multicast tree. While Chord represents a distributed hash table (DHT)-based overlay ring network. Chord is a well known overlay network while TBCP is a clean realization of an application level multicast tree. Implementations of both overlay networks are part of the GRIDKIT framework.

From our implementation of the design detailed in section 3 above, we set up two sets of incremental experiments that focused on validating the architecture described in the previous section. As a first step, the general concept was verified by implementing a sample application that could be used to show major aspects of the proposed system and its basic performance metrics. Since overlay networks are not only defined by the forwarding technique that they implement but also by their topology and their state, the components maintaining and realizing their topology and state are represented in the context of virtual overlay networks. The second set of experiments aims to show a non-static (dynamic) implementation of meta-routing. It presents a prototype developed for inter-overlay routing based on self-configuring routes.

4.1   A Basic Middleware Firewall

Overview
The proof-of-concept implementation presented in this sub-section shows the realization of interception of messages within an overlay and reinjection of messages in the very same overlay. Crucially, its aim is to a) illustrate the internals of a minimal configuration of a virtual overlay and b) evaluate the performance overhead that is introduced by the implementation of a virtual overlay.

Implementation
As detailed below, this experiment implements the three constituents of a virtual overlay described in section 3 above. It involves a selection and implementation of a message injection mechanism, an implementation of a message tagging technology and an implementation of a rule engine.

Message Injection. The fundamental concept of the proposed architecture is message interception and message injection. To prove this concept, a test application comprising two parts, a sender and a receiver was developed. Both components intercept messages before sending or receiving them. The intercepted messages get manipulated and then re-injected into (other or the same) overlay networks. In the initial stages of the experiment, a TBCP tree containing exactly two nodes was created, one node being the sender while the second node acted as a receiver. The sample application used a custom Log4J[10] appender to published messages to a multicast tree. Since broadcast messages were filtered within the sender and receiver in a multicast application that was extended to provide support for the interception of inbound and outbound messages, this could be considered a simplified firewall.

Message Tagging. In the first prototype implementation, the filter basically drops or passes messages according to their tags. To gain higher flexibility, the plugin processing the tags has to define a default behavior in case no matching tags can be found or in case conflicting tags are attached to a message. The mechanism of using a separate tagging engine which does not define the behavior of the stack creates flexibility in choosing a rule engine for a particular task, or to meet specific environmental constraints. It also allows the use of precompiled sets of tags to be attached to precompiled messages, which might be relevant in throughput-critical systems.

Rule Engine. As illustrated in Figure 5 below, the TBCP Overlay was extended to provide the interface IOverlayCallback. It also provides intercepted messages to the Virtual Overlay component using the IIntercept interface. The Virtual Overlay component uses a Tagging Engine component to wrap the rule engine via the interface ITag and forwards tagged messages to a chain of plugins using the IPlugin interface. The diagram below shows the components used. The chain of plugins only consists of two generic empty plugins as proof of the concept of the plugin chain as well as the DROPPlugin. The chain of plugins is realized using the IPlugin interface that each plugin has to implement.

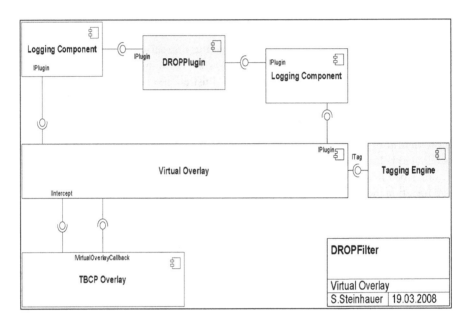

Fig. 5. Major components of the first prototype

It is also implemented by the Virtual Overlay component which re-injects messages into the TBCP Overlay after they have completed the entire chain. The prototype's major components are briefly described below.

The Tagging Engine. This rule tags all messages containing the word "DEBUG" with the tag DROP. A similar rule is used to tag all message having the word "FA-TAL" in them with the tag PASS. All other messages are not tagged at all. The rule engine automatically loads rules listed in a rule set definition file. The Tagging Engine also checks the rule set definition file for updates before tagging a message. This very simple approach allows runtime manipulation of the deployed rule set and was implemented to show that runtime adaptability can be achieved using the proposed system.

Evaluation

To evaluate the prototype, a basic system creating log messages was used. The generator sends two sets of 1000 numbered messages with priorities iterating over {DEBUG, INFO, WARN, ERROR, FATAL}. A small receiver application logged the message, including the time of creation, as well as the time of reception to a file. To provide reproducible and facilitate comparison of results without the need to consider time synchronization, the receiving and sending application executed on the same computer. All involved Java Virtual Machines (JVMs) were running with normal priorities as user applications. Two virtual machines were used to span a tree containing one root node and one non-root node. All measurements were carried out free of external network interruptions, only the loopback device was used. Two measurements were taken; one showing the native GRIDKIT framework delivering the messages without any filtering or tagging and one showing the performance of the GRIDKIT framework using the prototype presented in this section. Table 1 below shows the delay measured per message of the second set of 1000 sent messages.

Table 1. Quantifying the Overhead of Virtual Overlays

Measurement	Mean Msg. Delay in s	Std Deviation in s (%)	No. of Msgs. Sent	No. of Msgs. Received (%)
GRIDKIT & Prototype	0.058	0.013 (22)	1000	800 (80)
GRIDKIT	0.055	0.013 (23)	1000	1000 (100)

It is evident that the virtual overlay firewall performed its intended purpose since the expected number of messages (200 or 20%) did not reach the receiving node in the test using the prototype implementation. It also shows that all messages send using the native GRIDKIT implementation arrived at the identical receiving node. The difference between the average message delay when using the virtual overlay compared to not using it is around 0.003s. The standard deviation calculated for both measures is 13ms. In all instances, the measured delay from all messages sent using the altered framework was smaller than delays measured for the pure GRIDKIT implementation. This might indicate that the overhead added by the prototype implementation is smaller than other factors interfering with the message transmission. The main suspected factors are the virtual machine internal thread management as well as the process scheduling of the operating system.

This experiment shows a sample application that realizes the basic architecture of a virtual overlay. The performance metrics detailed above prove that the configurability and expressiveness that is achievable using the proposed system makes the overhead insignificant. The next two experiments build on the implementation presented above to present more complex scenarios.

4.2   An Enhanced Virtual Overlay

Overview

This experiment aims at showing that our approach is not limited to message filtering or static routes but that virtual overlays can use their own state and a meta-routing algorithm to reproduce GRIDKIT's Control, Forward and State overlay pattern introduced in section 3.

As illustrated in Figure 6 below, the namespace spanned by a Chord ring is used to globally address messages while messages sent to nodes in the Chord ring are actually routed via appropriate direct routes, which are in this example smaller Chord rings (with only 2 nodes).

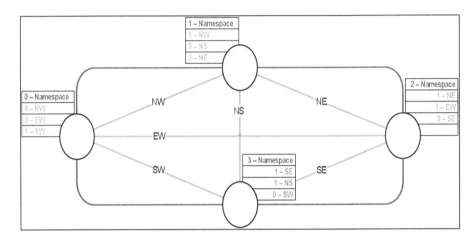

Fig. 6. Illustration of TBCP Trees and Chord Ring Setup

This gives developers the flexibility to create virtual overlays which do not route messages within the actual overlays but between multiple overlays.

Implementation

As shown in Figure 7 below, central to achieving this experiment's aim is the Routing Packet Overlay which uses a time controlled trigger to send information about each node it is deployed on in intervals. If the trigger fires, the Routing Packet Overlay obtains a list of all local Chord endpoints created by the Multi CHORD Overlay component. It then creates a message containing the global identifier (defined for the global namespace Chord ring) of the current node as well as the name and local identifier of the node in each Chord Overlay. The packet is sent via the local network named within the message. Thus the nodes in each local network can route messages correctly as they get to 'know' the global identifiers of the nodes on that network. This data is stored and managed in Routing Table.

The Multi CHORD Overlay component was developed to provide a unified interface to a multitude of Chord overlay networks. The component uses a network name to distinguish between the Chord overlay networks. In order to create a prototype which shows easily verifiable behavior, the Chord framework implementation was altered to support direct definition of node IDs.

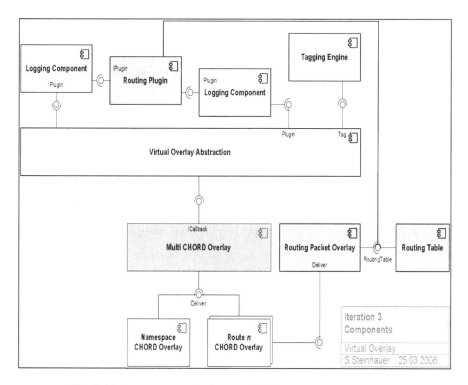

Fig. 7. Major components in the scenario "Enhanced Virtual Overlay"

Figure 7 above shows three major components developed as part of this prototype (Routing Packet Overlay, Routing Table and Routing Plugin).

Evaluation

This scenario shows how the given components work together to route messages in a multi-overlay environment through collaborative message routing between nodes. The evaluation scenario is based on an overlay network environment with two nodes being part of two different Chord networks. Since the overhead of creating and maintaining the routing data within the hybrid network significantly influences the performance, it is not quantified. A scenario to demonstrate the effectiveness of the proposed system in an expressive manner would have required a bigger network and setup work beyond the scope of this paper.

5 Related Work

In Cooper et al.'s paper 'Trading Off Resources between overlapping Overlays' [3], an architecture called ODIN-S is introduced which has a focus on different methods to mediate resource usage between coexisting overlay networks. It uses a set of ingoing and outgoing filter to intercept messages on a shared communication layer. In this approach overlay networks are not stand-alone entities but plugins running on top of a common transport system. This transport system communicates with a set of filters in order to control throughput and order of messages being sent through the overlay network. ODIN-S also assumes a homogeneous deployment of ODIN-S instances since it uses specific receiver originated messages to control the throughput of messages on sending nodes. In general the paper shows that manipulation of messages on their entry point into the overlay environment can be used to achieve QoS through the control of resource conflicts between coexisting overlay networks. Some generic ideas for the design of the proposed system were inspired by a project called P2 [2]. This project makes use of a declarative language to define overlays on top of a shared transport layer. The work stresses that declarative approaches can be efficient and expressive for describing the behavior of overlay networks. The novelty of the concept of virtual overlays, as detailed in this paper is that it addresses the more general management of collaboration and competition between multiple overlay structures.

6 Conclusion

This paper has presented an argument for the use of *virtual overlays* as a technique by which competition and collaboration between co-existing overlay network structures can be managed. Although a number of middleware frameworks e.g. GRIDKIT [1] and P2 [2] currently offer support for the co-existence of overlay networks, co-existing overlay networks inevitably interfere with each other's performance either through competition for resources or the lack of collaboration between them. More specifically, the paper has provided a high level overview of a middleware design which uses a meta-overlay to combine the strengths of multiple overlapping overlays (hybrid overlay networks) with a strong focus on dynamic adaptability, flexibility and configurability. We therefore argue that the use of virtual overlays to resolve resource conflicts, optimize performance via collaboration between multiple overlay structures and provide a higher-level abstraction that gives developers control over the overlay networks they deploy is the way forward in the design of next generation middleware. Areas of future work include research into deployment of multiple rule sets, development of a custom rule engine and rule language, self-configuration of rule sets and performance metrics in a large scale deployment environment.

References

1. Grace, P., Coulson, G., Blair, G., Mathy, L., Yeung, W.K., Cai, W., et al.: GRIDKIT: Pluggable Overlay Networks for Grid Computing. In: Proceedings of Distributed Objects and Applications (DOA), Cyprus (2004)
2. Loo, B.T., Condie, T., Hellerstein, H. M., Maniatis, P.: Implementing Declarative Overlays. In: Proceedings of ACM Symposium on Operating System Principles 2005 (SOSP), Brighton, UK (2005)
3. Cooper, F., B.: Trading Off Resources between overlapping Overlays. In: Proceedings of the ACM/IFIP/USENIX 7th Middleware Conference, Melbourne, Australia (2006)

4. Aberer, K., Alima, L.: The essence of P2P: A Reference Architecture for Overlay Networks. In: Proceedings of the 5th IEEE Conference on Peer-to-Peer Computing, Konstanz, Germany (2005)
5. Stoica, I., Morris, R., Karger, D., Kaashoek, F., Balakrsihnan, H.: Chord: A Scalable Peer-to-Peer Lookup Service for Internet Applications. In: Proceedings of the ACM SIGCOMM Conference, San Diego, CA, USA (2001)
6. Davis, A.M.: Operational Prototyping: A New Development Approach. IEEE Software 9(5), 70–78 (1992)
7. Rowstron, A., Druschel, P.: Pastry: Scalable Decentralized Object Location and Routing for Large Scale Peer-to-Peer Systems. In: Guerraoui, R. (ed.) Middleware 2001. LNCS, vol. 2218, pp. 329–350. Springer, Heidelberg (2001)
8. Mathy, L., Canonico, R., Hutchinson, D.: An Overlay Tree building Control Protocol. In: Proceedings of the 3rd International Workshop on Networked Group Communication, NGC, London (2001)
9. Coulson, G., Blair, G., Grace, P., Joolia, A.: A Component Model for Building Systems Software. In: Proceedings of IASTED Software Engineering and Applications (SEA), Cambridge, MA, USA (2004)
10. The Log4J Appender, http://logging.apache.org/log4j/docs/index.html
11. Conoboy, B., Fichtner, E.: IP Filter Based Firewalls HOWTO Tutorial (2002), http://www.obfuscation.org/ipf
12. IP Filter ver. 4.1.27, http://coombs.anu.edu.au/~avalon/
13. Toussaint, A. (ed.): Java Rule Engine API: JSR-94. Java Community Press (September 2003)
14. Friedman-Hill, E.: Jess Information, the Jess Engine for the Java Platform, http://www.jessrules.com/jess/index.shtml
15. JBoss: JBoss Rules Documentation Library, jboss.org, http://labs.jboss.com/jbossrules/docs
16. Hammurapi Group: Hammurapi Rules, http://www.hammurapi.biz/hammurapi-biz/ef/xmenu/products/hammurapirules/index.html

Tree-Based Analysis of Mesh Overlays for Peer-to-Peer Streaming

Bartosz Biskupski[1], Marc Schiely[2], Pascal Felber[2], and René Meier[1]

[1] Trinity College Dublin, Ireland
[2] University of Neuchâtel, Switzerland

Abstract. Mesh-based P2P streaming approaches have been recently proposed as an interesting alternative to tree-based approaches. However, many properties of mesh overlays remain little understood as they are difficult to study due to the lack of a predefined structure. In this paper we show that when data is streamed through mesh overlays, it follows tree-based diffusion patterns and thereby mesh-based streaming can be studied in a similar manner to tree-based approaches. We identify properties of the diffusion trees that emerge in mesh overlays and compare them to optimal diffusion trees. We show that the emerging diffusion trees exhibit suboptimal height and are unbalanced, which results in increased buffering delay of mesh-based P2P systems, particularly in heterogeneous environments. We present an algorithm that adapts the mesh overlay to shorten diffusion trees and to reduce the buffering delay.

1   Introduction

The use of peer-to-peer (P2P) overlays for multicast media streaming has gained significant attention in recent years as it alleviates scalability problems of centralised client-server architectures and weaknesses that prevent a wide adoption of IP Multicast. Two main approaches for building overlays for P2P multicast media streaming are tree-based [1] and mesh-based [2,3,4]. The former approach explicitly places peers in a single tree or multiple multicast trees, where they receive the stream from their parent(s) and forward it to their children. In the mesh-based approach, the P2P overlay is unstructured, formed by peers connecting to neighbours, which may be randomly selected. The media stream is typically split into small data blocks that are exchanged between neighbouring peers, resulting in their propagation throughout the overlay. The main advantage of mesh overlays compared to tree-based overlays is their much higher robustness to peer churn. In tree-based approaches, a peer can receive data only from its specified parent and when that parent fails or leaves the network, its whole sub-tree loses that data until the tree is reconstructed. In mesh-based streaming systems, data chunks can be obtained from any neighbour that holds it and thus when one neighbour fails, other neighbours may still provide the data. For that reason, many researches focus on mesh overlays for P2P streaming. However, one problem posed by mesh overlays is that they do not rely on any predefined

R. Meier and S. Terzis (Eds.): DAIS 2008, LNCS 5053, pp. 126–139, 2008.

network structure and thereby are more difficult to study than tree-based overlays. In this paper, we show that when data chunks are streamed over mesh overlays, tree-based diffusion patters dynamically emerge in the overlay. These tree-based patterns of diffusion can be studied in the same manner as tree-based overlay structures. The contribution of this paper is that we identify and analyse properties of the emerging tree structures in mesh overlays and, in order to evaluate their performance, we compare them to optimal diffusion trees in both homogeneous and heterogeneous environments. This provides insights into how mesh overlays can be adapted to reduce buffering delay in mesh-based streaming systems to a theoretical minimum. Based on this analysis we developed an algorithm that reduces diffusion tree heights in a mesh overlay and thus, also reduces buffering delay.

The paper is organised as follows: in Section 2 different approaches to the analysis of mesh-based streaming systems are presented. Section 3 shows how diffusion trees emerge in mesh overlays and analyses these diffusion trees. Finally, the adaptation algorithm is presented and evaluated in Section 4 before the paper concludes in Section 5.

2   Related Work

Many mesh-based P2P streaming systems have been proposed in the last few years [2,3,4], but none of them has been formally analysed due to their complexity.

Chunkyspread [5] is one example of an unstructured approach to media streaming. It uses a multi-tree (multi-description) based structure on top of an unstructured overlay. The structure is very dynamic as each peer periodically searches for new partners in its local environment. Peers exchange information (load, latency, creation of loops) with their neighbours to search for the best parent-child pairs for each tree. The constraints on these relationships are (1) to avoid loops, (2) to satisfy any tit-for-tat constraints, (3) to adapt load (shall be in a per peer defined range) and (4) to reduce latency. The loop-preventing algorithm which is run on the overlay ensures that chunks are distributed following a multi-tree structure. In this paper we argue, that trees do not need to be built explicitly, but that they are inherent to the mesh structure.

In contrast, SplitStream [1] is a tree-based P2P media streaming architecture that focuses on robustness. Different to our model, the stream is split into multiple stripes that can be distributed independently. A distinct tree is constructed for each of these stripes on all the participating peers. The robustness in SplitStream comes from the fact that each node is an inner node in at most one tree and a leaf node in all the other trees. Thus, if a peer fails, only one distribution tree is affected and has to be rebuilt. In our model a tree structure close to SplitStream is derived from a mesh-based approach. Peers are also inner nodes in only one tree and leaf nodes in all others. Due to the mesh structure, trees are dynamically built and adapted if nodes fail or bandwidth conditions change.

A comparative study of tree- and mesh-based approaches for media streaming is presented in [6]. Authors first propose an organised view of data delivery in mesh overlays, which consists of data diffusion and swarming phases, and later introduce delivery trees, which they discover in mesh overlays in a similar fashion to diffusion trees described in our paper. Our work is different in that we focus on formally analysing properties of diffusion trees rather than evaluating them by simulation. We also propose an overlay adaptation algorithm that improves properties of these trees.

A different approach to analysing P2P media streaming systems are fluid models. In [7] the authors present a stochastic fluid model that takes into account peer churn, heterogeneous peer upload capacities, peer buffering and delays. In this paper we analyse the distribution trees created in a mesh such that known adaptations for tree-based approaches can be applied to meshes.

In [8] tree-based P2P streaming systems are analysed and it is shown that moving high-bandwidth nodes close to the source is advantageous and leads to high performance gains in terms of total download capacity. We show in this paper that the same holds for mesh-based systems and that trees can be shortened by adapting the location of high-bandwidth nodes in diffusion trees.

3   Mesh-Based P2P Streaming

The mesh-based approach to data streaming originates from research on gossip and epidemic protocols, where nodes periodically exchange information among each other, which results in the eventual dissemination of all information to all nodes. The BitTorrent [9] file-sharing system popularised this approach for the dissemination of large volumes of data from a transmitter to all receivers. BitTorrent creates an unstructured overlay mesh to distribute a data file. A file is divided into chunks, which are exchanged by nodes in a pull-based fashion until nodes can reconstruct the original file.

In contrast to file-sharing systems, the transmitter in live P2P streaming protocols does not have access to the entire data as it is generated "live", and thus, it cannot split the whole data into chunks for distribution throughout the network. In order to leverage mesh-based delivery, streaming protocols require a delay between the stream creation time at the transmitter and the receiver playback time. The data stream produced within this delay is split into small chunks and distributed throughout the network similar to the way chunks of an entire file are distributed in mesh-based file-sharing protocols. Nodes maintain sliding windows that reflect this delay and capture which chunks have already been received and which are still missing. The buffers move forward with the speed of the original video transmission rate, which is discovered by all nodes from the video stream. The beginning of the buffer points at the chunk currently being played at the receiving node and the end of the buffer reflects the chunk currently generated at the transmitting node. Chunks that do not arrive in time (outside the sliding window) are lost and cause video playback degradation.

A mesh overlay is created in a random fashion by joining nodes connecting with selected nodes. The selection of neighbours can be based on different strategies, e.g., random or bandwidth-based. Neighbouring nodes maintain local knowledge about data chunks they possess by informing each other whenever they receive a new chunk. The missing chunks are requested from neighbours immediately or periodically, following a chunk selection algorithm. Different strategies such as most-recent-chunk-first, rarest-chunk-first or random can be used to schedule the chunk requests.

3.1   Mesh Overlay Properties

In our previous research on mesh overlay adaptation [10,11], we identified that completely random mesh overlays limit the network throughput by underutilising the available upload bandwidth at peers. Limited network throughput in turn reduces possible video streaming rates and the corresponding video quality. We showed properties of mesh overlays that, when satisfied, optimise the network throughput. This requires that each peer maintains two sets of neighbours — (1) children, which are the neighbours to which data is uploaded and (2) parents, which are the neighbours from which data is downloaded. The network throughput is optimised in such a directed mesh overlay when:

- Each peer has a constant (configurable) number of parents
- Each peer has a number of children proportional to its upload bandwidth

We showed in [10] that a mesh overlay satisfying these two conditions optimises the upload bandwidth utilisation and enables all peers to download at the maximum possible global video streaming rate. We also proposed algorithms for adapting the mesh overlay to satisfy these conditions. In this paper, we conduct our analysis on directed mesh overlays that satisfy these two conditions and thus we can provide a fair comparison to multiple-tree-based overlays that also optimise the network throughput. This paper is novel in that we show how diffusion trees emerge in these adapted directed mesh overlays; we analyse properties of diffusion trees and compare them to those of multiple-tree-based overlays; and finally, propose an algorithm that improves these properties.

3.2   Tree-Based View of Mesh Overlays

Mesh overlays are very dynamic and thus are difficult to analyse. In contrast, trees are well understood and it is easier to derive properties of trees. Meshes can be seen as a structure of multiple trees if we assume that bandwidth of all peers remain constant over time and that the chunk selection algorithm is deterministic. We assume that peers request missing chunks from parents immediately when they are notified of them, following a most-recent-chunk-first strategy, i.e., when a decision is made between two chunks, a chunk with a more recent timestamp is requested. This chunk request strategy is based on an observation that most recent generated chunks are also the rarest in the overlay and thus need to be given priority for distribution.

We assume that the stream rate is set to the maximum rate supported by the overlay such that all peers can receive it, i.e., equal to $\frac{\sum_i^N upload_i}{N-1}$, where N is the total number of peers including the source node (the source uploads, but does not download data). We also assume that the mesh overlay satisfies conditions discussed in Section 3.1 and that a peer's upload bandwidth is shared equally by all its connections. Under such assumptions, upload of all peers is saturated and the upload rate of each link is the same, equal to $\frac{\sum_i^N upload_i}{(N-1)*K}$, where K is a globally configurable number of parents of each peer. From this follows that each chunk is transferred over a link in time $\frac{s*(N-1)*K}{\sum_i^N upload_i}$, where s is the size of a chunk. The source node generates a new chunk every $\frac{s*(N-1)}{\sum_i^N upload_i}$ time units, so by the time a single chunk is transferred to a child, K new chunks are generated. Since it is desired that the source node sends different chunks to different children (to distribute chunks equally in the overlay), we use a round-robin strategy to push chunks from the source node to its direct children in which the ith child receives chunks with sequence numbers $t_0 + j * K + (i \bmod K)$, for some initial t_0 and $j = 0, 1, 2, 3, \ldots$. Peers, which are not direct children of the source node, request the most recently generated missing chunks, so they always request a missing chunk that travelled the least number of hops (and time). Effectively, K diffusion trees emerge, where each tree propagates every K^{th} chunk. This process of diffusion trees emerging in a mesh overlay, which has properties outlined in Section 3.1, is illustrated in Figure 1 for $K = 2$.

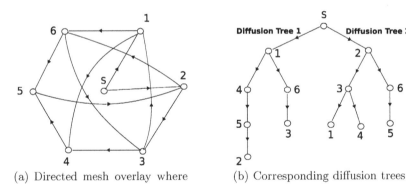

(a) Directed mesh overlay where each peer has 2 parents

(b) Corresponding diffusion trees

Fig. 1. Mesh overlay and its two diffusion trees

3.3   Analysis

In this section we show how optimal multiple trees are constructed in both homogeneous and heterogeneous environments and analyse their heights in order to compare them, in the next subsection, to diffusion trees emerging in mesh overlays.

Height of Optimal Trees in a Homogeneous Environment. First, we analyse a homogeneous environment, where all peers have the same upload capacity. Optimal K distribution trees can be created by placing each peer as an inner node in exactly one tree and as a leaf node in the other $K - 1$ trees. Thus, each peer has K parents, one in each optimal distribution tree. In a homogeneous environment, this means that the out-degree d of each peer is equal to K. Since a peer has children in only one tree, K and d are the number of children of each inner node in each tree. Thus, the height of each of K optimal distribution trees in a homogeneous environment with N nodes is equal to the height $H(d, N)$ of an evenly balanced tree with N nodes and out-degree d, which is calculated using a relation

$$\sum_{i=0}^{H(d,N)} d^i = N$$

based on the fact that there are d^i peers at tree level i. Solving this geometric sequence gives an equation for the height of a balanced homogeneous tree:

$$H(d, N) = log_d\left((d - 1) * N + 1\right) - 1 \tag{1}$$

Therefore, the height of each of K optimal trees in a homogeneous environment is given by $H(K, N)$. In this paper we also use an equation for the number of leaf nodes $L(d, N)$ in a balanced homogeneous tree with N nodes and out-degree d, given by

$$L(d, N) = d^{H(d,N)} = \frac{(d - 1) * N + 1}{d} \tag{2}$$

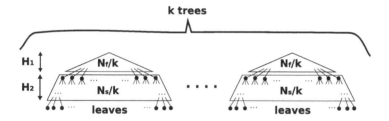

Fig. 2. Optimal construction of K trees consisting of fast and slow nodes

Height of Optimal Trees in a Heterogeneous Environment. We study the construction of optimal trees in a heterogeneous environment by using two types of peers — N_s slow peers and N_f fast peers, where a fast peer has upload bandwidth i times higher than a slow peer. In such a scenario, the optimal placement of peers that minimises the height of each of the K trees is presented in Figure 2. Similar to homogeneous environments, each peer is an inner node in exactly one tree and a leaf node in $K - 1$ trees. Additionally, fast nodes are placed at the top of the trees in order to reduce the height of the trees. Slow nodes have out-degree d, while fast nodes can upload i times faster, so their out-degree is

$i*d$. The out-degree of slow and fast nodes is derived from the fact that the total number of outgoing links of all peers must be equal to the total number of incoming links in the P2P overlay, while taking into account that the source node has out-going links, but does not have any incoming links. From this we have $N_s * d + N_f * i * d = K * (N_s + N_f - 1)$, which gives

$$d = \frac{K * (N_s + N_f - 1)}{i * N_f + N_s} \tag{3}$$

The height H_{het} of each heterogeneous tree constructed as in Figure 2 is calculated as $H_{het} = H_1 + H_2 + 1 + 1$, which is the sum of the height H_1 of the upper part of the tree composed of inner fast nodes only, the height H_2 of the lower part of the tree composed of slow inner nodes only, plus one level between the two parts of the tree and one level for the peers that are leaves in the tree (and which are inner nodes in other trees). The height H_1 is calculated using Eq. 1 as the height of a homogeneous tree of N_f/K fast nodes with out-degree $i*d$:

$$H_1 = H(i*d, \frac{N_f}{K}) = log_{i*d}\left((i*d-1)*\frac{N_f}{K}+1\right) - 1$$

The height H_2 is calculated as the height of a homogeneous tree of $\frac{N_s/K}{L_1*i*d}$ slow nodes with out-degree d

$$H_2 = H(d, \frac{N_s/K}{L_1*i*d}) = log_d\left((d-1)*\frac{N_s/K}{L_1*i*d}+1\right) - 1$$

where $L_1 = L(i*d, \frac{N_f}{K})$ is the number of leaves in the upper part, i.e., H_1. From these equations we derive a formula for the optimal height H_{het} of each optimal heterogeneous diffusion tree

$$H_{het} = log_{i*d}\left((i*d-1)*\frac{N_f}{K}+1\right) + log_d\left((d-1)\frac{N_s}{(i*d-1)*N_f+K}+1\right) \tag{4}$$

where d is the out-degree of a slow node given by Eq. 3.

3.4   Evaluation

We compare the optimal tree heights, calculated in Equation 4, to the average height of diffusion trees that emerge in mesh overlays and are calculated by our custom-built simulator of mesh overlays. The simulator relies on the assumptions outlined in Sections 3.1 and 3.2. We used 50,000 nodes and studied both a homogeneous environment and environments with different levels of heterogeneity. In experiments involving heterogeneity, 10% of all nodes are fast nodes with upload bandwidth 2 and 8 times higher than the remaining slow nodes. The overall upload bandwidth in all overlays is the same. The results are presented in Figure 3. The results show that the average height of diffusion trees in homogeneous mesh overlays is around 2 levels above the optimal height, for all K. The reason for

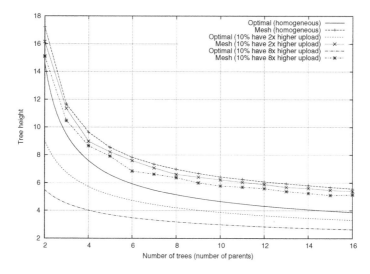

Fig. 3. Average tree height for different number of parents and different heterogeneity levels

that is that in the optimal tree each peer is an inner node in exactly one diffusion tree, whereas in the trees emerging in mesh overlays a peer is located randomly and can be an inner node in several trees. The results show that when the level of heterogeneity increases, the gap between the height of diffusion trees in the mesh overlay and optimum trees significantly increases. For the case with 10% of peers being 8 times faster than the remaining slow peers, the average height of a diffusion tree in the mesh overlay for $K = 2$ is 3 times higher than the optimum and drops to 2 times over the optimum for $K = 16$. Increased heterogeneity results in higher importance of the location of fast and slow peers in the tree. Worse performance for small K, in turn, is caused by higher variation in the height of diffusion trees - some leaves are much lower or higher than the others. This tree imbalance can be observed in Figure 4 that shows the cumulative distribution function (CDF) of the depth of leaf nodes in diffusion trees that emerge in a mesh overlay for both homogeneous and heterogeneous environments. The highest diffusion tree imbalance is for small K.

Chunk Propagation Delay. In order to measure the impact of the tree height on the buffering delay, we analyse the time required to propagate a chunk through the diffusion trees in mesh overlays. Since in a mesh overlay, a peer can be placed anywhere in each diffusion tree, its buffering delay needs to accommodate the maximum difference between chunk arrivals in each distribution tree, which is equal to the chunk propagation delay. The propagation delay can be calculated as

$$delay = \frac{H * s * K * (N - 1)}{\sum_i^N upload_i}$$

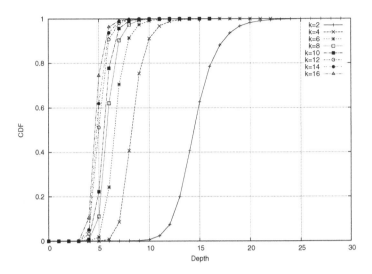

Fig. 4. CDF of the height of diffusion trees in mesh overlays in a heterogeneous (10% peers have 4x upload) environment

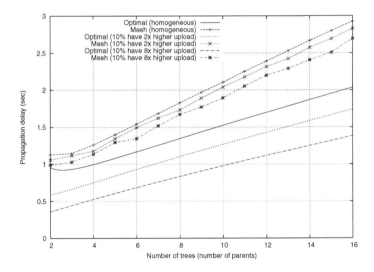

Fig. 5. Propagation delay for varying number of trees for mesh overlays and the optimal case

where H is the height of the tree, s the size of a chunk and the remaining part of the formula derives from the equation for the bandwidth of a link (see Section 3.2). It can be observed that this delay represents a trade-off between the height of a tree and the number K of distribution trees. Larger K produce shorter trees, however, it takes longer for a node to upload a chunk to all its children (since a node has more children). Smaller chunk sizes allow for their faster propagation, but more control messages are required to notify/request chunks. Propagation delay as a function of the number of diffusion trees (peer parents) is shown in Figure 5 (for an average upload bandwidth of 1,000kbps and a chunk size of 4KB). The results show that a small number of diffusion trees result in shorter buffering delays. However, small number of diffusion trees also means that the number of parents of each peer is small and this reduces robustness to peer failures.

4   Mesh Adaptation Algorithm

In the previous sections we showed that the heights of diffusion trees in mesh overlays are much higher than the optimal height. In this section we present an algorithm that adapts the location of high-bandwidth peers dynamically. To shorten tree lengths it is advantageous to place high-bandwidth nodes near the source and low-bandwidth peers near the leaves.

4.1   Algorithm

We assume that peers have accurate information about their bandwidth, either through user input or through passive measurement techniques, such as [12]. Furthermore, the assumption is made that techniques are deployed that prevent peers from cheating about their bandwidth. To do this, peers may for example team up to compare effective bandwidth of neighbours with their indicated bandwidth and drop links to cheaters if the difference is too high. Alternatively, a reputation system like [13] could be implemented.

Each chunk being distributed from the source s to a peer p contains a hop count of the path it travelled. Peers can use this hop count as an estimate of their distance to the source. As explained in previous sections, the goal of each peer is to climb up, respectively to its upload bandwidth, in one diffusion tree and to become a leaf node in all other diffusion trees. In order to achieve this, each peer periodically executes Algorithm 1, which improves a peer's position in one diffusion tree. Since each parent of a peer is responsible for delivering only one tree, the algorithm aims at improving the peer's position by replacing its current best parent (nearest to the source) with one of its grandparents that is closer to the source, subject to the conditions discussed below, effectively moving higher in one tree. Specifically, a peer p tries to find its parent $parent$ and a grandparent $grandparent$ (a parent of $parent$) that satisfies the following conditions:

1. distance($grandparent$) < distance(bestparent(p))
2. upload(p) > upload($parent$) OR bestparent($parent$) ≠ $grandparent$

The first condition requires that $grandparent$ is closer to the source than the current best parent. The second condition requires that the upload bandwidth of peer p is greater than the upload bandwidth of $parent$ (child of $grandparent$) or $grandparent$ is not the best parent of $parent$ ($parent$ does not climb up in that tree) and thus, $parent$ can give up that $grandparent$. If these two conditions

---

Algorithm 1. Adapting position of peer p in the mesh overlay

---

for all *parent* ← *parent*(p) **do**
  for all *grandparent* ← *parent*(*parent*) **do**
    if *parent* ≠ *source* **then**
      if *distance*(*grandparent*) < *distance*(*bestparent*(p)) **then**
        if *upload*(p) > *upload*(*parent*) **or** *bestparent*(*parent*) ≠ *grandparent*
        then
          exchangePosition(p, *parent*, *grandparent*)
        end if
      end if
    end if
  end for
end for

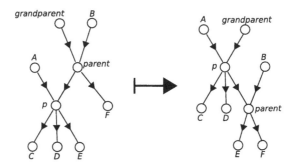

Fig. 6. Peers p and *parent* exchange their positions respectively to *grandparent*

are satisfied, then peer p climbs up one level by: replacing *parent* as a child of *grandparent*, becoming a new parent of *parent* and losing one child, which becomes a child of *parent* (Figure 6 shows the exchange protocol). This way, the number of children and parents of all peers involved (p, *parent* and *grandparent*) remain unchanged and thus, the properties of the overlay required for achieving the optimal network throughput, described in Section 3.1, remain satisfied. The presented adaptation algorithm effectively results in each peer climbing up in one tree as long as its parent in this tree has lower upload bandwidth and climbing down in other trees (by giving up its position in these other trees to its children that climb up in these trees). The algorithm does not affect the network throughput as it does not change the number of children or parents of any peer.

4.2 Evaluation

In this section, we show the results of our evaluation of the adaptation algorithm presented in Section 4.1. The algorithm was implemented in our custom-built simulator and executed on 50,000 nodes with different ratios of upload bandwidth of fast and slow nodes. First, an initial mesh was created and tree heights

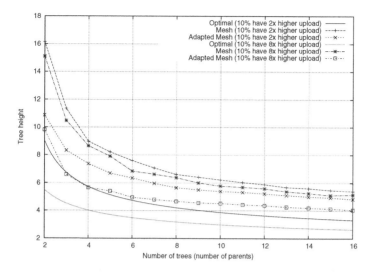

Fig. 7. Average tree heights for different proportions of upload bandwidth and 50,000 peers

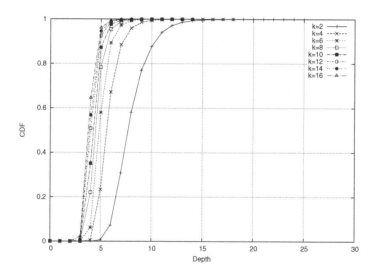

Fig. 8. CDF of the height of diffusion trees in adapted mesh overlays in a heterogeneous (10% peers have 4x upload) environment

calculated. Then, Algorithm 1 was executed to adapt the positions of all peers until no more adaptations were possible.

In all experiments 10% of all peers had i ($i = \{2, 8\}$) times higher upload bandwidth than the remaining peers. The number of trees K varied from 2 to 16. As can be seen in Figure 7, there is a significant benefit of placing high-bandwidth nodes near the source. The average tree heights decrease by about 35% for two trees ($K = 2$). The same improvement is in the buffering delay, which is proportional to the tree height. Figure 8 shows the cumulative distribution function (CDF) of the depth of leaf nodes in diffusion trees in adapted mesh overlays. This figure, when compared to the analogous Figure 4, shows that diffusion trees in the adapted mesh overlays are significantly more balanced. However, despite of much improvement, some imbalance in the diffusion tree heights remains and, for that reason, the height of diffusion trees (and the corresponding buffering delay) is suboptimal. To achieve optimal diffusion trees, a more system-wide adaptation is required, which is a focus of our future work.

5   Conclusions

In this paper we analysed data diffusion in mesh overlays. We showed that data chunks follow dynamically formed diffusion trees and analysed properties of these trees. The proposed structured view of meshes allows us to apply knowledge about trees directly to mesh-based streaming approaches. Our results show that diffusion trees in mesh overlays are unbalanced with suboptimal height and thereby, buffering delay in mesh overlays is suboptimal. With the increasing heterogeneity in an overlay, the diffusion trees become even more suboptimal due to imperfect placement of fast peers in the diffusion trees. This implies that a mesh adaptation algorithm that places fast nodes closer to the source in exactly one diffusion tree shortens the height and improves the balance of diffusion trees, thereby significantly reducing the data buffering delay. We presented such a mesh adaptation algorithm and showed that it improves tree heights. In future work the algorithm will be enhanced to better balance the height of diffusion trees, implemented in our prototypes and experimentally evaluated to show its effectiveness in real-world scenarios.

Acknowledgements

This work is supported in part by MiNEMA, ESF, Swiss National Foundation Grant 102819 and Enterprise Ireland under the Commercialisation Proof of Concept Programme (MeshTV).

References

1. Castro, M., Druschel, P., Kermarrec, A.M., Nandi, A., Rowstron, A., Singh, A.: SplitStream: High-bandwidth multicast in cooperative environments. In: SOSP 2003: Proceedings of the nineteenth ACM Symposium on Operating Systems Principles, New York, NY, USA, pp. 298–313 (2003)
2. Pai, V.S., Kumar, K., Tamilmani, K., Sambamurthy, V., Mohr, A.E.: Chainsaw: Eliminating trees from overlay multicast. In: Castro, M., van Renesse, R. (eds.) IPTPS 2005. LNCS, vol. 3640, pp. 127–140. Springer, Heidelberg (2005)
3. Magharei, N., Rejaie, R.: PRIME: Peer-to-peer receiver-driven mesh-based streaming. In: 26th Annual IEEE Conference on Computer Communications IEEE INFOCOM 2007 (2007)

4. Pianese, F., Perino, D., Keller, J., Biersack, E.: PULSE: an adaptive, incentive-based, unstructured p2p live streaming system. IEEE Transactions on Multimedia, Special Issue on Content Storage and Delivery in Peer-to-Peer Networks 9(6) (2007)
5. Venkatraman, V., Yoshida, K., Francis, P.: Chunkyspread: Heterogeneous unstructured end system multicast. In: Proceedings of 14th IEEE International Conference on Network Protocols (November 2006)
6. Magharei, N., Rejaie, R., Guo, Y.: Mesh or multiple-tree: A comparative study of live p2p streaming approaches. In: Proceedings of 26th IEEE International Conference on Computer Communication (INFOCOM), pp. 1424–1432 (May 2007)
7. Kumar, R., Liu, Y., Ross, K.: Stochastic fluid theory for p2p streaming systems. In: Proceedings of 26th IEEE International Conference on Computer Communication (INFOCOM), pp. 919–927 (May 2007)
8. Schiely, M., Renfer, L., Felber, P.: Self-organization in cooperative content distribution networks. In: Proceedings of IEEE International Symposium on Network Computing and Applications (NCA), pp. 109–116 (July 2005)
9. Cohen, B.: Incentives build robustness in BitTorrent. In: the 1st Workshop on Economics of Peer-to-Peer Systems, Berkeley, CA, USA (June 2003)
10. Biskupski, B., Cunningham, R., Dowling, J., Meier, R.: High-bandwidth mesh-based overlay multicast in heterogeneous environments. In: AAA-IDEA 2006: Proceedings of the 2nd International Workshop on Advanced Architectures and Algorithms for Internet Delivery and Applications, pp. 4–11. ACM Press, New York (2006)
11. Biskupski, B., Cunningham, R., Meier, R.: Improving throughput and node proximity of p2p live video streaming through overlay adaptation. In: Proceedings of the 9th IEEE International Symposium on Multimedia (ISM 2007), pp. 245–252. IEEE Computer Society, Los Alamitos (2007)
12. Strauss, J., Katabi, D., Kaashoek, F.: A measurement study of available bandwidth estimation tools. In: IMC 2003: Proceedings of the 3rd ACM SIGCOMM conference on Internet measurement, New York, NY, USA, pp. 39–44 (2003)
13. Nandi, A., Ngan, T.W., Singh, A., Druschel, P., Wallach, D.S.: Scrivener: Providing incentives in cooperative content distribution systems. In: Alonso, G. (ed.) Middleware 2005. LNCS, vol. 3790, pp. 270–291. Springer, Heidelberg (2005)

Managing Peer-to-Peer Live Streaming Applications

Raymond Cunningham, Bartosz Biskupski, and René Meier

Distributed Systems Group,
Department of Computer Science,
Trinity College Dublin

Abstract. A number of p2p live streaming systems [1], [2], [3], [4], [5], [6] and [7] have been proposed in recent years. Typically, the description of these systems focuses on how the live stream is transmitted from its source to a number of viewers within the particular p2p network and how these systems deal with the failure of one or more viewers during transmission of the stream. An important aspect of each of these systems that is typically overlooked is how individual stream transmitters and viewers of these streams are managed in terms of registration, configuration and maintenance. In this paper, a set of management related abstractions common to many p2p live streaming systems are identified. This paper describes the MeshTV architecture, capturing these abstractions, to simplify the management of p2p live streaming applications. The architecture has been evaluated through a number of experiments and has been assessed against existing related work.

1   Introduction

A number of Peer-to-Peer (p2p) live streaming systems [1], [2], [3], [4], [5], [6] and [7] have been proposed in recent years. Typically the description of these systems focuses on how the particular live stream is transmitted, for example, whether it uses an underlying tree based or mesh based topology and/or the assumptions made about the underlying network infrastructure (such as updates to intermediate network level routers, etc).

In contrast, this paper focuses on an architecture and the corresponding abstractions needed to ease the deployment and ongoing management of an application-level p2p live streaming system. Our architecture does not make any assumptions about the underlying network layer routing infrastructure. In general, the abstractions common to p2p live streaming systems can be broken into a number of categories:

- Coordination
- Management
- Communication.

The coordination category comprises a number of use cases such as the registration of participating peers (both a transmitter and one or more viewers)

R. Meier and S. Terzis (Eds.): DAIS 2008, LNCS 5053, pp. 140–153, 2008.
© IFIP International Federation for Information Processing 2008

which is typically not described in existing p2p live streaming systems. In addition, how the ongoing configuration of these participating peers is achieved is typically not described. An underlying assumption of most live streaming p2p overlay based systems is that the total system upload (i.e., the sum of the upload capacities at all peers) can be utilised correctly to enable all peers to download the stream at the stream rate at which the transmitter transmits. Thus, it is important for a running system to be able to verify this latter assumption.

The management category includes a number of different aspects of a p2p live streaming application such as the gathering of relevant statistics related to the live stream and the enforcement of a revenue model for a particular stream. These aspects are typically overlooked in favour of ensuring that the p2p live streaming system maximises a global system parameter such as the total upload utilisation. However, the particular system is typically unaware of what the total system upload capacity actually is.

The final abstraction covers the lower level management related issues of communicating the live stream from a transmitter to a number of interested viewers. Typically, how bootstrapping is achieved in most systems is not covered in detail as it is assumed to be a solved problem. However, the solution to this problem depends on the number of current peers in the system and the percentage of the peers that are joining and/or departing the system.

These abstractions and how they relate to the MeshTV architecture will be further elaborated in section 2. Section 2 is followed by a description in section 3 of a realisation of the lowest layer of the architecture and an evaluation of this realisation in section 4. These sections are followed by an assessment of related work and how this work fits into the MeshTV architecture in section 5. Finally, section 6 concludes the paper and discusses future work.

2   MeshTV Architecture

As illustrated in Figure 1, the MeshTV Architecture is broken into a number of layers corresponding to the categories identified in section 1. The upper most layer of the architecture is called the Stream Coordination layer and enables potential viewers of a particular stream to discover the stream (typically by browsing a list of streams) that a transmitter is transmitting or intends to transmit and for the particular peers that are providing the stream to be easily configured throughout the lifetime of the stream.

2.1   Coordination

Before a transmitter can begin transmitting a live stream, it is required to register its details (such as type of content, point of contact for the stream (i.e., underlying mesh/tree component endpoint), start time of transmission, etc) so that potential viewers of the stream can become aware of this stream. The registration of a particular stream occurs at a logically centralised stream manager that can record relevant details about the stream for later querying by interested

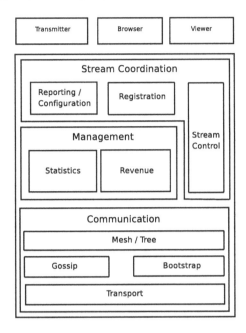

Fig. 1. MeshTV Architecture

potential viewing peers. Note that how to secure the registration of a transmitter (and a potential viewer) will not be addressed in this paper though a number of possible approaches exist such as [8] and [9].

As will be seen in the following sections, this logically centralised stream manager plays an important role in a number of the abstractions identified in this paper.

When the transmitter registers its information with the stream manager, the stream manager records information related to the transmission with the statistics management component and then generates a billing profile for the future transmission of the content by using the lower layer revenue management component. This profile may allow advertisements to be tailored to the content of a particular transmission or the transmitter may require a potential viewer to pay to watch its particular transmission.

In general, the configuration of the different components that constitute a live streaming application should be configured in one of two ways, depending on the number of peers in the topology. Firstly, when the number of nodes is below a known threshold configuration may be carried out directly by a particular peer such as the transmitter contacting each of the viewing peers directly to adapt their operation. For example, if the transmitter wishes to switch to a newer codec (to reduce bandwidth consumption) while transmitting using an older codec, the transmitter may contact each individual viewing peer aware of this change (assuming that the number of viewing peers is relatively small). Secondly, if the number of viewing peers is above the threshold, configuration could be carried out using a gossip protocol ([10], [11], [12]) to spread the burden of configuration across all the peers in the system.

This dual mode of operation for the configuration of different aspects of a peers behaviour is important as existing live streaming systems do not highlight how such configuration is achieved and focus on the operation of these when a certain number of participating peers are in the system. The approach to configure/tune a live streaming system with a total of 100 peers can be very different from a system with 1,000 peers which in turn can be different from a system with 10,000 peers.

An important part of the configuration/reporting component of the MeshTV architecture is how bandwidth related information/statistics (such as total upload bandwidth utilisation) is reported. For example, the total upload bandwidth utilisation is an important global system property that existing mesh based systems and multi-tree systems attempt to maximise. A human manager or a realisation of the MeshTV architecture may use this bandwidth related information to change relevant protocol parameters to better adapt to the current dynamic environment within which the particular stream is being transmitted.

In a similar way to how system wide configuration is achieved, the collection of bandwidth related statistics would also have a dual mode of operation with direct point to point communication being used for the live streaming systems with a small number of peers and aggregation [13], [14], [15] (with an underlying gossip protocol) being using for larger systems. This second (and more complex) approach using a number of aggregation rounds may be initiated by any peer in the system gossipping an initial aggregation message to its set of neighbours that then gossip this message onto their neighbours. As the aggregation message containing the aggregated statistics propagates throughout the system, each peer on receiving the aggregation message updates these statistics with local information related to its bandwidth usage. These local bandwidth related statistics are maintained by the statistics component of the management layer.

2.2 Management

There are two main parts in the management layer of the MeshTV architecture. As briefly discussed in the previous sub-section, the statistics management component is responsible for aggregating important statistics related to the transmission of the stream such as, for example, the total number of peers, the total amount of bandwidth downloaded at all peers and the average neighbour degree of each peer throughout the system. This statistical information could be used locally by the peer or be used to inform other peers (such as joining peers) about the state of the system.

An additional capability of the statistics component is to build a model of how the lower communication layer uses the peers upload bandwidth as the stream is transmitted. This upload bandwidth model would depend on the characteristics of a particular peer's set of neighbours and may require the peer to learn how much upload bandwidth it can currently offer to the overall live streaming system.

The second part of the management layer is the revenue component whose role is to ensure that a particular revenue model for the stream is enforced. There are a large number of possible revenue models for a stream that are possible such as one based on advertisements, a single advance up front payment or a split revenue model with the first number of minutes free followed by micro-payments for each subsequent minute of viewing.

Note that some of these revenue models require registration of the viewing peer while others may not. A transmitter may wish to change the revenue model of its stream based on the current demand with one revenue model being used at the beginning of a stream's transmission before being switched to another revenue model as demand increases.

The commencement of a stream is recorded with a local and/or remote statistics component before retrieving optional adverts from a local and/or remote revenue component. In the remote case, this information is recorded with the stream manager. The stream manager uses this information to provide a list of possible streams that can be viewed. Before returning this list of streams, the stream manager retrieves relevant statistics of the currently available streams (possibly using a profile of the viewing peer). Relevant statistics for a stream may include the current bandwidth consumed most recently by the stream, the current stream rate and number of viewers that are currently watching the stream.

In addition to the above statistics, the stream manager also retrieves details related to the cost of viewing each stream in the list of streams. This should allow different types of pricing to be achieved based on the type of viewer that is requesting the stream.

2.3   Communication

In this section, a number of lower level abstractions are presented that are related to the transmission and reception of the live stream.

After registering its details with the stream manager, the transmitter begins transmitting its content by sending it to the communication layer in the MeshTV architecture as illustrated in Figure 1. The mesh/tree component is considered as a decentralised component (which we consider as a single logical component for the purposes of this document) that manages the distribution of the stream content from the transmitter to the other viewing peers that are participating in the mesh/tree. Note that this distribution can be done over either a tree-based or mesh-based topology such as those covered in section 5.

Sending the content to the underlying topology requires that the mesh/tree component has a list of other peers to which it can transmit. When a transmitter begins to transmit the stream, the mesh/tree component of the transmitter contacts the bootstrap component of the communication layer to initialise a new mesh or tree for the transmission that is about to start. This in turn results in a mesh or tree peer being created that represents the transmitter on the underlying topology. The mesh/tree component (on the transmitter) then initialises its list of neighbouring nodes to be empty.

It is possible for the above steps to happen when a peer indicates its intention to transmit a stream during registration. This allows the underlying topology to be setup with an initial set of viewing peers before the stream begins transmission and possibly reduces the latency at the beginning of the transmission. This bootstrap component is considered as a logically centralised component that could be hosted or maintained by the transmitter or could be distributed across a number of peers.

When a MeshTV viewer chooses a particular stream from the stream manager, the stream manager records the addition of a new viewer with the statistics manager and then verifies with the revenue component that the viewer has the requisite credentials to view the stream. Thus depending on the type of stream that is of interest, the viewer may or may not need one or more components (such as the registration or revenue components). In a similar way to the transmitter initiating the mesh/tree component for the transmission of its content, the mesh/tree component (on behalf of a viewer) must also join the mesh/tree by utilising the services of the local bootstrap component. Firstly, the mesh/tree component sends a request to join the topology (previously created by the transmitter) to the bootstrap component for that topology which in turn results in the creation of a new peer on the topology that represents the joining viewer. As a result of this request, the mesh/tree component receives a number of potential neighbours that it then uses to initialise its neighbourhood.

A common abstraction that a number of live streaming systems use is that of a neighbourhood of peers that an individual peer uses to transmit the stream to and/or to receive the stream from. In the MeshTV architecture, the neighbourhood component provides functionality to ease the burden on a particular peer of maintaining a set of neighbouring peers such as providing one or more techniques for the detection of a failed neighbouring peer. In addition, the neighbourhood component can easily maintain a profile of the communication (bandwidth) capacity of each of its neighbouring peers which can then be used to inform the decision making of the mesh/tree component.

Finally, the neighbourhood component can be used in conjunction with the gossip component to provide the capability to communicate with all the peers in a large-scale system. This communication could be achieved over a specialised random mesh network or using the existing topology that is already in use by the live stream.

3   MeshTV Peer-to-Peer Protocol

In this section we show how the communication component of the MeshTV architecture can be realised using an existing p2p protocol. Complete details of this p2p protocol are available in [16]. In the following subsections we present each communication subcomponent in our system.

3.1   Mesh

The mesh overlay is formed by joining peers connecting to randomly selected neighbours and then periodically refining them using an exploration algorithm.

Each peer maintains two sets of neighbours - receivers, which are the neighbours to which it uploads data and senders, which are the neighbours from which data is downloaded. The transmitter splits the data stream into small data chunks, which are exchanged between neighbouring peers in an epidemic fashion. Peers maintain local knowledge about data chunks possessed by their senders and inform receivers whenever they receive (or generate, in case of the transmitter) a new data chunk. Whenever a sender of a peer notifies it about a newly received chunk, the peer requests this new chunk if it has not requested this chunk from another peer already.

The exploration algorithm is used to adapt the overlay to optimise the video streaming throughput by maximising the utilisation of available upload bandwidth of peers, which we consider the most scarce resource in the system. The algorithm is executed by each peer independently and its goal is to adapt the peer's set of senders to improve the download rate. The algorithm is executed by a peer periodically in a series of rounds and ensures that:

- A peer has a constant (configurable) number of senders.
- A peer replaces the sender from which it receives the worst download rate with a new sender provided by the bootstrap component that selects it randomly from all peers in the overlay.

The exploration algorithm adapts the mesh overlay so that *(i)* the upload bandwidth of all peers is efficiently utilised, *(ii)* download rates of nodes are improved and *(iii)* network latency between interacting peers is reduced. Upload bandwidth is utilised by matching a peer's number of receivers with its available upload bandwidth. The reason for this is that a peer continues to gain new receivers when it is underloaded and loses some receivers (i.e., receivers replace it with less loaded senders) when it is overloaded.

A peer joining the network initially acquires a random set of senders from its bootstrap component. The exploration algorithm will then continuously attempt to improve the peer's download rate by replacing the slowest senders with senders that can provide higher transfer rates, thereby effectively optimising its set of senders. This approach also decreases the network latency between neighbouring peers as a consequence of using TCP to transmit data chunks, and TCP's built-in congestion control. The reason for this is that when multiple connections share an overloaded link, TCP allocates more bandwidth to connections with lower network round-trip times (RTT) [17]. When a bottleneck occurs at the sender's uplink, more upload bandwidth is allocated to receivers with low latency. Similarly, when a bottleneck occurs at the receiver's downlink, more download bandwidth is allocated to senders with low latency. This causes receivers to replace distant senders (for which TCP allocates less bandwidth) with senders that are potentially closer.

3.2   Bootstrap

The MeshTV bootstrap component is used by the mesh component to provide a random sample of peers (potential neighbours) when a peer joins the system and whenever the exploration algorithm is executed. Bootstrap uses the gossip component, described below, to periodically obtain a new sample of peers.

3.3 Gossip

The gossip component in MeshTV is based on a peer sampling service [18] in which peers randomly exchange membership information between themselves. This results in each peer periodically obtaining a random subset of all peers in the system, which are then provided to the bootstrap component and are used to create and refine the mesh overlay.

3.4 Transport

The MeshTV p2p protocol uses TCP for transferring data chunks between peers. The use of TCP as a transport protocol enables the exploration algorithm to improve proximity between neighbouring peers as described in section 3.1.

4 MeshTV Evaluation

In this section, we present an initial evaluation of the communication layer of the MeshTV architecture encompassing the previously highlighted p2p protocol [16]. This evaluation was carried out in ns-2 [19]. In particular, we show that the p2p protocol optimises upload bandwidth utilisation, improves throughput and network proximity between neighbouring peers by using the combination of the mesh, bootstrap, gossip and transport components.

Ns-2 [19] provides a realistic model of the physical network and the TCP/IP stack (the MeshTV p2p protocol uses TCP New Reno) at the cost of reduced scalability limiting the number of nodes that have been simulated to 500. Our previous experience in evaluating larger overlays in less accurate flow-level simulators lead us to believe that the findings presented here are also valid for larger overlays [7]. The physical network topology created for simulations is a full mesh with bandwidth being limited on the access links (uplinks and downlinks). The node bandwidth distribution has been derived from Gnutella p2p system measurements [20] and nodes have been categorised into 4 groups: A, B, C and D (see Table 1). Network latencies between nodes are selected uniformly at random between 2ms and 300ms. MeshTV parameters used in the experiments are presented in Table 2. The mesh overlay in the experiments is initially random, formed by nodes selecting random senders.

4.1 Upload Utilisation

Figure 2 compares the average upload utilisation of the overlay with and without the adaptation (note the different scales on the y-axes). It shows that when the exploration algorithm is used, a node's upload reaches its maximum upload capacity as shown in Table 1. This means that nodes in all categories fully utilise their upload bandwidth. In contrast, when the exploration is not used,

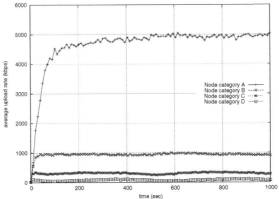

(a) Average upload rates with the exploration algorithm

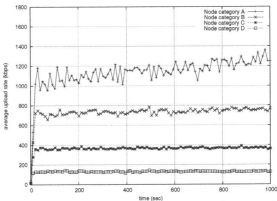

(b) Average upload rates without the exploration algorithm

Fig. 2. Optimising average upload rates

Table 1. Node bandwidth distribution

Category	Downlink	Uplink	Ratio
A	10 Mbps	5 Mbps	15%
B	3 Mbps	1 Mbps	25%
C	1.5 Mbps	384 Kbps	40%
D	784 Kbps	128 Kbps	20%

the upload bandwidth of nodes in the highest categories A and B is greatly underutilised. It can be observed from these figures and the given node bandwidth distribution that the total aggregated upload for adapted and not adapted overlays is about 550 Mbps and 260 Mbps respectively. This means that the upload bandwidth utilisation is improved by over 100% when the overlay is adapted by the exploration algorithm.

Table 2. Protocol parameters

Parameter	Value
stream rate	1500 Kbps
number of senders	5
exploration round length	5 sec
chunk size	4 KB
pipelined requests	8
sliding window size	30 sec

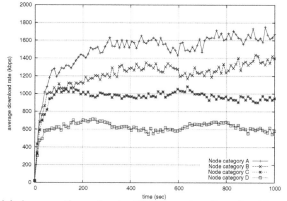

(a) Average throughput with the exploration algorithm

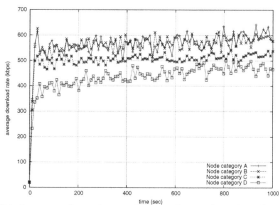

(b) Average throughput without the exploration algorithm

Fig. 3. Improving the average throughput

4.2   Throughput

The improved utilisation of the upload bandwidth results in nodes increasing their data throughput. Figure 3 compares the data rates with and without the exploration algorithm (note again the different scales on the y-axes). It shows that the data rates received in the adapted overlay are all much higher than in the case of a random mesh overlay. However, not only the upload bandwidth of senders, but also a node's own download capacity limits the received data rate. So, for instance, the download rate of nodes in category D is limited by their download bandwidth of 784 Kbps. Other node categories have higher download capacity and thus achieve higher download rates. MeshTV accommodates limited download bandwidth of some nodes and different data rates received by different node categories through the use of the Multiple Description Coding (MDC) technique and specifically MDC-FEC [21]. The MDC technique enables the original video stream to be split into a number of descriptions. A node can download any subset of all descriptions to recreate the video stream.

4.3   Node Proximity

Figure 4 shows how the exploration algorithm reduces the network latency between interacting nodes. Initially, the random mesh overlay has an average latency between neighbouring nodes roughly equal to 151ms as the latencies are assigned randomly between 2ms and 300ms. Since senders allocate more upload bandwidth to closer receivers, the overlay adapts, resulting in a reduction of the average latency to about 75ms, which is a 50% improvement. The exploration algorithm does not further reduce the distances between neighbouring nodes as this might degrade the data throughput. Connecting exclusively to the nearest senders implies two undesired effects. Nodes that share low-latency links with many other nodes might be overloaded and the overlay might be divided into disconnected clusters of nearby nodes. The exploration algorithm prevents these unwanted effects as it improves proximity only when this does not degrade the data throughput. This is because a high-latency underloaded node will provide higher data throughput than a low-latency overloaded node and thus will be preferred as a sender.

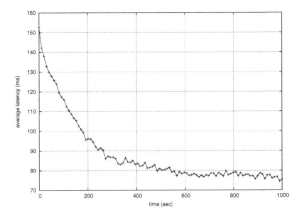

Fig. 4. Improving proximity of neighbours

5   Related Work

As would be expected from a number of research project solutions in the domain of p2p live streaming (such as Bullet [2], Splitstream [1], Chainsaw [3], Coolstreaming [6] and MeshCast [7]) these solutions has focussed on the challenging distributed system problems of achieving low latency and robustness in such a dynamic environment and not been on the management of streams or the generation of revenue.

Most of these systems are mesh based with the exception of Splitstream which uses a tree and Bullet which uses a hybrid approach of a tree for dissemination of the stream and a mesh for retransmission of lost or dropped packets.

A number of the systems use a form of gossip in the construction of their underlying topologies. For example, Bullet executes the RanSub algorithm [22] to deliver a uniform random subset of peers to each peer in the system. Coolstreaming also uses a gossip protocol to achieve membership management. MeshCast on the other hand uses a variant of the Newscast algorithm [12] to distribute a sampling of the peers in the system. The use of bootstrapping is not stressed in any of the descriptions of these systems though it is typically needed to enable the correct functioning of each system in the presence of new peers joining and existing peers departing.

Finally, a number of these systems attempt to model the communication capability of a neighbouring peer so that the overall system can better utilise the bandwidth (typically upload bandwidth) at all nodes. Bullet builds on top of TCP Friendly Rate Control [23] (with each peer periodically evaluating its senders and receivers and dropping or replacing them if they do not provide sufficient bandwidth to that peer. In coolstreaming, a peer estimates the performance of its neighbours to guide the scheduling of requests for parts of the stream. MeshCast also attempts to estimate its neighbouring peers upload capacity using its sender/receiver balancing algorithm.

6   Conclusions/Future Work

This paper described the MeshTV architecture which incorporates a set of abstractions that are common to a number of existing live streaming systems. This layered architecture divides these abstractions into three categories which have been labelled coordination, management and communication. A realisation of this architecture incorporating an existing p2p protocol was implemented in ns2.

Work is currently ongoing to provide an implementation of the MeshTV architecture (outside of the ns2 simulator) that incorporates one or more existing live streaming systems. On completion, this will enable a further evaluation of our architecture including the performance advantages and impact of using different higher layer components such as the statistics managment component. It will also be possible to investigate the performance impact on a set of peers that are executing two or more live streaming systems (e.g., as part of a wireless access point based home entertainment system hub).

Acknowledgements

This work was partly funded by the "Information Society Technology" Programme of the Commission of the European Union under research contract IST-507953 (DBE) and by Enterprise Ireland under the Commercialisation Proof of Concept Programme (MeshTV).

References

1. Castro, M., Drushel, P., Kermarrec, A., Nandi, A., Rowstron, A., Singh, A.: Splitstream: High-Bandwidth Multicast in Cooperative Environments. In: SOSP (2003)
2. Kostic, D., Rodriguez, A., Albrecht, J., Vahdat, A.: Bullet: high bandwidth data dissemination using an overlay mesh. In: Symposium on Operating System Principles (2003)
3. Pai, V.S., Kumar, K., Tamilmani, K., Sambamurthy, V.: Chainsaw: Eliminating trees from overlay multicast. In: Castro, M., van Renesse, R. (eds.) IPTPS 2005. LNCS, vol. 3640, pp. 127–140. Springer, Heidelberg (2005)
4. Jannotti, J., Gifford, D.K., Johnson, K.L., Kaashoek, M.F., O'Toole, J.: Overcast: Reliable multicasting with an overlay network. In: OSDI (2000)
5. Castro, M., Drushel, P., Kermarrec, A., Rowstron, A.: SCRIBE: A large-scale decentralised application level multicast infrastructure. IEEE JSAC, 1–9 (2002)
6. Zhang, X., Liu, J., Li, B., Yum, T.S.P.: Coolstreaming/donet: A data-driven overlay network for peer-to-peer live media streaming (2005)
7. Biskupski, B., Cunningham, R., Dowling, J., Meier, R.: High-bandwidth mesh-based overlay multicast in heterogeneous environments. In: AAA-IDEA 2006: Proceedings of the 2nd international workshop on Advanced architectures and algorithms for internet delivery and applications, p. 4. ACM, New York (2006)
8. Hiclanan, K., Elgamal, T.: The SSL protocol. Internet draft, Netscape Communications Corp. Technical report (1995)
9. Kohl, J.T., Neuman, B.C.: The Kerberos network authentication service (V5). Technical Report 1510 (1993)
10. Jelasity, M., Babaoglu, O.: T-man: Gossip-based overlay topology management. In: 3rd International Workshop on Engineering Self-Organising Applications (2005)
11. Rao, A., Lakshminarayanan, K., Surana, S., Karp, R., Stoica, I.: load balancing in structured p2p systems. In: 2nd International Workshop on Peer-to-Peer Systems (2003)
12. Jelasity, M., van Steen, M.: Large-scale newscast computing on the Internet. Technical Report IR-503, Department of Computer Science Vrije Universiteit, Amsterdam, The Netherlands (2002)
13. Jelasity, M., Montresor, A.: Epidemic-style proactive aggregation in large overlay networks. In: Proceedings of the 24th International Conference on Distributed Computing Systems, pp. 102–109 (2004)
14. Jelasity, M., Montresor, A., Babaoglu, O.: Robust aggregation protocols for large-scale overlay networks. In: International Conference on Dependable Systems and Networks, pp. 19–28 (2004)
15. Kempe, D., Dobra, A., Gehrke, J.: Gossip-based computation of aggregate information. In: 44th IEEE Symposium on Foundations of Computer Science, pp. 482–491 (2003)

16. Biskupski, B., Cunningham, R., Meier, R.: Improving throughput and node proximity of p2p live video streaming through overlay adaptation. In: Proceedings of the 9th IEEE International Symposium on Multimedia (ISM 2007), pp. 245–252. IEEE Computer Society, Los Alamitos (2007)
17. Lakshman, T.V., Madhow, U.: The performance of TCP/IP for networks with high bandwidth-delay products and random loss. IEEE/ACM Trans. Netw. 5(3), 336–350 (1997)
18. Jelasity, M., Guerraoui, R., Kermarrec, A.M., van Steen, M.: The peer sampling service: experimental evaluation of unstructured gossip-based implementations. In: Jacobsen, H.-A. (ed.) Middleware 2004. LNCS, vol. 3231, pp. 79–98. Springer, New York (2004)
19. McCanne, S., Floyd, S.: ns—Network Simulator, http://www.isi.edu/nsnam/ns
20. Saroiu, S., Gummadi, P.K., Gribble, S.D.: A measurement study of peer-to-peer file sharing systems. In: Proceedings of Multimedia Computing and Networking (2002)
21. Goyal, V.K.: Multiple description coding: Compression meets the network. IEEE Signal Processing Magazine 18(5), 74–93 (2001)
22. Kostic, D., Rodriguez, A., Albrecht, J., Bhirud, A., Vahdat, A.: Using random subsets to build scalable network services. In: Proceedings of 4th USENIX Symposium on Internet Technologies and Systems (USITS) (2003)
23. Floyd, S., Handley, M., Padhye, J., Widmer, J.: Equation-based congestion control for unicast applications. In: SIGCOMM 2000, Stockholm, Sweden, August 2000, pp. 43–56 (2000)

Dynamic Adaptability for Smart Environments

Daniel Retkowitz and Mark Stegelmann

Department of Computer Science 3 (Software Engineering)
RWTH Aachen University
Ahornstr. 55, 52074 Aachen, Germany
{retkowitz,stegelmann}@i3.informatik.rwth-aachen.de

Abstract. Software reuse and hardware integration are key factors to offer flexible, low-cost smart environments. Until now, we have been using a static process called the SCD-process to allow a tool-supported realization of such smart environments. The SCD-process is comprised of three different phases: specification, configuration, and deployment. As an initially specified environment is expected to change during runtime and the user may wish to influence certain aspects of the configuration, the static process had to be adapted. This paper describes a new process that supports continuous specification activities and allows for an automated adaptation of the smart home's configuration based on a model-driven approach. We enriched the specification of services with binding policies and constraints to allow for a flexible reconfiguration and a service-specific adaptation. The new configuration mechanism facilitates dynamic reconfiguration based on context information and the extended service specification. In addition, we present a visual tool, which is used to assist the developer and the end-user.

1   Introduction

Ambient intelligence, ubiquitous and pervasive computing, are some of the more recent topics in computer science. Approaches in these fields aim at creating so called *smart environments* by separating computing from today's desktop PCs to make applications and their functionalities available anywhere, independent of PC hardware [1]. This way, users can access services wherever they are. Any available device should be usable to realize service functionality. Devices installed in the user's current environment, together with mobile or wearable devices may be used by the software.

Related to home environments, ambient intelligence is realized by so called *eHomes* or *smart homes*. We refer to *eHome systems* as a combination of devices and software running in such an eHome. This software is running on a residential gateway that controls all home appliances. Top-level services are applications that offer certain functionalities to the user. Top-level services are based on integrating services that reduce the level of abstraction down to device driver services, which control actual hardware devices. In today's homes, a lot of appliances are available, but in general, these appliances are not interconnected.

R. Meier and S. Terzis (Eds.): DAIS 2008, LNCS 5053, pp. 154–167, 2008.

To facilitate comprehensive services based on multiple appliances, that offer complex functionalities, it is necessary to develop flexible and adaptive software. To achieve this goal at low overall costs, the eHome software has to be built from standard components, that are automatically composed according to the user's needs and the individual home environment.

The goal of our research is to enable such low-cost eHome systems by composing eHome services from reusable software components. In our prototypes these software components are developed according to the OSGi component model [2]. We currently employ the Equinox framework of the Eclipse platform [3] as an OSGi runtime environment for our service bundles, as the components in OSGi are called. The customization of the eHome software is achieved later on by composition of the services in a process of specification, configuration, and deployment. This process is called the *SCD-process* [4].

In [4], a tool called *eHomeConfigurator* is presented, which enables the SCD-process by employing a model-driven approach based on Fujaba. Fujaba is a tool for specifying a software's data model and application logic using different UML diagrams [5]. Furthermore, it allows to generate Java source code from such a specification. In this paper, we present a redesigned SCD-process, which is capable of handling the dynamics in smart environments and incorporates several major improvements. We also present a newly developed tool based on the Ecliplse platform mentioned above.

The rest of the paper is structured as follows. In Section 2 we describe a scenario to illustrate the need for a support of dynamic changes in smart environments. Next, in Section 3, we explain the different concepts which form the basis of the new continuous SCD-process. After that, in Section 4, we discuss the realization details and we show how we implemented the new concepts. Then we present the current state of our new tool in Section 5. In the following Section 6, a short overview of related work is given. Finally, in Section 7, we give a conclusion and point out some open problems and future work.

2   Scenario

Before discussing the details of our system architecture, we will take a closer look at an example scenario. We will see that changes appear frequently in smart environments, which imposes certain requirements on the SCD-process.

John is coming home from work. At home, he sits down in his living room. Since he has a music service selected in his personal profile, his favorite music starts playing when he enters the room. After some time he walks into the kitchen to prepare some food. The music in the living room stops playing when John leaves the room. Once he enters the kitchen, his new location is detected by the eHome and the music service starts playing John's music again in his new location using the speakers integrated in the kitchen wall. The music service resumes playing from the last position where John was listening in the living room. A few minutes later John's wife Mary comes home, too. When she walks through the living room, her personal video conferencing service notifies her about an incoming call from Anne. She takes the call and a live picture of Anne appears on the TV. She can hear Anne's voice from the speakers in the living room. Anne talks about their last joint vacation and wants to show Mary some of the pictures she took. Mary's video conferencing service is capable of presenting different media data. Using her PDA, Mary selects the TV to display Anne's picture presentation. The pictures appear on the TV and the live picture of Anne is reduced and displayed in the lower corner of the screen. Mary wants John, who is still in the kitchen, to see the pictures too. So she adds the display in the kitchen to be used for media data output of her video conferencing service. Now the picture presentation is also displayed in the kitchen. After Mary has seen several pictures she decides to create prints of some of them. So she picks up her PDA again and connects the printer in the living room to her video conferencing service. The printer is also capable of processing visual media data and starts printing the selected pictures.

This example scenario shows some standard situations we assume in future smart environments. To design a software system that is sufficiently flexible and adaptable to support such scenarios, we had to come up with a novel development process. In the next section we will describe our approach based on a modified SCD-process in more detail.

3   System Architecture

The SCD-process as described in [4] aims at reducing development costs per eHome by increasing the amount of possible service reuse. Thus services are developed once and enriched with a specification. This allows for a later automatic integration of the services into different eHome configurations. The service specification describes which functionality each service provides to other services and which functionality is required to do so.

3.1   Service Layers

We distinguish between three types of services: driver, integrating, and top-level services. Driver services represent low-level driver software needed to access the different hardware devices. Top-level services are applications that offer functionality to the user. So called integrating services may be used to add multiple layers of abstraction to the basic, driver-based hardware access. In many cases the functionality that is required by a top-level service does not directly match a functionality provided by a driver service, because both services are on very different layers of abstraction. In such cases adequate integrating services have to be found to adapt both layers to each other.

In Figure 1 the three types of services are shown by the example of the video conferencing scenario from Section 2. In Figure 1(a) the Video Conferencing top-level service is depicted, which requires several functionalities as Audio Input, Audio Output, etc. to operate properly. For each required functionality the cardinality shows how many instances of this functionality are required at least

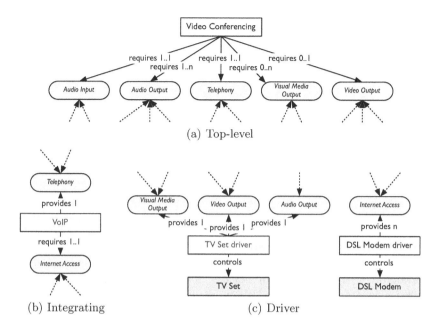

(a) Top-level

(b) Integrating   (c) Driver

Fig. 1. Service Layers

and at most. Figure 1(b) shows an integrating service. In this example the depicted VoIP service is used for voice over IP telephony. Accordingly it provides Telephony functionality and furthermore requires Internet Access, since network access is required. Finally, in Figure 1(c) two driver services are depicted. A DSL Modem Driver which provides Internet Access and a TV Set Driver which offers Visual Media Output, Video Output, and Audio Output.

Any service used in the eHome system is specified as indicated above. This way, services can be composed by the system later on in the configuration phase according to their specified functionalities. In the described example the Video Conferencing service may use the VoIP service to fulfill its Telephony requirement. The VoIP service in turn may use the DSL Modem Driver to fulfill its Internet Access requirement.

3.2 Process Requirements

An automatic support for the SCD-process is one of the main requirements for the application of eHome services. The user will not accept a system that requires permanent interaction. Most of the tasks have to be performed automatically. Ambient intelligence implies that the environment acts and reacts automatically according to context changes. Nevertheless, the user permanently wants to be in control of the situation, i. e. the system must not act in a way the user does not expect. In case the system makes a decision the user does not agree with, it should be possible to manually apply changes so that the user has means to influence the system's behavior. Especially when considering home environments, these are key issues for the acceptance of eHome systems.

3.3   Continuous SCD-Process

As we have seen in Section 2, the nature of dynamics at runtime of an eHome system can be quite diverse. To cope with the described dynamics, we redesigned the SCD-process described in [4] to meet the new requirements discussed above. Our approach focuses on considering runtime changes concerning user movement through different locations and device mobility. Whenever changes occur in the eHome environment, the different phases of the SCD-process have to be re-executed to adapt the software to the new situation. Any change of the user's location or desires or any change of available devices implies corresponding changes in the specification and hence also the configuration and the deployment. We refer to the new adapted process as *continuous SCD-process*.

To facilitate an automated adaption of the eHome system to context changes, the availability of certain sensor devices that allow to detect these changes is required. The scenario presented above requires e. g. some means of automated person and device detection. The demonstration environments described in [4] and [6], which we use as testbeds, provide these capabilities e. g. by means of video cameras or remote controls for the different users to log in. We assume that appropriate technologies will be available for future eHomes at low prices.

In Figure 2, the new overall eHome process is illustrated. On the left-hand side of the figure the service-specific part is depicted. This part consists of the service development phase and the phase of service specification. These phases are performed by a software developer. The resulting service components can be used in any eHome based on our framework.

The right-hand side of Figure 2 depicts the eHome-specific part of the overall process, i. e. the SCD-process which represents the runtime phase of the system. For each eHome the SCD-process demands a specification of floor plans,

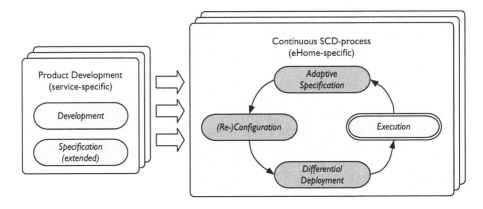

Fig. 2. Overall process incorporating the new continuous SCD-process

the desired top-level services, and the available devices. This is the specification phase of the SCD-process. The division into two independent specification phases, the product-specific service specification and the eHome-specific specification, allows to minimize the expert knowledge required by the end-user. After the eHome-specific specification phase the configuration phase follows next. In this phase any changes of the specification are processed and a recomposition of services according to their provided and required functionalities is performed. Depending on the service specification the composition is performed automatically or manually. In case a service requires manual binding, so far the user has to create the appropriate bindings in the graphical service representation of the visual specification tool described in Section 5 in order to start the service. In the future, this way of interaction could be extended e. g. by offering a graphical user interface for PDAs such that users can carry PDAs as remote controls for their current environments. Furthermore composition constraints are checked to keep the configuration valid. In Section 4, further details on the configuration algorithm are presented. Finally, when the eHome software has been configured, the configuration has to be deployed. In the deployment phase service instances are created or destroyed according to the configuration and the bindings between these instances are registered.

4   Realization

As described in [7] we pursue a model-driven approach to realize eHome systems. Our data model, which is partially shown in Figure 3, is specified as UML class diagram. The runtime behavior of our framework is described using so called UML story diagrams to express the configuration logic. All defined classes and methods are translated to compilable Java source code via Fujaba. Thus no actual configuration code has to be written by hand.

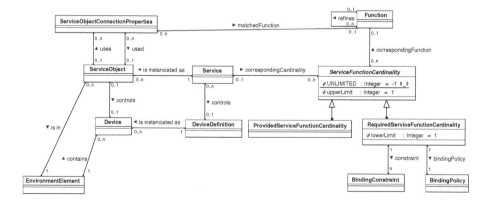

Fig. 3. Part of the data model UML class diagram

4.1   Data Model

In the data model, `Services` are used to represent the eHome-independent service specifications. These services are linked through `ServiceFunctionCar-dinality` objects to `Functions`. The `RequiredServiceFunctionCardinality` objects express that the service requires some functionality. `ProvidedService-FunctionCardinality` objects respectively mean that the service provides some functionality. Furthermore, lower and upper cardinality bounds are stored, whereas lower bounds are only used for required functionalities. A driver service additionally `controls` a specific `DeviceDefinition`.

During the eHome-specific configuration phase the specified required and provided functionalities are used to match services. This way the needed service runtime instances called `ServiceObjects` can be determined. To connect two of these `ServiceObjects`, `ServiceObjectConnectionProperties` are used. Top-level `ServiceObjects`, selected by the user, are contained in `Environ-mentElements` thereby describing the `ServiceObject`'s location. *Context-aware* [8] or so-called *personal services*, adapt to the user's context, e. g. his surroundings. Such `ServiceObjects` thus are always associated to their user's current location.

4.2   Dynamic Service Composition

The continuous nature of the new process requires some way to determine which match a connection between two `ServiceObjects` is based on. This information is stored in the model by the `matchedFunction` relation from `ServiceObject-ConnectionProperties` to `Function`. Thus it is feasible to extend and respectively reduce prior compositions of `ServiceObjects` according to the service's specification.

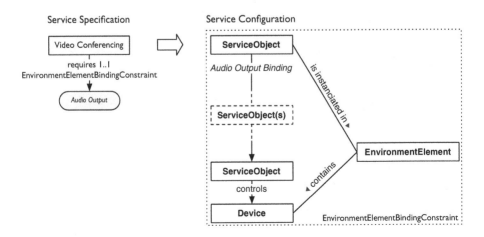

Fig. 4. Abstract visualization of a binding constraint

Binding Policies. To specify for each required functionality if it should be bound automatically or manually by the user, so-called binding policies were introduced.

A *binding policy* constitutes a strategy concerning the establishment of bindings for a specific Function required by a Service. We offer three types of policies covering different configuration strategies. The *automatic binding policy* manages all bindings to services providing the required function automatically. The *manual binding policy*, in contrast, only allows manual binding modifications. To automatically establish bindings until the lower cardinality limit is reached and allow manual interaction beyond that point, an *automatic mandatories policy* can be selected.

Binding Constraints. To implement a flexible concept of fine-grained, context-aware services, binding constraints were introduced. We call a *binding constraint* a declarative description of a graph pattern that has to be matched in the configuration in order to establish the binding. If the configuration graph conforms to the pattern the binding constraint *is satisfied*.

Realizing a constraint for personal services is straightforward. The data model contains all information necessary for such a pattern. An abstract visualization of the constraint is shown in Figure 4. The binding constraint is satisfied if all Devices that are used via the Audio Output binding are from the user's current location. As constraints are specified for each required Function separately the developer may choose to omit this restriction for some functionality that does not have to be chosen from the user's current location. Telephony support e. g. typically does not have to be located in the same room as the user, even for personal services. This kind of supporting services are usually not bound to a specific location.

Binding constraints are a fundamental concept within our approach. They can be used to impose various effects on the dynamic composition mechanism. We will extend this concept in the future to support further context-aware features.

4.3   Adaptive Configuration

To incorporate environment specification changes as discussed in Section 3 the possibility to choose from different binding policies was introduced. As shown in Figure 3, each BindingPolicy object is related to a certain RequiredService-FunctionCardinality. These objects in turn are bound to a Function. Thus this information can be easily derived by the binding policies' implementations.

In Figure 5 an excerpt of the method addBinding(ServiceObject) is shown. This method is responsible for the automatic creation of bindings between ServiceObjects and is used by the automatic binding policy and by the automatic mandatories policy. The particular method fragment depicted creates bindings to existing service compositions that may provide the specified function. In the topmost activity, being a so-called *for-each activity*, candidate ServiceObjects meeting this requirement are determined. For this purpose, first those Services that according to their specification may offer function are ascertained. Then

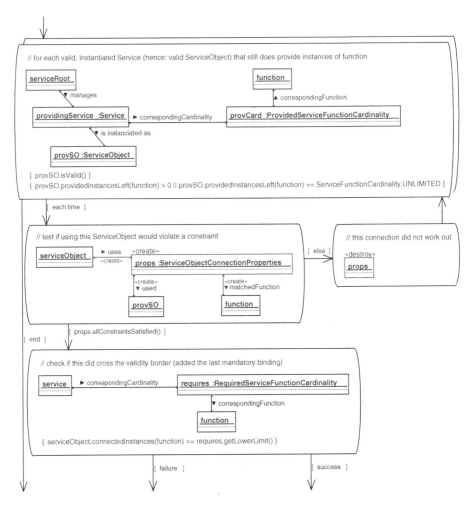

Fig. 5. Activity diagram fragment of `addBinding(ServiceObject)`

each `provSO` object that is an object of such a service is examined if it is valid and is able to provide an instance of the required `function`. As some functionality required by a `ServiceObject` may be unavailable at times, a `ServiceObject` does not always have to be valid. We define a `ServiceObject` to be *valid* if all mandatory required functionality is provided by `ServiceObject`s that are valid themselves and all binding constraints for connections between the `ServiceObject`s are satisfied. To check the latter, the binding has to be established, as `BindingConstraints` are defined for existing configuration graphs. Thus for each of the found `provSO`s a `ServiceObjectConnectionProperties` object is created in the left activity below. This object indicates that `provSO` is used to provide `function`. If at least one binding constraint is violated the binding is destroyed in the activity to the right and the next `provSO` is determined in the topmost activity. Execution continues with the bottommost activity if all constraints are satisfied. If the connection did add the last mandatory binding the `ServiceObject`'s validity may have changed. The validity is thus reevaluated. Else the method ends as a binding was added by the policy. If none of the existing `ServiceObjects` qualifies as provider for the required `Function` the left arrow marked with *end* is followed. The method continues by creating new `ServiceObjects` of `Services` that may provide the function.

5   Tool Support

To provide tool support for the continuous SCD-process we created a visual specification tool (cf. Figure 6). We chose the Eclipse Graphical Editing Framework (GEF) for implementing the user interface. GEF [9] is a framework focusing on providing an easy way to build Eclipse-based graphical editors for existing models. As Fujaba is able to generate code for our model and the configuration logic, GEF was a natural choice for realizing the tool.

The *Service Editor* shown in the left screenshot of the figure is used by the service developer. Here services, functions, device definitions, and their relations can be modeled as described in Section 4. In the right screenshot the

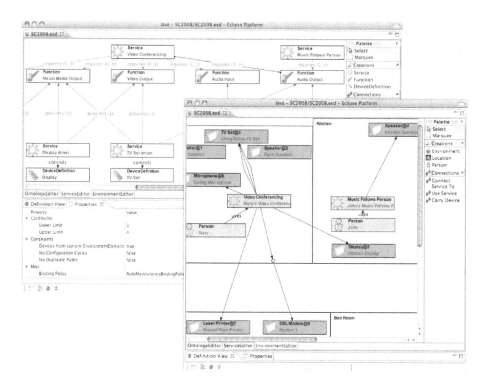

Fig. 6. Screenshots of the visual specification tool

Environment Editor is depicted. It is used for the specification phase of the continuous SCD-process. Environments and locations can be created to specify floor plans. Afterwards, the hardware devices may be placed and desired top-level services can be selected and associated to the prior defined locations. The tool palette of the Service Editor allows users to specify what service objects should be used as personal services and what devices they currently carry. To manually link service objects to each other or to some devices the user may also use the tool palette. After each change in the editor the configuration code is executed to reconfigure the runtime graph accordingly. The amount of required user interaction can be reduced if person and device detection and localization is available. Corresponding context changes can then be automatically detected. For the future we plan to integrate user profiles, such that desired services can be automatically inferred from the profile data.

The *Service Editor* depicts the service specifications for the scenario detailed in Section 2. Each service is specified along with its required and provided functions. In addition, driver services are linked to their respective devices. Binding policies and binding constraints can be chosen for each required functionality. This is shown in the properties view visible at the bottom of the left screenshot.

The right screenshot visualizes the configuration at the end of the example scenario. Mary resides in the living room. John is in the kitchen. The composition is a result of the successive environment changes and the user-generated specification changes described.

6   Related Work

As mentioned before there is a lot of research activity going on in the field of ambient intelligence and the related topics. Some of this research focuses on smart environments. Nevertheless there are numerous other areas of application. Related to software engineering, the concepts of software components and services are addressed frequently.

In [10], Cervantes and Hall discuss the concepts of service and component orientation and a service-oriented component model which is used in their project, called *Gravity*. The authors' initial goal, which is detailed in [11], is to provide an automatic service dependency management framework for user-oriented applications. As these applications are composed of services that continuously arrive or depart during runtime, the applications constantly have to be reassembled. Gravity allows to eliminate dependency management code needed to deal with such compositional issues using a tool called *Service Binder*. The Service Binder prototype is realized for the OSGi framework. Using XML descriptors similar to our service specifications each OSGi component is enriched with meta-data descriptions of its required and provided services. Cardinalities and static or dynamic policies can be specified to define the runtime reconfiguration behavior. The continuous SCD-process, we described in this paper, also aims at dynamic recomposition. Yet, the composition behavior defined by binding policies and binding constraints differs from the policies of the Gravity project. In contrast to our approach, no means of user interaction are provided by Gravity. This is an important aspect of our approach as the user has to be in control of the system even if the process should be executed as automated as possible. For each component instance the Service Binder creates instance managers that locally try to maintain the instance's validity according to the respective instance descriptor. In contrast, our graph-based approach relies on a centralized composition mechanism that may leverage local as well as global context information. This includes locations of persons, services, and devices. Context-restrictions based on the model may be described as binding constraints.

In [12], Botarro and Gérodolle describe several extensions to the original Service Binder addressing some of its limitations, like service selection ambiguity for equivalent service providers, support for context-awareness, and remote distribution of services. The *Extended Service Binder* introduces service provider rankings based on dynamic properties and transparent service access to remote services to the original concept. At the moment, we are exploring approaches that may help reducing selection ambiguity based on semantic service description.

In [13,14], Broens et al. propose a middleware called Context-Aware Component Infrastructure (CACI) that allows transparent binding management for personalized mobile component-based applications. The authors distinguish between context producing entities (e. g. GPS receivers, RFID beacons) and context consuming entities (e. g. context-aware applications). Bindings between these are called context bindings, and they are established dynamically and maintained at runtime. Using the CACI Component Description Language (CCDL), developers may define which context bindings are required by their application. Every context binding is specified with several parameters including a binding policy. The policy may be set to be either dynamic, semi-dynamic, or static. A dynamic policy indicates that the binding is to be updated if *better* context producers become available at runtime. Semi-static context bindings are only replaced if the context producer gets unavailable. Static bindings are only bound once. Compared to our binding specification approach CCDL lacks the possibility to specify if a context producing entity should be bound automatically or if user interaction is desired. In fact, no manual modifications can be applied by the user. No tool is provided for visualization and interaction.

In [15], the authors present an approach to behavioral service composition that is based on semantic web services. The user's needs are specified as so called abstract user tasks. Abstract user tasks do not refer to actual component instances. To realize these tasks, a matching algorithm is applied to compose semantic web services, which implement a certain behavior. Both abstract user tasks and semantic web services are specified as OWL-S processes. These process definitions are modeled as finite state automata, which are used by the matching algorithm to reconstruct the abstract user tasks based on available service behavior. In our approach, we do not consider service behavior to perform the matching. Instead we focus on context information, user interaction, and especially the reconfigurability of service compositions. In the approach discussed above, no reconfiguration issues are addressed.

7   Conclusion and Outlook

Smart homes require flexible and adaptive software composed from standard components. To offer smart home software to end-users at a reasonable price, the individual eHome-specific software is composed from these components at runtime. Service composition is a complex task, which has to be solved by a service gateway capable of managing, running, and adapting compositions automatically. If the end-user is bothered with technical configuration tasks in everyday life, smart homes will not be accepted by the general public. However, users want to be in control of their environments. Therefore, complementary means of user interaction have to be offered.

In this paper we described a dynamic process for composing standard service components, such that the resulting compositions meet the individual requirements for specific eHomes. The continuous SCD-process is capable of handling the dynamics occurring during runtime of eHome systems. To automate service composition, a detailed service specification has to be provided. We achieve this by specifying binding policies and binding constraints. This allows the service developer to define an adequate composition behavior for each specific service. We described a dynamic reconfiguration mechanism and how we implemented the according algorithm in a model-driven approach. Finally, we gave a short overview of a new tool supporting the eHome development process.

Currently, we are adapting the final deployment phase of the SCD-process to connect our tool to the eHomeSimulator [6], which is a virtual eHome environment we use as a testbed. This enables us to simulate environments containing numerous different devices and to evaluate more complex scenarios and the dynamic behavior at runtime. So far, preliminary tests indicate that the adaptive recomposition at runtime does not produce any significant performance overhead in comparison to the prior static approach used in [4]. In the near future, we will carry out a more extensive performance analysis to evaluate complex scenarios with a larger number of simultaneous users. We currently also work on further extensions of the service specification. Especially the specification of service functionalities using semantic labels is to be extended, to better support the matching algorithm and to allow for a more flexible service composition in heterogeneous environments. Other future extensions could be automated support for conflict resolution, optimization of the global configuration with respect to resource usage or other parameters, and also support for service versioning and updating at runtime.

References

1. Weiser, M.: The Computer for the 21st Century. Scientific American 265(3), 66–75 (1991)
2. The OSGi Alliance: OSGi Service Platform Core Specification. Release 4 (August 2005), http://www.osgi.org/osgi_technology/download_specs.asp#Release4
3. des Rivières, J., Wiegand, J.: Eclipse: A platform for integrating development tools. IBM Systems Journal 43(2), 371–383 (2004)

4. Norbisrath, U., Mosler, C.: Functionality Configuration for eHome Systems. In: Proceedings of the 16th International Conference on Computer Science and Software Engineering, CASCON 2006, ACM Digital Library (2006)
5. Fischer, T., Niere, J., Torunski, L., Zündorf, A.: Story Diagrams: A new Graph Rewrite Language based on the Unified Modeling Language. In: Ehrig, H., Engels, G., Kreowski, H.-J., Rozenberg, G. (eds.) TAGT 1998. LNCS, vol. 1764, pp. 296–309. Springer, Heidelberg (2000)
6. Armac, I., Retkowitz, D.: Simulation of Smart Environments. In: Proceedings of the IEEE International Conference on Pervasive Services 2007 (ICPS 2007), pp. 257–266. IEEE Press, Los Alamitos (2007)
7. Norbisrath, U., Armac, I., Retkowitz, D., Salumaa, P.: Modeling eHome systems. In: MPAC 2006: Proceedings of the 4th International Workshop on Middleware for Pervasive and Ad-Hoc Computing (MPAC 2006), 6 pages. ACM Press, New York (2006)
8. Abowd, G.D., Dey, A.K., Brown, P.J., Davies, N., Smith, M., Steggles, P.: Towards a Better Understanding of Context and Context-Awareness. In: Gellersen, H.-W. (ed.) HUC 1999. LNCS, vol. 1707, pp. 304–307. Springer, Heidelberg (1999)
9. Moore, B., Dean, D., Gerber, A., Wagenknecht, G., Vanderheyden, P.: Eclipse Development using the Graphical Editing Framework and the Eclipse Modeling Framework, 1st edn. IBM (Redbooks) (February 2004)
10. Cervantes, H., Hall, R.S.: Automating Service Dependency Management in a Service-Oriented Component Model. In: Crnkovic, I., Schmidt, H., Stafford, J., Wallnau, K. (eds.) Proceedings of the 6th ICSE Workshop on Component-Based Software Engineering (CBSE6), pp. 379–382 (May 2003)
11. Hall, R.S., Cervantes, H.: Gravity: supporting dynamically available services in client-side applications. In: ESEC/FSE-11: Proceedings of the 9th European Software Engineering Conference held jointly with 11th ACM SIGSOFT International Symposium on Foundations of Software Engineering, pp. 379–382. ACM Press, New York (2003)
12. Bottaro, A., Gérodolle, A.: Extended Service Binder: Dynamic Service Availability Management in Ambient Intelligence. In: FRCSS 2006: Future Research Challenges for Software and Service (April 2006)
13. Broens, T.H.F., van Halteren, A.T., van Sinderen, M.J.: Infrastructural Support for Dynamic Context Bindings. In: Havinga, P., Lijding, M., Meratnia, N., Wegdam, M. (eds.) EuroSSC 2006. LNCS, vol. 4272, pp. 82–97. Springer, Heidelberg (2006)
14. Broens, T.H.F., Quartel, D.A.C., van Sinderen, M.J.: Towards a Context Binding Transparency. In: Pras, A., van Sinderen, M. (eds.) EUNICE 2007. LNCS, vol. 4606, pp. 9–16. Springer, Heidelberg (2007)
15. Mokhtar, S.B., Georgantas, N., Issarny, V.: Ad Hoc Composition of User Tasks in Pervasive Computing Environments. In: Gschwind, T., Aßmann, U., Nierstrasz, O. (eds.) SC 2005. LNCS, vol. 3628, pp. 31–46. Springer, Heidelberg (2005)

Brokering Planning Metadata in a P2P Environment

Johannes Oudenstad[1], Romain Rouvoy[2], Frank Eliassen[2,3], and Eli Gjørven[3]

[1] Norwegian Defence Research Establishment
P.O. Box 25, N-2027 Kjeller
johannes.oudenstad@ffi.no
[2] University of Oslo, Department of Informatics
P.O. Box 1080 Blindern, N-0314 Oslo
{rouvoy,frank}@ifi.uio.no
[3] Simula Research Laboratory
P.O.Box 134, N-1325 Lysaker
eligj@simula.no

Abstract. In self-adaptive systems, metadata about resources in the system (*e.g.*, services, nodes) must be dynamically published, updated, and discarded. Current adaptive middleware approaches use statically configured, centralized repositories for storing and retrieving of such metadata. In *peer-to-peer* (P2P) environments, we can not assume the existence of server nodes that are always available for hosting such centralized services. However, the metadata repository is the keystone of the adaptation middleware and the consistency of adaptations relies on its reliability.

To address this limitation in our QuA planning-based adaptation middleware, we introduce a P2P broker, which is a metadata advertisement service based on P2P technology. This P2P broker can be plugged into the QuA middleware to support the construction of self-adaptive applications in a P2P environment. We use a structured P2P protocol that distributes the service metadata over a set of nodes based on service type and property information. The P2P broker is therefore capable of handling node failures by providing replication of the metadata. We present a working prototype of the P2P broker as well as results from initial experiments. These results show that the metadata distributes well over the nodes in the network, thus enabling scalability and robustness to node failures.

Keywords: Peer-to-peer systems, resource brokering, self-adaptive middleware, service planning.

1 Introduction

As computing systems become larger and more complex, the idea of self-adapting systems is spreading to many areas of computing and communication, such as multimedia applications, mobile applications, advanced communication protocols, and management of low level operating system resources. In particular, a self-adapting system is able to reason about itself at run-time and, when necessary, to make changes to itself in order to better satisfy the current environment requirements. However, while distributed applications traditionally were built from client-server architectures, many current distributed applications are now built from *peer-to-peer* (P2P) architectures. These

R. Meier and S. Terzis (Eds.): DAIS 2008, LNCS 5053, pp. 168–181, 2008.
© IFIP International Federation for Information Processing 2008

systems consist of equal, autonomous peers entering an application when suitable for themselves, and then generally leaving without warning. Generally, approaches to adaptation middleware assume the existence of server nodes that can be expected to almost always be available, and in particular to be continuously available for long periods of time. As these approaches do not fit the P2P paradigm, we investigate self-adaptive middleware that is able to exploit other types of architectures at the middleware level. Thus, this paper contributes to the integration of component- and planning-based adaptation middleware in a P2P environment.

In this paper, we focus on the problem of dynamically locating metadata about resources, such as services, nodes, in the system as they become available in the network. We present the design of a resource broker based on a P2P infrastructure, and describe how this broker is used by our planning-based adaptation middleware QuA [1]. In the QuA middleware, adaptation is driven by metadata associated to services (*e.g.*, service performance or cost). Thus, the middleware aims at providing the best possible *Quality of Service* (QoS) to users under variable execution contexts. However, this adaptation requires quick and simple means to query for metadata in the system. And, existing approaches to resource discovery, such as Twine [2], do not satisfy our requirements as they do not provide the strong association of types to resources, as required in the QuA middleware. Therefore, we propose to achieve this task with our P2P broker, which exploits diverse connectivity between participants in a network and the cumulative bandwidth of network participants. Using a P2P infrastructure, we benefit from the seamless distribution of the metadata across the network nodes to improve the planning processing performance. Thus, a main challenge for the design of the P2P broker is to find a mapping from the metadata associated to services with the goal of obtaining an even distribution over P2P nodes. Besides, the replication of metadata using the P2P network ensures the metadata high-availability in terms of access time, fault tolerance, and network participants connectivity.

In the remainder of the paper, we introduce the QuA planning middleware (cf. Section 2), and we discuss related work in the domain of resource brokering (cf. Section 3). Then, we present the design of our P2P broker for the QuA planning middleware (cf. Section 4), and an evaluation of its performances (cf. Section 5). Finally, we discuss the perspectives of this work before concluding (cf. Section 6).

2   Foundations of the QuA Planning Middleware

The QuA middleware [1] supports planning-based adaptation, which means that applications are specified by their behavior, and are planned, instantiated, and maintained by the middleware in such a way that the behavioral requirements are satisfied throughout the application life-time.

Central to this middleware is *mirror-based service reflection* [3], which supports introspection and intercession on a service through all the phases of its life-cycle, including pre-runtime. Each service is represented by a *service mirror*, which is an object reflecting the service behavior (known as *service type*) and its implementation (known as *blueprint*). Each service mirror has a map of <*name,value*> property pairs, where the list of property types allowed in the map is determined by the QuA type specified by the service mirror. The property type determines the value range of a property of that type and the matching operators that can be applied for filtering service mirrors. Thus, the task of *service planning* consists in planning the initial configuration or the dynamic re-configuration of a service. The planner is responsible for evaluating alternative service mirrors in order to find and select the service implementation with the highest util-ity that satisfies both the functional and qualitative specifications of a service request. Service mirrors can be advertised to and obtained from a pluggable middleware *broker service*. The QuA broker is a trader-based discovery service. The resources traded in the broker are the service mirrors discussed above. Component and application developers alike must advertise the service mirrors to the broker. The broker has a responsibility of hosting all the service mirrors advertised in a repository. In the service planning phase, the planner asks the broker for service mirrors matching a type description and property constraints (if any), and the broker is responsible of returning the service mirrors that match the description.

An instance of the QuA platform consists of a small *core* that may be extended with specialized, domain-specific services. A QuA *capsule* represents the local runtime environment that a QuA platform instance depends on. A capsule hosts one or more *repositories*, where *blueprints* referred to by service mirrors can be stored and retrieved. Capsules themselves are advertised as service mirrors, and can be discovered by service planners looking for nodes to interpret QuA blueprints and instantiate services from it. For this purpose, each blueprint specifies a dependency to the required type of QuA platform, such as a QuA:Java or QuA:Smalltalk platforms.

Thus, a challenge for the design of the P2P broker is to map service mirrors to P2P nodes, and to provide efficient filtering both on type of functionality and properties.

3   Related Work

The discovery of metadata in QuA is based on required service types and potentially required static properties of implementations of those service types. We limit the dis-cussion of related work to resource discovery approaches similar to that of QuA—*i.e.*, resource discovery through some form of marketplace often referred to as a trader or a broker. We therefore focus on systems where resources are traded based on type con-formance and matching of properties.

Two representative systems for resource discovery that are similar to the approach of QuA are Jini [4] and the ODP/CORBA trading service [5]. Jini is able to operate in a ubiquitous environment, as it has mechanisms for discovering the trading function—*i.e.*, the lookup server—dynamically. Once a binding has been established to the lookup ser-vice, Jini trading operates in a similar way to that of the QuA broker. The ODP-trader is part of a middleware framework and also operates similarly to the QuA broker. A more recent trading-like resource discovery service is the *Universal Description Discovery and Integration* (UDDI) registries of Web Services [6]. A service provider publishes the services it is willing to share with others in a UDDI registry, which announces their availability to interested customers. A service consumer accesses the UDDI registry to retrieve the relevant announcements, which describes where and how the services can be invoked. The main difference between Jini, ODP trader, UDDI registry, and QuA is the way resources are modeled. In ODP, resources are modeled as service offers, while in UDDI resources are modeled as WSDL documents. But more importantly, neither Jini, ODP trader, nor UDDI registries have been designed for a P2P system architecture.

Twine [2] builds on the *Intentional Naming System* (INS), which focuses on resource discovery in the mobile domain. Resources in Twine are represented by a resource description consisting of *<attribute,value>* pairs. Twine creates trees of these pairs as hierarchical structures of attribute types are possible. On resource advertisement, *strands* are constructed from the trees for each possible prefixed subsequence of attributes and values in each attribute hierarchy, where the top-level attribute in the hierarchy is the prefix. When resources are queried for, one of the longest strands from it tree is extracted at random, and the node that has responsibility for the given key is asked for resources that fit the resource description. Twine relies on Chord [7] to distribute responsibility for resources among participating nodes. However, Twine is not intended for use in component-based middleware, and has no need for strong association of types to resources.

JXTA [8] uses messaging for advertisement of resources fitting a P2P environment, allowing for creation of module types in advertisements. In our context, it is crucial to find all advertised metadata describing services of a given type in the network. Even if the introduction of the *Shared Resource Distributed Index* (SRDI) makes it more likely that information that belong together are grouped to one rendezvous peer, JXTA provides no guarantees for finding all the published pieces of metadata describing a specific type. Furthermore, nodes willing to take the role as *supernodes* (rendezvous peer or gateway peer) might not be available in all situations.

It is therefore interesting to investigate the feasibility of designing and implementing a broker component for QuA based on P2P technology.

4   Design of the P2P-Based Broker Service

In QuA, both service blueprints and capsules are described by service mirrors, which are frequently retrieved in the planning and re-planning phases of applications. During these phases, the QuA planner uses the trading features of the broker to filter out the most useful service mirrors.

Our design approach consists in creating a P2P network and distributing the service mirrors evenly on participating nodes. The network is self-organizing, and the nodes will at all times agree upon which nodes are responsible for the different service mirrors. Service mirrors are also replicated to additional nodes, which makes the metadata highly available and independent of any central entity.

The main design issues of the P2P broker include choice of P2P technology and its integration into the QuA architecture (cf. Section 4.1), the mapping of service mirrors to P2P nodes (cf. Section 4.2), and the replication scheme that makes service mirrors highly available (cf. Section 4.3).

4.1   Choice of P2P Technology

While ideally the design should be independent of any specific P2P technology, it is important for service planners to be able to discover all possible service mirrors

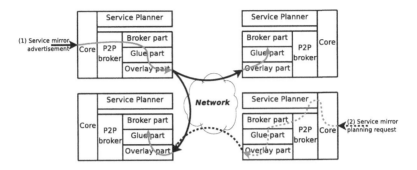

Fig. 1. P2P broker and planner services in QuA

describing services of a specific type. For this reason it is preferable to use a structured P2P overlay. Unstructured P2P technologies, such as the well known Gnutella protocols, make use of broadcasts of query messages to find resources in the network. To avoid these broadcasted messages strangling the network, a maximum number of hops is usually specified for these messages. Because of the way these systems construct their networks, this feature provides no guarantee for finding all resources that exists in a network matching a specific query. This is in conflict with the requirement of finding *all* service mirrors matching a service type and a set of properties when requested by the service planner. In structured P2P overlays, each participating node is assigned a *unique identifier* (UID) from a global identifier space. Every node is typically responsible for a contiguous area of the identifier space and receives all messages sent to any UID in this space. This area usually consists of a set of UIDs that are numerically closer to the node's own UID than to the UID of any other node. When a node joins or leaves the network, the neighboring nodes in the UID space are affected by this as their area of responsibility grows or shrinks.

By mapping service mirrors to UIDs, we effectively assign responsibility for them to nodes in the network. The node that is responsible for this area of the UID space will at any time be responsible for that service mirror. In our design, a collection of P2P brokers constitute a distributed system that works as a whole to provide a service that is common and equal to all interconnected instances of the software.

Figure 1 depicts four instances of QuA deployed on four nodes of a P2P network. Each instance is composed of a Core hosting two pluggable services: the P2P broker and the Service planner. The Service planner uses the local P2P broker to retrieve service mirrors that are suitable for an adaptation. The local P2P broker interacts with networked P2P brokers to find all the relevant service mirrors. The P2P broker itself is composed of three parts. The P2P part contains the implementation broker logic. Communication with other P2P brokers is maintained by the Overlay part, while the Glue part glues those parts together and assists in calculating replication of the data.

4.2   Mapping of Service Mirrors to Nodes

To be able to distribute the metadata evenly on the nodes participating in the network, we need a way to map service mirrors to nodes. As there already exists hashing mechanisms in the P2P technologies that handle the creation of keys that fit in the UID space based on some input (*e.g.*, a string of characters) the problem boils down to extracting data from the service mirrors to use as basis for the generation of keys. It has been shown by many projects, including the PAST persistent storage project [9], that structured P2P overlays can be used to effectively distribute storage of large quantities of data between nodes. Our problem is different because the QuA planner searches for all service mirrors conforming to a service type and property constraints and not for a specific mirror. In practice, this means that instead of creating unique keys for each service mirror (like *e.g.*, PAST creates a key for each individual file), we need to group service mirrors together in a way that makes it easier to find all the relevant service mirrors when they are needed.

Both CAN [10], Chord [7], Pastry [11], and Tapestry [12] create keys and UIDs with a hashing function to ensure an even distribution of UIDs in the identifier space. These hashing functions always create the same UID from the same input. Thus, an intuitive way of mapping service mirrors to nodes uses only the service type specified by the service mirror as basis for key generation. Both nodes advertising and querying for service mirrors find out which service type the service mirror specifies, and uses the string representation of the type as a basis for calculation an overlay specific key for the resource (known as *key-base*). A consequence of this approach is that all service mirrors associated to the same service type, will be mapped to the same key and hence to the same node. Unfortunately, this means that when there are many service mirrors specifying the same service type, such as when there are many instances of a specific capsule type, they will all be mapped to and thus hosted on the same node. Furthermore, each time a service planner asks the broker for capsules that can host a service, all those queries will end up as incoming messages at the node responsible for that key-base.

Besides, if in its request to the broker, the service planner specifies a property constraint, such as a version or a location constraint, then the receiving node has to search through all the service mirrors to find the capsules that match the constraint. If several service planners plan concurrently, this may be time consuming. This problem will become cumbersome for any service type referenced by many service mirrors, and often retrieved by service planners. In order to address this issue, we associate more than one key to each resource advertised. By using more storage space for each resource, and distributing it on participating nodes, the search space and thus the time for queries can be reduced. In addition, as explained below, the requests for service mirrors for specific service types will be distributed over more keys, and implicitly over more nodes, ultimately ensuring a better distribution of queries. We achieve this by creating more than one key-base when the advertised service mirror specifies values for *enumerated properties*—*i.e.*, properties that have an enumerated type.

In general, a service mirror can be characterized by the pair $[T, < p_0, \ldots, p_n >]$ where T is the type specified by the service mirror, $< p_0, \ldots, p_n >$ is an ordered list of the enumerated properties, and each p_i draws its value v_i from an enumeration domain D_i. Then, we can define a set of key-bases in the advanced mapping method, where each key-base is defined as:

$$\text{key-base} = T + x_0 + \cdots + x_i + \cdots + x_n$$

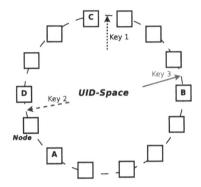

Fig. 2. Mapping of service mirrors to nodes

where T is the type of the service, $x_i \in \{v_i, \emptyset\}$ (where $v_i \in D_i$, while $\emptyset$ is the empty string representing a wild card), and the operator $+$ indicates string concatenation. To ensure that key-bases based on enumerated properties are generated in the same way in all participants of the network, property values are alphabetically ordered based on the names of the property types for the service type associated to the mirror.

The P2P broker receiving the initial advertisement of a new mirror goes through the property set of the service mirror and finds all enumerated properties that are specified. Then, by following the property type ordering, it creates key-bases for all possible combinations of the service type and values of the enumerated property types where the values are either the value specified by the service mirror, or a wild card. Key-bases for each combination of property value or wild card are created in order to later match the key-base generated from any broker query when requesting a particular service mirror. This means that a P2P broker that receives a resource query for a service type and some properties, creates *one* key-base based on the service type wanted and the enumerated properties specified in the service mirror. This key-base will be in the form:

$$\text{key-base} = T + v_0 + \cdots + v_i + \cdots + v_n$$

where T is the type of the service, $v_i \in D_i$ (D_i is the enumerated domain of property i), and the operator $+$ indicates string concatenation.

We illustrate this idea by the following example (see Figure 2). The network of P2P brokers can be seen as a *distributed hash table*, where each node has responsibility for a unique part of the UID-space. To simplify, we assume that there is only one enumerated property type for a capsule, specifying the type of code hosting capabilities it has. We also assume that a capsule, whose type is QuA-capsule, exclusively hosts either Java or Smalltalk code. In other words, the value range of the property *hosting capabilities* is strictly enumerated to Java and Smalltalk.

In our example, there are three possible key-bases that can be created from the type and the enumerated property, of which any announced mirror at most can produce two. The three resulting key-bases are QuA-capsule, QuA-capsule:Java[1]

---

[1] The ":" delimiter is placed between type and property for readability, and is not supposed to be there following the definition of the form of key-bases given above.

and QuA-capsule:Smalltalk. Now, as we have more than one key-base for each service mirror, we associate one key with each key-base (cf. Figure 2). For example, key 1 is QuA-capsule, key 2 is QuA-capsule:Java, and key 3 is QuA-capsule:Smalltalk. If node A advertises its own capsule as a resource, and the capsule has capabilities of hosting Smalltalk code, both node C and node B would assume responsibility of hosting that resource, but under different conditions. Node C would now respond to all queries for a capsule without any preferences to hosting capabilities. Node B would respond to all queries for a capsule that has capabilities of hosting Smalltalk code. Further, node C would host one service mirror for each capsule advertised. Node B would only host service mirrors for capsules with Smalltalk capability, and node D would host service mirrors for capsules with Java capabilities. The reader may notice that it is possible for more than one key belonging to a service mirror to be associated with one node. However, the probability of this happening decreases linearly with the number of nodes joining the system. Further, the broker is able to distinguish resources based on key-bases anyway.

The multi-key mapping technique described above has two main advantages with regards to filtering of service mirrors in the broker. Service description including enumerated properties are processed by the responsible node that match the requested properties. This ensures that service mirrors exhibiting at least one incompatible property are excluded from the research. And, because of the multi-key advertising, the different service requests (most often) end up at different nodes, increasing parallelism of metadata filtering during service planning.

4.3   Replication of Service Mirrors

As nodes join and leave a network of P2P brokers, the areas of responsibility for nodes change dynamically. As a result, when a P2P broker of a given node is asked for service mirrors conforming to a service description, the node that is responsible for the corresponding key might not be the same as the one that processed the advertisement message initially. In the same way, when nodes responsible for service mirrors leave the network, that information will be lost if it is not taken care of by some replication mechanism. If not, the design will not ensure metadata robustness to node failure. Thus, we support built-in replication in the system to handle both the self-organization and the metadata robustness concerns.

A key feature of any structured P2P network is that the placement of nodes in the global identifier space relative to each other is organized. This means that it is always possible to calculate who is the closest neighbor in a given direction in the UID-space. These systems also have strict algorithms on routing messages, always routing to the node responsible for the given area that the destination UID of the message lies within. The combination of these two properties gives the opportunity to use the immediate neighbors of a given node, node B, as its replicating nodes. If node B unexpectedly leaves the network, one of its immediate neighbors, node R1, will become in control of the area of the UID-space node B was responsible for (cf. Figure 3). In effect, node R1 will receive all messages regarding the objects that node B just recently had. In some cases where node B had multiple resources associated with different keys, the responsibility of resources may be spread amongst several immediate neighbors. In any

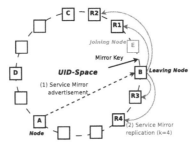

Fig. 3. Replication in the P2P broker

case, replicating data on the nearest neighbors to node B solve the problem. In addition, each node must recalculate its immediate neighbors and area of key-responsibilities frequently so that replicas remain up to date.

In a special case, node B may leave and a node E may join the network with an UID that lies between node B and node R1 in the key-space. In this case, constant monitoring of the routing state of node R1 discovers the arrival of node E. By recalculating the responsibility-area of UIDs, R1 and E are able to figure out which keys node E is responsible for, and arrange for R1 to send the relevant data to it.

Now consider Figure 3 that basically illustrates how replication would work in a Pastry network. A resource gets advertised at node A. Node A calculates the UID[2] that corresponds to the service mirror and sends an advertising message to the network. Node B is the node responsible for that UID, so node B receives the message. The first thing node B does is to *replicate* the service mirror by sending a message to the k replicating nodes R (k is known as the replicating factor).

Replication like this has already been implemented with PAST [9,11] over the Pastry technology, and it can be shown that it is possible to implement over a Chord, Tapestry, or CAN network, even though the CAN identifier space differs significantly from the others (at least for a high number of dimensions).

4.4   Outdated Information in Service Mirrors

Although our design ensures that the metadata is highly available even with nodes join-ing and leaving the network due to the replication scheme, we can not be sure that the information in the service mirrors do not get outdated. As nodes that host blueprints or even instantiated and running components that have been advertised to the P2P bro-ker leave the network, the service mirrors describing these services will become out of date. Likewise, service mirrors describing capsule resources will also contain outdated information when the nodes hosting those capsules disappear from the network.

We assume that, on average, nodes stay for a while once they have joined the net-work of P2P brokers. As QuA is used for planning and frequent re-planning of adaptive applications, the time used to plan and re-plan applications has to be kept at a minimum

---

[2] Or possibly multiple UIDs from multiple key-bases if running the advanced mapping method, but in this example it is only one key.

in any case. Whenever the service planner discovers that a service mirror contains out-dated information, it will ask the P2P broker to discard those service mirrors. Further, we believe that the problem of outdated information on where to find blueprints can be solved by creating a P2P-based blueprint repository. By combining this with a policy to only use a local broker to advertise and query for instantiated and running compo-nents, we believe that we have an efficient and satisfactory solution for highly available metadata.

5 Evaluation

The evaluation of the P2P broker reported in this section has been performed using the Java implementations of QuA and FreePastry [13]. We have conducted performance measurements on a desktop PC with the following software and hardware configura-tion: Intel Core 2 Duo 2,38 GHz processor, 3GB of RAM, Ubuntu linux distribution, Java Virtual Machine Sun JDK version 1.6.01 build 105. Our experiments focused on validating the following properties of the P2P broker: *scalability*, *self-organization*, and *robustness* to metadata loss by node failure. In particular, we evaluated the algorithm that maps service mirrors to UIDs in order to validate the even distribution of service mirrors among the P2P nodes (cf. Section 5.1). We ran the entire test setup on a sin-gle computer to disable the interferences created by the network. The P2P broker we designed balances the load of storing service mirrors, resolving queries, and filtering service mirrors on nodes that have responsibility for hosting the corresponding service mirrors. Replication factor is set to 4, which means that the four closest nodes to the responsible node are told to replicate the resources. Thus, we expect that the system as a whole will be scalable if the responsibility for service mirrors are well distributed. As a consequence, we also evaluated the resilience of the system to node failures (cf. Section 5.2) before discussing our results (cf. Section 5.3).

5.1 Service Mirrors Distribution

The first experience aims at demonstrating the scalability of the distribution of service mirrors among distributed nodes. Thus, Figure 4 shows the results of an experiment where $81,000$ service mirrors specifying different service types are advertised in a P2P network of 300 nodes. This configuration reflects the deployment of a set of QuA appli-cations and their respective configurations. For different node UIDs along the X-axis, the Y-axis shows in the blue dotted graph the number of service mirrors each node is responsible for, the replicated ones in the green dashed graph, and either responsible for or replicated in the red graph. Although the graph shows that the responsibilities for service mirrors are not perfectly evenly distributed, it shows that the metadata is shared among all participating nodes. This distribution is justified by the way Pastry distributes keys responsibility to nodes. For example, when 300 nodes are randomly assigned UIDs in an UID-space of 2^{128}, the nodes form clusters in the UID-space. The nodes at the edges of these clusters get responsibility for a high number of keys, while those at the center of the cluster will have neighbors close by on both sides, and will have a smaller key-space to be responsible for.

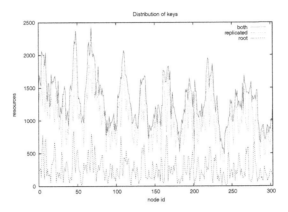

Fig. 4. Distribution of service mirrors over nodes

5.2   Service Mirrors Availability

To demonstrate that the system is able to reorganise the distribution when new nodes are joining, we performed series of experiments where an initially small network is joined by a stream of new nodes. In Figure 5, we observe the evolution of 3 resources (qua:/VideoBuffer, qua:/Component1, and qua:/Printer), which are initially advertised to a network composed of 11 nodes. The X-axis depicts time-stamps, while the Y-axis shows UIDs in the UID-space in base 10. 100 nodes are individually joining this initial configuration following a rate of about 1 node per second. Immediately upon joining the network, each joining node tries to discover all service mirrors. The responsible node for answering service mirror requests is allocated to the closest node with regards to the resource key requested. Monitoring shows how the responsibility for responding to the queries shift as new nodes join the network. Thin lines in the graph can be explained by the delay introduced by FreePastry to re-organize the distribution and re-allocate responsibilities.

Similarly, as depicted in Figure 6, we have performed experiments where we have started each scenario with an initial network composed of 100 interconnected nodes. Subsequently, each node leaves the network unexpectedly at a random time (60 seconds on average). Initially, 3 service mirrors were advertised to the network (qua:/VideoBuffer, qua:/Component1, and qua:/Printer). In these experiments, a number of nodes are constantly querying the three resources to monitor their availability. As nodes responsible for certain service mirrors left the network, we observed that the closest node in the UID-space answered queries as expected.

5.3   Discussions

This section discusses the results we obtained with regards to the observed properties: *scalability*, *self-organization*, and *robustness* to metadata loss by node failure.

Distribution and Scalability. As mentioned in Section 5.1, the service mirror distribution we obtained is not perfectly even. The reason is that the resources are assigned

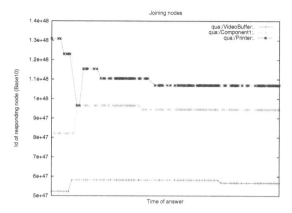

Fig. 5. Service mirrors responsibility when nodes join

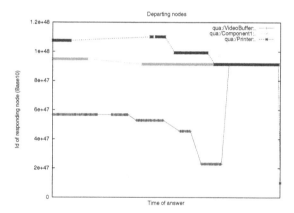

Fig. 6. Service mirrors responsibility when nodes leave

keys that are fairly well distributed in the UID-space, but node identifiers are clustered. Given that the resources are replicated to the closest nodes in the UID-space, some nodes get responsibility for a larger range of keys than other nodes. Nevertheless, even if the distribution is not perfect, the P2P-broker seems to be able to take advantage of Pastry's properties with respect to distribution of resources. This make the P2P-broker able to scale as the numbers of nodes and resources increases.

Self-organization. In Figure 5 and Figure 6, thin lines depict the reorganization of responsibilities and replicas when the network topology evolves. These thin lines represent temporary unavailability of resources and forces the QuA planner to wait for the service mirrors. The temporary unavailability of resources is due to FreePastry, which tries to send a message via a route that is unavailable because of a recent node failure. When the node failure is discovered, FreePastry routes the message along a different path. This delay can be reduced by decreasing the message timeout values for messages in the FreePastry implementation. However, if the timeout is set too low, messages will be frequently re-sent even if an answer to the message is underway, and consequently much resources will be wasted on sending duplicate messages.

Robustness. Figure 5 and Figure 6 validate the replication scheme. In particular, it is capable of replicating resources to new nodes to try to keep the invariant that $k + 1$ nodes should hold every resource in the system. However, the dynamism of the P2P environment breaks regularly this invariant and the replication scheme has to detect these situations to restore the system back into a consistent state. The capacity of the replication scheme to handle node failures depends on the frequency of node failures. In particular, [11] has shown that the lazy repair algorithms of Pastry allows the network, over time, to completely recover from a drop of 10% of $100,000$ nodes. When increasing the frequency at which nodes leave the network, we reach a point where the replication scheme fails. Observations show that this happen when the number of nodes equals the replication factor—*i.e.*, the number of nodes replicating each service mirror—dropped out in a time interval close to the *keep-alive* refresh interval of FreePastry.

6   Conclusions

In this paper, we have introduced the design and the implementation of a P2P broker for the QuA planning-based adaptation middleware. The QuA middleware uses the broker to retrieve metadata in the form of service mirrors describing implementation alternatives conforming to a service description. The description includes the type of service required and constraints on other properties of the service implementation. The broker is also used to advertise new service mirrors.

While the original broker for QuA was designed for a traditional client-server architecture, this paper has investigated the feasibility of implementing the QuA implementation broker using P2P technology. A particular challenge addressed in this paper was the mapping of service mirrors to nodes in the network to provide an even distribution of metadata over the nodes. While enabling better scalability of query processing, this paper has also shown that the QuA broker can tolerate node failures.

Our perspectives include large-scale deployment of the QuA middleware to evaluate the performance of the P2P broker using a time metric (*e.g.*, response-time, throughput).

Acknowledgements

The authors thank the partners of the MUSIC project and reviewers of the DAIS conference for valuable comments. This work was partly funded by the European Commission through the project MUSIC (EU IST 035166).

References

1. Eliassen, F., Gjørven, E., Eide, V.S.W., Michaelsen, J.A.: Evolving Self-Adaptive Services using Planning-Based Reflective Middleware. In: 5th Int. Middleware Workshop on Adaptive and Reflective Middleware (ARM). AICPS, vol. 190, p. 6. ACM, New York (2006)

2. Balazinska, M., Balakrishnan, H., Karger, D.: INS/Twine: A Scalable Peer-to-Peer Architecture for Intentional Resource Discovery. In: Mattern, F., Naghshineh, M. (eds.) PERVASIVE 2002. LNCS, vol. 2414, pp. 195–210. Springer, Heidelberg (2002)
3. Bracha, G., Ungar, D.: Mirrors: Design Principles for Meta-level Facilities of Object-Oriented Programming Languages. In: 19th Annual ACM SIGPLAN Conference on Object-Oriented Programming, Systems, Languages, and Applications (OOPSLA), Vancouver, BC, Canada, pp. 331–344. ACM, New York (2004)
4. Sun Microsystems: Jini Architecture Specifications - v2.1 (2005), `http://www.sun.com/software/jini/specs`
5. Bearman, M.: Tutorial on ODP Trading Function. Faculty of Information Sciences Engineering. University of Canberra, Australia (February 1997)
6. OASIS: UDDI Version 3.0.2 (February 2005), `http://uddi.xml.org`
7. Stoica, I., Morris, R., Karger, D., Kaashoek, M.F., Balakrishnan, H.: Chord: A scalable peer-to-peer lookup service for internet applications. In: Int. Conference on Applications, technologies, architectures, and protocols for computer communications (SIGCOMM), San Diego, CA, USA, pp. 149–160. ACM, New York (2001)
8. Sun Microsystems: JXTA Protocol Specification - v2.0. 2.5.3 edn. (October 2007), `https://jxta-spec.dev.java.net`
9. Druschel, P., Rowstron, A.: PAST: A large-scale, persistent peer-to-peer storage utility. In: 8th Int. Workshop on Hot Topics in Operating Systems (HotOS), CNF, Schloss Elmau, Germany, pp. 75–80. IEEE, Los Alamitos (2001)
10. Ratnasamy, S., Francis, P., Handley, M., Karp, R., Schenker, S.: A scalable content-addressable network. In: Int. Conference on Applications, technologies, architectures, and protocols for computer communications (SIGCOMM), San Diego, CA, USA, pp. 161–172. ACM Press, New York (2001)
11. Rowstron, A., Druschel, P.: Pastry: Scalable, Decentralized Object Location, and Routing for Large-Scale Peer-to-Peer Systems. In: Guerraoui, R. (ed.) Middleware 2001. LNCS, vol. 2218, pp. 329–350. Springer, Heidelberg (2001)
12. Zhao, B.Y., Huang, L., Stribling, J., Rhea, S.C., Joseph, A.D., Kubiatowicz, J.: Tapestry: A resilient global-scale overlay for service deployment. IEEE Journal on Selected Areas in Communications 22, 41–53 (2003)
13. Zhao, B.Y., Huang, L., Stribling, J., Rhea, S.C., Joseph, A.D., Kubiatowicz, J.: FreePastry. Rice University, Houston, USA. and Max Plank Institute for Software Systems, Saarbrücken, Germany, `http://freepastry.org`

Adaptive Web Service Migration

Holger Schmidt[1], Rüdiger Kapitza[2], Franz J. Hauck[1], and Hans P. Reiser[3]

[1] Institute of Distributed Systems, Ulm University, Germany
{holger.schmidt,franz.hauck}@uni-ulm.de
[2] Dept. of Comp. Sciences, Informatik 4, University of Erlangen-Nürnberg, Germany
rrkapitz@cs.fau.de
[3] LASIGE, Departamento de Informática, University of Lisboa, Portugal
hans@di.fc.ul.pt

Abstract. In highly dynamic and heterogeneous environments such as mobile and ubiquitous computing, software must be able to adapt at runtime and react to the environment. Furthermore it should be independent of a certain hardware platform and implementation language.

In this paper, we propose an infrastructure for self-adaptive migratable Web services (SAM-WS) for implementing applications for such environments. A SAM-WS supports stateful migration and adaptation to particular application context by being able to dynamically change the interface, locally available state and implementation in use. Despite adaptation and migration it maintains a unique ID during the whole life time. This allows clients to have a location-independent reference to a specific Web service instance. Although our prototype implementation is based on Apache Axis, the concept can be easily ported to any Web service framework without platform modifications. We provide an example application and performance measurements for different system platforms ranging from a standard device to resource-restricted mobile devices.

Keywords: Web Service, Migration, Adaptation.

1 Introduction

In ubiquitous computing (UbiComp) [1], a large number of small devices are interconnected in a dynamic and ad-hoc fashion. Applications for such devices should be platform independent because of the heterogeneous hardware and system software. They have to be adaptive and reactive to cope with the inherent environment dynamics. This is especially the case for mobile applications that are not attached to a specific device. Thus, a UbiComp infrastructure should provide mechanisms to automatically handle heterogeneity and reduce complexity of handling adaptivity and reactivity in the applications.

Mobile processes are an approach to simplify development of applications that change their interaction patterns and location during lifetime. A developer uses a description language (such as proposed by *Kunze et al.* [2]) to specify the behaviour and the interactions of the application. State-of-the-art infrastructures have limitations in terms of supporting adaptation and handling heterogeneity.

R. Meier and S. Terzis (Eds.): DAIS 2008, LNCS 5053, pp. 182–195, 2008.

Adaptation might be necessary for the local state of a process, the current functionality, and the implementation variant. These concerns need to be adjusted according to runtime environment properties, such as the hardware architecture, operating system, available memory, and local devices. Supporting heterogeneity means that processes have to be able to migrate between heterogeneous nodes, without requiring the developer to manually implement code for converting incompatible data representations. Interoperability between different vendor implementations of the infrastructure calls for using standardised protocols.

In previous work, we proposed the concept of a *self-adaptive* mobile process [3]. It can be seen as an ordered execution of services and is able to adapt itself in terms of state, functionality and implementation to the current context (which is represented by the runtime environment) and to migrate either for locally executing services or for accessing particular context, while maintaining its unique identity. We suggest an implementation of mobile processes with Web service technology on the basis of the model-driven architecture (MDA) [4]: developers specify behaviour and interactions of an application using a self-adaptive mobile process description, which is mapped on a self-adaptive migratable Web service (SAM-WS). In this paper, we focus only on the infrastructure for implementing such SAM-WSes without details on the MDA code generation process.

The novel contribution of our infrastructure is that it combines Web service technology with mobility mechanisms that support adaptation and heterogeneity. The key difference to related work on migratable Web services [5,6] is the support for adaptation to the application context by dynamically changing the service interface, the available state and the implementation while maintaining a persistent Web service identity. Unlike our previous work on context-aware migration of CORBA objects [7], in this paper we propose the use of standard Web service technology as core mechanism, which simplifies interoperability between heterogeneous infrastructures of different vendors and allows disconnected operation. On the basis of our dynamic code loading infrastructure [8], the platform contains a novel dynamic deployment service that allows service migration to machines on which the needed code is unavailable and thus has to be loaded on demand. We support client-transparent migration by providing persistent Web service references for the whole life cycle by introducing a persistent Web service identity. Although our prototype is implemented using Apache Axis, the concept provides a generic life cycle service specification for Web services.

The paper is structured as follows. First, we discuss related work. In Section 3, we present our design of adaptive Web service migration: basic principles, requirements and logical entities. After an in-depth description of our infrastructure in Section 4, we sketch a basic example application and show performance measurements in Section 5. We conclude and draft future work in Section 6.

2   Related Work

There are several projects targeting adaptation and context-sensitivity of Web services. For instance *Erradi et al.* developed a policy-based middleware for adaptive composite Web services [9]. Adaptation is based on dynamic Web service composition in these systems, wheras we replace the original Web service with an adapted one. Thus, our approach allows optimal resource usage by adapting a Web service to a device-tailored one. The Web service composition approach for adaptation can be used for integrating legacy services in our approach.

There exists a lot of work in the area of object migration, in particular for mobile agents (objects with an autonomous activity). However, many systems, such as *Aglets* [10] rely on native Java serialisation and are therefore restricted to a homogeneous environment and do not support adaptation to the context.

In previous work, we presented a concept for weak object migration on basis of the CORBA life cycle service [11]. For implementing mobile objects we use CORBA value types, i.e., objects with call-by-copy semantics. Thus, the developer does not have to care about externalisation and internalisation of the mobile object as this is handled transparently by the CORBA system. Our implementation does not support adaptation to the current application context.

There also exist systems that support adaptive object migration. For instance, *Almeida et al.* developed a dynamic reconfiguration service for CORBA [12]. The developer has to implement methods for internalising and externalising the object state, which may lead to error-prone implementations.

Recently, we introduced a concept for context-aware object migration on basis of the CORBA life cycle service [7]. To the best of our knowledge, this service is the only one allowing dynamic adaptive object migration regarding state, interface and code at runtime. However, it is restricted to CORBA and does not enable Web service migration and disconnected operation.

Hammerschmidt and Linnemann developed a service for stateful Web service migration [5]. However, as the approach builds on native Java serialisation, it is limited to homogeneous Java environments. The system does not provide concepts for adaptation of the state, interface and code. Furthermore, *Ishikawa et al.* describe a system for supporting Web service integration for pervasive computing [6]. In this approach mobile agents implement workflows. The agents can move to Web service locations in order to obtain efficient local access. However, their system does not support adaptation and is restricted to Java as it uses native Java serialisation.

Our system enables the implementation of mobile workflows (see example in Section 5). However, in contrast to a mobile workflow management system such as proposed by Satoh [13], which transfers documents, our system allows the complete migration of services. This enables tailored adaptation of the application to the current context and an on-demand instantiation of the application on devices that are not aware of the application in advance.

3   Design of Adaptive Web Service Migration

In this section, we first give an overview on basic principles on which our concept for adaptive Web service migration builds. Then, we present requirements that we identified and present necessary logical entities.

3.1   Basic Principles of Self-adaptive Web Service Migration

Web Service migration is the concept of moving a Web service from one machine to another at runtime. This requires transferring the Web service's implementation code. In this paper, we introduce *stateful self-adaptive migratable Web services* (SAM-WS), which have the advantage of supporting dynamic adaptation on the basis of current run-time environment and explicitly specified criteria. Our infrastructure introduces a concept for uniquely referencing a Web service independent of its location on basis of a location tracking service (see Section 4.5). For this purpose, the service URL is augmented with a globally unique ID (GUID). This allows the coexistence of several Web service instances at a particular location. We allow adaptation of the Web service's provided functionality (i.e., interface), the used internal state (i.e., set of variables) and the implementation code. Neither adaptation nor migration influence the GUID of the Web service, which allows continuous identification and addressing of the Web service. The GUID is automatically generated at deployment time.

For implementing self-adaptation, we introduce the concept of *Web service facets*. These represent a particular characteristic of the migratable Web service with a specific configuration of interface, state and implementation. Figure 1 shows a Web service facet providing interface A, using internal state a, b, and c and running an implementation in Java which adapts itself in context of migration to a Web service facet providing interface B, using internal state b, c, d and running an implementation in C++. As mentioned before, it is important to note that the globally unique ID is preserved during migration. The assignment of service state from one Web service facet to another one is realised using a name matching algorithm: If a Web service facet #1 contains state attributes with name b and c, the states b and c within another Web service facet #2 are considered the same (see Figure 1). Thus, after adaptation from Web service facet #1 into Web service facet #2, the state b and c of facet #2 has to be set to the prior state b and c of facet #1 (type incompatibilities result in an error).

Stateful adaptive Web service migration requires transferring the service state from the source to the target. By enabling a replacement of the implementation upon migration of the Web service, transfer states have to be interpretable by any possible implementation. Thus, we differentiate *implementation-dependent* and *implementation-independent* state of a Web service. We define implementation-independent state as the part of the service state that should be interpretable by any possible implementation of a specific functionality. For example, in

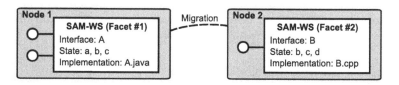

Fig. 1. Adaptive migration from one Web service facet into another one

case of a hash table functionality this would be only the key-value pairs. We consider state such as internal variables of managing structures for the hash function as implementation-dependent state which varies from one implementation to another. In case of migration, such implementation-dependent state can only be interpreted by the same target implementation. Thus, we transfer implementation-independent state only. However, implementation-independent state cannot be automatically determined. Thus, the developer of a SAM-WS has to tag implementation-independent state manually (see Section 4.1).

Additionally, for enabling SAM-WSes, we introduce a differentiation of *active* and *passive service state*. By adapting a Web service to a specific Web service facet, parts of the service state can be left out and other parts can be added. We call leaving out parts of the service state *passivation* and allow a subsequent *activation* of this state within another Web service facet. Therefore, passive state has to be stored for later use (see Section 3.3).

3.2   Requirements for Web Service Migration

We identified several requirements for our infrastructure:

Ubiquitous computing environments are characterised by *high dynamics* and *heterogeneous infrastructure*. Dynamics require supporting run-time decisions, e.g., selecting appropriate migration targets. Additionally, dynamic loading of locally unavailable code should be supported for allowing migration to any possible target location (even if the code is not known there before). The heterogeneous infrastructure requires platform- and language-independent techniques for communication and for state transfer. We think that by building on XML, Web service technology is appropriate for such environments.

Due to the heterogeneous infrastructure, we advocate requiring *self-adaptation* according to the application context. For example, this enables dynamic replacement of the implementation and thus running the same functionality on a mobile device with a lean and restricted implementation as well as on a workstation with a fully-fledged implementation.

For intuitive usage of SAM-WSes these should offer *client-side transparency*. Clients should notice neither migration nor adaptation of the Web service. This requires *continuous addressing* of the migratable Web service for the whole life cycle without client notice. Every SAM-WS should have a service-specific management interface, which every possible Web service facet has to support for providing some kind of stable interface part.

Furthermore, there should be *application development support*. For instance, developers should be offered an interface that provides high-level migration and adaptation support based on criteria, which allow the specification of target locations, context requirements and adaptation requirements.

3.3   Logical Entities and Collaboration

This section provides a brief overview of logical entities for SAM-WS migration. Figure 2 shows the interaction.

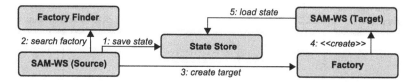

Fig. 2. Collaboration of logical entities for adaptive Web service migration

When a SAM-WS decides to migrate (this could be triggered internally or externally), it has to store the Web service's active state into a *state store* service for later use (passivation, see Section 3.1). To guarantee a consistent state transfer, migration has to be coordinated with request execution (see Section 4.3). Then, the SAM-WS tries to discover possible migration targets with the help of a *factory finder* service. Therefore, the SAM-WS passes criteria to the factory finder service (e.g., required context and provided interface at the target) according to which appropriate *factory* services (i.e., migration targets) are returned. These factory services enable the remote deployment of arbitrary Web services (if code is existent and executable for the particular platform). The factory service allows the creation of the criteria-specified Web service facet at the desired location. Last, the newly created Web service is updated with the necessary state from the state store service, the original Web service is undeployed and references to the Web service are updated to the new location (see Section 4.5).

4   Infrastructure for Adaptive Web Service Migration

In this section, we sketch our infrastructure for supporting SAM-WSes. First, we give details on the adaptive Web service migration process with its compulsory entities within our prototype for Apache Axis[1]. However, our concept is generic and can be applied to other Web service containers as well. Then, we show development steps for implementing SAM-WSes. Furthermore, we present advanced concepts for coordination of migration with request execution, dynamic loading of code and continuously addressing a SAM-WS for its whole life time.

4.1   Process of Adaptive Web Service Migration

Figure 3 shows the collaboration of implementation entities for adaptive Web service migration. However, before migration is processed it has to be coordinated with request execution (see Section 4.3). In the first step, the SAM-WS's move method is called[2]. The method can either be called directly by a client or by the SAM-WS itself, which provides a mechanism to enable autonomous behaviour. For specifying the migration target, the URI to the preferred factory finder service as well as (key, value)-pairs of non-functional criteria describing

---

[1] http://ws.apache.org/axis/

[2] The SAM-WS implements the interface AWSMService within our prototype.

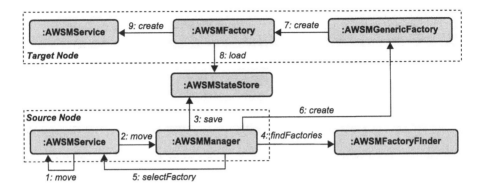

Fig. 3. Collaboration of implementation entities for adaptive Web service migration

appropriate migration targets (e.g., required context and interface) have to be passed as parameters.

AWSMManager. For simplifying development, we provide a local `AWSMManager` Web service, which manages further migration steps. It provides a `move` method that is called by the migrating SAM-WS. As parameters, the SAM-WS passes the given factory finder URI and criteria describing appropriate migration targets. Additionally, a self-reference, which is used for state introspection, and the service ID have to be passed.

Before migrating the SAM-WS, the implementation-independent state has to be extracted. Therefore, this state has to be described within the WSDL description to allow a language-independent specification (see Fig. 4). Within our prototype implementation running in Java we allow annotating implementation-independent state and provide a tool, which automatically generates the WSDL description. On the basis of the WSDL description, the implementation-independent state can be extracted automatically. Then, the state has to be stored (i.e., passivated) to the state store service for future use (see below).

```
1   <wsdl:definitions xmlns:wsdl="...">
2     <wsdl:types>...</wsdl:types>
3     <wsdl:portType name="Test">
4       <wsdl:operation name="getX"> ...
5       </wsdl:operation>
6     <wsdl:service name="TestService">
7       <wsdl:port>...</wsdl:port>
8       <awsm:states xmlns:awsm="...">
9         <state>x</state> ...
10      </awsm:states>
11    </wsdl:service>
12  </wsdl:definitions>
```

Fig. 4. WSDL description with implementation-independent state

```
1  public interface AWSMStateStore {
2    public String getStates(int id, String stateNames[]);
3    public String getStates(int id);
4    public void store(int id, String xmlState);
5  }
```

Fig. 5. Java interface of the `AWSMStateStore` Web service

The infrastructure has to select an appropriate migration target. A factory finder service assists in this selection by, given a list of criteria, returning appropriate factory services as a list (see below). The `AWSMManager` invokes a call-back method at the migrating SAM-WS to support an application-specific selection.

Last, our `AWSMManager` creates and deploys the necessary SAM-WS facet at the new location according to the given requirements, undeploys the original SAM-WS and updates the SAM-WS reference (see Section 4.5).

AWSMStateStore. The `AWSMStateStore` Web service provides methods for storing and retrieving state with respect to a specific service ID. As already mentioned in Section 3.1 this is needed for implementing passive state of the SAM-WS, which is non-existent within a particular facet, but may be used again within another facet. Figure 5 shows the interface of the `AWSMStateStore`. For retrieving only necessary parts of the current Web service facet, the `AWSMStateStore` service provides a custom `getStates` method with a parameter for specifying such parts of the state. For interoperability reasons with other Web service platforms, we use an XML string representation for passing state. This XML state representation is automatically generated within our `AWSMManager` on the basis of the WSDL description containing the implementation-independent state and parsed within the `AWSMStateStore`.

We provide a basic `AWSMStateStore` Web service implementation that internally stores the XML state data in the memory. However, on the basis of the `AWSMStateStore` interface, there can also be more complex implementations, e.g., using a database or peer-to-peer mechanisms for decentrally storing data.

AWSMFactoryFinder. The `AWSMFactoryFinder` implements a kind of factory service repository and represents an abstract service location. Factory services can be discovered as soon as they make an initial registration at the `AWSMFactoryFinder`. The factory finder service has a `register` method, which receives the WSDL-URI of a factory service and a corresponding set of criteria that the factory service provides (see Fig. 6). For interoperability reasons with other platforms, these criteria are transferred as an XML string representation. This data is stored in some kind of factory service repository with provided criteria. For deleting factory services there is an `unregister` method accepting the affected factory service's WSDL-URI as a parameter.

The `AWSMFactoryFinder` service provides an interface with methods for searching for factory services according to given criteria. We allow the specification of required context (e.g., physical/network location, CPU power, memory)

```
1  public interface AWSMFactoryFinder {
2    public void register(String xmlCriteria, String wsdlAddress);
3    public void unregister(String wsdlAddress);
4    public String[] findFactories(String xmlCriteria);
5  }
```

Fig. 6. Java interface of the `AWSMFactoryFinder` Web service

and provided functionality. These capabilities of the `AWSMFactoryFinder` enable two types of Web service migration: *Context-based migration* targets at running the SAM-WS on a platform that provides the desired context and *functionality-based migration* targets at running a specific Web service facet, e.g., for implementing the next step within mobile workflows (i.e., the mobile workflow is implicitly implemented by a SAM-WS, workflow steps are implemented by adaptation to specific Web service facets; see Section 5). Internally, for searching for appropriate factory services, the `AWSMFactoryFinder` selects adequate factory services from its repository and returns the corresponding WSDL-URIs.

We also allow using UDDI for discovery of factory services. In contrast to UDDI, our factory finder service eases the integration of policies according to which factories are returned (e.g., unordered list and best-fitting first).

AWSMGenericFactory and AWSMFactory. The logical factory service entity from Section 3.3 is split into two entities in our prototype implementation. The `AWSMGenericFactory` Web service is responsible for creating a SAM-WS-facet-specific `AWSMFactory` Web service. We need this delegation mechanism for integration of our dynamic code loading infrastructure [8], because it allows loading the `AWSMFactory` code before creation (see Section 4.4). Direct registration of an `AWSMFactory` at the `AWSMFactoryFinder` is possible as well.

The `AWSMFactory` enables dynamic deployment of necessary SAM-WS facets. Therefore, it offers a **create** method, which takes the SAM-WS ID as well as mandatory criteria as parameters. On the basis of the passed criteria, an appropriate SAM-WS facet is selected and instantiated. By using the given ID, the necessary state is retrieved from the `AWSMStateStore` and initialised within the new SAM-WS facet with keeping the original ID. Then, the Web service facet is deployed to allow remote access. Therefore, a deployment descriptor as well as the WSDL interface is generated automatically at runtime if required.

4.2 Development of Self-adaptive Mobile Web Services

For developing a SAM-WS, the developer has to decide which kind of facets a service should offer. Then, she has to implement them for each platform that should be supported, according to these conventions:

– Only implementation-independent state should be considered for migration and adaptation. It has to be marked either by our Java annotation *@ImplementationIndependentState* or within the WSDL file (see Section 4.1)

- Implementation-independent state defined within one SAM-WS facet is mapped to another facet by name matching (see Section 3.1)
- The implementation has to implement the `AWSMService` interface, which provides life-cycle methods of the SAM-WS (`move`, `copy`, `remove`)
- The implementation has to implement the `StatefulService` interface, which provides introspection methods of the SAM-WS (`getState`, `setState`).

For easing development efforts, we provide an abstract `AWSMServiceImpl` class, which contains generic code for introspection (on the basis of annotations and WSDL), generation of the globally unique ID and migration methods. Thus, the developer only has to inherit from this class and to ensure specification of state and state consistency among the different SAM-WS facets.

Then, the developer has to generate standard Web service packages of the SAM-WS facets for the required platforms (e.g., standard Web archive for Apache Axis). These packages are deployed and registered at our dynamic code loading infrastructure for loading these packages on demand (see Section 4.4).

4.3   Coordination

For maintaining consistent state with migration and adaptation, coordination is required. First, migration should only be possible if no other requests are currently handled by the SAM-WS. We use an interceptor at the server side for counting the number of currently active requests. Safe migration is possible if the current migration or adaptation request is the only active. Thus, such a request can only execute as soon as the request counter is equal to 1. As soon as a migration or adaptation is requested, all subsequent requests are deferred. After all previous requests have returned, the migration is started, and after successful migration, the deferred requests are forwarded to the new location.

In our prototype implementation for Apache Axis, we implemented a `SOAPHandler` by extending Apache Axis' abstract class `BasicHandler`. There, an `invoke` method is called with passing a `MessageContext` object from the Apache Axis container for every SOAP request and response. The `MessageContext` object contains the affected service and service method. This allows the sole interception of a specific SAM-WS; otherwise, other Web services would be affected as well. The `SOAPHandler` has to be registered at the container.

4.4   Dynamic Loading of Code

For enabling migration to Web service containers where the necessary code is locally unavailable, we integrated a dynamic code loading service. Dynamic code loading is an essential part of service migration, especially in a dynamic environment without guarantee of local existence of required code.

We developed a decentralised code loading service (P2P-DLS) [8]. It allows any peer to offer and to obtain platform-specific code. We proposed a dynamic loading infrastructure that is independent from the peer-to-peer mechanism in use. Based on our generic concept, we developed a JXTA-based service [14].

For supporting dynamic code loading within our infrastructure, we integrated the P2P-DLS into the `AWSMGenericFactory` (see Section 4.1). The generic factory service queries the P2P-DLS for appropriate location-dependent Web service facet implementations. The `AWSMGenericFactory` service identifies the necessary code by the interface name, and loads this code on demand for instantiating factories, which are specific for deploying a particular Web service facet.

For addressing security issues regarding dynamic code loading standard security mechanisms like code signing could be easily integrated.

4.5   Addressing Self-adaptive Mobile Web Services

Even though a SAM-WS is mobile as well as self-adaptive it can be continuously addressed using the SAM-WS service URL, which also contains the service ID. We implemented a location tracking service that is able to manage current locations of a defined set of SAM-WSes. Therefore, Web services initially register a public service address at the location tracking service and identify themselves using their current service address with the globally unique ID. The public service address, which is located at the location tracking service container, is used as permanent Web service reference; invocations are redirected by the Web service container using the location tracking service data. Whenever a Web service changes its location, it notifies the location tracking service about the new location (i.e., reference is updated). For client-transparency SAM-WSes should implement a management interface being stable within each facet (see Section 3.2).

For improving performance in our prototype for Apache Axis, we implemented an `HTTPRedirector` for client-side interception of SOAP requests over HTTP. This redirector has to be deployed at client-side, which results in every invocation going through the interceptor. Current locations of SAM-WSes, which are given in a redirect response, are cached. Thus, further invocations are directly forwarded without redirection (an error, i.e., a `404 Not Found` response, leads to invoking the original service URL again).

5   Example Application

Our approach provides a basis for the development of flexible and dynamic applications, e.g., for UbiComp. We present a mobile reporter application, in which reporters spontaneously initiate a mobile workflow: reporters enter data into a local Web service, which migrates onto a reviewer's machine for checking the data, and then migrates on a publisher's machine for publishing the content. Reporters become reviewers after a number of accepted reports. This requires dynamic deployment, which is also enforced by the fact that participants may spontaneously join and therefore have to deploy the application on demand.

Such an application can be implemented using SAM-WSes. Web service facets represent different roles within the mobile workflow: reporter, reviewer and publisher facet (see Fig. 7). In contrast to standard workflow systems, the workflow in our system comes along with the code, which can preserve computing resources

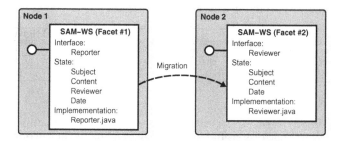

Fig. 7. Self-adaptive migration from reporter facet into reviewer facet

for workflow interpretation on resource-limited devices. Our transparent concept for addressing the SAM-WS enables service observation whenever required.

We measured the time for migrating from the reporter into the reviewer facet. The measurements were performed on an AMD Athlon with 1.73 GHz and 1GB RAM with two Apache Axis 1.4 containers (migration source/target) running on Apache Tomcat 5.5.12 with Java 1.5.0_08. Table 1 shows the overall result and the time for each of the process steps. We measured the performance of 30 Web service migrations and calculated the average time needed.

Overall, self-adaptive migration takes some time; especially WSDL generation as well as deployment are noticeable at the migration target. However, WSDL generation performance can be improved using caching mechanisms. Deployment at the migration target within the Apache Axis container takes around 72% of overall migration time. We are confident that future generations of Apache Axis provide improved deployment performance, which may rigorously improve overall migration time.

For comparison, we measured the time for migration without adaptation of the reporter facet. As migration steps are the same, overall time is comparable: 10229 ($\pm$582) ms. The moderately increased migration time compared to Table 1 results from the fact that the complete state is transferred, whereas in case of migration into the reviewer Web service facet the `reporter` state is omitted.

Considering embedded and mobile devices, we have done the same performance measurement for two somewhat outdated ARM-based as well as for a

Table 1. Migration from reporter into reviewer facet on standard device

Migration source (reporter facet)				
State extraction	State storage	Find factories		Sum
3$\pm$13 ms	101$\pm$103 ms	35$\pm$29 ms		139 ms
Migration target (reviewer facet)				
WSDL generation	State loading	Deployment	State setting	Sum
2378$\pm$58 ms	90$\pm$34 ms	7399$\pm$32 ms	19$\pm$17 ms	9886 ms
			Overall: 10184 ms	
			$\pm$580 ms	

Table 2. Migration from reporter into reviewer facet on embedded/mobile devices

Device	CPU	Memory	Migration Time
Embedded System	Strong ARM 233 MHz	256 MB	80±4 s
Handheld (HP Jornada)	Strong ARM 200 MHz	32 MB	230±12 s
Subnotebook (Asus EeePC 4G)	Intel Celeron M 900 Mhz	512 MB	9±0.5 s

current x86-based device (see Table 2). On outdated devices our Apache Axis approach does not perform well, but the measurement on the current device with much more computing power result in better figures. As our concept relies on standard Web service technology, this can be improved even further by optimised Web service containers for small devices.

6 Conclusion and Future Work

In this paper, we proposed a novel infrastructure for self-adaptive migratable Web services. These Web services enable the implementation of UbiComp applications by supporting very flexible adaptation to particular application context (dynamic change of the interface, locally available state and implementation in use). This allows an adaptation of a fully-fledged implementation on a powerful device to a restricted implementation on a resource-limited device. We implemented a prototype for the Apache Axis Web service container. As our system builds on top of standard Web service technology without any modifications, we allow interoperable implementations for other Web service containers as well. However, for supporting coordination and continuous addressing of the SAM-WS clients as well as containers have to support interception of invocations. We prove the feasibility of our approach with a basic reporter example application and performance measurements for different platforms.

For future work, we plan to implement a prototype for another Web service platform. We do not expect interoperability problems, as we designed our infrastructure to only rely on standard Web service technology. For an improved appliance in ubiquitous computing scenarios we will investigate the implementation of our concept using the Java Micro Edition.

Our approach for self-adaptive migratable Web services provides a very flexible concept. This may lead to error-prone applications whenever migrating into unanticipated facets (this may, e.g., result in unavailable state). Therefore, we will examine concepts for defining rules for the specification of allowed migration of Web service facets into other ones. For supporting this specification process we are investigating an MDA-like approach as proposed in our recent work [3].

References

1. Weiser, M.: The computer for the 21st Century. Sci. American 265(3), 66–75 (1991)
2. Kunze, C.P., Zaplata, S., Lamersdorf, W.: Mobile Process Description and Execution. In: Eliassen, F., Montresor, A. (eds.) DAIS 2006. LNCS, vol. 4025, Springer, Heidelberg (2006)

3. Schmidt, H., Hauck, F.J.: SAMProc: Middleware for Self-adaptive Mobile Processes in Heterogeneous Ubiquitous Environments. In: MDS 2007, ACM Press, New York (accepted for publication, 2007)
4. OMG. MDA Guide Version 1.0.1. OMG Doc. omg/2003-06-01 (2003)
5. Hammerschmidt, B.C., Linnemann, V.: Migratable Web Services: Increasing Performance and Privacy in Service Oriented Architectures. IADIS Int. J. on Comp. Sci. and Info. Sys. 1(1), 42–56 (2006)
6. Ishikawa, F., Yoshioka, N., Tahara, Y., Honiden, S.: Mobile Agent System for Web Services Integration in Pervasive Networks. In: IWUC 2004, pp. 38–47 (2004)
7. Kapitza, R., Schmidt, H., Söldner, G., Hauck, F.J.: A Framework for Adaptive Mobile Objects in Heterogeneous Environments. In: Meersman, R., Tari, Z. (eds.) OTM 2006. LNCS, vol. 4276, Springer, Heidelberg (2006)
8. Kapitza, R., Schmidt, H., Bartlang, U., Hauck, F.J.: A Generic Infrastructure for Decentralised Dynamic Loading of Platform-Specific Code. In: Indulska, J., Raymond, K. (eds.) DAIS 2007. LNCS, vol. 4531, Springer, Heidelberg (2007)
9. Erradi, A., Tosic, V., Maheshwari, P.: MASC -.NET-Based Middleware for Adaptive Composite Web Services. In: ICWS 2007, pp. 727–734 (2007)
10. Lange, D.B., Oshima, M.: Programming and Deploying Java Mobile Agents with Aglets. Addison-Wesley, Reading (1998)
11. Kapitza, R., Schmidt, H., Hauck, F.J.: Platform-Independent Object Migration in CORBA. In: Meersman, R., Tari, Z. (eds.) OTM 2005. LNCS, vol. 3760, Springer, Heidelberg (2005)
12. Almeida, J., Wegdam, M., van Sinderen, M., Nieuwenhuis, L.: Transparent Dynamic Reconfiguration for CORBA. In: DOA 2001, IEEE, Los Alamitos (2001)
13. Satoh, I.: Network Processing of Documents, for Documents, by Documents. In: Alonso, G. (ed.) Middleware 2005. LNCS, vol. 3790, pp. 421–430. Springer, Heidelberg (2005)
14. Gong, L.: JXTA: A Network Programming Environment. IEEE Internet Comp. 5(3), 88–95 (2001)

A Model-Driven Approach for Developing Adaptive Software Systems

Thomas Hamann, Gerald Hübsch, and Thomas Springer

Technische Universität Dresden, Department of Computer Science,
Institute for Systems Architecture, Computer Networks Group
{Thomas.Hamann,Gerald.Huebsch,Thomas.Springer}@tu-dresden.de

Abstract. Context-awareness and adaptation are highly interrelated key concepts to build applications for heterogeneous and dynamic execution environments. While gathering, distribution, abstraction, and management of context is examined in research for several years, development of context-aware, adaptive applications, and the relations between context and adaptation are rarely considered. We present a model-driven approach for developing adaptive software. It comprises a design methodology, a set of software engineering artefacts, and a runtime platform for adaptive, multimodal software. Our approach focusses on modelling context information, context providers, and their relations to system functionality and user interface adaptation. We developed an adaptive plant maintenance application to show the feasibility of our methodology.

1 Introduction

Today, mobile and wireless technologies are an integral part of distributed computing environments building up a convergent platform for traditional as well as innovative services and applications. As a consequence new service and application areas are enabled, but also new challenges for application development arise from a mobility induced frequently changing infrastructure and the heterogeneity of: device capabilities; reliability and performance of network connections; user requirements and computing context.

Adaptation and context-awareness are closely interrelated key concepts for software executed in pervasive computing environments. The term adaptation describes the adjustment of a system to specific conditions or changes in its environment. The question to ask is: What is adapted to what? referring to *object* and *target* of the adaptation. Objects from an application's viewpoint are its processed data, communication for data exchange, and internal structure (functional components, their interconnections, and placement). The target of adaptation is the environment (i.e. available resources, user information and preferences, and context of system usage), characterized by *context information* (or short: context), which represents information about the state and changes of the environment.

A typical example illustrating the need for adaptation is an adaptive plant maintenance application. Maintenance workers have to visit the plant locations

R. Meier and S. Terzis (Eds.): DAIS 2008, LNCS 5053, pp. 196–209, 2008.

to carry out their tasks. In this scenario, workers as well as management could benefit from adapting mobile and wireless technologies. Mobile workers could access location and task information or construction documents for particular plant equipment while being connected to a wireless network. Accessed data as well as its presentation could be adapted to the capabilities of the devices a worker is using and to the environmental conditions (e.g. selecting relevant document parts only for reducing the amount of transferred data or choosing the interaction modalities according to available modalities and ambient noise and light conditions). Moreover, application functionality could be reduced according to the processing power and storage capacity of the used device. The other way around, the management could track mobile worker's positions, capture their current activity and situation, to dispatch incoming service requests to a worker (a) with an empty task queue, (b) nearby the requesting customer or (c) with appropriate expertise.

This paper is organized as follows: Related work is discussed in section 2. Section 3 introduces our adaptive software design methodology. While section 4 discusses its major artefacts representing tasks, application data, and context. These models are refined over various abstraction levels and are transformed into code. The runtime environment for execution of the latter is described in section 5. After a prototype-based validation of our approach in section 6 we conclude the paper with a summary of our ideas and an outlook to future work.

2   Related Work

The presented approach has relations to several research domains. Beside the concept of model-driven development, especially the definition of domain-specific languages and approaches for developing adaptive applications in conjunction with concepts for context-awareness are relevant.

The modelling of context considered in adaptation processes and the adoption of a context middleware service are addressed in many research projects during the last years. Recent projects [11,5] covered the creation of comprehensive and generic context models with the goal of identifying and integrating characteristics of context. Especially, ontology-based modelling is addressed [3,7,4] with focus on knowledge sharing and reasoning. In [3,7], approaches for defining a common context vocabulary based on a hierarchy of ontologies are described. An upper ontology defines general terms while domain-specific ontologies define the details for certain application domains. Both approaches use a centralized architecture and work on local scenarios from the smart home or intelligent spaces domain. Furthermore, implications of modelling for context service design, integration of heterogeneous context sources and distribution support are not addressed. In our approach we adopt ontologies for modelling context information, but the major focus of our models is to create a common basis for context providers and context consumers. Especially, a dynamic discovery and binding of context providers should be supported. Moreover, the models are used for generating code for context access.

Besides modelling and integration issues, architectural aspects are considered. Current context-aware systems are mostly centralized. Thus mobile clients either rely on a server providing them with context or gather required context on their own. The Java Context Aware Framework (JCAF) [1] is a Java-based approach for a generic context middleware service. Service components communicate in a peer-to-peer manner with support of an event-based notification mechanism. Nexus [6] deals with the efficient management of heterogeneous context information in large-scale infrastructures. Especially scalability is addressed by a federated context middleware and special-purpose servers for optimized management of large amounts of context. Moreover, approaches like [9] and [10] concentrate on the abstraction process of context and the integration of sensing devices. Our context service as part of a runtime environment follows a peer-to-peer approach. It adopts concepts from architecture and abstraction but is based on the abstraction of context providers which can be hierarchically organized to derive more abstract context.

Our modelling approach is based on the concepts of Model-Driven Architecture (MDA) and UML. As abstract view to our applications we use a task model. Its basic classes are adopted from an approach described in [15]. User interaction modelling builds on concepts developed for device-independent [8,17] or multimodal user interfaces [2,12].

3   Design Methodology for Adaptive, Multimodal Applications

Development of adaptive software involves interrelated steps, which require specific expertise provided by different developers. According to the model-driven software development approach, these steps are carried on models of different abstraction layers. Hence, the development process are performed by developers acting in different roles that must be coordinated. Our approach is embedded into a design methodology (cf. 1), which defines a set of artefacts (mainly models), developer roles and a process model, to coordinate the development process.

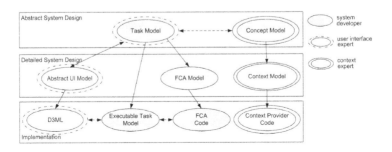

Fig. 1. Design methodology for adaptive, multimodal systems

The development process starts with a *requirements analysis*. Focusing on requirements concerning system functionality and user interaction as well as their adaptation this phase lays the foundation for later system specification.

In the *abstract system design* phase two models are created. The *task model* specifies control and data flow as well as temporal relationships between tasks. Whereas, the *concept model* comprises the application data and knowledge, including context relevant for adaptation of the system. The task model refers to the concept model for the definition of application data, input and output parameters as well as for involving context for adaptation.

Both models are transformed into the models of the next development phase – the *detailed system design*. Depending on their nature tasks are either transformed into the *Abstract UI model (AUI)* or the *Functional Core Adapter model (FCA)*. Context-related concepts from the concept model are transformed into the *context model* for specification of context provision based on context providers.

The detailed system design models are used for code generation in the *implementation phase*. All code is generated toward a well defined runtime environment, which is part of the presented solution. It contains a task execution engine, a user interface engine, and a context infrastructure. The *executable task model* is derived from the task model. It governs the control and data flow of the application and it refers to *D3ML* representations of the interaction tasks and *FCA code*, for executing tasks respectively. It also calls to the *context provider code* that is generated from the context model to access context for adapting user interactions and control flow. The corresponding context providers are managed by the context service at runtime.

We assume that the roles of a *system developer*, a *user interface expert*, and an *context expert* are necessary to perform all steps of our development methodology. While the task and concept models can be designed by a system developer, special expertise is needed to consider the requirements for adaptation and the relations to context in that design phase. Since refinement of the AUI model and D3ML code comprises multimodal interaction as well as user interface adaptation, this is the responsibility of a user interface expert. The creation and refinement of the context model and the context provider code is the task of the context expert, for the latter requires detailed knowledge of the underlying context service.

4 Models

Models are the formal basis to capture software design at a conceptual level. Just like UML is tailored to the specific requirements of object-oriented software design, dedicated models are needed to account for the peculiarities of adaptive software. We have devised a set of five models to enable modelling of all aspects that are necessary to create task-driven, adaptive multimodal applications. They can be used to model the interrelated aspects of domain modelling (concept model), context provision (context model) and context consumption in the form of application logic (task model, functional core adapter model) and adaptive multimodal user interfaces (abstract user interface model) – sections 4.1 to 4.5.

Following the philosophy of model-driven software-engineering, the models support the range from a highly abstract level down to generated code as the most concrete level. Transitions between the different levels are implemented as model-to-model and model-to-code transformations – based on MOF QVT [14] or JET [16]. Technology independence is achieved across all models and levels of abstraction.

4.1   Concept Model

The common base of all models is represented by the concept model. It allows for modelling of application data and knowledge based on ontologies. Therefore the Ontology Definition Metamodel (ODM) [13] was chosen for integrating the Web Ontology Language (OWL) into object-oriented design. Thus application developers can rely on the expressiveness of XML Schema, RDFS, RDF, and OWL-DL when modelling data that is being processed in and presented by software.

Furthermore the model may contain contextual concepts and their data types, which might be relevant for adaptivity. This allows for two major advantages: (1) uniform modelling of application data and context knowledge, and (2) paving the way for logic-based reasoning over context.

4.2   Task Model

In our approach, we use a task model to express the dynamic aspects of adaptive applications from both the user and the system perspective. Following the approach presented in [15], our task model features three task types. *User Tasks* are performed solely by the user (e.g. perceiving and evaluating system output). *Interaction Tasks* represent interactions between the user and the application via a user interface. Their complexity can vary from entering a simple piece of information, e.g. a single numeric value, to complex tasks such as editing a plant maintenance report. *System Tasks* are performed entirely by application logic (e.g. validating the maintenance report and storing it in a database).

The temporal relationship between tasks is modelled by directed edges that represent the control flow. They are triggered when a system task completes or when the user completes an interaction task. Control flow parallelism is modelled by Fork, Merge and Join Nodes. Data transport to and from tasks is modelled by object flows. Like control flows, object flows are directed edges between tasks. They transport concepts defined in the concept model (see section 4.1) and are connected to tasks by input and output pins (cf. 2).

Context-awareness is supported by three novel concepts that we have introduced in task modelling. These concepts are *event consumers*, *context queries* and *guard conditions*.

Event consumers represent event subscriptions in the task model. By event consumers, subscriptions to the following two types of events can be modelled.

Context events are issued by context providers. They allow push access to context. For example, a context provider may trigger an event when a sensed temperature exceeds a critical value. *Observer events* allow monitoring state changes of concepts. Whenever a change occurs, an observer event is triggered. It conveys the new state to subscribed tasks. Due to the abstraction introduced by the concept model, the origin of the state change is not visible to the tasks, allowing homogeneous processing of observer events. For example, an observer event may be thrown when a system task updates a concept by writing the result of a calculation or when the value sensed by a context sensor changes.

Tasks can consume events in two ways. Event consumers can be bound to a system task by a control flow. In this case, the system task has the role of an event handler. When the subscribed event occurs, a new instance of the system task is created and its execution is started. Event consumers that are subscribed to observer events can be connected to input pins via an object flow. Upon an observer event, the value of the input pin is updated with the new state of the observed concept.

Whenever context must be fetched by an application, means to actively pull information from the concept model are needed. In our task model, these means are provided by concept queries. A concept query is bound to a concept in the concept model and connects to a task via an object flow and an input pin. The task can access the value of the input pin regardless of the data sources bound to the input pin.

Guard conditions can be bound to control flows and object flows that originate from event consumers. Guard conditions are formulated over concepts. In case of control flows, the control is passed to a task only if the guard condition of the control flow is fulfilled. Using identical modelling techniques, control flows can therefore be controlled by context and application data. For example, assume that the number of records stored in a database is modelled as a concept. A guard condition that requires the number of records in the database to be zero can prevent the invocation of a system task that deletes the database if it contains any records.

Guard conditions bound to object flows that originate from event consumers serve as filters for observer events. They can be formulated over the concept transported by the observer event. If the guard condition is not fulfilled, the observer event does not update the value of the input pin.

Fig. 2 shows the novel modelling concepts for context-aware task modelling in a task model consisting of two interaction tasks (InteractionTask1, InteractionTask2) and two system tasks (SystemTask1, SystemTask2). User tasks are omitted for reasons of brevity. InteractionTask1 and InteractionTask2 can be interacted order independent. SystemTask2 is the event handler for the context event consumer bound to it. An observer event consumer for the numeric concept SensedValue is connected to InteractionTask2. The guard condition filters out all events with negative or zero values of SensedValue, i.e. only positive values of SensedValue are written to the input pin of InteractionTask2. The InteractionTask2 can only be completed by the user if the value of the concept SensedValue is larger than ten.

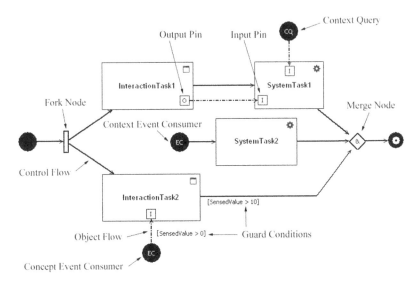

Fig. 2. Task model

4.3   Abstract User Interface Model

The abstract user interface model (AUI) allows modelling abstract multimodal user interfaces based on abstract interactors as proposed in [2] and [12]. These are representation- and technology-independent descriptions of user interface widgets. They are composed to complex abstract user interfaces, which can be transformed into multiple, technology-specific representations, including versions for different modalities. In most cases, technology independence alone is not sufficient to create highly usable user interfaces from abstract user interfaces. For this reason, AUI refinements that take the context in which a user interface presented into account are needed [8].

In our approach, AUI refinement is based on the concept of manual adaptation to so called *context profiles*. A context profile is a list of name-value pairs that characterize a complex condition (a *situation*) in terms of device properties, built-in sensors, and available input and output mechanisms. Fig. 3 shows two context profiles. The *PDA* profile describes a device whose keyboard, display, microphone, and speaker can be utilized for user interaction. The keyboard must be thumb keyboard with English layout. The display must have QVGA resolution, which is typical for most PDAs, and landscape format. Audio output can be via earphone or speaker. The *Hands-Free/PDA* profile describes a typical hands-free situation in which the keyboard can not be used for input. The display must have QVGA resolution in portrait format.

Context profiles can be bound to refined versions of the *initial AUI model*. The initial AUI model is generated by a task-to-AUI transformation of interaction tasks. For each interaction task, a generic AUI interactor is generated.

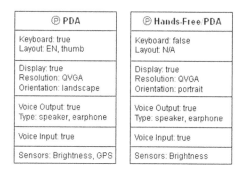

Fig. 3. Context profiles

Fig. 4 shows the transformation of a login dialog task model and the initial AUI model to which it is transformed.

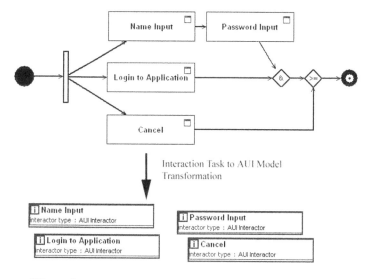

Fig. 4. Interaction task to initial AUI model transformation

AUI refinement is performed on copies of the initial AUI model. The developer binds each copy to at least one context profile and starts its refinement process. In this process, concrete interactor types (text input field, select control, button, ...) must be assigned to the generic interactors generated by the task-to-AUI transformation. Furthermore, layouts for an appropriate visual appearance of the user interface in the situation described by the context profile can be added (cf. 5). Interactors can also be removed from a refined model if they are inappropriate for the situation, e.g. if the device does not support its rendering. Modality-specific properties like voice input grammars, voice prompts, etc. can be set as properties of a concrete AUI interactor where applicable.

(a)   (b)

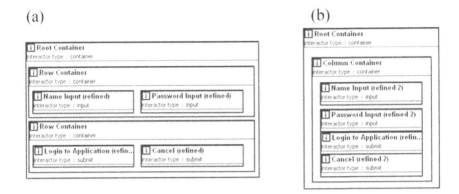

Fig. 5. Refined AUI models of the login dialog for (a) landscape and (b) portrait displays

At runtime, evaluation of context profiles is performed by the context service to select the appropriate version of the user interface. A context profile is transformed into a context query, which is evaluated against a concept that describes the properties of the execution environment. This concept is added automatically to every concept model.

4.4   Functional Core Adapter Model

Besides enhancing the two particular aspects task and user interface a more generic way exists for achieving context-awareness of the designed software. This means is provided by the model representing the functional core adapter (FCA) – the interface to the business logic of the software.

The FCA model provides two element types – *FCA methods* and *FCA calls*. Methods contain the mapping to methods of the business logic, including their arguments and results. Calls are instantiations of those methods and therefore refer to the methods.

4.5   Context Model

Building upon the concept model as common ground the context model refers to its conceptual facet only. Subject of this model is the provision of context. A variety of context sources exists all differing in retrieval, storage, and presentation of their information. Hiding that heterogeneity the sources are described in a uniform way – as so-called context providers – to allow for matching with potential context consumers.

The context model describes the various types of context providers, which may be of two different kind – low- or high-level. Low-level providers that retrieve sensed, profiled or stored context directly from a hardware or software context source (e.g. sensor, monitor, database) can be described by characterizing their provided context. Thus the data types and concept from the concept model are referred to by the context model. High-level providers apply various derivation schemes for retrieving their provided context and thus must consume other context prior to the derivation of more abstract (or high-level) context. Therefore high-level providers need additional description of their consumed context.

5   Runtime Environment

The afore mentioned modelling concepts are mapped onto our runtime environment, which is targeted toward resource-constraint mobile and embedded devices – implemented in Java ME (CDC 1.1) based on the OSGi platform. Its main components are: task process engine, context service, and multimodal services component (cf. 6). For brevity reasons we focus on the context service only.

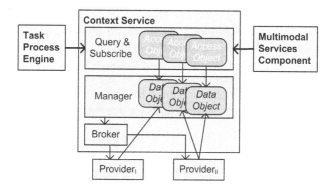

Fig. 6. Runtime architecture – main components

The context service provides on-demand access to context. Service instances running on different devices connect to each other and form a distributed context service. Thus, allowing for context access between sources and consumers – the adaptive software – even on different devices.

Context propagated from the sources to the consumers is represented based on a metamodel [13], which is adopted from the topic map and entity-relationship metamodels. It defines three model element types: *Entities* represent either real-world objects or abstract concepts (e.g. a process). *Attributes* contain the specific features of the entities and can be of simple or structured type – arranged in so-called *attribute groups*. *Associations* are relationships between two entities.

The different facets of designtime context models are reflected in the runtime too. There are context, data, and usage models. Provided and consumed context is specified by so-called context patterns each of them being a triple (m, t, r) with: a meta type m (entity, attribute, or association), a domain-specific type t, and an optional restrictive expression r. The pattern $(ENTITY,'person','')$ would refer to all entities of type 'person' without any restriction.

Runtime Context Model: For uniform management each context source is wrapped in a so-called context provider – a lightweight component with uniform interface. Due to the nature of its underlying context source (e.g. wireless sensor, database, application) a provider may be subject to software de-/installation, plug-and-play, or wireless connectivity problems and thus dynamically available.

A provider is self-descriptive since a single service instance cannot be expected to a priori "know" all potential providers that may be encountered during its life cycle. Upon detection a provider is examined by the broker component using the provider API to retrieve its description. The main part of this description consists of the provided and consumed context, each represented by a set of context patterns.

Runtime Usage Model: Context consumers specify their needs by using context patterns too. They are passed as call parameters to the Query & Subscribe API resulting in either synchronous responses or asynchronous notifications – both containing references to the current context.

The context usages of the task, AUI, and FCA models are implicitly contained in the context patterns and the specific API calls performed by the respective code at runtime. In figure 6 this is shown by the arrow from the task process engine and the multimodal services component accessing the Query & Subscribe component.

Runtime Data Model: Since the context service is executed on resource-constraint devices it does without expensive model validation mechanisms. Instead the service performs a matching algorithm based on consumed and provided context patterns. This matching is applied for binding suitable providers when a consumer specifies a pattern in an API call.

Java classes exist corresponding to all data types defined in the concept model – either by mapping to native Java classes or by generating application-specific ones. The dynamic availability of providers applies to their provided context too. Instead of caching context we opted to decouple the information access in order to prevent consumption of stale context. Therefore, context is kept in data objects that are hidden from the consumers by access objects. The latter are maintained by the Query & Subscribe component whereas the former are updated by the providers, while being created by the manager component.

When the provider of a certain data object becomes unavailable subsequent consumer calls to its access object will cause the binding to an alternative provider. When this is unsuccessful the consumer receives an according notification.

6   Validation

We have successfully validated our approach by developing a context-aware plant maintenance application. This application consists of three tools that (a) support

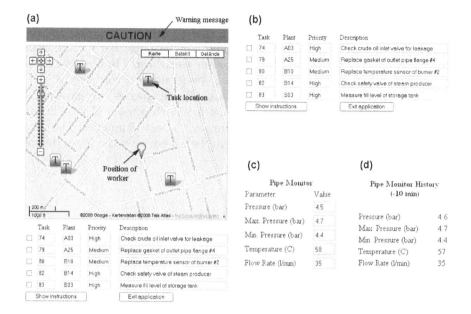

Fig. 7. Screen shots of the plant maintenance application: (a) task organization tool, (b) task organization tool without location context, (c) sensor monitoring tool, (d) sensor history tool

maintenance workers in organizing their work and (b) allow the remote monitoring of plant parameters and (c) their history. It exploits all features of context-aware software design provided by our models.

The task organization tool (cf. 7a) demonstrates the use of location information and UI adaptation. In our scenario, a list of tasks is assigned to a maintenance worker by his manager. A maintenance task is composed of information about the location (name and geo-coordinates of the plant) where the task is to be performed, its priority, a short description, and list of detailed instructions. This information is conveyed by a warning message area, an electronic map, and a task list. Symbols in the map indicate the task locations. Observer events generated by a location context provider, which wraps the GPS sensor of the PDA running the application, are utilized to update the marker that indicates the worker's position on the map (cf. 7a). The warning message area is updated from "OK" to "CAUTION" whenever the worker is in the proximity of plants that process inflammable or explosive substances. This update is initiated by observer events that are produced by a remote context provider that consumes the output of the location context provider and determines the hazard classification of the area around that geo-coordinate.

UI adaptation is demonstrated in fig. 7b. When location information is not available, e.g. because there is no GPS signal or because the PDA is not equipped with a GPS sensor, a reduced UI of the task organization tool is loaded. It omits the map and the warning message area since they require location information.

Several components of a plant are monitored by sensors. A sample remote monitoring tool (Pipe Monitor, cf. 7c) aggregating pressure, temperature and flow rate information from a hot water pipe has been realized for validation purposes. The values shown by the Pipe Monitor are delivered by observer events from corresponding sensors and update the system output accordingly.

To demonstrate pull access to context via context queries, we have implemented sensor history providers for the pipe monitor's sensors. Sensor history providers can be queried for the sensor readings of the last 15 minutes. The query results returned by the history providers can be accessed by the Pipe Monitor History tool (cf. 7d).

7   Conclusion and Outlook

We have presented a software development methodology for adaptive, multimodal applications. It comprises a process model, a set of models and transformations and a runtime environment. Especially, we presented a concept for modelling system and user interface adaptation based on context. Thus, with our approach, the relation between context and adaptation processes is explicitly definable. Using a model-driven approach, these definitions can be transformed semi-automatically into code, which significantly eases the development of adaptive software. Our validation example has demonstrated the feasibility of the approach presenting a context-aware application able to adapt its functionality and user interaction to the execution environment. Therefore, we have involved several context sources, which are managed by a peer-to-peer context service.

In the future we will extend the existing methodology and development environment. Furthermore, we plan to implement further applications to validate how our model-driven approach can reduce development effort.

References

1. Bardram, J.E.: The Java Context Awareness Framework (JCAF) – a service infrastructure and programming framework for context-aware applications. In: Gellersen, H.-W., Want, R., Schmidt, A. (eds.) PERVASIVE 2005. LNCS, vol. 3468, pp. 98–115. Springer, Heidelberg (2005)
2. Burmeister, R., Pohl, C., Bublitz, S., Hugues, P.: Snow - a multimodal approach for mobile maintenance applications. In: 15th IEEE International Workshops on Enabling Technologies: Infrastructure for Collaborative Enterprises, pp. 131–136 (2006)
3. Chen, H., Finin, T., Joshi, A.: An ontology for context-aware pervasive computing environments (2003)
4. Christopoulou, E., Goumopoulos, C., Kameas, A.: An ontology-based context management and reasoning process for ubicomp applications. In: sOc-EUSAI 2005: Proceedings of the 2005 joint conference on Smart objects and ambient intelligence, pp. 265–270. ACM Press, New York (2005)

5. Fuchs, F., Hochstatter, I., Krause, M., Berger, M.: A meta-model approach to context information. In: Proceedings of Third IEEE International Conference on Pervasive Computing and Communications Workshops, pp. 8–14. Cambridge University Press, Cambridge (2005)
6. Grossmann, M., Bauer, M., Hönle, N., Käppeler, U.-P., Nicklas, D., Schwarz, T.: Efficiently managing context information for large-scale scenarios. In: Proceedings of the 3rd IEEE Conference on Pervasive Computing and Communications, Kauai Island, Hawaii (March 2005)
7. Gu, T., Pung, H.K., Zhang, D.Q.: Toward an osgi-based infrastructure for context-aware applications. IEEE Pervasive Computing 3(4), 66–74 (2004)
8. Hübsch, G., Springer, T., Spriestersbach, A., Ziegert, T.: An Integrated Platform for Mobile, Context-Aware, and Adaptive Enterprise Applications, pp. 1105–1124. Physica-Verlag (2005)
9. Henricksen, K., Indulska, J., McFadden, T., Balasubramaniam, S.: Middleware for distributed context-aware systems. In: Meersman, R., Tari, Z. (eds.) OTM 2005. LNCS, vol. 3760, pp. 846–863. Springer, Heidelberg (2005)
10. Korpipää, P., Mäntyjärvi, J., Kela, J., Kernen, H., Malm, E.-J.: Managing context information in mobile devices. IEEE Pervasive Computing 2(3), 42–51 (2003)
11. Livingstone, K.H.S., Indulska, J.: Towards a hybrid approach to context modelling, reasoning and interoperation. In: Ubi-Comp 1st International Workshop on Advanced Context Modelling, Reasoning and Management, pp. 54–61 (2004)
12. Mueller, W., Schaefer, R., Bleul, S.: Interactive multimodal user interfaces for mobile devices, page 90286.1 (2004)
13. Object Management Group, Inc. Ontology definition metamodel. OMG Adopted Specification ptc/2007-09-09, OMG (November 2007)
14. Object Management Group, Inc. MOF QVT. Final Adopted Specification ptc/05-11-01, OMG (November 2005)
15. Paterno, F., Mancini, C., Meniconi, S.: ConcurTaskTrees: A diagrammatic notation for specifying task models. In: INTERACT 1997: Proceedings of the IFIP TC13 International Conference on Human-Computer Interaction, London, pp. 362–369. Chapman and Hall, Ltd., Boca Raton (1997)
16. Popma, R.: JET tutorial part 1 (introduction to jet). Technical report, Azzurri Ltd. (2003)
17. Ziegert, T., Lauff, M., Heuser, L.: Device independent web applications – the author once - display everywhere approach. In: Koch, N., Fraternali, P., Wirsing, M. (eds.) ICWE 2004. LNCS, vol. 3140, pp. 244–255. Springer, Heidelberg (2004)

Model-Based Performance Instrumentation of Distributed Applications

Jan Schaefer[1,2], Jeanne Stynes[2], and Reinhold Kroeger[1]

[1] Wiesbaden University of Applied Sciences
Distributed Systems Lab
Kurt-Schumacher-Ring 18, D-65197 Wiesbaden, Germany
{jan.schaefer,kroeger}@informatik.fh-wiesbaden.de
[2] Cork Institute of Technology
Department of Computing
Rossa Avenue, Bishopstown, Cork, Ireland
jeanne.stynes@cit.ie

Abstract. Problems such as inconsistent or erroneous instrumentation often plague applications whose source code is manually instrumented during the implementation phase. Integrating performance instrumentation capabilities into the *Model Driven Software Development* (MDSD) process would greatly assist software engineers who do not have detailed knowledge of source code instrumentation technologies. This paper presents an approach that offers instrumentation support to software designers and developers. A collection of instrumentation patterns is defined to represent typical instrumentation scenarios for distributed applications. A UML profile derived from these patterns is then used to annotate UML models. Based on suitable code generation templates, the annotated models are transformed into instrumented source code for different instrumentation APIs. A prototypical implementation, including an adaptation to Web services, was evaluated in a lab environment.

1 Introduction

In recent years, *Model Driven Software Development* (MDSD) has become increasingly popular[1] because several MDSD tools have reached a sufficient level of maturity. In MDSD, code generators are used to generate application source code from technical models based on transformation templates. Using this approach, source code for specific types of platforms and applications can be created efficiently. Today, several Open Source MDSD code generator frameworks are available and used in professional projects, in particular *AndroMDA*[2] and *openArchitectureWare*[3] have become popular in recent years. Because of diverse application requirements, extensions containing specific templates and UML profiles for these frameworks are constantly being developed. So far, these extensions

---

[1] http://www.voelter.de/data/articles/cgn.pdf
[2] http://www.andromda.org
[3] http://www.openarchitectureware.org

R. Meier and S. Terzis (Eds.): DAIS 2008, LNCS 5053, pp. 210–223, 2008.

cover mainly middleware infrastructure aspects (e.g. for EJB, CORBA, Spring, Hibernate). Extensions supporting mandatory application management aspects like security and performance are still rare.

Performance is an important aspect of applications, even more so in heterogeneous distributed systems. Thus, continuous performance tests, performance validation – especially after modifications or redesigns – and *Service Level Management* (SLM) at runtime are necessary tasks during the lifecycle of applications. This can be achieved by applying *Performance Instrumentation*, which can be defined as the process of adding non-functional code to an application to provide performance analysis information at runtime.

Instrumentation is usually performed during the implementation and testing phases, when software developers analyse the application's source code. Once relevant positions have been identified (e.g. based on their importance for the application), instrumentation statements are inserted into the source code. Manual instrumentation always carries the potential of errors or unwanted side-effects: the instrumentation might be incomplete, too detailed (and therefore slow down the application) or too sparse. Tools supporting developers during the instrumentation process greatly reduce the probability that these common mistakes will occur. More importantly, enhanced tool support removes the developers' need to acquire detailed knowledge of the applied instrumentation technology before the instrumentation process is carried out.

An instrumentation has to be integrated with the underlying application architecture, which can become a time-consuming and difficult task if the performance aspect is not considered until the end of the development process. Unfortunately this occurs frequently even though application performance and responsiveness are major acceptance factors for end users. Once applications are deployed or have evolved over time, there may exist immobile technical or architectural dependencies that must be observed if monitoring capabilities or performance-related changes have to be implemented. Such dependencies can be avoided by implementing performance monitoring capabilities as early as possible, preferably before the first pieces of source code are written. In this paper, logging and performance measurements (e.g. execution times of work units) are considered as the primary goals of performance instrumentation.

Based on Pooley's definition [1] of *Software Performance Engineering*, a performance engineering process integrating instrumentation with the MDSD methodology can be defined as follows: UML application models are annotated with an UML instrumentation profile. The resulting annotated models are transformed into instrumented source code using specific templates developed for a MDSD framework. This enables software designers to define performance monitoring capabilities in UML application models during the design phase without detailed knowledge of the instrumentation technologies that are used in the generated code. If standardised instrumentation APIs such as *log4j*[4] and *Application Response Measurement*[5] (ARM) are targeted during code generation,

---

[4] http://logging.apache.org/log4j
[5] http://www.opengroup.org/arm

the runtime performance data produced by the instrumented application can be processed easily by enterprise management systems such as *IBM Tivoli*[6] or *HP Business Technology Optimization Software*[7]. Therefore, the focus of this paper is on modelling and transformation of performance annotations.

This introduction is followed by a presentation of the state of the art in application performance instrumentation in section 2. Section 3 introduces the unique instrumentation approach developed for this paper. A performance engineering process incorporating this approach is presented in section 4, followed by its prototypical implementation in section 5 and a case study in section 6. This paper closes with a conclusion and a look at possible future work in section 7.

2   Related Work

Instrumentation can be required and performed during almost any phase of an application's lifecycle. This section introduces common approaches to software-based instrumentation that support developers in the process.

Apart from the risk of erroneous instrumentation, manual source code instrumentation can lead to a possibly unwanted mixture of functional (business logic) and non-functional (instrumentation) source code. Thus, instrumentation approaches using *Aspect-Oriented Programming* (AOP), where no instrumentation code has to be written repeatedly once templates are created, have been implemented in recent years [2] [3]. However, aspect compilers such as *AspectJ* which are used by these approaches often support granularity at method invocation level only. Another drawback is the lack of correlation functionality (i.e., the absence of facilities for semantically related instrumentation points to reference each other). This is not a problem for independent logging instrumentation but, especially in distributed systems, end-to-end monitoring based on related measurements can be mandatory to track requests on their way through complex workflows. Also, current AOP-based instrumentation approaches can be used only from the implementation phase on.

Binary code instrumentation is necessary if the source code of the to be instrumented application is not available or must not be modified. This approach is often used in conjunction with the Java programming language [4], because Java offers standardised interfaces for modifications to bytecode even at runtime (e.g. engaging bytecode running in the *Java Virtual Machine* (JVM) [5] [6]). Although arbitrary positions in binary code can be addressed in general, this instrumentation approach suffers from similar limitations as AOP. Correlation facilities are not provided, and obviously this approach can only be used if binary code for the targeted application already exists. The abstraction ability of binary code (or machine code for that matter) is too limited because it is supposed to be a concrete (platform-specific) implementation of the application.

In recent years, the need for instrumentation led to the development of middleware frameworks that already contain fixed instrumentation capabilities as

---

[6] http://www.ibm.com/software/tivoli
[7] http://www.managementsoftware.hp.com

developed by the vendor. For example, IBM instrumented[8] their *DB2 Universal Database*[9] (version 8.2 or later) and *WebSphere Application Server*[10] (version 5.1.1.1 or later). And starting with Java 5, even the standard edition JVM contains *Java Management Extensions*[11] (JMX), which support state monitoring of applications at runtime.

Another approach suited to instrumenting framework-based client/server applications uses the widely supported *message handler* framework (also known as *interceptor* or *listener* framework). It is part of the CORBA [7] and *Java API for XML Web Services* (JAX-WS) [8] specifications and supported by application servers such as the *Apache Tomcat*[12] and *JBoss*[13] application servers. This approach relies on instrumented components that are plugged into the frameworks by configuration transparently to the application [9] [10]. This approach can even be combined with legacy middleware technologies if supported by a connector such as an *Enterprise Service Bus* (ESB).

All these instrumentation alternatives cannot be integrated with the MDSD process because they do not feature modelling capabilities. However, several approaches for integrating performance aspects with UML models have been developed. The definition of the *UML Profile for Schedulability, Performance, and Time*[14] (UML-SPT, now known as MARTE) sparked a vast collection of research projects with the intention to implement the SPE requirements [11]. So far, work based on the UML-SPT primarily focussed on systems with strict timing and performance constraints (e.g. real-time systems). The process of creating a complete application model with performance annotations for each component can become very time-consuming. Nevertheless, this is common practice, especially for developing embedded systems. This design detail may be mandatory for simulating and validating system properties prior to implementation [12], but it removes the advantage of relieving developers during the instrumentation process if the supporting solution increases the modelling effort drastically. In addition, the modelling effort required for complying with the UML-SPT is greater than what is required for basic application monitoring.

Performance prediction is based on models like *Petri Nets* [13] [14], *Queueing Models* or *Markov Chains* [15] [16]. These approaches focus on stochastic methods for predicting qualitative (correctness) and quantitative (performance) applications properties or even complex systems. Pooley proposes generating such models from UML models, which is used seldom in a traditional software development process as software designers and developers are usually unfamiliar with this task. Furthermore, in order to be of practical relevance, queueing models have to be calibrated based on runtime measurement data, which must be

---

[8] http://www.ibmsystemsmag.com/i5/june05/features/9060p3.aspx
[9] http://www.ibm.com/db2
[10] http://www.ibm.com/websphere
[11] http://java.sun.com/javase/technologies/core/mntr-mgmt/javamanagement
[12] http://tomcat.apache.org
[13] http://www.jboss.org/products/jbossas
[14] http://www.omg.org/technology/documents/formal/schedulability.htm

collected using some sort of monitoring anyway [17]. If the sample data used for this purpose is too limited or generally inappropriate, the results of the subsequent analysis will not reflect the real system behaviour. Thus, queueing models cannot replace but can complement a concrete instrumentation.

3   Model-Based Performance Instrumentation

As mentioned in section 1, this paper focuses on the integration of logging and performance measurement capabilities with the MDSD process. This section presents the approach to integrate an abstract representation of instrumentation information with application models.

3.1   Instrumentation Patterns

Figure 1 presents a service invocation as an instrumentation scenario example which could be instrumented by defining two related execution time measurements. The server-side measurement corresponds to the execution time of the service ($t_{2\rightarrow3}$), the client-side measurement represents the response time visible to the client ($t_{1\rightarrow4}$). If these measurements were linked, they would allow an analysis of execution and response time of each processed request.

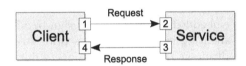

Fig. 1. Instrumentation Scenario

This paper defines a collection of *Instrumentation Patterns* representing abstract instrumentation scenarios. By referring to this pattern collection, software designers can determine possible instrumentation scenarios in their application models. The pattern collection offers additional guidance to designers because the relationships between determined instrumentation points might not always be recognisable.

The pattern collection can be split into two groups: *Basic Patterns* and *Complex Patterns* [18]. Basic patterns are the building blocks of complex patterns. In addition to the patterns introduced in this paper, new patterns can be defined based on either basic or complex patterns.

Instrumentation points and their purpose are described in more detail by their *Role* in a pattern. Each pattern defines a set of roles detailing the responsibilities of the associated points (e.g. instrumentation points can take either "start" or "stop" role in a measurement). An instrumentation point can be part of multiple basic patterns, which themselves can be part of multiple complex patterns.

The instrumentation of an application – the collection of all its pattern instances – can be seen as a directed graph: instrumentation points are vertices of this graph and their connecting edges can be annotated to further describe the relationships between the instrumentation points. A pattern (a subgraph) is described by one (basic pattern) or more (complex pattern) tuples. Basic instrumentation patterns describe simple workflow elements that can occur in applications. Figure 2 displays the three basic patterns defined by this paper.

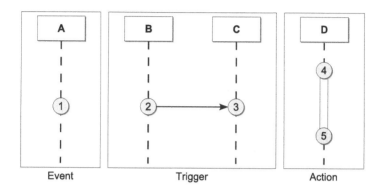

Fig. 2. Basic Instrumentation Patterns

The *Event Pattern* is the simplest instrumentation pattern. It is used for defining single, unrelated instrumentation points. Thus, it is usually represented by a log or status message (see example A in figure 2). The name of the only role in this pattern is *source*, because the point in this pattern is the source of the event.

The *Trigger Pattern* defines an event that sets off an arbitrary number of other events. A triggered event is causally dependent on its trigger event. The trigger event and the triggered event can be processed by a single system component or by multiple (distributed) components. `Triggers` support synchronous and asynchronous application execution scenarios. (see example B/C in figure 2). The are two roles in this pattern: *activator* and *receiver*. A trigger event also can be blocked (e.g. in a queue).

The *Action Pattern* defines two related `Events` (a start and a stop `Event`) which are processed by a single system component or a pair of related components. An `Action` spans a certain period of an application's execution time (see example D in figure 2) and can be seen as a specialisation of the `Trigger` pattern. The `Action` pattern also has two roles, namely *start* and *stop*.

The *RPC Pattern* shown in figure 3 is an example of a complex pattern. [19] contains a more detailed description of the pattern collection including the *Multitrigger* and *Sequence* patterns. The RPC pattern represents a synchronous or asynchronous message exchange. The activities on client and server component can be seen as related work units. Thus, the server-side activity is semantically nested in the client-side activity. This describes a classic *Remote Procedure Call*

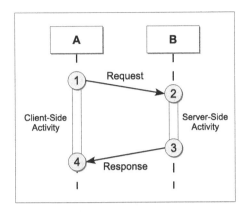

Fig. 3. RPC Pattern

(RPC) interaction in which server activities are triggered by client invocations. This pattern is a composition of four basic patterns: two `Actions` (*client-side activity* and *server-side activity*) and two `Triggers` (*request* and *response*).

3.2 UML Instrumentation Profile

The abstract graphical pattern representation must be mapped to appropriate UML entities to enable software designers to use these patterns in application models. The *UML Instrumentation Profile* shown in figure 4 represents a mapping of the patterns introduced in section 3.1 to UML. The stereotypes in this profile contain abstract instrumentation information required for logging and performance measurements.

The abstract *Pattern* stereotype contains shared tagged values, which are required by all basic and complex instrumentation patterns. The `id` attribute (or tagged value) contains a unique (human-readable) name of the *Instrumentation Entity*, which can be either a point or a pattern. The `id` can be used to name the

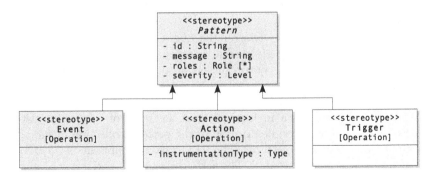

Fig. 4. Basic instrumentation stereotypes

entity. The `message` attribute contains a message describing the entity. Depending on the instrumentation APIs provided by the code generator, the `message` might reemerge in the generated instrumentation code. `roles` is an enumeration literal containing the role(s) that an entity takes in patterns (see section 3.1). The role merely can be used to supply additional detail to instrumented entities which allows the code generator to generate specific instrumentation code (e.g. for a selected middleware platform). The `severity` is also an enumeration literal and defines the importance level of the output of this instrumented entity. Based on the common features of today's logging frameworks, the abstract pattern supports the levels `Info`, `Debug`, `Warn`, `Error`, `Fatal` and `Trace`. The default importance level is set to `Debug`.

The *Event* stereotype does not introduce additional tagged values. It can be attached to UML operations. During code generation, the `Event` is typically implemented by a logging statement.

The *Action* stereotype introduces an additional tagged value named `instrumentationType`. The instrumentation type is an enumeration literal that can be set to either `Logging` or `Measurement`. Depending on its value, source code for logging or response time measuring will be generated.

The *Trigger* stereotype and the complex stereotypes are not graphically representable in UML class diagrams, which have been investigated for this paper, using UML notation. This diagram type supports static associations between classes, but it is impossible to mark source and target instance of an operation invocation nor patterns spanning multiple UML entities. The case study in section 6 discusses this limitation further.

4   Performance Engineering Process

This section introduces a performance engineering process, illustrated in figure 5, that is compatible with the Software Performance Engineering approach described by Pooley in [1]. It is based on UML, the UML instrumentation profile as introduced in section 3.2 and the *openArchitectureWare* (oAW) MDSD code generation framework for Java source code generation, but the methodology can be transferred to other frameworks and programming languages easily. For illustration purposes, the subsequent description uses oAW-specific terminology.

Before the instrumentation process is started, the instrumentation profile is imported into the software designer's UML modelling tool. During creation and analysis of the UML application models, the designer can annotate designated instrumentation points using the stereotypes of the instrumentation profile. Once this process has been finished, the instrumented model is exported to XMI.

The code generation workflow of the oAW framework is configured to import and parse the instrumented model using the profile metamodel. The oAW code generator component generates pure Java source code for uninstrumented UML elements (using generic *JavaBasic Templates* provided by the *Fornax Platform*[15]) and instrumentation code for instrumented elements (using custom *In-*

---

[15] http://www.fornax-platform.org

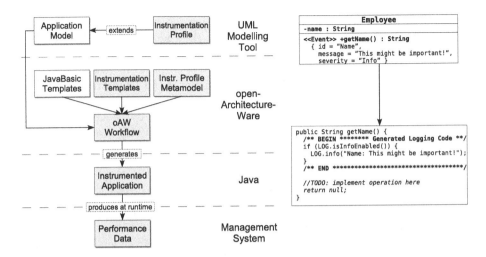

Fig. 5. Performance Engineering Process

strumentation Templates developed for processing stereotyped UML elements). Figure 5 also exemplifies a UML class extended with the *Event* stereotype and the resulting instrumented Java source code.

Once the generated instrumented application source code is completed by implementing the application's business logic, the *Instrumented Application* generates *Performance Data* at runtime, which can be processed (i.e. displayed, analysed) using a *Management System*. In case common instrumentation APIs and libraries are used for generating the instrumentation code, existing enterprise management systems can be used for the analysis.

The approach presented in this paper does not dictate following the MDSD approach during development of all application components. Modelling and instrumentation can also take place in the beginning only, followed by more traditional source code-based development afterwards. However, the presented approach can be integrated seamlessly into a MDSD process.

5   Prototypical Implementation

An overview of the oAW-based code generation process has already been given in section 4. Custom instrumentation templates have been developed for generating instrumentation code. oAW features an AOP mechanism supporting the extension of existing templates. The instrumentation templates extend the Fornax JavaBasic templates just as the instrumentation profile extends UML. The oAW workflow presented in figure 5 is clarified by figure 6.

The instrumentation extension developed for oAW contains templates that support code generation for the logging and time measurement instrumentation goals. The prototypical implementation creates a source code representation of the instrumentation patterns introduced in section 3.1 to the well-known log4j

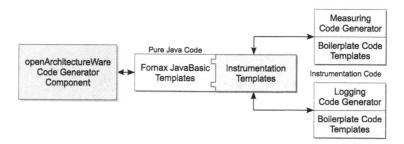

Fig. 6. oAW Code Generator Instrumentation Extension

(for logging) and ARM 4.0 (for measuring) APIs. ARM is a widely acknowledged *Open Group* standard for performance measurements within distributed applications. Within ARM, *Response Times* are execution time measurements of work units termed *ARM Transactions* within distributed applications. To avoid dependencies on global time, each measurement has to start and end within the same process. However, the standard allows the correlation of semantically related measurements, even across host boundaries. For this purpose, ARM defines *ARM Correlators*, which are unique tokens assigned to each ARM transaction. ARM is capable of recording single ARM transactions, which is a requirement for the instrumentation of critical applications, and supports direct integration of applications with enterprise management systems. This creates a comprehensive end-to-end monitoring capability, including the measurement of application performance, availability, usage and end-to-end transaction response times. To effect this integration, ARM calls must be present in the application source code, which are processed by an ARM library during application execution. ARM defines C and Java APIs.

Both code generators retrieve the required instrumentation statements from textual code templates. These templates have been developed based on the *Velocity*[16] template engine, so the targeted instrumentation APIs can be exchanged without modifying the code generators' source code. For `Events`, logging statements are placed at the beginning of generated methods stubs; for `Actions`, two measurement statements are placed at beginning and end of method stubs. ARM measurement data map to the corresponding instrumented source code locations containing `start()` and `stop()` calls on the transaction object. Therefore, a response time value as defined in the ARM 4.0 API can only express the time span referenced by two instrumentation points located in the same application instance and thus on the same host.

Depending on the instrumentation stereotypes and tagged values of each instrumentation point detected in a parsed UML model, the instrumentation templates invoke the appropriate code generator for generating either measuring or logging statements. The positions, in which these statements are placed, are shown in figure 7.

---

[16] http://velocity.apache.org

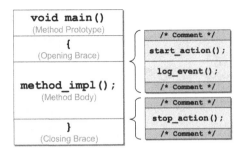

Fig. 7. Instrumentation Code Insertion Positions

6   Case Study: Web Services

The performance engineering process has been applied to several examples in a lab environment (i.e. without real-world application and work load). One example is presented in this section to demonstrate the applicability of the process to modern middleware-oriented applications and the flexibility of the developed prototype.

As discussed in section 3.2, complex patterns like the RPC pattern cannot be applied to UML class diagrams graphically. On the other hand, the RPC pattern as presented in section 3.1 is essential when instrumenting distributed applications. In order to solve this conflict, an adaptation has been developed which uses roles to textually represent the RPC pattern in UML class diagrams, so that the code generator can generate appropriate instrumentation code.

For the adaptation to Web service facilities, the client-side and the server-side Actions were outfitted with their respective roles (as introduced in section 3.1) in the UML diagram, which were then interpreted by the code generation templates appropriately. First, JAX-WS-based Web service communication, which is supported by major Web service frameworks such as *Apache Axis 2*[17], *Apache CXF*[18] and even *Java 6*[19], was analysed for facilities supporting ARM correlation of distributed measurements. Figure 8 shows the resulting exchange of a correlation token (CT) between client and Web service based on the *Web service context* and *message handler* facilities. The generated instrumentation code inserts an ARM correlator into the Web service context, which is attached as metadata to the outgoing request by a message handler. On the service side, another message handler extracts the correlator and puts it into the context. The generated instrumentation code for the service then uses the received correlator as parent correlator for its ARM measurement.

The case study showed that the model-based instrumentation approach can be applied to middleware-oriented applications, although adaptation is required for each additional framework to be supported. The amount of modifications

---

[17] http://ws.apache.org/axis2

[18] http://incubator.apache.org/cxf

[19] http://java.sun.com/javase

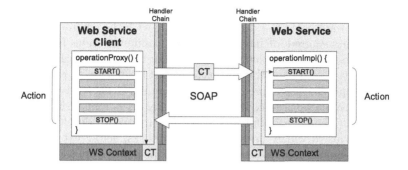

Fig. 8. JAX-WS Facilities in Web Service Interaction

required for adapting the code generator, however, was small so this does not pose a grave disadvantage. A look at the MDSD template collection hosted by Fornax confirms that the adaptation requirement is a general limitation of MDSD code generation: generic templates result in generated source code that requires comprehensive manual additions (thus limiting the benefit of code generation), and specific templates are limited in their applicability. There simply is no generic yet flexible solution appropriate for a broad palette of instrumentation scenarios.

Although the prototype is based on and integrated with openArchitecture-Ware, the presented approach can also be implemented in alternative MDSD code generation frameworks, programming languages and middlewares. Depending on the extension capabilities of the target platforms, the oAW-independent Java code generators and velocity templates might even be reusable.

7 Conclusion and Future Work

This paper presented an approach to model-based performance instrumentation of distributed applications in accordance with Pooley and modern MDSD-based software engineering processes. The performance aspect has been integrated into the MDSD process so that software designers can continue to use their existing UML modelling tools to instrument application models. With the collection of instrumentation patterns presented here in mind, designers are able to identify interactions within the models that are possible candidates for instrumentation. A drawback of the UML instrumentation profile based on these patterns is that it is a custom development. However, existing profiles for integrating performance annotations with UML models (such as the UML-SPT/MARTE) lacked essential features due to their emphasis on real-time systems modelling. The custom-designed profile defined here suffers from the risk of being outdated by standards developed in the future.

The prototypical implementation of the architecture was evaluated in a case study which demonstrated the overall usability and adaptability of the approach. The tests showed that comprehensive code generation can be achieved for specific usage scenarios (here: JAX-WS-based Web services) with only minor modifications to the otherwise generic templates. This can have a great impact on the productivity of a software project: a developer familiar with the environment executes the adaptations required for integrating a new communications framework, and all peers can use and profit from the generated instrumentation. Further evaluation of the methodology and the prototype is part of an ongoing research project which allows applying the approach presented here to an enterprise application.

Although template-based code generation only offers limited flexibility, projects such as the Fornax Platform, which concentrates on developing and providing extensions to widely used MDSD frameworks, help create a toolbox for MDSD which should contain something useful for almost any software development project. So far, the available extensions are mostly middleware-specific. Increasing acceptance and usage of MDSD technologies in professional software development, however, might spark the interest in extensions for generating source code for non-functional application properties like management and security, which could be combined with existing templates. This would effectively add an additional layer on top of the currently available communication- and infrastructure-centric templates.

As UML class diagrams are the most popular diagram type today, they were initially investigated for applicability of the instrumentation profile. The result showed that class diagrams are not ideally suited for instrumenting distributed applications. For example, dynamic interactions between distributed entities (e.g. Remote Procedure Calls) cannot be described sufficiently. But for developing the performance engineering process, class diagrams were the best choice, based on the fact that most available resources for MDSD frameworks rely on this diagram type. The evaluation of additional diagram types for integration with the instrumentation patterns and the profile (e.g. UML sequence and state diagrams) has already been started.

References

1. Pooley, R.: Software engineering and performance: A roadmap. In: ICSE 2000: Proceedings of the Conference on The Future of Software Engineering, pp. 189–199. ACM Press, New York (2000)
2. Krishnamurthy, R.: Performance Analysis of J2EE Applications Using AOP Techniques (2004), http://www.onjava.com/pub/a/onjava/2004/05/12/aop.html
3. Weimer, C.: IDE-gestützte Generierung von Quellcode zur Instrumentierung von Anwendungen. FH Wiesbaden (2005)
4. WO 03/062986 A1: Flexible and extensible java bytecode instrumentation system. Patent (July 2003)
5. Buytaert, D., Maebe, J., Eeckhout, L., Bosschere, K.D.: Building Java program analysis tools using Javana. In: OOPSLA 2006: Companion to the 21st ACM SIGPLAN conference on Object-oriented programming systems, languages, and applications, pp. 653–654. ACM Press, New York (2006)
6. US 2002/0152455 A1: Dynamic instrumentation of an executable program. Patent (October 2002)
7. Wegdam, M., van Halteren, A.: Experiences with CORBA interceptors (2000), http://www.comp.lancs.ac.uk/computing/rm2000/papers/20-aacentcweg.pdf

8. Pulavarthi, R.: Writing a Handler in JAX-WS (2006), http://java.sun.com/mailers/techtips/enterprise/2006/TechTips_June06.html

9. Schmid, M., Thoss, M., Termin, T., Kroeger, R.: A Generic Application-Oriented Performance Instrumentation for Multi-Tier Environments. In: 10th IFIP/IEEE International Symposium on Integrated Network Management (IM 2007), pp. 304–313. IEEE, Los Alamitos (2007)

10. Debusmann, M., Schmid, M., Kroeger, R.: Measuring End-to-End Performance of CORBA Applications using a generic instrumentation Approach. In: Corradi, A., Daneshmand, M. (eds.) Proceedings of the Seventh IEEE Symposium on Computers and Communications ISCC 2002, IEEE, Los Alamitos (2002)

11. Smith, C.U., Williams, L.G.: Performance and Scalability of Distributed Software Architectures: An SPE Approach (2002)

12. Gomez-Martinez, E., Merseguer, J.: A Software Performance Engineering Tool based on the UML-SPT. In: QEST 2005: International Conference on the Quantitative Evaluation of Systems (Proceedings), p. 247. IEEE Computer Society, Los Alamitos (2005)

13. Anglano, C.: Performance modeling of heterogeneous distributed applications. In: MASCOTS 1996: Proceedings of the 4th International Workshop on Modeling, Analysis, and Simulation of Computer and Telecommunications Systems, p. 64. IEEE Computer Society, Washington (1996)

14. Dehnert, J., Freiheit, J., Zimmermann, A.: Workflow Modeling and Performance Evaluation with Colored Stochastic Petri Nets (2000)

15. Bolch, G., Greiner, S., de Meer, H., Trivedi, K.S.: Queueing Networks and Markov Chains: Modeling and Performance Evaluation with Computer Science Applications, 2nd edn. Wiley-Interscience, Chichester (2006)

16. Theelen, B., Voeten, J., van Bokhoven, L., van der Putten, P., Niemegeers, A., Jong, G.: Performance Modeling in the Large: A Case Study (2001)

17. Xu, J., Oufimtsev, A., Woodside, M., Murphy, L.: Performance modeling and prediction of enterprise JavaBeans with layered queuing network templates. SIGSOFT Softw. Eng. Notes 31(2), 5 (2006)

18. Kroeger, R., Machens, H.: Trace Framework - Tracing in heterogenen Umgebungen. Technical report, Wiesbaden University of Applied Sciences (November 2002)

19. Schaefer, J.: Model-based Instrumentation of Distributed Applications. Master's thesis, Cork Institute of Technology (2008)

Implementing a Data Distribution Variant with a Metamodel, Some Models and a Transformation

Eveline Kaboré and Antoine Beugnard

Department of Computer Sciences, TELECOM Bretagne, Technopôle Brest-Iroise
CS 83818 – 29238 Brest Cedex 3, France
{eveline.kabore,antoine.beugnard}@enst-bretagne.fr

Abstract. In this paper, we show how model transformations can be used to implement data distribution features in the software design process of a component. This approach is based on a single metamodel that defines data distribution abstractions and on the design of alternatives that are used to implement each data distribution variant. A model transformation is associated with the metamodel and the component metamodel we consider as the target. We show that this approach facilitates the derivation of different implementation strategies from the model of a component. We illustrate our approach with the example of distributed communication component software that implements one centralized and two peer-to-peer variants and we demonstrate the reusability of the transformation.

1 Introduction and Motivation

Models are widely used in science and have become an essential tool for software designers and programmers. Models have been used in many development methods such as SADT [1], JSD [2], etc. They allow the description of different aspects of a system: structural, functional, behavioural, temporal, etc. Models also allow the description of the system to be developed at different stages with various levels of detail.

The Unified Modeling Language(UML) is the last avatar of a standard modelling notation. The way models are produced and elaborated is mainly beyond the scope of modelling, which relies on good-practice, know-how and more or less formalized methods. One of the latest great advances in software engineering has been the introduction of patterns (especially design patterns) as a semiformalization of good (or bad) practice.

The formalization and the clarification of the process of elaborating models are the next challenges. Considering the processes of elaborating and renaming models as an activity that can be described with a dedicated language is, in our view, a revolution.

We show in this article how models, metamodels (that can be defined as model types) and model transformations can be used to automate the design and implementation process of a distributed software component.

R. Meier and S. Terzis (Eds.): DAIS 2008, LNCS 5053, pp. 224–237, 2008.

We are working on a specific component model dedicated to communication [3,4] and the way to derive an implementation thanks to a process based on model transformations [5,6]. Many models and metamodels have been developed and a design process (Fig.1.) has been implemented as a set of model transformations. The first transformations that were defined introduced the general architecture of the implementation. In this paper, we describe the way we have automated the design choice related to data placement and distribution.

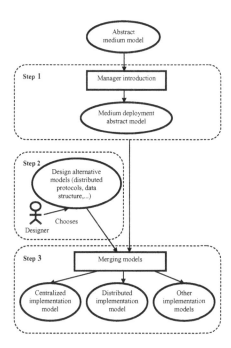

Fig. 1. A view of the full design process of a medium

We argue that if models can describe *the product* to develop and metamodels the *abstractions and constraints* that are used and reused to define models, model transformations can be used to describe *the process* to follow. Hence, we have analysed the different design choices that are available when implementing communication components. Among them, we have isolated data placement strategies. We then looked for the abstractions required to describe data placement and elaborated a dedicated metamodel. The validation of this metamodel was made thanks to the definition of some data placement models such as "centralized placement" "peer-to-peer Pastry placement strategy" or "peer-to-peer Chord placement strategy".

In order to apply these design choices we had to define a model transformation that was compatible with our target: communication components. The transformation was hence defined using the two metamodels: the communication component and the data placement metamodels. This choice guarantees that the transformation is reusable since applicable to all models that conforms: any communication component model or any data placement model. Finally, this approach also ensures extensibility since new data placement models - if conforming - could be added.

The paper is organized as follows. The next section summarizes the definition and the deployment target of communication components in order to ensure a better understanding of metamodels and transformation. Section 3 presents our approach defining the implementation parts of data distribution problems as a sequence of transformations in a communication component design process. Section 4 presents some related work. We conclude the paper in section 5 with some perspectives of this work.

2   Communication Component: Medium

Definition. A medium is a special component which implements any level communication protocol or system. A medium can implement, for example, a consensus protocol, a multimedia stream broadcast or a voting system. A medium includes classical component properties such as explicit interface specification, reusability or replaceability, but a medium is not a unit of deployment. A communication component is a *logical* architectural entity built to be *distributed*. An application is the result of inter-connecting a set of components and mediums. This is particularly interesting as it can allow the separation of two concerns: local concerns described by components and communication concerns described by mediums.

Example. As an illustration, we reuse the example published in [5] of an airline company with travel agencies located worldwide. A medium can implement the reservation system and offer services to initialize information on seats, to reserve seats and to cancel reservations. A reservation application can then be built by inter-connecting the reservation medium and components representing the company and the agencies as illustrated in Fig.2.

Deployment Target. In the previous section, we saw that, at the abstract level, the medium is represented by a single software component. The goal of the design process is to make the distribution of this abstraction possible. The

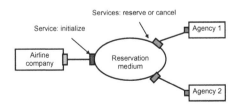

Fig. 2. An example of a communication component: reservation medium

single software component which represents the medium at the abstract level is split into small implementation components called *role managers*. Each *role manager* is locally associated with a local component and the medium becomes a logical unit composed of all the *role managers*. From a local point of view, each *role manager* implements the services used by its associated component. From a global point of view all the *role managers* communicate through middleware and cooperate to realize all the medium services.

Thus, at the deployment level the single software communication component which represents the medium at the abstract level disappears completely and the medium becomes an aggregation of distributed *role managers*. The data manipulated by the medium at the abstract level are distributed between role managers.

The next section presents our approach to implement data distribution features as a sequence of transformations. We note that the definition of technical details related to elements which are used to ensure data distribution and access services is beyond the scope of this paper.

3   Our Approach

3.1   Analysis

Identifying the Source and the Target of the Transformation

Identifying the Source. The introduction of managers is beyond the scope (step 1 in Fig.1.) of this paper. Thus, in the context of this paper, the source of the transformation is a medium deployment abstract model in which:

1. A *manager* is associated with each role
2. Each *manager* implements all the services offered by the medium to its associated role
3. Each role is separate from the other elements constituting the medium
4. The medium is defined by the aggregation of *managers* as illustrated in Fig.3. for the reservation medium.

Identifying the Target. The target of the transformation is a medium implementation model in which:

1. Items (1) - (4) in the source specification are verified
2. The entity representing the medium in the source specification is deleted
3. Each data managed by the medium in the source specification is distributed between *managers*

The description of the target does not provide design alternatives that will be used to implement data distribution features. It just specifies the set of constraints that each final implementation model of the medium should satisfy. Both source and target descriptions are detailed in [7].

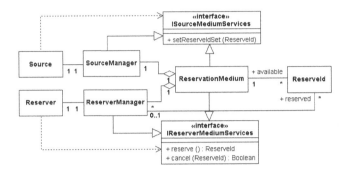

Fig. 3. Structure of the reservation medium after the introduction of managers

Identifying and Separating Design Alternatives. We decompose the problem of implementing data distribution issues into three design alternatives at the moment. Other design alternatives related to data distribution such as synchronization or context adaptation aspects can be added in future work.

First Design Alternative: Data Distribution Topology Choice. This involves in specifying the set of managers that can participate in the distribution of each data and those that can only have access to it.

Second Design Alternative: Distributed Protocol Choice. This specifies the distributed protocol (*Chord [8], Pastry [9]*, etc.) that will be used to implement the distribution strategy of each data.

Third Design Alternative: Distributed Protocol Implementation Algorithm. The last step is the choice of algorithm that will be used to implement each distributed protocol services. As an illustration, in the case of the *Chord* protocol, the designer can choose the algorithm proposed by *MIT* [10] or the algorithm proposed by the *MACEDON* [11] framework to implement the protocol.

3.2 Automation

In this section, we sketch out metamodels and transformations that we use to describe and automate the introduction of design alternatives identified in the previous section in the medium deployment abstract model.

Metamodelling. We define a different metamodel for the source, the target and distributed protocols in order to ensure a better understanding of metamodels. Each metamodel is specified with two elements: a UML class diagram describing the generic structure of the concept and a set of OCL specifications describing the properties of the concept which cannot be expressed in the class diagram. For the sake of brevity, we only show the generic structure of each metamodel in this paper. The full definition of all the metamodels is available in [12].

Medium Deployment Specification Metamodel. Figure 4 shows the generic structure of a medium during deployment. A *manager* (*</RoleName>Manager*) is
associated with each role (*</RoleName>*). Each *manager* implements the interface of the services offered by the medium (*I<RoleName>MediumServices*)
to its associated role and the medium (*<MediumName>Medium*) is defined by
the aggregation of *managers*.

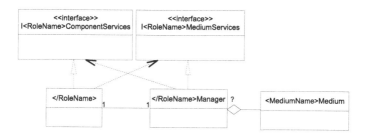

Fig. 4. Generic structure of a medium at deployment level

Medium Implementation Specification Metamodel. Figure 5 shows the generic
structure of a medium during implementation. The medium class disappears
completely and the medium data are distributed between managers. The gray
colour delimits our metamodel of a distributed data. Each distributed data is
represented by two elements. The first element (*DataManager*) ensures the data
distribution services and the second (*DataObject*) element ensures the data access services.

Distributed Protocol Metamodel. We define a distributed protocol by a set of
objects called *ProtocolObject* (Fig.6.). A *ProtocolObject* is an object that can

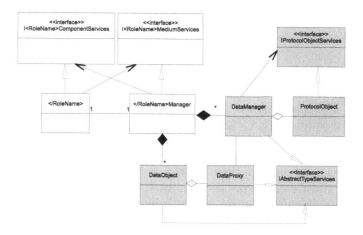

Fig. 5. Generic structure of a medium at implementation level

execute the behaviour of a distributed protocol. Each *ProtocolObject* is implemented by a specific algorithm (*ProtocolObjectAlgorithm*). The main goal of the distributed protocol metamodel involves defining a common interface for all the distributed protocols that will be used in the context of mediums. Such interfaces are proposed in [13,11,9]. The *IProtocolObjectServices* interface exported by the distributed protocol definition metamodel is similar to the interface defined in [13]. This interface defines services for three main distributed application abstractions: DHT (Distributed Hash Tables), DOLR (Decentralized Object Location and Routing) and CAST (group anycast/multicast). The *IProtocolObjectServices* interface offers the following services: *route* (to route a message), *forward* (to forward a message), *deliver* (to deliver a message), *join* (to join the distributed application) and *leave* (to leave the distributed protocol).

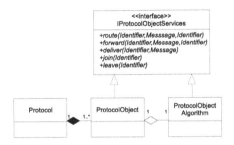

Fig. 6. A view of the distributed protocol specification metamodel

A definition of a distributed protocol model which conforms to the distributed protocol metamodel involves:

1. The description of each *ProtocolObject* and at least one of its implementation algorithms
2. The implementation of each service offered by the *IProtocolObjectServices*.

We illustrate the definition of a *Chord* protocol model in [14].

Model Transformation

Principle. The entry point of the transformation is a well defined medium deployment abstract model (Fig.1. and Fig.3.) in this paper. In the full design process of the medium, we perform a first transformation in order to transform this model into an abstract implementation model in which all the UML associations between the medium class and the medium data classes are replaced by the appropriate abstract types specified by the designer [15]. In the case of the reservation medium for example, the available reservation identifiers (**available** property in Fig.3.) can be represented by a **list**. Since we do not discuss abstract types choice in this paper, this transformation will not be described in this section. After the introduction of abstract types, we perform five successive transformations in order to introduce data distribution topologies, distributed protocols and distributed protocol algorithms into the abstract implementation model of the medium. These transformations leads to a generic implementation model implementing the actual data distribution variant. The designer completes this generic implementation model by defining each offered service's actual implementation algorithm to produce the final implementation model of the medium. The following example describes a data distribution variant that will be used to illustrate transformations in the remainder of this section.

An Example of a Data Distribution Variant. We will use the reservation medium to illustrate transformations in this section. We suppose that the available reservation identifiers (**available** property) are represented by a list. The goal is to distribute this list between managers associated with agencies (*ReserverManager*) using the *Chord* protocol. The *manager* associated with the airline company (*SourceManager*) can only access the list. The Chord protocol will be implemented by the *MIT* algorithm. These information are defined in a medium decision model in the full implementation process in order to allow the automatic execution of transformations [15].

T_1. Introducing each Data Distribution Topology into the Abstract Implementation Model of the Medium. The input model of this step is the medium abstract implementation model obtained after the introduction of abstract types. We aim at introducing each data distribution topology into this model. We define a transformation based on the medium deployment and implementation metamodels and the distributed data metamodel for this purpose. This transformation leads to an abstract implementation model of the medium in which : a *DataManager* is associated with each *manager* participating in each data distribution and a *DataObject* is associated with each *manager* accessing each distributed data. Here is an informal summary of its main operations.

```
Preconditions:
 1.Verify if each distribution node is defined in the medium model.
Actions:
  For each data managed by the medium class:
   1.Create and associate a generic DataManager object with each manager
     participating to data distribution.
   2.Create and associate a generic DataAccess object with each manager
      using the data
Postcondition:
  Verify if a DataManage and/or a DataObject is associated with each
  manager according to the implementation variant.
```

As an illustration, in the example of the reservation medium, the transformation associates a *ListDataManager* to *ReserverManager* and a *ListObject* with both *SourceManager* and *ReserverManager* (Fig.7.).

T_2. Introducing Distributed Protocol in the Abstract Implementation Model of the Medium In this step we define another transformation based on the same

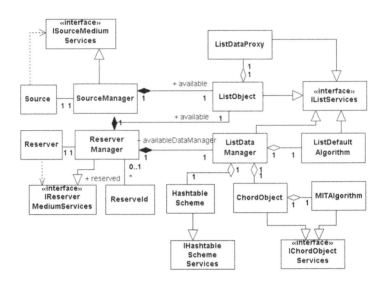

Fig. 7. A view of the reservation medium after T_1, T_2 and T_3

metamodels as T_1 to introduce the distributed protocol that will be used to ensure each data distribution strategy in the abstract implementation model generated by T_1. Its operations can be summarized as follows:

```
Preconditions:
 Verify if the model of each distributed protocol conforms to
 the distributed protocol metamodel
Actions:
1. Create and associate a generic ProtocolObject with each DataManager
   according to the distribution variant.
Postcondition:
 Verify if a generic ProtocolObject is associated with each DataManager
   according to the distribution variant.
```

T_3. *Introducing Distributed Protocol Algorithms into the Abstract Implementation Model of the Medium* This transformation perform the following operations in order to introduce the implementation algorithm of each distributed protocol object into the model generated by T_2 as illustrated in Fig 7.

```
Preconditions:
  Verify if each distributed ProtocolObject implementation algorithm is
  well defined according to the distributed protocol metamodel.
Actions:
 Create and associate a generic ProtocolObjectAlgorithm with
 each protocol object according to the distribution variant.
Postcondition:
  Verify if a generic ProtocolObjectAlgorithm is associated
  with each ProtocolObject according to the distribution variant.
```

T_4. *Generating Abstract Methods Implementation Algorithms in the Abstract Implementation Model of the Medium* In this step, we define a transformation to generate a default algorithm in order to implement each abstract method contained in the abstract implementation model produced by T_3. Here is an example of a piece of code generated by this transformation in order to implement the *add* primitive of the **list** for the reservation medium example.

```
class ListObject inherits IListServices
{     ... method get (index : Integer ): Object from IListServices is do
          if (self.dataProxy != void) then
              then result := self.dataProxy.get(id) end
          end end   ... }
class ListDataProxy inherits IListServices
{     ... method get (index : Integer ): Object from IListServices is do
          var dataManager : ListDataManager init getListDataManager()
          if (dataManager != void) then
              then result := dataManager.get(id) end
          end end   ...}
```

T_5. *Configuring the Medium* The previous step leads to an abstract implementation model of the medium in which all the generic elements needed to provide each data distribution and access service are well defined. In this step, we define a last transformation based on the same metamodels as the previous transformation in order to instantiate and associate the appropriate value with each generic element. Four generic operations called *managerConnection, managerDisconnection, initialization and termination* are defined in [7] in order to associate a specific behaviour with a manager during its connection, disconnection, initialization and termination. The last transformation redefines these operations in order to reach its goal. Here is an informal summary of the main operations performed by the last transformation as an example of generated code for the reservation medium.

```
Precondition:
 Verify if all the abstract methods are implemented in the input model.
Actions:
 1.Redefine the managerConnection, managerDisconnection, initialization
   and termination operations in each Manager class.
 2.For each distributed data:
   2.1.Generate instructions in the managerConnection operations to
       instantiate the appropriate protocol objects and protocol object
       algorithms according to the design choice
   2.2.Set the data manager and the data object values
   2.3.Generate instructions in the managerDisconnection operations to
       disconnect protocol objects
   2.4.Generate instructions in the initialization operations to
       initialize protocol objects
   2.5.Generate instructions in the termination operations to terminate
       protocol objects.
Postcondition:
```

Verify if the output is a good medium implementation specification
model according to the medium decision model and the medium
implementation specification metamodel

```
class ReserverManager inherits IReserverMediumServices
{...operation managerConnection() is do ....
      available := ListObject.new
      available.dataProxy := ListDataProxy.new
      availableProtocolObject := ChordProtocolObject.new
      availableProtocolObject.protocolObjectAlgorithm := MITAlgorithm.new
      availableDataManager := ListDataManager.new
      availableDataManager.protocolObject := availableProtocolObject
      availableDataManager.listDefaultAlgorithm :=
                ListDefaultAlgorithm.new // other instructions end }
```

Transformation Definition Platform. Transformations are implemented, tested
and executed on the Kermeta [16] platform. Each metamodel is implemented
by two Kermeta files. The first file implements all the structural aspects of the
metamodel. The second file implements all the properties of the metamodel. It is
then possible to check if a specific model is conform to the metamodel in which it
is defined. Each transformation is implemented by three Kermeta files. The first
file implements the preconditions, the second file implements the operations and
last file implements the postconditions of the transformation. A full definition
of metamodels and transformations in Kermeta is available in [12].

4   Related Works

Most methodologies are informally described. They suggest a process which, in
most formalized cases, rely on contracts [17] or mathematical refinements like
the B-method [18]. B defines a language and a refinement methodology. It is
an algebraic specification language that is supported by tools that help refine
specification safely. Each step of the process generates the proof requirement
that the developer has to demonstrate, either manually or automatically. Some
critical systems have been developed in B (in 1998 the control system of line 14
of the Parisian subway was fully developed and proved in B). Our approach is
more empirical and uses the so-called "semi-formal" approach. It may be easier
to learn and may tackle different kinds of design problems such as distribution.
We do not try to prove design steps, but just to automatize them and give
enough confidence in the transformations thanks to pre and post-conditions.

In a recent paper, H. Sneed [19] criticizes the model driven approach. He
argues that model-driven tools magnify the mistakes made in the problem definition; create an additional semantic level to be maintained; distort the image of
what the program is really like; complicate the maintenance process by creating
redundant descriptions which have to be maintained in parallel; are designed for
top-down development that creates well-known maintenance problems. These
drawbacks are mainly associated with tools. All these criticisms have already

been raised when assembler was replaced by high level programming languages. We agree that tools are not mature. Our experiment shows that transformations may help make explicit the process and simplify the maintenance, if models are well defined enough.

Other experiments [20] tend to prove that model composition (hence a bottom-up approach) is possible. This compositional approach resembles Aspect Oriented Modelling [21]. This approach recommends separating concerns and offers an operation of weaving that composes/weaves each concern with the functional specification. Our approach differs since the "weaving" operation we use is a transformation that is adapted to the kind of concern composed. Instead of using a universal weaving operation we propose a more flexible (but less re-usable) approach in which a balance may be found between the metamodel definition of the concern and its composition operation implemented as a transformation.

Model transformations are widely used in UML models. Most of them cover a small part of the development life cycle. Some transformations are dedicated to code generation. They usually produce the skeleton (structural part) of the source code that has to be completed manually. Another current use is in applying design patterns [22]. Once again, the structural part is rather well implemented[1], but the collaboration part is still research in progress.

5   Conclusion

This paper shows how model transformations can be used to describe the implementation process of data distribution issues in a distributed software component. To do this we have defined metamodels that capture the required concepts of data distribution. We have also realized a sequence of model transformations that weave a variant of the data distribution design choice into the model of the distributed component.

The transformations describe the process of introducing actual design alternative models in the specification of the component. The approach makes explicit the data distribution implementation process. We argue that it is of great interest in the sense that it facilitates traceability (the sequence of transformations), reuse (applicability of transformations to many different models) and the evolution of the full process (adding more variant models).

As an illustration, we have applied our approach to implementing data distribution in the context of mediums. We have described a set of transformations and metamodels that can be used to introduce distributed protocols.

But the concern of data distribution is only one step in a larger design process. We have described an approach based on the definition of a sequence of design concerns. As an example we have selected the choice of an abstract type for the

---

[1] Pattern purists would say that patterns are not dedicated to be automatically applied. In the absolute, we agree, but why not consider applying patterns in well defined contexts?

collection of data, the choice of distribution strategies (described in this paper) and the choice of data representation format.

Transformations are implemented, tested and executed with the Kermeta platform. The implementation of the full design process relies on 6 metamodels and 5 main transformations. Each metamodel is implemented by two Kermeta files. The first file implements all the structural aspects of the metamodel. The second file implements all the properties of the metamodel. It is then possible to check if a specific model is conformed to the metamodel in which it is defined. Each transformation is implemented by three Kermeta files. The first file implements the preconditions, the second the operations and the last file the transformation postconditions. We also provide a library containing some abstract types (list, set, bag, etc.), distributed protocols (chord, pastry, etc.) and data representation format models (hashtable, array, matrix, etc.).

Transformations can be used to implement any abstract type, distributed protocol and data representation format model which conforms to our metamodels in any well defined medium initial specification model. As an illustration, we have used transformations to automatically derive various centralized and distributed implementation variants of the reservation medium presented in this paper and two other mediums: a voting medium and a message broadcast medium.

The actual generated implementation models of mediums are not fully executable in the sense that they do not provide a full executable code of distributed protocols. They just call protocol APIs to ensure that all distributed feature are well implemented. Thus, in the short term, our main perspective is to build middleware in order to allow the execution of the generated models in conjunction with existing executable distributed protocol frameworks such as MACEDON. We also aim to define other design alternatives metamodels and models to enrich our library. After that, we aim to extend transformations to define auto-adaptable mediums that embed many variants and that could change their internal deployed structures according to environment evolutions.

References

1. Connor, M.: Sadt - structured analysis and design technique. Technical Report 9595-7, Softech (May 1980)
2. Jackson, M.: System Development. Prentice-Hall, Englewood Cliffs (1983)
3. Cariou, E., Beugnard, A.: The specification of UML collaboration as interaction component. In: Jézéquel, J.-M., Hussmann, H., Cook, S. (eds.) UML 2002. LNCS, vol. 2460, pp. 352–367. Springer, Heidelberg (2002)
4. Matougui, S., Beugnard, A.: Two ways of implementing software connections among distributed components. In: International Symposium on Distributed Objects and Applications, Agia Napa, Cyprus (October 31 - November 2, 2005)
5. Cariou, E., Beugnard, A., Jézéquel, J.M.: An archictecture and a process for implementing distributed collaborations. In: The 6th IEEE International Enterprise Distributed Object Computing Conference (EDOC 2002), Ecole Polytechnique Fédérale de Lausanne (EPFL), Switzerland (September 17 - 20, 2002)

6. Kaboré, E., Beugnard, A.: Conception de composants répartis par transformations de modèle. In: Journées de l'Ingénierie Dirigée par les Modèles, Toulouse, France, pp. 117–131 (March 29–30, 2007)
7. Cariou, E.: Contribution à un processus de réification d'abstraction de communication. Thèse de doctorat, Université de Rennes 1 (June 2003)
8. Stoica, I., Morris, R., Karger, D., Kaashoek, M.F., Balakrishnan, H.: Chord: A scalable peer-to-peer lookup service for internet applications. In: ACM SIGCOMM Conference, San Diego (2001)
9. Rowstron, A., Drusche, P.: Pastry: Scalable, distributed object location and routing for large-scale peer-to-peer systems. In: Guerraoui, R. (ed.) Middleware 2001. LNCS, vol. 2218, pp. 329–350. Springer, Heidelberg (2001)
10. Massachusetts Institute of Technology: lsd (2004), http://www.pdos.lcs.mit.edu/chord/
11. Rodriguez, A., Killian, C., Bhat, S., Kostic, D., Vahdat, A.: Macedon: Methodology for automatically creating, evaluating, and designing overlay networks. In: USENIX/ACM Symposium on Networked Systems Design and Implementation (NSDI 2004) (2004)
12. Kaboré, E.: Metamodel definitions (2008), http://stockage.univ-brest.fr/~kabore/
13. Dabek, F., Zhao, B., Drushcel, P., Kubiatowicz, J., Stoica, I.: Towards a common api for structured peer-to-peer overlays. In: Kaashoek, M.F., Stoica, I. (eds.) IPTPS 2003. LNCS, vol. 2735, Springer, Heidelberg (2003)
14. Kaboré, E., Beugnard, A.: On the benefits of using model transformations to describe components design process. In: Twelfth International Workshop on Component-Oriented Programming (WCOP 2007), at ECOOP 2007, Berlin, Germany (July 2007)
15. Kaboré, E., Beugnard, A.: Automatisation d'un processus de conception par transformations de modèles. L'Objet 13(4), 105 (2007)
16. Muller, P.A., Fleurey, F., Jézéquel, J.M.: Weaving executability into object-oriented meta-languages. In: Briand, S.K.L. (ed.) MoDELS 2005. LNCS, vol. 3713, pp. 264–278. Springer, Heidelberg (2005)
17. D'Souza, D., Wills, A.C.: Objects, Components and Framework with UML: The Catalysis Approach. Addison-Wesley, Reading (1998)
18. Abrial, J.R.: The B-Book, Assigning Programs to Meanings. Cambridge University Press, Cambridge (1996)
19. Sneed, H.M.: The drawbacks of model-driven software evolution. In: Workshop on Model-Driven Software Evolution, IEEE - CSMR 2007 11th European Conference on Software Maintenance and Reengineering "Software Evolution in Complex Software Intensive Systems", Amsterdam, the Netherlands, March 20-23 (2007)
20. Muller, A., Caron, O., Carré, B., Vanwormhoudt, G.: On some properties of parametrized model application. In: Hartman, A., Kreische, D. (eds.) ECMDA-FA 2005. LNCS, vol. 3748, pp. 130–140. Springer, Heidelberg (2005)
21. Mens, K., Lopes, C., Tekinerdogan, B., Kiczales, G.: Aspect-oriented programming. In: Bosch, J., Mitchell, S. (eds.) ECOOP 1997 Workshops. LNCS, vol. 1357, Springer, Heidelberg (1998)
22. Sunyé, G., Guennec, A.L., Jézéquel, J.-M.: Design pattern application in UML. In: Bertino, E. (ed.) ECOOP 2000. LNCS, vol. 1850, pp. 44–62. Springer, Heidelberg (2000)

Facilitating Gossip Programming with the GossipKit Framework

Shen Lin, François Taïani, and Gordon S. Blair

Computing Department
Lancaster University, UK
{s.lin6,f.taiani,gordon}@comp.lancs.ac.uk

Abstract. Gossip protocols have been successfully applied in the last few years to address a wide range of functionalities. So far, however, very few software frameworks have been proposed to ease the development and deployment of these gossip protocols. To address this issue, this paper presents GossipKit, an event-driven framework that provides a generic and extensible architecture for the development of (re)configurable gossip-oriented middleware. GossipKit is based on a generic interaction model for gossip protocols and relies on a fine-grained event mechanism to facilitate configuration and reconfiguration, and promote code reuse.

Keywords: Gossip protocol, component framework, middleware, flexibility, event-driven architecture.

1   Introduction and Problem Statement

Gossip-based algorithms have recently become extremely popular. The underlying concept of these algorithms is that individual nodes repeatedly exchange data with some randomly selected neighbours, causing information to eventually spread through the system in a "rumour-like" fashion. Gossip-based protocols offer three key advantages over more traditional systems: 1) they provide a scalable approach to communication in very large systems; 2) thanks to the randomised and periodic exchange of information, they offer self-healing capacities and robustness to failures; and 3) since gossip peers are selected at random and each node communicates with a limited number of peers, they offer natural load-balancing abilities. Because of these benefits, gossip-based protocols have been applied to a wide range of problems such as peer sampling [9,17], ad-hoc routing [14], reliable multicast[1,2], database replication [10], failure detection [11], and data aggregation [12].

In spite of this success, however, very few attempts have been made at developing gossip-based middleware architectures. T-Man [5] and Gossiping Framework [6] proposed by Kermarrec and Steen [6] are two of the early gossip-dedicated frameworks that have been proposed in this area. They both rely on a common periodic gossip pattern to support a variety of gossip protocols. Although these frameworks can help develop gossip-based systems to a significant extent, we contend that they only partially address the issues faced by the developers of

R. Meier and S. Terzis (Eds.): DAIS 2008, LNCS 5053, pp. 238–252, 2008.

gossip-based applications. First, the common periodic gossip pattern they rely on only captures the features of proactive gossip protocols but does not support reactive gossip algorithms. Second, these frameworks tend to be monolithic, thus precluding a flexible and easily extensible architecture. Finally, these frameworks are not designed to support runtime reconfiguration.

This paper introduces GossipKit, a fine-grained event-driven framework we have developed to ease the development of (re)configurable gossip-based systems that operate in heterogeneous networks such as IP-based networks and mobile ad-hoc networks. The goal of GossipKit is to provide a middleware toolkit that helps programmers and system designers develop, deploy, and maintain distributed gossip-oriented applications. GossipKit has a component-based architecture that promotes code reuse and facilitates the development of new protocols. By enforcing the same structure across multiple and possibly co-existing protocols, GossipKit simplifies the deployment and configuration of multiple protocol instances. Finally, at runtime, GossipKit allows multiple protocol instances to be dynamically loaded, operate concurrently, and collaborate with each other in order to achieve more sophisticated operations.

The contributions of this paper are threefold. First, we identify a generic and modular interaction pattern that most gossip protocols follow. Second, we propose an event-driven architecture based on this pattern that can be easily extended to cover a wider range of gossip protocols. Third, we evaluate how our event-driven architecture provides a fine-grained mechanism to compose gossip protocols within the GossipKit framework.

The remainder of the paper is organised as follows. Section 2 discusses related work. Section 3 presents a study of existing gossip protocols and explains how this study informed the key design choices of GossipKit. Section 4 gives an overview of GossipKit's architecture. Section 5 describes our current implementation, while an evaluation is provided in Section 6. Finally, Section 7 concludes the paper and points out future work.

2   Related Work

Two categories of communication frameworks have been proposed to support gossip protocols: Gossip Frameworks, which directly support gossip-based systems, and Event-driven communication systems, which tend to be more generic and more flexible. In this section we analyse the strengths and weaknesses of both of them from the viewpoint of gossip protocol development.

Gossip frameworks are specifically designed to support gossip protocols. Typical examples of such frameworks are T-Man [5] and Gossiping Framework [6] proposed by Kermarrec and Steen [6]. These two frameworks assume that most gossip protocols adopt a common proactive gossip pattern. In this gossip pattern, a peer P maintains two threads. One is an active thread, which periodically pushes the local state S_P to a randomly selected peer Q or pulls for Q's local state S_Q. The other is passive, which listens to push or pull messages from other peers. If the received message is pull, P replies with S_P; if the received message is push, P updates S_P with the state in the message.

To develop a new gossip protocol within this common proactive gossip pattern, one only needs to define a state S, a method of peer selection, an interaction style (i.e. pull, push or pull-push), and a state update method. This inherently supports a large range of proactive gossip protocols such as peer sampling service, data aggregation, and topologic maintenance, which have all been implemented in such gossip frameworks.

However, the monolithic design of these frameworks makes them inadaptable to protocols that use a reactive gossip pattern (e.g. SCAMP [9]) or those implementing sophisticated optimisations such as feedback based dissemination decision [13] and premature gossip death prevention [14]. Furthermore, these frameworks neither support reconfiguration nor concurrent operation of multiple gossip protocols at runtime.

Event-driven communication systems aim to provide a flexible composition model based on event-driven execution. They are developed to support general-purpose communication and can be used for gossip protocols. Examples of such communication systems are Ensemble [3], Cactus [4] and their predecessors Isis [7] and Coyote [8]. In these environments, a configurable service (e.g. a Configurable Transport Protocol) is viewed as a composition of several functional properties (e.g. reliability, flow control, and ordering). Each functional property is then implemented as a micro-protocol that consists of a collection of event handlers. Multiple event handlers may be bound to a particular event and when this event occurs, all bounded event handlers are executed.

Event-driven communication systems offer a number of benefits for developing gossip protocols. First, individual micro-protocols can be reused to construct families of related gossip protocols (implemented as services) for different applications instead of implementing each new protocol from scratch. Second, reconfigurability can be achieved by dynamically loading micro-protocols and re-binding event handlers to appropriate events. Finally, the use of event handlers present a fine-grained decomposition of protocols.

However, event-driven frameworks are known to be notoriously difficult to program and configure as argued in [16]. In large part, this is because these frameworks do not by themselves include any domain-specific features (e.g. interaction patterns and common structure) for individual protocol types.

In order to address the above shortcomings, GossipKit adopts *a hybrid approach that combines domain-specific abstraction and the strengths of event-driven architecture*. The remaining sections of this paper present its design and prototype implementation.

3   GossipKit's Key Design Choices

GossipKit is based on three key design choices: (i) application-dependent interfaces; (ii) a common-interaction pattern, and (iii) an event-driven architecture. These choices result from a detailed analysis of a number of existing gossip-based

protocols. In the following, we discuss in turn each of our choices, and explain
how they derive from this analysis.

3.1   Application-Dependent Interfaces

Gossip-based solutions have been proposed for a wide range of problems, and for
each specific problem, external modules are expected to interact with the gossip
protocol in very specific ways. For instance, a gossip-based routing protocol
has to provide a way for external applications to trigger a route request to be
gossipped, whilst a peer sampling service must instead expose the set of collected
peers. There is no elegant way to map those fundamentally different services onto
a unique common generic interface. Instead we have identified a *set* of generic but
domain-specific interfaces that can each support a category of gossip protocols
in a particular application domain (e.g. ad-hoc routing, or peer-sampling). This
approach allows us to uncouple the varied semantics of gossip-based services
from the unified implementation framework we have developed. We will revisit
this topic in Section 4.1, where we will describe in more detail the mapping
between these domain-specific interfaces and our underlying framework.

3.2   Common Interaction Pattern

Although different types of gossip protocols provide divergent interfaces to external applications, we have found that, internally, they all follow the same interaction pattern. This common interaction pattern can be captured using a modular
approach and combines the proactive gossip pattern that has been identified in
existing gossip frameworks [5,6], with the reactive gossip patterns observed on
gossip protocols such as [9] and [14]. This common interaction model is shown
in Fig. 1. In this figure, the modules involved in the interaction are presented as
boxes, and interactions between modules as arrowed lines. The direction of the
arrows indicates which module initiates the interaction, and the labels show in
which sequence these interactions take place.

Initially, a gossip dissemination can either be raised periodically (e.g. a periodic pull or push of gossip message), or upon a receipt of an external request

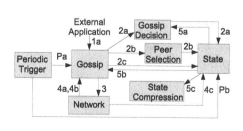

Fig. 1. Common Interaction Model

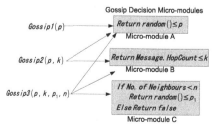

Fig. 2. Various Gossip Decision modules composed by micro-modules

(e.g. an ad-hoc routing protocol requesting a reactive gossip protocol such as [14] and [21] to gossip a route request). These two interactions are represented as (Pa) and (1a) in Fig. 1, respectively.

The second phase prepares the gossip action. Some gossip protocols may use various policies to decide whether to gossip at the current state (2a). For instance, a reactive gossip protocol may decide not to gossip the same message twice or forward the message with a given probability [9]. If a decision is made to forward the gossip message, the protocol instance will then select the peers it wishes to gossip with from its state (2b). Different policies exist for selecting peers. For instance, a subset of peers can be selected from the local state randomly or based on their lifetime [17]. Note that peer selection may be optional in our model: for instance the nodes of a wireless single-hop network always reach all their neighbours with a single radio broadcast, [20], gossip protocols operating in these environments therefore usually achieve gossiping behaviour through randomised gossip decisions. In addition to gossip decision and peer selection, many gossip protocols will need to decide which content is to be gossiped (2c). In particular, a proactive gossip protocol typically requires to retrieve the gossip content from its local state (e.g. a temperature reading) if it needs to send periodically its state (push-style gossip) or reply to a request of its state (pull-style gossip).

The third phase is gossip dissemination (3). It utilises the underlying network to send gossip messages to either the selected (e.g. in wired networks) or neighbouring (e.g. in MANETs) peers.

On receipt of a gossip message from the network, a gossip protocol may react in three different ways, depending on the type of the received message: *i)* it might forward the message to peers that it knows (4a), thus repeating phase 2 (2a, 2b and 2c); *ii)* it might respond with its own state (4b), and again loop on phase 2); and *iii)* it might extract the remote state contained in the message, either merging [17] or comparing [2] the remote state with its own (4c). Besides this reactive behaviour, a gossip protocol may also update its own state periodically (Pb). For instance: a peer sampling protocol [17] may select peers by periodically their observed lifetime. Finally, a gossip protocol might invoke three different interactions during the state update process: 1) it might need to decide whether to merge the remote state with its local one (5a) based on certain probabilistic policies [9]; 2) it might compress the merged state (5b) to fit a predefined limit on the state size [2]; and 3) it might request for the missing information through the Gossip module (5c) after comparing the content in the remote state with its local one [1,2].

Note that this overall interaction model can be invoked recursively — each module presented in Fig. 1 can itself be implemented as a gossip protocol that follows the interaction model. For instance, the Peer Selection module can itself be a gossip-based peer sampling service protocol.

In practice, the modules in Fig. 1 are rather coarse-grained, and may vary widely between gossip protocols, making them hard to reuse. To maximise reuse, our framework therefore allows each module to be composed from finer-grained micro-modules, as shown on Fig. 2. More precisely, we have noticed that five modules (*Gossip, Peer Selection, Gossip Decision, State Compression*, and *State*)

can often be decomposed into finer-grained and reusable entities we have termed
micro-modules. These micro-modules each implement a distinct algorithm, and
can be combined to create more sophisticated behaviours. Fig. 2 shows for instance three gossip-decision policies used in a gossip-based ad-hoc routing protocol ($Gossip1(p)$, $Gossip2(p, k)$, and $Gossip3(p, k, p_1, n)$) [14].

   $Gossip1$, $Gossip2$, and $Gossip3$ differ by how they decide whether to forward
the received routing request message (i.e. they use different Gossip Decision
modules): $Gossip1$ forwards the message with probability p; $Gossip2$ is the same
as $Gossip1$ except that it forwards the message with probability 1 in the fist k
hops; and $Gossip3$ is the same as $Gossip2$ except that it forwards message with
probability $p_1 > p$ if it has less than n neighbouring peers.

   Rather than using separate implementations, these three different gossip decision strategies can be implemented by combining the three micro-modules shown
on Fig. 2. $Gossip1$ can directly use micro-module A; $Gossip2$'s Gossip Decision
module can be realised by combining with a Boolean OR the return values of
Micro-modules A and B ; and $Gossip3$ can similarly be composed from micro-
module A, B, and C. These different compositions are described in an XML
configuration file that we will present in Section 6.1.

3.3   Event-Driven Architecture

To support the common interaction pattern we have just presented, we argue that
any generic architecture should satisfy the following two criteria: First, it should
facilitate the implementation of the various modules we have just described by
making micro-modules easy to implement and configure. Second, Gossip protocols exist that we have not considered, and new ones will appear in the future,
hence it requires extra modules and interactions beyond those we have identified,
making extensibility a key requirement.

   Both requirements can be fulfilled using an event-driven architecture. Traditional event-driven architectures such as Ensemble and Cactus allow flexible protocol configuration through bindings between event handlers and events.
In such event-driven frameworks, our micro-modules (e.g. the Gossip Decision
micro-modules in Fig. 2) can be viewed as event handlers that are bound to
certain events. On the basis of these traditional event-driven architectures, GossipKit can be further improved to capture micro-module composition (e.g. the
ones mentioned in Section 3.2) using extended event-bindings. For instance, to
compose a 'Gossip Decision' module in GossipKit, several micro-modules can be
bound to events raised by the 'Gossip' module (Fig. 1). The 'Gossip' module can
then combine the values returned by each micro-module with a Boolean OR as
part of the binding, and decide whether to forward the message.

   Similarly, extensibility is addressed by using events to minimise explicit coupling between modules as argued in [8]. This allows our framework to be easily
extended by plugging in new micro-modules (i.e. event handlers) and reconfig-
uring event bindings to support new interaction patterns.

4   GossipKit's Architectural Overview

The three design choices we presented in Section 3 have resulted in an architecture consisting of five components, as shown in Fig. 3. In the figure, an interaction between two components is represented as a pair of connected interface and receptacle. The API components implement the domain-specific interfaces described in Section 3.1. The remaining components realise the common interaction pattern described in Section 3.2. The remainder of this section discusses these components and their interactions in detail.

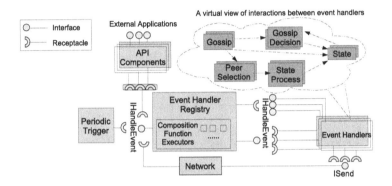

Fig. 3. GossipKit Architecture

4.1   API Components

API components uncouple the gossip protocols implemented by the framework from external applications. Each type of API component provides a generic interface to access a particular category of gossip protocols. API components also act as a bridge between their method-based interface and the events used by the framework. Fig. 4 for instance shows how the API component for the peer sampling service provides an IGetPeers interface to retrieve peer information from the local peer. When IGetPeers is invoked (operation 1 in Fig. 4), the API component generates a GetPeers event to the event handler registry (operation 2). The registry dispatches this event to the proper event handler (operation 3, see Section 4.3 below), which then retrieves the peer sampling information stored locally, and returns the information to the API component as the event handling result (operation 4 and 5). Finally, the API component returns the resulting peer sample to the external application through IGetPeers interface (operation 6).

4.2   Periodic Trigger Component

The periodic trigger component is only needed when the framework is used to support proactive gossip protocols. This component periodically dispatches

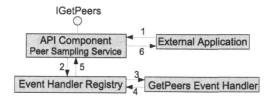

Fig. 4. Interaction of API Component with External Application

events to trigger specific event handlers that perform different styles of gossiping, such as pull, push or pull-push. The event-dispatching period (the gossip frequency) is set at deployment time, and can be reconfigured dynamically.

4.3   Event Handler Registry

The event handler registry acts as a broker between event handlers and event producers (components that raise events). On the invocation of an event, the event registry finds and executes the registered event handlers that are bound to this particular event type. To this aim, the registry maintains a table that records event handler IDs with the events they can handle. This table is populated each time an event handler's IHandleEvent interface is connected to the registry using the handler's meta-data. The event handler registry also provides an IHandleEvent interface to event producers to trigger the events.

Interestingly, the event handlers themselves can use the IHandleEvent interface to raise and delegate internal events to others handlers, thus providing a consistent event-based environment and facilitating interoperability between different gossip protocols.

Finally, the event handler registry can dynamically load composition functions to compile and interpret descriptions of micro-module composition, such as the ones mentioned in Section 3.2.

4.4   Event Handler Plugins

As mentioned in Section 3.3, our modules (i.e. Gossip, Peers_Selection, Gossip_Decision, State_Compression, and State in Fig. 1) can be further decomposed into finer-grained micro-modules. In our architecture, these micro-modules are implemented through a collection of event handler plugins (Fig. 3). These micro-modules are directly invoked by the event handler registry to handle events generated by the rest of the framework (including other micro-modules) using the extended bindings we've presented earlier. Micro-modules for the Gossip module have also access to network component to send messages (see below).

4.5   Network Component

This component provides network level communication to other components, and as such is responsible both for sending messages generated by the Gossip module and for delivering message events received from the network to the event handler registry. Through this component, our framework can operate on heterogeneous transport layers such as UDP, TCP, or ad-hoc routing, or any virtual transport layers such component-based virtual overlays [19].

5   Implementation

GossipKit's prototype implementation[1] is based on the Java version of OpenCom [15], a lightweight, efficient and reflective component engine. Java's portability enables GossipKit to operate on various platforms, from desktop computers through to PDA. We implemented the micro-modules and event handler plugins shown in Fig. 3 as individual OpenCom components, while we realised events with a plain Java class. This class contains: (i) a header string, which identifies the event type used by the handler registry to find appropriate event handlers, (ii) a body containing data to be processed by event handlers, (iii) a source ID denoting the peer that generated the event, and (iv) a target ID that identifies the target peer the event should be routed to.

Our periodic trigger component features a basic yet efficient task scheduler that allows the coexistence of multiple gossip protocols working at different frequencies. Our scheduler uses a single thread shared for protocols, and thus significantly reduces resource utilisation on constrained systems. We will revisit this issue at Section 6.3 when we discuss the memory measurement of GossipKit.

6   Evaluation

We evaluated five key properties of GossipKit—(i) configurability, (ii) reusability, (iii) memory usage, (iv) extensibility, and (v) reconfigurability—by implementing three gossip protocols from two categories: the peer-sampling services SCAMP and PSS [9,17], and the reliable multicast 'Bimodal Multicast' [2]. To assess GossipKit's ability to support concurrent execution of multiple protocol instances, we also configured Bimodal Multicast to operate on SCAMP and PSS.

6.1   Configurability

In event-driven systems, manually configuring event bindings is often time-consuming. To ease this, GossipKit uses an XML-based configuration format (Fig. 5) that describes each protocol as a high-level component composition. This format uses the common interaction pattern we have identified earlier (Fig. 1) as a template that guides users through the selection process of interactions and module instances required to form a gossip-based protocol/application.

---

[1] Source code available at: www.lancs.ac.uk/postgrad/lins6/sub/GossipKitWeb/GossipKit.html

GossipKit's XML configuration format abstracts away the details of our event-driven architecture, and allows GossipKit to automatically map high-level protocol configurations to appropriate event generators and event handlers. GossipKit's configuration format contains the following key entities: 1) coexisting protocol instances are described using <protocol> elements; 2) the micromodules that make up each gossip protocol are described in <micromodule> elements, and can be parametrised individually using the <parameters> element; and 3) a dedicated non-XML syntax is used to describe textually compositional or recursive modules: for instance the Peer_Selection module for Bimodal Multicast is described as protocol(PSS) in Fig. 5 to indicate that PSS is used recursively to select peers; and the compositional GossipDecision module of *Gossip*3 in Fig. 2) would be described as micromodule(A OR B OR C).

From our experience, configuring a new protocol from existing elements takes approximately 15 minutes. For illustration, the remainder of this subsection shows how the PSS protocol can be configured to use push-style gossip and life-time based peer selection from existing events and micro-modules.

Before discussing PSS, we must first explain the various event types that label inter-module interactions in Fig. 6. As explained in Section 5, each event's type is encoded in a string-based header to help the event handler registry dispatch the event to the correct handlers. For instance, a State module can handle Get and Add events while a Gossip module can handle Gossip events. In addition to this base type, a header string can carry extra information to indicate the type of data either carried by the event, or that is to be retrieved from the state (i.e. our events are similar to *generics*). For instance, Get<PeerID> will instruct the State module to get a list of PeerIDs instead of the whole state. This mechanism is recursive, which allows for cascading events, such as when a Gossip module receives a Gossip<Add<PeerID>> event, and dynamically raises a Add<PeerID> event to be sent over the network.

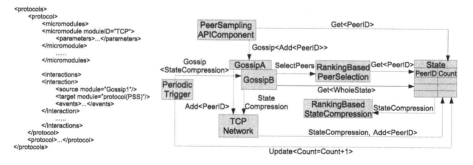

Fig. 5. XML Config   **Fig. 6.** Use case study: configuring the PSS protocol

In Fig. 6, the State is configured as a set of PeerIDs with associated lifetime counts. A local peer P joins the network by sending a Gossip<Add<PeerID>> event to an existing network peer Q, and retrieves its local peer sample with a Get<PeerID> event. On a join, GossipA is configured to forward the returned content (i.e. in this case P's PeerID) to a given target (i.e. in this case Q) by sending the event Add<PeerID> on the network. When it receives this event, Q extracts P's PeerID from the event body and adds it to its state. The Periodic Trigger module dispatches two events periodically: 1) The first event increments the Count associated with each PeerID in State; while 2) the second triggers GossipB to push the content of the local state to selected peers. GossipB invokes the Ranking_Based_Peer_Selection micro-module to select peers based on their lifetime, and forward them its own state, obtained using Get<WholeState>. GossipB then sends this information within a StateCompression event to the selected peers. Each recipient then appends the received state to its own, before, the Ranking_Based_State_Compression micro-module compresses the size of the resulting state by discarding the PeerIDs entries with the oldest lifetime.

6.2 Reusability

We evaluated the reusability of GossipKit using a quantitative approach suggested in [18]. This approach measures the byte code size of the Java classes that make up different configurations of components. To evaluate the reused development effort, we initially considered to measure both the reused byte code size and the cyclomatic complexity [22], but as shown in Fig. 7, the byte code size and the cyclomatic complexity (measured using CyVis[2]) provide roughly the same indication of development effort. In the following we therefore limit ourselves to byte code measurements.

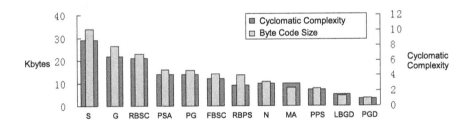

Fig. 7. Byte Code size and cyclomatic complexity provide the same measurements

In table(a) of Fig. 8, the columns under the protocol name SCAMP, PSS, and Bimodal Multicast list the number of each component type used for configuring these protocols. The highlighted rows show the components that were used more than once during configuration. These results show that most components have been frequently reused during the development of the three protocols. Furthermore, GossipKit does not only promote component reuse for developing gossip protocols that belong to the same category (SCAMP and PSS belong to the peer sampling category), but also for those belong to different categories (PSS and Bimodal Multicast). Finally, we compared the total effort of developing these

---

[2] http://cyvis.sourceforge.net/

Config. / Components (IDs)	No. of Components Used			Framework size with 3 protocols (Kbytes)	Side by side size with 3 protocols (Kbytes)
	SCAMP	PSS	Bimodal Multicast		
Multicast APIComponent (MA)	0	0	1	2.43	2.43
PeerSampling APIComponent (PSA)	1	1	0	4.82	9.64
Gossip (G)	2	2	3	7.88	39.4
LimitBased GossipDecision (LBGD)	0	0	3	1.35	4.05
Probabilistic GossipDecision (PGD)	2	0	0	1.00	2.00
PeriodicGossip (PG)	1	1	1	4.68	14.04
Probabilistic PeerSelection (PPS)	1	0	use PSS or SCAMP	2.32	2.32
RankingBased PeerSelection (RBPS)	0	1	use PSS or SCAMP	4.00	4.00
Network (N)	1	1	1	3.21	9.63
State (S)	1	1	1	10.18	30.54
RankingBased StateCompression (RBSC)	0	1	0	6.86	6.86
FilterBased StateCompression (FBSC)	0	0	1	4.26	4.26
Total				52.99	129.17

Table (a) Reusability Measurement in Byte Code Size

Protocol	Memory size (bytes)		
	GossipKit	OpenCom	Java
PSS	14744	6160	15415
SCAMP	704	6600	24623
Bimodal Multicast	8216	8352	14786

Table (b) Runtime Memory Footprint Size Measurement

Fig. 8. Reusability and Memory Usage Measurements

three protocols in GossipKit (framework size) against the effort for developing each individual protocol without the support of GossipKit (side-by-side size). The result in table(a) of Fig. 8 shows that, overall, GossipKit helps save about 60% of development effort when implementing the three protocols.

6.3   Memory Usage

GossipKit aims to facilitate the development of a wide range of gossip protocols across heterogenous networks and devices. To assess GossipKit's suitability for mobile devices with strict memory constraints, we measured the dynamic memory footprint of the components that make up the protocol configurations at runtime, using the JProfiler[3] tool. The results in table(b) of Fig. 8 indicate that the configurations map well onto mobile devices, as minimum configurations of protocols in GossipKit require less than 100Kbytes. In addition, JProfiler shows the memory usage of the PeriodicGossip component that adopts a single thread implementation remains 16 bytes regardless to the number of concurrent protocol instances running in GossipKit, validating our choice of avoiding memory-intensive multi-threading mentioned in Section 5.

6.4   Extensibility

To assess GossipKit's extensibility, we used a case study to evaluate the effort required to add a new gossip-based protocol to the three existing ones. More precisely we developed a gossip-based number averaging protocol [6] based on the existing configuration for PSS. Fig. 9 shows that this new protocol can reuse most of PSS's modules and XML configuration file: One only needs to implement two extra modules (with development effort of 3.7 Kbytes measured in byte

---

[3] http://www.ej-techonologies.com

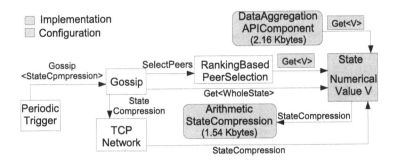

Fig. 9. Extending the PSS implementation into a number averaging protocol

code size) that are presented as shaded rectangles, to remove several redundant interactions and to change several configurations that are presented as shaded and rounded rectangles (the modifications on the configuration file only takes about 1 minute). Furthermore, we consider that it is less frequent for users to implement new components as the component collection expands because of GossipKit's support on code reuse. For instance, the newly implemented two modules will remain available for other data aggregation protocols and will not need to be re-implemented in the future.

6.5   Reconfigurability

GossipKit supports fine-grained reconfiguration to adapt to environment changes — different protocol behaviours can be achieved by replacing a single component. For instance, a peer sampling service with a life-time based peer selection can be replaced by a probabilistic peer selection module, and a particular network component can be replaced by different routing schemes. This form of component replacement relies on the mechanisms directly provided by OpenCOM. A discussion of these mechanisms is however out of the scope of this paper.

7   Conclusion and Future Work

This paper has presented GossipKit, an event-based gossip protocol framework that aims to facilitate the development of configurable and reconfigurable middleware and supports multiple gossip protocols potentially operating in parallel under different types of networks. We have presented a prototype implemented using a reflective component model (OpenCom), and we have discussed some of the benefits we have observed when implementing several gossip protocols with our framework. Our evaluation indicates that GossipKit promotes code reuse, simplifies configuration for deploying gossip protocol middleware, reduces the overhead for runtime reconfiguration, and minimises the resource usage at runtime to a certain level.

In the future, we plan to explore a broader range of gossip protocols in order to identify more domain-specific features and to improve the genericity of the common interaction model. We are also currently developing a domain specific visual language based on the existing XML-based configuration to further reduce the configuration effort and to guard users from potentially incorrect configurations. Furthermore, we plan to utilise the self-organising features of gossip protocols to improve GossipKit towards a self-adaptive framework so that it can automatically reconfigure itself and adapt to changes in its environment.

Acknowledgement

This work has been partially supported by the ESF MiNEMA programme.

References

1. Eugster, P., Guerraoui, R., et al.: Lightweight Probabilistic Broadcast. In: IEEE International Conference on Dependable Systems and Networks(DSN 2001) (2001)
2. Birman, K., Hayden, M., et al.: Bimodal multicast. TR99-1745, May 11 (1999)
3. Renesse, R., Birman, K., Hayden, M., et al.: Building Adaptive Systems Using Ensemble. Cornell University Technical Report (1997)
4. Hiltunen, M., Schlichting, R.: The Cactus Approach to Building Configurable Middleware Services. In: Proceedings of the Workshop on Dependable System Middleware and Group Communication (DSMGC 2000), Nuremberg, Germany (October 2000)
5. Jelasity, M., Babaoglu, O.: T-Man: Gossip-based overlay topology management. In: EngineeringSelf-Organising Systems: 3rd International Workshop (2005)
6. Kermarrec, A., Steen, M.: Gossiping in Distributed Systems. In: Proc. of SIGOPS Operating System Review (2007)
7. Birman, K., Abbadi, A., Dietrich, W., et al.: An Overview of the ISIS Project. In: IEEE Distributed Processing Technical Committee Newsletter (January 1985)
8. Bhatti, N., Hiltunen, M., Schlichting, R., Chiu, W.: Coyote: A System for Constructing Fine-Grain Configurable Communication Services. ACM Transactions on Computer Systems (November 1998)
9. Ganesh, A., Kermarrec, A.-M., Massoulie, L.: SCAMP: Peer-to-Peer Lightweight Membership Service for Large-Scale Group Communication. In: Proc. of the 3rd International workshop on Networked Group Communication (2001)
10. Agrawal, D., Abbadi, A.E., Steinke, R.: Epidemic algorithms in replicated databases. In: Proc. 16th ACM Symp. on Principles of Database Systems (1997)
11. van Renesse, R., Minsky, Y., Hayden, M.: A gossip-style failure-detection service. In: Proc. IFIP Intl. Conference on Distributed Systems Platform and Open Distributed Processing (1998)
12. Gupta, I., van Renesse, R., Birman, K.: Scalable fault-tolerant aggrgation in large process groups. In: Proc. Conf. on Dependable Systems and Networks (2001)
13. Demers, A., Greene, D., Hauser, C., et al.: Epidemic algorithms for replicated database maintenance. In: Proc. of the sixth annual ACM Symposium on Principles of distributed computing (1987)
14. Haas, Z., Halpern, J., Li, L.: Gossip-based Ad-Hoc Routing. IEEE/ACM Transactions on Networking (TON) (2006)

15. Clarke, M., Blair, G., Coulson, G., et al.: An efficient component model for the construction of adaptive middleware. In: Proc. of IFIP/ACM International Conference on Distributed Systems Platforms and Open Distributed Processing (2001)
16. Hiltunen, M., Taiani, F., Schlichting, R.: Reflections on Aspects and Configurable Protocols. In: The 5th Int. Conf. on Aspect Oriented Software Development (2006)
17. Jelasity, M., Guerraoui, R., Kermarrec, A., et al.: The Peer Sampling Service: Experimental Evaluation of Unstructured Gossip-Based Implementations. In: Proc. of the 5th ACM/IFIP/USENIX international conference on Middleware (2004)
18. Flores-Cortes, C., Blair, G., Grace, P.: A Multi-protocol Framework for Ad-Hoc Service Discovery. In: Proc. of the 4th International Workshop on on Middleware for Pervasive and Ad-Hoc Computing, Australia (2006)
19. Grace, P., Coulson, G., Blair, G., et al.: GRIDKIT: Pluggable Overlay Networks for Grid Computing. In: Proc.of International Symposium on Distributed Objects and Applications(DOA), Larnaca, Cyprus (2004)
20. Friedman, R., Gavidia, D., Rodirgues, L., et al.: Gossiping on MANETs: the Beauty and the Beast. ACM Operating Systems Review (2007)
21. Hou, X., Tipper, D.: Gossip-based sleep protocol (GSP) for energy efficient routing in wireless ad hoc networks. In: Proceedings of Wireless Communications and Networking Conference (2004)
22. McCabe: A Complexity Measure. IEEE Transactions on SE (1976)

Cost-Efficient Deployment of Collaborating Components

Máté J. Csorba, Poul E. Heegaard, and Peter Herrmann

Norwegian University of Science and Technology (NTNU),
Department of Telematics, N-7491 Trondheim, Norway
{Mate.Csorba,Poul.Heegaard,Peter.Herrmann}@item.ntnu.no

Abstract. We study the problem of efficient deployment of software components in a service engineering context. Run-time manipulation, adaptation and composition of entities forming a distributed service is a multi-faceted problem challenged by a number of requirements. The methodology applied and presented can be viewed as an intersection between systems development and novel network management solutions. Application of heuristics, in particular artificial intelligence in the service development cycle allows for optimization and should eventually grant the same benefits as those existing in distributed management architectures such as increased dependability, better resource utilization, etc. The aim is finding the optimal deployment mapping of components to physically available resources, while satisfying all the non-functional requirements of the system design. Accordingly, a new component deployment approach is introduced utilizing distributed stochastic optimization.

1 Introduction

Today, computer applications tend to be highly distributed and dynamic. In addition, they are executed on hardware systems that change their topology and performance dynamically. This calls for flexible methods to deploy the software components realizing a networked application on the available hosts to achieve preferably high performance and low cost levels.

By such a software component we mean an executable stand-alone package of software that has a well-defined interface and can communicate with other components via message exchange. Furthermore, we define a service as a collaboration of distributed components running in a (possibly also highly distributed) hardware environment on different hosts, using distinct network elements for interconnection. A specific service can be observed from different views. We investigate the problem of efficient component deployment from the view of the service creator who is in most cases the provider of the service as well. We do so based on the starting point we use for our investigation, i.e. we start from a service specification, from a model that is a product of the service designer. Usually the parameters we are interested in are performance and cost effectiveness, which are both substantial from the provider's perspective if it comes to the deployment of a new service.

The problem of cost-efficient component deployment is challenged by multiple dimensions of Quality of Service (QoS), or in other words, non-functional requirements

R. Meier and S. Terzis (Eds.): DAIS 2008, LNCS 5053, pp. 253–268, 2008.

that need to be taken into account. To name a few there might be a fluctuation in the number of users of the service deployed who might also have arbitrary utility functions for the service as well as different usage scenarios. Additionally, the QoS requirements identified might change over time, the system designed might provide several services. This complicated combination of factors forms the basis of the problem we aim to solve. Namely, finding the optimal deployment mapping of components to physically available resources, while satisfying all the non-functional requirements of the system design.

The resulting deployment mapping has a large influence on the QoS that can and will be provided by the system. The most basic example of improving QoS by choosing a better deployment architecture is to consider only the latency of the service. The easiest way to satisfy latency requirements is to identify and deploy the components that require the highest volume of interactions onto the same resource, or to choose resources that are at least connected by links with sufficiently high capacity.

Several approaches have been followed to solve this problem, e.g. binary integer programming [1] or graph cutting [2]. Usually, complexity becomes NP-hard using these methods with more than 2-3 hosts. Others try to capture constraints and restrict the solution space [3]. However, due to the exact solution algorithms computational complexity is still an issue. What is even more restrictive in these approaches is that they do not attempt to work with more than one QoS dimension at a time, while our objective is to deal with vectors of QoS properties in one run. Furthermore, we aim to be able to aid the deployment of several different services at the same time using the same framework.

Approximative solutions are devised by Malek et al., such as greedy algorithms, genetic programming for example in [4]. Malek et al. however approaches the deployment problem from the user's perspective by maximizing an overall utility function. On the contrary, we aim to investigate the deployment problem from the service provider's perspective. Besides, autonomous replication management is targeted by Meling in a framework based on group communication systems [5]. Widell et al. discuss an alternative solution based on a stochastic optimization method called the Cross Entropy (CE) Method [6].

Generally, we require a method that is capable to adapt to changes in the environment in a highly efficient way. Also, as module allocation problems are proven to be NP-complete (cf. [7]), except in some special cases, heuristics are needed for providing an efficient solution. Accordingly, we chose a bio-inspired system, swarm intelligence as a basis for our method to solve the deployment problem in a fully distributed manner. As we omit any centralized database or building block and propose to use the analogy of pheromones for storing information in a distributed way the logic presented is robust and highly adaptive with respect to changing QoS provided by the service execution platform. Eventually, our aim is to develop a method for run-time component (re-)deployment support that allows execution of services within the allowed region of external parameters defined by the service requirements.

The remainder of this paper is organized as follows. The next section will introduce our system model and position our work. Sect. 3 briefly presents the Cross-Entropy Ant System (CEAS) that is used throughout the paper as the basis of our heuristic optimization method. Sect. 4 provides our solution to the target scenario and a summary of our algorithm. Sect. 5 comes with a more tangible example and compares our results to previous solutions. In the last section we conclude and touch upon our future work.

2   Support for Deployment Mapping

Our deployment approach fits to the engineering method SPACE which is devoted to the rapid and correct engineering of distributed services [8]. As depicted in Fig. 1(a), in the process of developing a service, one creates first a purely functional service model. This specification is collaboration-oriented, i.e., the overall service specification is not composed from descriptions of the physical software components realizing the service but from models of distributed sub-functionalities which — in interaction — fulfill the complete service behavior. This specification style enables the development of service models by reusing building blocks from domain specific model libraries to a much higher degree than it would be possible when applying component-based descriptions (e.g., [9]). As modelling language, we use UML collaborations and activities.

After performing correctness checks on the service model (see [10]), it is transformed to a component-oriented design model by a model transformation tool [11] which is specified by UML state machines. In the next step, code generators create executable Java code from the design model enabling a fully automated transformation of collaboration-oriented service models to executable programs. This process is well described in [12].

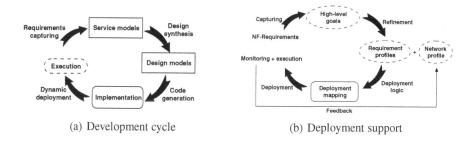

(a) Development cycle   (b) Deployment support

Fig. 1. Development with SPACE and the deployment support

For the efficient deployment of the implementation, we extend the development cycle as shown in Fig. 1(b). The service models are amended by *high-level non-functional (NF) goals* defining the non-functional requirements (NFR) of a service in a rather abstract manner. In parallel with the transformation from the service to the design models, these NF goals are refined into *requirement profiles* specifying the non-functional requirements of the service components. Moreover, a *network profile* is added, thus required and provided properties are collected describing the system and its target environment. Based on these inputs our deployment logic can be launched with the profiles specifying the goals and the *net-map* specifying the search space.

For capturing QoS requirements that are relevant to our system, we follow the collaboration-oriented style and capture NFRs in design time. NFRs usually represent qualities such as security, performance, availability, portability, etc. In fact, in our view the

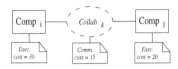

Fig. 2. Collaboration with NFRs

deployment logic should be able to handle any properties of the service, as long as we can provide a cost function for the specific property. In that matter we will exploit the advanced scalability of CEAS and the method of pheromone sharing.

In Fig. 2 a simple example of a collaboration between two components is depicted enriched with NFRs for both the components and for the collaboration binding them. This basic collection of requirements contains two types of cost values, an execution and a communication cost. The execution cost is added to the local cost of a node that contains the particular component after deployment. The communication cost is imposed on the connection between the two components participating in the collaboration. This simple example of collaboration-oriented specification and capturing of requirements will be illustrated in the example in Sect. 5.

Existing component deployment strategies and solutions use various centralized databases and decision logics. Relying on a fully centralized logic requires the burden of keeping the central database constantly updated and at the same time introduces a single point of failure in the system. Moreover, a performance bottleneck may arise at the node storing the central database and accommodating the decision logic both communication wise and storage wise.

In a distributed cooperative algorithm (semi-)autonomous agents cooperate to achieve certain common goals. Since in a distributed environment autonomous agents do not have an overview of the system as a whole, their decisions have to be based on information that is available locally to the place where they reside. To enable cooperation between agents, some sort of shared memory is required at each place an agent can visit. In our deployment logic, the information is distributed across all the nodes participating in the deployment. In this way, we achieve a completely robust, scalable and fault tolerant mechanism. Furthermore, to achieve a complete solution, our aims are twofold. First, the logic shall be able to obtain an initial deployment mapping based on the service model. Second, once the service is running, the logic shall be capable of monitoring online and execute the necessary changes to satisfy the requirements it is launched with.

The objective is to find the optimal, or at least a satisfactory, mapping in reasonable time between a number of component instances c, onto nodes n. A component, $c_i \in \mathbf{C}$ ($\mathbf{C}$ is the set of components available for (re-)deployment) can be a *client process*, or a *service process*, while a node, $n \in \mathbf{N}$ ($\mathbf{N}$ is the set of nodes) can be a *transit node*, e.g. a traditional IP router, a *server node*, which is capable of accommodating a service component, a *client node*, which is an aggregation point for client components, or a *mixed node* that can accommodate both client and service components.

The cost function $F(M)$ of the mapping $M : \mathbf{C} \rightarrow \mathbf{N}$ should be minimized under the constraints given by the *mapping scopes* $\mathbf{R}_i \subseteq \mathbf{N}$ for each component instance i. $\mathbf{R}_i$

is determined by the intersection of access restrictions, service provider policies (e.g. service level agreements of ISPs), provided and requested capabilities (soft costs) and provided and requested capacity requirements (hard costs, e.g. bandwidth limitations). Attached components, i.e. components restricted to a specific node will have an $\mathbf{R}_i$ set consisting of a single node, thus reducing the search space.

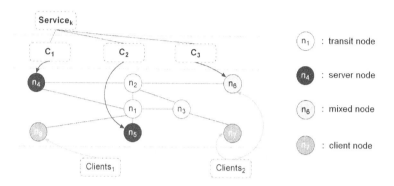

Fig. 3. Component mapping example

An illustration of the model can be found in Fig. 3. Suppose we develop a service, $Service_k$, which is implemented by three service components $\mathbf{C} = \{c_1, c_2, c_3\}$ and the service is expected to be accessed by two distinguishable set of clients. Besides the *requirement profiles*, the service provider must provide the *net-map* for the decision logic as well, specifying the available nodes and links. Thus, the set of nodes becomes $\mathbf{N} = \{n_1, n_2, \ldots, n_8\}$. Client nodes in this case are considered to be aggregation nodes, i.e., they represent a single point of access to the network for the clients of the service, with a different meaning from the traditional notion of node. So, the designer can specify where in the provided *net-map* the clients are located and can insert additional parameters describing the clients of the service, such as the expected amount of clients, the expected service demand, etc. as NFRs. Constraints that will influence the optimal deployment can be assigned to nodes and links. For links, constraints appear as the costs of using the particular link for connection between two components that need to interact. Constraints assigned to nodes, for instance, can represent memory sizes restricting placement of component instances to a place. Besides, node properties can be interrelated, i.e., for example if a mixed type node (n_6) accommodates a service component it can influence the rest of the properties, e.g. lower the amount of allowed clients at the node by modifying the memory constraint.

Next, we introduce the stochastic optimization background, which we use for providing solutions to the component deployment and redeployment problem.

3   Cross Entropy Ant System

The deployment problem in this paper is approached by use of a distributed, robust and adaptive routing system called the Cross Entropy Ant System (CEAS) [13]. The

CEAS is an Ant Colony Optimization (ACO) system as introduced by Dorigo et al. [14], which is a multi-agent system for solving a wide variety of combinatorial optimization problems where the agents' behavior are inspired by the foraging behaviour of ants. Examples of successful application in communication system are load-balancing (Schoonderwoerd et al. [15]), routing in wired networks by AntNet [16], and routing in wireless networks by AntHocNet [17]. The key idea is to let many agents, denoted *ants*, iteratively search for the best solution according to the problem constraints and cost function defined. Each iteration consists of two phases; the *forward* ants search for a solution, which resembles the ants searching for food, and the *backward* ants that evaluate the solution and leave markings, denoted *pheromones*, that are in proportion to the quality of the solution. These pheromones are distributed at different locations in the search space and can be used by forward ants in their search for good solutions; therefore, the best solution will be approached gradually. To avoid getting stuck in premature and sub-optimal solutions, some of the forward ants will explore the state space freely ignoring the pheromone values.

The main difference between the ant based systems is the approach taken to evaluate the solution and update the pheromones. For example, AntNet uses reinforcement learning while CEAS uses the *Cross Entropy (CE) method for stochastic optimization* introduced by Rubinstein [18]. The CE method is applied in the pheromone updating process by gradually changing the probability matrix $\mathbf{p}_r$ according to the cost of the paths. The objective is to minimize the cross entropy between two consecutive samples $\mathbf{p}_r$ and $\mathbf{p}_{r-1}$. For a tutorial on the method, [19] is recommended.

The CEAS has demonstrated its applicability through a variety of studies of different path management strategies, such as shared backup path protection (SBPP) [20], p-cycles [21], resource search under QoS constraints [22], and adaptive paths with stochastic routing [23]. Implementation issues and trade-offs, such as management overhead imposed by additional traffic for management packets and recovery times are dealt with using a mechanism called elitism [24] and self-tuned packet rate control [25], [26]. Additional reduction in the overhead is accomplished by pheromone sharing [27] where ants with overlapping requirements cooperate in finding solutions by (partly) sharing information.

In this paper, the CEAS is applied to obtain the best deployment of a set of components, $\mathbf{C}$, onto a set of nodes, $\mathbf{N}$. The nodes are physically connected by links used by the ants to move from node to node in search for available capacities. A given deployment at iteration r is a set $\mathbf{M}_r = \{\mathbf{m}_{n,r}\}_{n \in \mathbf{N}}$, where $\mathbf{m}_{n,r} \subseteq \mathbf{C}$ is the set of components at node n at iteration r. In CEAS applied for routing the path is defined as a set of nodes from the source to the destination, while now we define the path as the deployment set $\mathbf{M}_r$. The cost of a deployment set is denoted $F(\mathbf{M}_r)$. Furthermore, in the original CEAS we assign the pheromone values $\tau_{ij,r}$ to interface i of node j at iteration r, while now we assign $\tau_{mn,r}$ to the component set m deployed at node n at iteration r. In Sect. 4 we describe the search and update algorithm in details.

In traditional CEAS applied for routing and network management, selection of the next hop is based on the *random proportional rule* presented below. In our case however, the *random proportional rule* is applied for deployment mapping. Accordingly, during the initial exploration phase, the ants randomly select the next *set of components* with uniform probability $1/E$, where E is the number of components to be deployed, i.e. the size of $\mathbf{C}$, while in the normal phase the next hop is selected according to the *random proportional rule* matrix $\mathbf{p}_r = [p_{mn,r}]$, where

$$p_{mn,r} = \frac{\tau_{mn,r}}{\sum_{l \in \mathbf{M}_{n,r}} \tau_{ln,r}} \qquad (1)$$

The pheromone values in (1) are determined considering the entire history of cost values $\mathbf{F}_r = \{F(\mathbf{M}_1), \ldots, F(\mathbf{M}_r)\}$ up to iteration r. The backward ants update the pheromone values at the nodes where one or more components in $\mathbf{M}_r$ are deployed. The pheromones are updated according to

$$\tau_{mn,r} = \sum_{k=1}^{r} I(l \in \mathbf{M}_{n,r}) \beta^{\sum_{x=k+1}^{r} I(x \in \mathbf{M}_k)} H(F(\mathbf{M}_k), \gamma_r) \qquad (2)$$

where $I(x) = 1$ when x is true and 0 otherwise. $H(f, \gamma) = e^{-f/\gamma}$ is the performance function and $\beta \in (0, 1)$ is the weight parameter, or in other words the memory factor in the auto-regressive formulation of the performance function. The auto-regressive formulation $h_r(\gamma_r) = \beta h_{r-1}(\gamma_r) + (1 - \beta) H(F(\mathbf{M}_r), \gamma_r)$ is the key in CEAS for avoiding any centralized control and synchronized iterations. This reformulation allows the cost value $F(\mathbf{M}_r)$ to be calculated immediately after a single ant ends its forward movement, i.e. the ant manages to find a mapping for all the components originally assigned to it. Now, iteration r represents the total number of updates, in other words, the total number of backward ants returned. The reformulated performance function, $h_r(\gamma_r)$ can be approximated by

$$h_r(\gamma_r) \approx \frac{1 - \beta}{1 - \beta^r} \sum_{i=1}^{r} \beta^{r-i} e^{-\frac{F(\mathbf{M}_i)}{\gamma_r}} \qquad (3)$$

see [13]. Thus, a digest of the search history is applied, where older cost values gradually disappear, i.e. *evaporate*. This evaporation is achieved using the memory factor β that provides geometrically decreasing weights for the output of the performance function. The control parameter, γ_r can be determined by minimizing γ subject to $h(\gamma) \geq \rho$, where ρ is the search focus parameter (typically 0.05 or less). For more details about the parameters and solutions to (2) and (3) see [28].

4   Application of Ant-Based Deployment Mapping

The deployment logic can be considered as an optimization task continuously executed by independent ant-like agents in the target network hosting the service we model. The continuous ant behavior contributes to the advantage of our approach, namely that the same logic can be used for an initial static mapping and for an online redeployment mechanism.

At first, every ant is assigned a task of deployment of $\mathbf{C}$ components. Thereafter, ants are started continuously and proceed with a random-walk on the provided *net-map* randomly selecting each next node to visit. Behavior at a visited node depends on if the ant is an *explorer* or a *normal* ant. A *normal* ant selects a subset of **C** governed by the pheromone levels at the node it currently resides in and stores its selection $\mathbf{m}_{n,r}$ in a mapping list $\mathbf{M}_r$, which is carried along by the ant. Similarly, an *explorer* ant selects a subset $\mathbf{m}_{n,r}$ based on a random decision instead of the distributed pheromone database. *Explorer* ants are used for exploring the available *net-map*, both initially and later as well for covering up fluctuations in the network, e.g. new nodes appearing. More precisely, the effects of *exploration* are twofold. First, as optimization starts *explorer ants* are used to cover up a significant amount of the problem space via random sampling. The required number of initial *exploration* iterations depend on the problem size, but it can be estimated by sampling the pheromone database size. After that, the *normal* phase starts, in which case only a fraction of the ants generated are flagged as *explorers*, thus allowing for the required responsiveness to changes in the environment, while *normal* ants are focusing on finding the optimum.

Once an ant has deployed all its assigned components the resulting mapping $\mathbf{M}_r$ can be evaluated by applying the cost function $F(\mathbf{M}_r)$ derived from the service specification. A more concrete example on $F(\mathbf{M}_r)$ can be found in Sect. 5. Once the mapping is evaluated, the ant goes back along the nodes in its path that has been stored in the hop-list $\mathbf{H}_r$ and updates pheromone values according to Equation (2) corresponding to the pairs of component sets and nodes it has selected during its journey. After that, a new iteration starts as a new ant is emitted, unless a stopping criteria is met. A stopping criteria can be constructed by observing the moving average of the evolving cost value, i.e. detecting convergence to a suggested solution. Another option is sampling the size of the distributed pheromone database during an iteration. After convergence a very strong pheromone value will emerge in the database, while inferior solutions will evaporate. The described process is summarized in Algorithm 1.

Algorithm 1. Deployment mapping of $\mathbf{C} = \{c_1, \ldots, c_E\}$ component instances

---

1. Select the initial node $n \in \mathbf{N}$ where the search will start randomly.
2. Select a set of components $\mathbf{m}_{n,r} \subseteq \mathbf{C}$ which satisfies $n \in \mathbf{R}$ for every $c_i \in \mathbf{m}_{n,r}$ according to the random proportional rule (*normal* ant), Equation (1), or in a totally random manner (*explorer* ant). If such a set cannot be found, goto step 5.
3. Update the ant's deployment mapping set, $\mathbf{M}_r = \mathbf{M}_r + \{\mathbf{m}_{n,r}\}$.
4. Update the set of components to be deployed, $\mathbf{C} = \mathbf{C} - \mathbf{m}_{n,r}$.
5. Select next node, n randomly and add n to the hop-list $\mathbf{H}_r = \mathbf{H}_r + \{n\}$.
6. If $\mathbf{C} \neq \emptyset$ then goto 2., otherwise evaluate $F(\mathbf{M}_r)$ and update the pheromone values, Equation (2) corresponding to the $\{\mathbf{m}_{n,r}\} \in \mathbf{M}_r$ mappings going backwards along $\mathbf{H}_r$.
7. If stopping criteria is not met then increment r, initialize and emit new ant and goto 1.

Generally, we have a trade-off between convergence speed and solution quality. Nevertheless, while deploying a service in a dynamic environment, which is our goal, a pre-mature solution that satisfies both functional and non-functional requirements often suffices. Thus the optimality requirement can be relaxed while taking restoration time requirements into consideration. Besides, it has been proven that ACO systems do in fact find the optimum at least once with probability close to one and when this has happened they converge to the optimum in a finite number of iterations. Since CEAS can be considered as a subclass of ACO the optimal deployment mapping will eventually emerge.

5   Analysis of a Problem

As a representative example, we consider the scenario originally from Efe dealing with heuristical clustering of modules and assignment of clusters to nodes [29]. This scenario has also been investigated by Widell et al., and a comparison to results of several other authors can be found in [6]. This scenario, even though artificial and may not be tangible from a designer's point of view, is sufficiently complex to test our deployment logic. The problem is defined in our approach as a collaboration of $E = 10$ components (labelled $c_1 \ldots c_{10}$) to be deployed and $K = 14$ collaborations between them k_j, $j = 1 \ldots K$, as depicted in Fig. 4. We consider three types of requirements in this specification. Besides the execution and communication costs, we have a restriction on components c_2, c_7, c_9, regarding their location. They must be bound to nodes n_2, n_1, n_3, respectively.

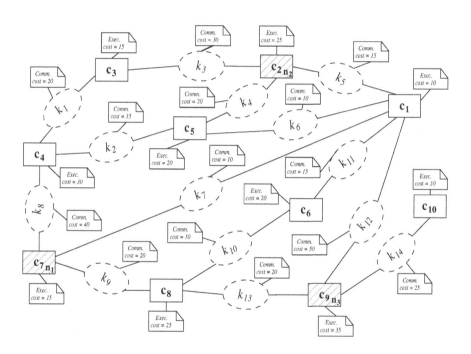

Fig. 4. Collaborations and components in the example scenario

Furthermore, to be able to use similar mechanisms for specifying the *net-map* for the deployment logic, we propose to use the same object paradigm UML employs to reduce complexity. Thus, we specify the underlying physical map of hosts as a diagram, depicted in Fig. 5.

In this example, the target environment consists only of $N = 3$ identical, inter-connected nodes with a single provided property, namely processing power and with infinite communication capacities. Accordingly, we only observe the total load

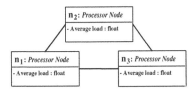

Fig. 5. The target network of hosts in the example scenario

$(\hat{l}_{n,r},\ n = 1 \ldots N)$ of a given deployment mapping at each node. The communication cost between two components is considered significant only if it appears between two separate nodes, and we will strive for a global optimal solution of equally distributed load among the processing nodes and the lowest cost possible, while taking into account the NFRs, execution cost f_{c_i}, $i = 1 \ldots E$ and communication cost f_{k_j}, $j = 1 \ldots K$. f_{c_i} and f_{k_j} are derived from the service specification, thus, the total offered execution load can be calculated before optimization starts as $\sum_{i=1}^{E} f_{c_i}$. This way, the logic can be aware of the target load

$$T = \frac{\sum_{i=1}^{E} f_{c_i}}{N} \tag{4}$$

By looking at the example in Fig. 4 and Fig. 5 for this service we have $T \cong 68$. Given a mapping $\mathbf{M}_r = \{\mathbf{m}_{n,r}\}$, the total load can be obtained as $\hat{l}_{n,r} = \sum_{c_i \in \mathbf{m}_{n,r}} f_{c_i}$. Furthermore, the overall cost function $F(\mathbf{M}_r)$ becomes

$$F(\mathbf{M}_r) = \sum_{n=1}^{N} |\hat{l}_{n,r} - T| + \sum_{j=1}^{K} I_j\, f_{k_j} \tag{5}$$

for mapping $\mathbf{M}_r$ suggested by ant r, where

$$I_j = \begin{cases} 1, & \text{if } k_j \text{ external} \\ 0, & \text{if } k_j \text{ internal to a node} \end{cases} \tag{6}$$

Optimization governed by the cost function $F(\mathbf{M}_r)$ starts with aligning pheromone values with the sets of deployed components. With the underlying set of nodes (**N**) each ant will form N discrete sets from the set of available components (**C**) that need to be deployed and evaluate the outcome of that deployment mapping (**M**$_r$) at the end of its run. However, the ants only need to carry a list of the unrestricted components, i.e. with the exception of components c_2, c_7, c_9 that are bound to a node by a constraint, leaving the rest of 7 components for mapping. A flag is assigned to each of the remaining components giving 2^7 as the number of possible combinations for a set at a node. Thus, the pheromone database at each node has to accommodate 2^7 floating point numbers in this case. After normalizing the pheromones in a node we can observe the probability distribution of component sets mapped to that particular node by the ant system. Eventually the optimal solution(s) will emerge with probability one after convergence.

The pheromone database is indexed by a component set identifier. For example, Id. 36, which is equivalent to $'0100100'B$, indicates that the free components c_4 and c_8 are deployed on that node. In Fig. 6, pheromone levels (normalized as probabilities) for two sets of components at node n_1 are depicted. After the initial phase of 10000 explorer ants doing random search the emergence of the solution deemed optimal can be seen in Fig. 6(a) for the set of components c_4, c_8 in addition to c_7 attached in advance. Also, in Fig. 6(b) evolution of the pheromone corresponding to a suboptimal set of components, c_4, c_6, c_8 and c_7 deployed at n_1, is shown (observe the different scales on the Y-axis).

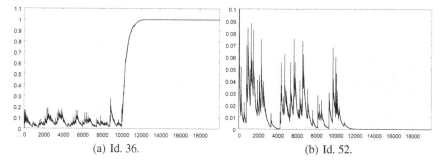

(a) Id. 36.   (b) Id. 52.

Fig. 6. Pheromones at node n_1

The optimal deployment mapping can be observed in Table 1. The lowest possible deployment cost, according to (5) is $17 + (200 - 100) = 117$.

Table 1. Optimal deployment mapping in the example scenario

node	components	$l_{n,opt}$	$|l_{n,opt} - T|$	internal collaborations
n_1	c_4, c_7, c_8	70	2	k_8, k_9
n_2	c_2, c_3, c_5	60	8	k_3, k_4
n_3	c_1, c_6, c_9, c_{10}	75	7	k_{11}, k_{12}, k_{14}
$\sum$cost			17	100

The rare event of finding the optimal deployment with the lowest cost during a random search can be observed in Fig. 7. The exploration phase consists of the first 2000 ants, conducting a random search and resulting in a random cost figure. However, after exploration ends, from ant number 2001, the real optimization phase starts and the overall deployment cost is converging to the optimal value of 117. At the same time, we propose usage of a pheromone database that is allocated dynamically in the memory for storing pheromone values based on a threshold level that evaporates all the pheromone entries under a certain significance level. In Fig. 7, 1% threshold is applied, i.e. pheromones smaller than 1% of the highest value are deemed insignificant and are eliminated from the database.

The database size tops at 2^7 as the solution space is starting to be covered by exploration ants and thus it can be used as an indicator to switch to the optimization phase. Likewise, when the overall cost converges to the optimal value (117) the size of the database approaches one (if there is a single solution like in the example) as the single optimal solution prevails, allowing for convergence detection.

We can compare our results to the results obtained using the centralized CE method. A comparison between different solutions to the original problem from Efe can be found in [6]. Widell et al., in accordance with the original CE method, uses a selected distribution to generate a sample iteration, which is in case of the component deployment problem a particular deployment mapping. The generated samples are then used for updates in the parameter of the selected distribution. The updates are based on an assessment of the quality of the sample iteration. Sampling and updating is repeated until convergence is detected, which, due to stochasticity though might not be the optimal mapping of components. In fact, the number of ant runs in distributed CEAS can be compared to full iterations in the centralized CE method, as a single ant's lifetime (from leaving the nest until its return) is equivalent to the number of samples taken multiplied with the number of iterations.

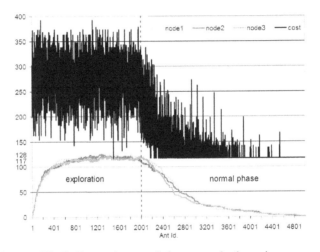

Fig. 7. Observed cost and pheromone database sizes

For example, in [6] using 100 samples the mean number of iterations required for finding the optimal solution with 80% confidence is 41, which in turn is approximately equivalent to $100 \cdot 41 = 4100$ ant runs. We can see that using the same CE focus parameter, i.e. $\rho = 0.01$, and a memory factor of $\beta = 0.998$ (cf. Sect. 3), we can expect convergence times to average at 1200 ant runs for arbitrary number of explorations (Fig. 8) using our distributed CEAS approach. Here, we only compared our results to the most efficient solution by Widell et al. However, it is difficult to compare the two approaches in terms of number of iterations because they differ in the methodology, i.e. multiple samples in one iteration in Widell's work versus one iteration as a sample in CEAS. Nonetheless, we have found that our approach is capable of finding the optimal solution (cf. Table 1) with at least the same confidence, requires less iterations, thus it is resource conserving and last but not least it is a completely distributed logic compared to the original CE-based method and the other strictly centralized solutions, e.g. clustering, bin-packing, etc.

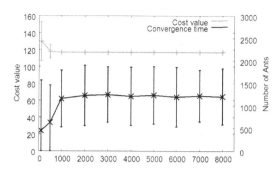

Fig. 8. The observed cost and the number of ants required for convergence as a function of the number of explorer ants

In Fig. 8, results of running the deployment logic with different amounts (shown on the x-axis) of explorer ants are depicted. The mean values of 200 subsequent executions in each setting can be observed with the standard deviation of the results included as error bars. The deployment logic is currently implemented in a simulator written in the Simula/DEMOS language [30] for evaluation purposes.

It can be noted that above a sufficient amount of initial exploration of the problem the logic is quite robust in finding the optimal solution and stable in convergence time as well. However, in our algorithm we do not set the number of explorers to a constant number, instead we propose to use the dynamic database size as an indication for sufficient exploratory runs. Also, an advantage of our approach is that it can provide alternative solutions weighted by their cost and corresponding pheromone values will indicate the deployment mapping for those solutions. So, in a system where convergence time is very critical, even premature results can be used for near optimal deployment.

6 Closing Remarks

We presented a novel approach for the efficient deployment of software components taking into account QoS requirements captured during the modelling phase in the service engineering approach, SPACE. The procedure starts from high-level QoS goals and through requirement profiles utilizes swarm intelligence to provide solutions and to aid dynamic deployment. The logic itself can be executed in a fully distributed manner, thus it is not prone to deficiencies of existing centralized algorithms, such as performance bottlenecks and single point of failures. Our approach does not require a centralized database, instead it uses the analogy of pheromones distributed across the network of hosts. Furthermore, the logic, as it is presented here, is applied to provide the optimal, initial mapping of components to hosts, i.e. the network is considered rather static. However, our eventual goal is to develop support for run-time redeployment of components, this way keeping the service within an allowed region of parameters defined by the requirements. As the results with CEAS show our logic will be a prominent candidate for a robust and adaptive service execution platform.

Our work is conducted in cooperation with the ISIS (Infrastructure for Integrated Services) project funded by the Research Council of Norway comprising of multiple participants both from industry and academia. The methodology and algorithms presented are in-line with the objectives of ISIS that are to create a well-established service engineering platform for collaboration-oriented models, covering a development cycle from the requirements to seamless execution in a heterogenous and dynamic environment.

In our future work we will investigate applicability and utility of different deployment strategies based on the existing logic. Also, we plan to experiment with stochastic optimization methods other than the CE method. Another issue is database size management locally to the nodes hosting the service. The first step to address this issue was the introduction of dynamically allocated databases, which will be investigated further. Especially, in case of deployment of multiple services at the same time, which is one of the topics in our future research. We presented a novel approach for the efficient deployment of software components taking into account QoS requirements captured during the modelling phase in the service engineering approach, SPACE. The procedure starts from high-level QoS goals and through requirement profiles utilizes swarm intelligence to provide solutions and to aid dynamic deployment. The logic itself can be executed in a fully distributed manner, thus it is not prone to deficiencies of existing centralized algorithms, such as performance bottlenecks and single point of failures. Our approach does not require a centralized database, instead it uses the analogy of pheromones distributed across the network of hosts. Furthermore, the logic, as it is presented here, is applied to provide the optimal, initial mapping of components to hosts, i.e. the network is considered rather static. However, our eventual goal is to develop support for run-time redeployment of components, this way keeping the service within an allowed region of parameters defined by the requirements. As the results with CEAS show our logic will be a prominent candidate for a robust and adaptive service execution platform.

Our work is conducted in cooperation with the ISIS (Infrastructure for Integrated Services) project funded by the Research Council of Norway comprising of multiple participants both from industry and academia. The methodology and algorithms presented are in-line with the objectives of ISIS that are to create a well-established service engineering platform for collaboration-oriented models, covering a development cycle from the requirements to seamless execution in a heterogenous and dynamic environment.

In our future work we will investigate applicability and utility of different deployment strategies based on the existing logic. Also, we plan to experiment with stochastic optimization methods other than the CE method. Another issue is database size management locally to the nodes hosting the service. The first step to address this issue was the introduction of dynamically allocated databases, which will be investigated further. Especially, in case of deployment of multiple services at the same time, which is one of the topics in our future research.

References

1. Bastarrica, M.C., et al.: A Binary Integer Programming Model for Optimal Object Distribution. In: Int'l. Conf. on Principles of Distributed Systems, Amiens (1998)
2. Hunt, G.C., Scott, M.L.: The Coign Automatic Distributed Partitioning System. In: Proceedings of the 3rd Symposium on Operating Systems Design and Implementation, New Orleans (1999)

3. Kichkaylo, T., et al.: Constrained Component Deployment in Wide-Area Networks Using AI Planning Techniques. In: Int'l. Parallel and Distributed Processing Symposium (2003)

4. Malek, S.: A User-Centric Framework for Improving a Distributed Software System's Deployment Architecture. In: Proceedings of the doctoral track at the 14th ACM SIGSOFT Symposium on Foundation of Software Engineering, Portland (2006)

5. Meling, H.: Adaptive Middleware Support and Autonomous Fault Treatment: Architectural Design, Prototyping and Experimental Evaluation. PhD Thesis, Norwegian University of Science and Technology, Department of Telematics (May 2006)

6. Widell, N., Nyberg, C.: Cross Entropy based Module Allocation for Distributed Systems. In: Proceedings of the 16th IASTED International Conference on Parallel and Distributed Computing and Systems, Cambridge (2004)

7. Fernandez-Baca, D.: Allocating modules to processors in a distributed system. IEEE Transactions on Software Engineering 15(11) (1989)

8. Kraemer, F.A., Herrmann, P.: Service Specification by Composition of Collaborations - An Example. In: Proceedings of the 2006 IEEE/WIC/ACM international conference on Web Intelligence and Intelligent Agent Technology, Hong Kong (2006)

9. Herrmann, P., Kraemer, F.A.: Design of Trusted Systems with Reusable Collaboration Models. In: Proceedings of the Joint IFIP iTrust and PST Conferences on Privacy, Trust Management and Security, Moncton. Springer, Boston (2007)

10. Kraemer, F.A., Slåtten, V., Herrmann, P.: Engineering Support for UML Activities by Automated Model-Checking - An Example. In: Proceedings of the 4th International Workshop on Rapid Integration of Software Engineering Techniques (RISE 2007), University of Luxembourg (2007)

11. Kraemer, F.A., Herrmann, P.: Transforming Collaborative Service Specifications into Efficiently Executable State Machines. Electronic Communications of the EASST 6 (2007)

12. Kraemer, F.A., Herrmann, P., Bræk, R.: Aligning UML 2.0 State Machines and Temporal Logic for the Efficient Execution of Services. In: Meersman, R., Tari, Z. (eds.) OTM 2006. LNCS, vol. 4276, Springer, Heidelberg (2006)

13. Helvik, B.E., Wittner, O.: Using the Cross Entropy Method to Guide/Govern Mobile Agent's Path Finding in Networks. In: Proceedings of 3rd International Workshop on Mobile Agents for Telecommunication Applications (2001)

14. Dorigo, M., et al.: The Ant System: Optimization by a colony of cooperating agents. IEEE Transactions on Systems, Man, and Cybernetics Part B: Cybernetics 26(1) (1996)

15. Schoonderwoerd, R., et al.: Ant-based Load Balancing in Telecommunications Networks. Adaptive Behavior 5(2) (1997)

16. Di Caro, G., Dorigo, M.: AntNet: Distributed Stigmergetic Control for Communications Networks. Journal of Artificial Intelligence Research 9 (1998)

17. Di Caro, G., Ducatelle, F., Gambardella, L.M.: AntHocNet: An Adaptive Nature-Inspired Algorithm for Routing in Mobile Ad Hoc Networks. European Transactions on Telecommunications (ETT) - Special Issue on Self Organization in Mobile Networking 16(5) (2005)

18. Rubinstein, R.Y.: The Cross-Entropy Method for Combinatorial and Continuous Optimization. Methodology and Computing in Applied Probability (1999)

19. de Boer, P.T., Kroese, D.P., Mannor, S., Rubinstein, R.Y.: A Tutorial on the Cross-Entropy Method. Annals of Operations Research 134 (2005)

20. Wittner, O., Helvik, B.E.: Distributed soft policy enforcement by swarm intelligence; application to load sharing and protection. Annals of Telecommunications 59 (2004)

21. Wittner, O., Helvik, B.E., Nicola, V.F.: Internet Failure Protection using Hamiltonian p-Cycles found by Ant-like Agents. Journal of Network and System Management, Special issue on Self-Managing Systems and Networks (2005)

22. Wittner, O., Heegaard, P.E., Helvik, B.E.: Scalable Distributed Discovery of Resource Paths in Telecommunication Networks using Cooperative Ant-like Agents. In: Proceedings of the Congress on Evolutionary Computation, Canberra (2003)
23. Heegaard, P.E., et al.: Self-managed virtual path management in dynamic networks. In: Babaoğlu, Ö., Jelasity, M., Montresor, A., Fetzer, C., Leonardi, S., van Moorsel, A., van Steen, M. (eds.) SELF-STAR 2004. LNCS, vol. 3460, Springer, Heidelberg (2005)
24. Heegaard, P.E., et al.: Distributed asynchronous algorithm for cross-entropy-based combinatorial optimization. Rare Event Simulation and Combinatorial Optimization, Budapest (2004)
25. Heegaard, P.E., Wittner, O.: Restoration performance vs. overhead in a swarm intelligence path management system. In: Proceedings of the Fifth International Workshop on Ant Colony Optimization and Swarm Intelligence, Brussels (2006)
26. Heegaard, P.E., Wittner, O.J.: Self-tuned refresh rate in a swarm intelligence path management system. In: de Meer, H., Sterbenz, J.P.G. (eds.) IWSOS 2006. LNCS, vol. 4124, Springer, Heidelberg (2006)
27. Kjeldsen, V., Wittner, O., Heegaard, P.E.: Distributed and Scalable Path Management by a System of Cooperating Ants (submitted, 2008)
28. Wittner, O.: Emergent Behavior Based Implements for Distributed Network Management. PhD thesis, Norwegian University of Science and Technology, NTNU, Department of Telematics (2003)
29. Efe, K.: Heuristic models of task assignment scheduling in distributed systems. Computer (June 1982)
30. Birtwistle, G.: Demos - a system for discrete event modelling on simula (1997)

STUNT Enhanced Java RMI

Oliver Haase, Wolfgang Reiser, and Jürgen Wäsch

Computer Science Department,
Konstanz University of Applied Sciences,
Constance, Germany

Abstract. Java RMI uses HTTP tunneling for NAT traversal. While HTTP tunneling is a valid technique for traditional client–server–architectures, it is too heavy-weight for highly distributed systems such as peer-to-peer applications. In this paper, we propose a STUNT enhanced RMI mechanism that takes advantage of the hole punching NAT traversal technique that many successful peer-to-peer applications use. Because the modified communication behavior is made part of the RMI server stub, our approach is fully transparent to the RMI client.

Keywords: Java RMI, NAT traversal, STUNT, TCP hole punching.

1 Introduction

Java's platform independence and built-in networking support have made it an interesting language for distributed computing. One key feature for the development of distributed Java applications is the Java Remote Method Invocation (RMI) technology [6]. The main idea behind RMI is to provide a communication mechanism that allows developers to use the method invocation paradigm to communicate between remote objects. This simplifies the development process because programmers do not need to deal with communication protocols, on-the-wire data representation, and connection management. The RMI communication protocol, Java Remote Method Protocol (JRMP), which is used for all communication between RMI clients and servers, builds on top of the TCP/IP protocol stack. In order to seamlessly connect RMI clients and servers throughout the Internet, the ubiquitous reachability of all involved entities via TCP/IP is essential.

Since the early days of the Internet—when every node had its own globally unique IP address and could be addressed directly—things have changed as a result of security considerations and a shortage of IP addresses. The old addressing model has been replaced with a new addressing model consisting of one global address realm and innumerable private address realms linked by Network Address Translators (NAT) [10].

Although this model is suitable for traditional client–server communication where at least the server is in the global address realm and can be reached directly, it makes it complicated for scenarios where the server, or both server and client, reside in different private networks. This kind of scenario is clearly on

R. Meier and S. Terzis (Eds.): DAIS 2008, LNCS 5053, pp. 269–274, 2008.

the rise with the spread of peer-to-peer technologies beyond use of file-sharing. Therefore, a solution to make RMI communication work even in the presence of NAT is essential for RMI to become a viable technology for modern peer-to-peer and other highly distributed applications.

The RMI built-in solution for NAT traversal, HTTP tunneling, requires significant administrative overhead and in many cases is in conflict with corporate security policies. In addition, the approach is not feasible for home users whose entire network sits behind the Internet service provider's NAT box. Another drawback is the bandwidth inefficiency due to the tunneling overhead.

Our primary focus is to develop a light-weight RMI NAT traversal technique with minimimal overhead that works with no changes to RMI clients and minimal changes to RMI servers. Therefore, we propose an enhanced RMI mechanism for NAT traversal that is based on a technique known as *hole punching* (first mentioned in [8]). Even though the name suggests otherwise, hole punching does not compromise the security of private networks, but rather empowers applications to communicate within the security policies of different types of NATs (e.g., cone NAT, restricted cone NAT, port restricted cone NAT, symmetric NAT [5]). There are a number of commerical applications which use hole punching techniques — Skype [12,11] is certainly one of the best known of them.

In order to use hole punching, nodes must have the capability to identify the presence and type of NAT they are behind, as well as their public IP address/port combination. One way to gather all this information is to use a public *STUNT* (*Simple Traversal of UDP Through NATs and TCP too*) server. STUNT is a protocol presented by Guha et al. in [3,4] which extends the STUN protocol [9] with TCP capabilities.

This paper shows the use of the hole punching technique to establish an RMI communication between two NATed RMI parties. In order to make this hole punching technique work, both parties have to go through several steps in their communication process. They first have to determine whether they are behind a NAT and which their public IP address/port combination is. After they have collected this information with the help of a public *STUNT server*, both parties have to publish the results through a public *Rendezvous Server*. To set up a communication, party *A* polls the data of the public communication endpoint of the other party from the Rendezvous Server. This polling automatically triggers a mechanism which pushes party *A*'s public IP address/port combination to party *B*. After this step, both parties have each other's address data which enables them to perform the actual hole punching process [8] to set up the communication between *A* and *B*.

In the following, we describe how to integrate STUNT-based hole punching into the RMI communication concept. Our solution makes use of a custom `RMI-SocketFactory` to modify the RMI connection behavior: after a failed direct RMI connection attempt, both RMI client and RMI server go through the STUNT-enhanced RMI communication process to set up a connection between the NATed RMI parties using hole punching.

2   STUNT Enhanced Java RMI Solution

Integrating TCP hole punching into Java RMI evidently changes the way Java RMI communication usually takes place. One of our top goals, however, is to change the RMI mechanism *without the need to modify any RMI client*, i.e., whether it uses a regular or a STUNT enhanced RMI server object should be transparent to the client. For the server object it is acceptable to implement behavior specific to STUNT enhanced RMI; the changes to regular RMI should nevertheless be minimal.

To show how we achieved the above mentioned transparency, a few words about Java RMI are helpful: An RMI client stub, i.e., the local proxy of the remote server object, consists of two parts, the RMISocketFactory and the actual RemoteReference. The RMISocketFactory controls the instantiation of the sockets used for RMI communication, and hence controls the communication behavior itself. This technique makes the RMISocketFactory the ideal hook point to alter the RMI communication while still complying to standard RMI on the API level. We thus replace the standard RMISocketFactory with a custom RMISocketFactory to transparently change the RMI communication behavior on the client side. The second component of the server stub, the RemoteReference, defines the IP address or the hostname of the RMI server object. When the server object is exported, i.e. when the client stub is created, the value of the Java property *java.rmi.server.hostname* is copied into the RemoteReference. Setting this property to a publicly reachable IP address pushes the desired address into the RemoteReference.

An RMI client obtains a server stub in one of two ways: It either (1) gets it as a return value or return parameter from another remote server object, or (2) it uses the *RMI registry*, the RMI specific naming service. Because the communication process in case (1) is a mere subset of the process in case (2), we focus on case (2) in the following.

The RMI registry is both an API specification and a reference implementation which is part of Sun Microsystem's Java SE. For security reasons (or a lack of proper authentication and authorization mechanisms), the reference implementation needs to run on the same machine as the RMI server object, a restriction which is not acceptable for our solution exactly because the server machine can sit behind a NAT box. Part of our solution is therefore a custom RMI registry that can register server objects from other machines. Again, for an RMI client, this change is transparent because the client uses the standard API to locate and query the custom RMI registry.

2.1   Communication Process

The sequence diagram in figure 1 shows the STUNT enhanced RMI communication process. This process is divided into server (ⓐ to ⓒ) and client (① to ⑥) behavior.

In step ⓐ, the server interrogates a STUNT server to learn its public IP adress and NAT type. It then sets the *java.rmi.server.hostname* property to its

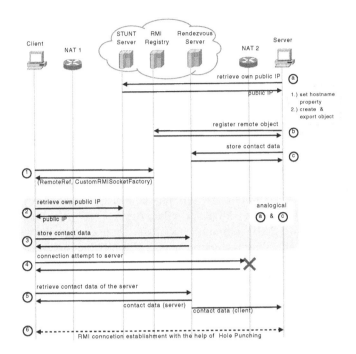

Fig. 1. STUNT RMI communication process

public IP address, creates and exports the server object and registers it with the naming service, i.e. the custom RMI registry (step ⓑ). Please note that when exporting the server object, the RMISocketFactory part of the stub is set to our custom RMISocketFactory. The server is now ready for incoming remote method invocations.

The client uses the standard RMI API to locate the naming service and look up the stub for the remote server object ①. After this step, the custom RMIClientSocketFactory controls the further communication process, *while the client still executes regular remote method invocations.* Steps ② and ③ are analog to steps ⓐ and ⓒ on the server side; the client interrogates its public IP address and NAT type, and has this data stored in the rendezvous server. In step ④, the client tries to directly connect to the remote object. This connection attempt succeeds only if the remote object is either in the same private network or belongs to the public Internet. If the direct connection attempt fails, the client contacts the rendezvous server (step ⑤) to retrieve the remote server object's contact address. The rendezvous server not only returns the remote object's public IP address, but also pushes the RMI client's public IP address to the RMI server object. After both hosts have received the other party's contact address they hole-punch their NAT boxes to establish a connection between each other. More specifically, each party's attempt to contact the other side establishes a temporary mapping in their NAT box that allows the other party to traverse the far side's NAT box.

2.2   Components

Our STUNT enhanced RMI mechanism comprises the following entities, some of which are standard off-the-shelf components, while others require custom implementations.

STUNT Server: The STUNT Server implements an extended version of the STUN protocol which includes TCP capabilities. The STUNT server determines the global IP addresses and ports which are assigned by the outermost NAT, assert its type and transmits them back to the host. Public STUNT servers are readily available in the Internet, and can be employed without changes.

Naming Service: Part of our solution is a RMI registry compliant custom naming service, which is enhanced with security features like access control to ensure that remote objects can be managed in a secure way. Keeping the naming service compliant to the standard registry ensures that clients can still use the *LocateRegistry* interface to connect to the service. This naming service must be publicly reachable and can, e.g., be a part of the rendezvous server.

Rendezvous Server: The rendezvous server is a publicly reachable server, providing a mapping service which maps global unique identifiers onto communication endpoint information. As shown in figure 1, both STUNT-RMI client and STUNT-RMI server register their contact address with this server. Appropriate unique identifiers are URIs with the form `<user>@<host>` because these URIs are unique and valid despite NAT boundaries. In order to keep the mapping table clean and to prevent entries from becoming stale, we propose to add a lease time for each entry and to set appropriate intervals to clear out old data.

Custom `RMISocketFactory:` As mentioned before, the `RMISocketFactory` is responsible for the RMI client/server communication behavior. In our solution the RMISocketFactory implements the STUNT enhanced communication behavior as shown in figure 1.

3   Conclusion and Future Work

All of the necessary components—except for the STUNT server several instances of which are publicly available in the Internet—are currently under development. As soon as the implementation work is completed, we will evaluate the solution in terms of operability, performance, and scalability. The results will be made public to the research community.

In a previous project, we have developed a neighbor-centric peer-to-peer infrastructure based on Java RMI communication [7]. That project has been the main driver for the light-weight NAT traversal solution presented in this paper. Consequently, the implementation of the STUNT enhanced RMI approach will be integrated into our peer-to-peer infrastructure. We believe, however, that our solution has the potential to be useful for other Java RMI based projects, infrastructures, and middlewares. Or to put it differently, we believe that the lack of a light-weight, zero-configuration NAT traversal solution is a major obstacles for a more widespread use of Java RMI in large-scale, industry grade distributed applications. We therefore plan to make the resulting software and servers available for public use.

References

1. Biggadike, A., Ferullo, D., Wilson, G., Perrig, A.: NATBLASTER: Establishing TCP connections between hosts behind NATs. In: Proceedings of ACM SIGCOMM ASIA Workshop (2005)
2. Ford, B., Srisuresh, P., Kegel, D.: Peer-to-peer communication across network address translators. In: Proceedings of the 2005 USENIX Annual Technical Conference (2005)
3. Francis, P., Guha, S.: Simple traversal of UDP through NATs and TCP too (STUNT), http://nutss.gforge.cis.cornell.edu/
4. Francis, P., Guha, S., Takeda, Y.: NUTSS: A SIPbased approach to UDP and TCP network connectivity. In: SIGCOMM 2004 Workshops (2004)
5. Francis, P., Guha, S.: Characterization and Measurement of TCP Traversal through NATs and Firewalls. In: Proceedings of Interet Measurement Conference (IMC) (2005)
6. Grosso, W.: Java RMI - Designing & Building Distributed Applications. O'Reilly & Associates (2002)
7. Haase, O., Todt, A., Wäsch, J.: A Peer-To-Peer Ring Infrastrucure for Neighbor-Centric Applications. In: Enokido, T., Barolli, L., Takizawa, M. (eds.) NBiS 2007. LNCS, vol. 4658, Springer, Heidelberg (2007)
8. Holdrege, M., Srisuresh, P.: RFC3027 - Protocol Complications with the IP Network Address Translator (2001), http://tools.ietf.org/html/rfc3027
9. Huitema, C., Mahy, R., Rosenberg, J., Weinberger, J.: RFC3489 - STUN - Simple Traversal of User Datagram Protocol (UDP) Through Network Address Translators (NATs) (2003), http://tools.ietf.org/html/rfc3489
10. Holdrege, M., Srisuresh, P.: RFC2663 - IP Network Address Translator (NAT) Terminology and Considerations (1999), http://tools.ietf.org/html/rfc2663
11. Schmidt, J.: The hole trick – How Skype & Co. get round firewalls. Heise Security (2006) [online 2007-11-21], http://www.heise-security.co.uk/articles/82481
12. Skype Limited: Guide for Network Administrators (2005) [online, 2007-11-21], http://www.skype.com/security/guide-for-network-admins.pdf
13. Sun Microsystems, Inc.: JXTA Java Standard Edition v2.5: Programmers Guide (2007) [online 2007-12-03], https://jxta-guide.dev.java.net

Facilitating Complex Web Service Interactions through a Tuplespace Binding

Daniel Wutke, Daniel Martin, and Frank Leymann

Institute of Architecture of Application Systems
University of Stuttgart
Universitaetsstrasse 38, 70569 Stuttgart, Germany
{wutke,martin,leymann}@iaas.uni-stuttgart.de
http://www.iaas.uni-stuttgart.de

Abstract. The SOAP messaging framework, as one key technology of the Web service technology standard stack, defines a standardized message format for Web service interactions, a set of rules governing their processing and a mechanism that describes how SOAP messages can be transmitted over different network transport protocols, called *SOAP bindings*. The most prominent example for a Web service transport today, is the Hypertext Transfer Protocol (HTTP), which however suffers from certain drawbacks such as being inherently synchronous in nature and not providing decoupling of message sender and receiver in reference or time. In this paper, we present tuplespace technology as an alternative Web service transport that is characterized by a number of properties that are not found in current Web service transports: asynchronism, strong decoupling of sender and receiver and support for advanced message exchange patterns, such as one-to-many interactions, directly on the transport level. We describe the representation of SOAP messages in tuple form and exemplify how to use the operations provided by the tuplespace interface to realize certain Web service message exchange patterns.[1]

Keywords: Web Services, Message Exchange Patterns, Tuplespaces, Web Service Binding.

1 Introduction

Web service technology has gained broad acceptance in research and industry due to enabling loosely coupled interactions between communication partners which can be conducted over potentially multiple different network transport protocols while retaining end-to-end quality of services. Web services are defined by a set of specifications that enable standards-based service description, discovery, invocation, and composition through the use of WSDL, UDDI, SOAP, BPEL and others.

---

[1] This work is funded by the European Commission under the TripCom project (IST-4-027324-STP).

R. Meier and S. Terzis (Eds.): DAIS 2008, LNCS 5053, pp. 275–280, 2008.

The SOAP messaging framework [1] defines a standardized XML-based message format and a set of rules that govern how SOAP processing nodes along the message path from initial sender to ultimate receiver should process a SOAP message. In addition, SOAP defines a mechanism to bind SOAP messages to different network protocols to enable their transmission between SOAP processing nodes over a network through so-called *SOAP bindings*. For this purpose, they define a serialization of the SOAP infoset in such a way that it can be transmitted by a sender over the chosen network transport protocol and reconstructed by the receiver (or the next hop/node in case of multi-hop interactions). Furthermore, they describe how the services of the underlying transport protocol (i.e. its interface) are used to transmit the chosen serialization of the SOAP infoset between SOAP processing nodes and describe potential failure scenarios that can be anticipated within the binding.

Tuplespaces have their origin in the *Linda coordination language*, defined in [2] as a parallel programming extension for programming languages for the purpose of separating coordination logic from program logic. A tuplespace is conceptually similar to a piece of memory shared among all participants of an interaction which provides clients with synchronized access to *tuples* (i.e. an ordered list of typed fields) via a simple interface: tuples can be stored (using the *out* operation), retrieved destructively (*in*) and retrieved non-destructively (*rd*). Tuples are retrieved associatively using a template matching mechanism, i.e. by providing values of a subset of the typed fields of the tuple to be read.

The remainder of the paper is organized as follows: first we motivate the work presented by elaborating on certain unique properties of tuplespaces when compared to existing Web service transports (Section 2). Subsequently, the SOAP binding for the tuplespace transport is presented, consisting of (i) a description of how the information contained in a SOAP envelope can be mapped to tuples to facilitate their transmission over a JavaSpaces transport (Section 3) and (ii) how message exchange patterns can be mapped to Linda communication primitives (Section 4). Section 5 concludes the paper.

2 Tuplespace Binding for Web Services

As of today, HTTP [3] is still the most widely accepted Web service transport. Due to the nature of HTTP being designed for direct, synchronous client-server interactions, it shows certain drawbacks with regard to decoupling sender and receiver in reference and time. As a result of tight referential coupling when conducting Web service interactions over HTTP, the sender of a message is required to explicitly address the concrete address (also referred to as *endpoint*) where a particular service implementation can be reached. If the location of the service implementation changes, a corresponding change has to be performed on the client. Furthermore, due to HTTP not offering decoupling in time, both message sender and receiver have to be available at the same time. If e.g. the receiver of a Web service invocation request is not available at the time of request sending, the message cannot be received and thus not processed. To overcome aforementioned shortcomings with regard to decoupling message sender and receiver in reference and time, a number of SOAP bindings have been proposed that build on messaging network transport protocols such as SMTP, XMPP or JMS which all employ the mechanism of store-and-forward to achieve decoupling in time (the sender hands over the message to transmit to the messaging system which delivers it as soon as the "next hop" becomes available). In addition, message recipients are addressed by logical identifiers instead of concrete addresses (e.g. an e-mail address in case of SMTP or a queue/topic name in JMS) which enables referential decoupling.

Although tuplespaces are in their use and behavior somewhat similar to messaging technology (see e.g [4] for a comparison), they are characterized by certain unique properties. In contrast to message-oriented middleware, where sender and receiver communicate by exchanging messages over queues and topics identified by logical addresses, in tuplespaces data is exchanged by senders publishing the data they want to communicate to a shared space (the counterpart to a queue/-topic in messaging) on which potentially multiple receivers are listening. Data is consumed by the receiver in an associative manner, meaning that the receiver of a data tuple describes its content by example, e.g. the data types of certain tuple fields or their value. As a result, tuplespace-based communication is based on a *pull* mechanism (i.e. the receivers actively select what they want to receive by template-based consumption of tuples) as opposed to a *push* mechanism employed in messaging (i.e. the sender addresses a certain queue/topic, from which it expects the receiver to consume). Furthermore, in tuplespace-oriented communication, data is regarded as a published object instead of a message directed to a certain receiver. This means that when a sender publishes a piece of information to a tuplespace, the (one single) data tuple is available for all receivers listening on the tuplespace (which in particular also includes the sender of the tuple). This enables certain communication patterns that are difficult to realize based on other – e.g. messaging-based – Web service transports such as the Request-for-bid pattern described later in the paper. For instance, after publication of a message, the sender of the message can destructively consume the message again, update its contents and re-publish it. In addition, data can easily be directed to a set of receivers (similar to broadcast/multicast communication) or processed by a set of potential competing consumers in style of the *replicated-worker* pattern [5].

3   Mapping SOAP Messages to Tuples

To enable communication of SOAP envelopes over a network transport protocol, (i) the SOAP envelope to be transmitted needs to be encapsulated in an object that can be transmitted using the communication primitives of the respective transport protocol and (ii) information necessary for message identification, delivery and correlation has to be added and made accessible to evaluation by the transport. In case of tuplespace-based communication, data is encapsulated in tuples; the individual tuple fields are defined as follows. The field identified by the *Content* property contains a representation of the actual SOAP envelope, comprising both SOAP headers and SOAP body. The encoding of the SOAP message is specified by the *Content type* property. In most cases, the preferred content type is "application/soap+xml" where the SOAP message is transferred as a XML string in UTF-8 encoding; however other encodings are possible such as e.g. "multipart/related" in case of a MIME encoded SOAP message with binary attachments. The *MEP* property identifies the message exchange pattern that governs the exchange of the respective message. Possible values for this property are e.g. the identifiers of the WSDL 2.0 specification [6]. Each tuple with an encapsulated SOAP message is uniquely identified via the *Message ID* property. If the SOAP envelope contains a WS-Addressing [7] header block, the WS-Addressing Message ID is propagated to the tuple level to allow its use for template matching. To enable correlation of messages as part of interactions that involve more that one message exchange between communication partners, the *Correlation ID* property of a message can contain the Message ID of another message which is "in relation" to the given message. How a message relates to the message with the given correlation ID is defined through the *Relationship type* property. Valid values for the relationship type property are dependent on the message exchange pattern the message belongs to; WS-Addressing relationship type values are reused where possible. To enable addressing one particular Web service provider in case multiple Web service providers are connected to the same tuplespace, the *Service name* property must contain the name of the destination service in form of a Uniform Resource Identifier (URI). To allow service providers to correctly dispatch incoming SOAP messages to a service implementation (if the service provider for instance offers more than one operation), the *SOAP action* property conveys the semantics of the SOAP message in the content property in form of a URI. The *Binding version* property describes the version of the binding to be used to allow for further development and extension of the binding while still retaining backwards compatibility in implementations. In case the message encapsulated in the content property is a SOAP fault, the *Is fault* property contains a boolean *true* value, otherwise it has the value of a boolean *false*. Propagating this information to the tuple level enables e.g. convenient retrieval of all fault or non-fault messages. In case a SOAP processor encounters any errors while processing the SOAP message, e.g. while parsing the message the *Unprocessable* property is set to a boolean value *true*. This facilitates simple retrieval of unprocessable messages by administrators for debugging purposes and can be used to prevent repeated consumption of unprocessable messages.

4   Mapping WS Interaction Patterns to Linda Coordination Primitives

In the following paragraphs, the mapping of Web service *message exchange patterns* (MEP) to sequences of tuplespace operation calls is exemplified through the *In-out* MEP described as part of the WSDL 2.0 specification [6] and the

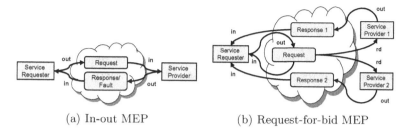

(a) In-out MEP   (b) Request-for-bid MEP

Fig. 1. Web service MEPs mapped to Tuplespace operations

custom *Request-for-bid* MEP that leverages the advanced functionality provided
by the tuplespace transport.

The *In-out* MEP as shown in Figure 1(a) comprises two message exchanges.
First, the service requester sends a request message to the service provider. The
service requester addresses the service provider either directly using the
WS-Addressing *Destination* property which is propagated to the tuple level as
the *Service name* property or indirectly using the *Action* property. This information is either extracted from the WSDL description of the Web service to be addressed or exchanged via out-of-band mechanisms and defined by the Web service
requester. The request message is stored in the tuplespace by the service requester
using the *out* operation and retrieved by the service provider using a blocking *in*
operation. While certain tuplespace implementations such as JavaSpaces support
asynchronous notifications as an alternative to blocking and non-blocking tuple
consumption operations, a presentation of the message exchange patterns which
makes use of these is left out for the sake of simplicity. The template used by the
service provider to retrieve request messages matches on the *Service name* and the
Action property of the request message. The destructive consumption operation
(*in*) is used rather than its non-destructive variant (*rd*), since the message should
be delivered to the service provider only once. When the request message has
been processed by the service provider, it constructs a corresponding response or
fault message by extracting the *Message ID* information (and the *Reply Endpoint*
WS-Addressing header if found in the SOAP message encapsulated in the request
tuple) from the request message. The *Correlation ID* property of the response
message is set to the *Message ID* of the request message to relate the response
message to the original request message and the *Relationship type* property is set
to the URI representing a response message in a request-response interaction. The
Web service provider stores the created response (or fault) message encapsulated
in the content field of the response tuple in the tuplespace using the *out* operation. The service requester retrieves a response message for its original request
message by issuing a blocking *in* operation, waiting for a message that contains
the necessary correlation information that identifies the message as a response to
the client's original request message.

The *Request-for-bid* MEP as shown in Figure 1(b) is an example for a complex
Web service MEP that can be implemented effiently on top of a tuplespace. It
is a composite pattern that consists of a *One-to-many* interaction and multiple

In-out interactions. First, as part of the one-to-many interaction, potentially multiple service providers non-destructively consume a request message (*rd*); each service provider processes the request message and evaluates whether to send a corresponding response message to the service requester. If a service provider decides to respond to the request message, it acts as described in the *In-out* pattern. The MEP is terminated by the service requester by destructively retrieving (*in*) the request message from the tuplespace.

5   Conclusions

In this paper, we have motivated and presented a SOAP Web service binding for a tuplespace transport. We have payed special attention to pointing out which properties of tuplespaces motivate their use as a Web service transport. Furthermore with the example of the In-out and Request-for-bid MEPs, we have demonstrated the suitability of the presented transport to efficiently implement both the standard Web service message exchange patterns described in the WSDL 2.0 specification, as well as custom, more complex message exchange patterns. A more extensive description of the binding, further MEPs and a prototypical implementation of the proposed Web service tuplespace binding based on the *JavaSpaces* interface by SUN Microsystems is available in [8].

References

1. Gudgin, M., Hadley, M., Moreau, J.J.: SOAP Version 1.2 Part 1: Messaging Framework. W3C Recommendation April 27, 2007 (2007)
2. Gelernter, D.: Generative Communication in Linda. ACM Transactions on Programming Languages and Systems 7(1), 80–112 (1985)
3. Fielding, R., Gettys, J., Mogul, J., Frystyk, H., Masinter, L., Leach, P., Berners-Lee, T.: RFC 2616: Hypertext Transfer Protocol HTTP/1.1 (June 1999)
4. Martin, D., Wutke, D., Scheibler, T., Leymann, F.: An EAI Pattern-Based Comparison of Spaces and Messaging. In: Proc. of EDOC 2007 (2007)
5. Freeman, E., Hupfer, S., Arnold, K.: JavaSpaces Principles, Patterns, and Practice. Pearson Education, London (1999)
6. Chinnici, R., Gudgin, M., Moreau, J.J., Schlimmer, J., Weerawarana, S.: Web Services Description Language (WSDL) Version 2.0 Part 1: Core Language. W3C Working Draft 26 (2004)
7. Gudgin, M., Hadley, M., Rogers, T.: Web Services Addressing 1.0 - Core. W3C Recommendation (May 2006)
8. Schwind, A.: Space-Based Web Services: Konzepte und prototypische Implementierung mit Linda-Spaces. Master Thesis, DIP-2692, Universität Stuttgart, Fakultät Informatik, Elektrotechnik und Informationstechnik, Germany (December 2007)

A Comprehensive Context Modeling Framework for Pervasive Computing Systems

Roland Reichle[1], Michael Wagner[1], Mohammad Ullah Khan[1],
Kurt Geihs[1], Jorge Lorenzo[2], Massimo Valla[3], Cristina Fra[3],
Nearchos Paspallis[4], and George A. Papadopoulos[4]

[1] University of Kassel, Distributed Systems Group
{wagner,reichle,khan,geihs}@vs.uni-kassel.de
[2] Telefónica Investigación y Desarrollo
jorgelg@tid.es
[3] Telecom Italia Lab
{massimo.valla,christina.fra}@telecomitalia.it
[4] Department of Computer Science, University of Cyprus
{nearchos,george}@cs.ucy.ac.cy

Abstract. Context management in pervasive computing environments must reflect the specific characteristics of these environments, e.g. distribution, mobility, resource-constrained devices, or heterogeneity of context sources. Although a number of context models have been presented in the literature, none of them supports all of these requirements to a sufficient extent at the same time. In this paper, we present a comprehensive and integrated approach for context modeling in pervasive computing environments. It combines the advantages of existing approaches and addresses the need for supporting effective software development. The proposed context model follows an ontology-based approach and has three layers of abstraction, i.e. conceptual layer, exchange layer, and functional layer. This layered approach facilitates a model-driven development of context-aware applications. Throughout the paper we compare our solution with the related work in order to clearly demonstrate why we needed to develop a new context management framework and where we have adopted existing ideas.

Keywords: Context Awareness, Context Modeling, Ontology, Model-Driven Development, Pervasive Computing.

1 Introduction

In recent years, context awareness has attracted a lot of attention, especially in the realms of mobile and pervasive computing. Context-aware applications are capable of monitoring and exploiting information about external operating conditions. Typically, such systems are also self-adaptive, in the sense that they can dynamically adapt as a response to changes in the execution context. Automating the development of such systems is an important challenge.

R. Meier and S. Terzis (Eds.): DAIS 2008, LNCS 5053, pp. 281–295, 2008.
© IFIP International Federation for Information Processing 2008

A context model provides an unambiguous definition of the context artifacts, their representations, semantics and usage. It takes into account the general characteristics of context information, such as its temporal nature, ambiguity, impreciseness, incompleteness and privacy. Furthermore, a context model must also address special requirements of pervasive computing environments like distribution, mobility, heterogeneity of context sources and resource-constrained devices. Often, pervasive applications require high-level context information that is derived from low-level context values. Therefore, support for automatic context reasoning has to be provided as well.

As it will be shown throughout this paper, existing context modeling approaches address a sub-set of these challenges only, or cover some of them only to a limited extent. Moreover, most of them view context modeling either from a pure conceptual or a pure functional perspective. However, when engineering context-aware systems, a software developer needs to deal with many aspects at the same time, e.g. define the semantics and relations between context elements at a conceptual view, realize the information exchange between heterogeneous nodes, and provide the concrete implementation of the context management functionality at a specific node.

The main contribution of this paper is a new comprehensive and integrated context modeling approach that is based on a new context ontology and three layers of abstraction: conceptual, exchange and functional. These three layers cover the identified requirements of context management in pervasive computing environments and, at the same time, facilitate the analysis and design of context-aware applications as part of a comprehensive, model-driven software engineering process. The presented context model is a result of a research EC IST project called *Self-Adapting Applications for Mobile Users in Ubiquitous Computing Environments (MUSIC)* [3]. The goal of MUSIC is to develop a comprehensive open-source computing infrastructure and an associated software development methodology that facilitate the development of self-adapting, context-aware applications in ubiquitous and pervasive computing environments.

The rest of this paper is organized as follows: Section 2 studies requirements for context modeling in pervasive computing environments, while Section 3 discusses existing approaches. The MUSIC context model is described in Section 4, and discussed in Section 5. Finally, Section 6 presents our conclusions and points to future work.

2   Requirements

This section identifies requirements for a context model that aims to ease the development of context-aware applications in mobile and pervasive computing environments. A comprehensive list of requirements has been derived through a process where a set of case studies featuring both real (commercial) and fictional scenarios were studied and evaluated in the scope of mobile and pervasive computing [3]. The requirements identified from the case studies are:

- *Ease of development:* While at a conceptual level modeling the semantics and the relations between context information is very important, the run-time representation of the context data must aim for efficiency. Appropriate development support must be provided to the software developers to ease their tasks considering the whole development process and incorporating all views and aspects. In this respect, Model-Driven Development (MDD) is favored.
- *Considering the characteristics of mobile and pervasive computing environments:* Mobile and pervasive computing environments imply further complexity as they are characterized by distribution, heterogeneity, unpredictability, unreliable communication links, etc. Furthermore, the limited capabilities of mobile devices, e.g. in respect to processing power, memory and energy consumption, have to be taken into account.
- *Need for machine-interpretable representation of context information:* A typical approach to tackle heterogeneity and to provide a machine-interpretable representation of context information is the use of semantic annotations. They are attached to the actual context data to enable automatic exploitation and transformation of information in distributed context sharing scenarios. Furthermore, they can be utilized to enable automatic context reasoning.
- *Dealing with special context properties:* Unlike data in conventional database systems, context data is characterized by properties such as incompleteness, ambiguity, uncertainty, and temporal nature.
- *Dealing with context information partitioning:* In adaptive systems, sharing of context information is a natural requirement. However, because of the nature of mobile and ubiquitous computing, it is possible that the nodes carrying the context information are partitioned. The context models should cope with such circumstances and enable the merging of the data when needed.
- *Evolution and extensibility:* Context models should not be monolithic, but rather be flexible and extensible. New applications and possibly new context nodes shall be allowed to enter the system. As the applications and their context needs evolve, so should the context model.

This list describes the requirements that originate from our chosen scenarios. As they are not intended to focus on a small number of rather specific applications, but more on pervasive applications in general, they are naturally quite high-level. Although we believe that the list is rather comprehensive for pervasive applications, we do not claim completeness. Other applications may have different or additional requirements. In addition, more general requirements apply to context modeling, just like they apply to software systems in general. These include *platform independence, privacy and security issues, support for automatic test execution, logging, simulated operation* and *visualization* of the system state.

3   Discussion of Existing Context Models

In search for an existing context model that would satisfy all of the above requirements, we carefully examined the related work in this research field. Our investigations revealed that research in the area of context modeling is well established and many ideas have been developed for addressing the above requirements individually.

3.1 Existing Approaches on Context Modeling

In order to provide application dependent context information through a context framework, a uniform way of representing and sharing context is required. Strang and Linnhoff-Popien [16] evaluate the most relevant context approaches based on the data structures used for representing and exchanging context information: key-value pair, markup scheme, graphical, object oriented, logic based and ontology based models. According to their evaluation, the most promising assets for context modeling for ubiquitous computing environments are found in ontology based models. In these models, the semantic context information is represented using one of the ontology markup languages, for example OWL (Web Ontology Language) [10]. We share their opinion and consider ontologies as an appropriate way to deal with the heterogeneity implied by ubiquitous computing environments. An ontology defines a common vocabulary to share context information among devices, services and users. This makes it possible to reason about various context types, thanks to machine-interpretable definitions on basic concepts in the domain and relations among them.

There are several projects that also apply ontologies as a central concept for modeling context information. For instance, Chen *et al.* [1] defined a context ontology based on OWL to support ubiquitous agents in their Context Broker Architecture (CoBrA). Their approach targets home area intelligent environments and applies sensor information detection and context awareness as a way of dealing with users' activities, intentions and movements between different home areas.

Ranganathan *et al.* [13] developed a middleware for context awareness and semantic interoperability in which they represented the context ontology in DAML+OIL [8]. One of the main shortcomings of this approach is that it does not deal with the specialized context characteristics, such as incompleteness, and that its extensibility is limited.

Context-Driven Adaptation of Mobile Services (CoDAMoS) [12] defines a generic ontology to model context in Ambient Intelligence infrastructures that suits very well the requirements of mobile computing. This ontology is based on four general entities. (1) The user is the central entity, including the user's profile, preferences, mood and current activity. The rest of the entities should adapt to the user, not vice versa. (2) The environment in which the user interacts, including information such as temperature and lighting. (3) The platform that describes the hardware and software of a device, including device resources such as memory and bandwidth. (4) The service that provides specific functionality to the user.

The Service-Oriented Context-Aware Middleware (SOCAM) [4] [17], is an architecture for building context-aware services based on a two-level context model. This middleware acquires context information from different sources and interprets it. The context ontology is divided into a two-level hierarchy, distinguishing between common and specific context information. The upper level describes global concepts of the ontology and captures general knowledge about location, type of entity, person or activity. On the other hand, the lower level is divided into several pervasive computing sub-domains, each one of which defines specific details and properties for each scenario. Depending on the situation and the available devices, an appropriate sub-domain is selected from the lower level. When environment changes are detected, the lower level ontology can be dynamically plugged into and unplugged from the upper ontology, thus dynamically changing this association. This mechanism appears to be very reasonable also with respect to resource limited devices. An ontology resulting from the extension of the top-level ontology with a domain-specific ontology can be kept quite small in comparison with a single huge ontology capturing all potentially involved concepts.

Strang et al. [15] describe a context modeling approach using ontologies as a formal foundation. They introduce their Aspect-Scale-Context (ASC) model and show how it is related to other models. A Context Ontology Language (CoOL) is derived from the model, which is used to enable context-awareness and contextual interoperability during service discovery and execution in a distributed architecture. One highlight of the ASC model is that it explicitly addresses heterogeneity with regard to different representations (called scales) of context information.

Apart from the ontology-based approaches, there are several other projects on context modeling that fulfill several of the requirements that were stated in the previous section. One example is CML from Henricksen and Indulska [6] [7]. They also incorporate ontologies to address particular aspects like privacy. The formal foundation of their context modeling approach is an enhancement of the ORM language. With the situation abstraction they provide elaborate support for reasoning on context information. Their context model can also deal with special characteristics of context information, such as temporal nature, incompleteness, ambiguity, etc. Additionally, the context modeling approach is complemented by a model-driven development approach (which provides an API for the application developer) and a methodology for the development of context-aware application [7]. In this approach, context information is addressed from three levels, i.e. conceptual, management and implementation level.

The Comprehensive Structured Context Profiles (CSCP) [5] was developed based on RDF to represent context by means of session profiles. However, this approach does not deal with all our required context characteristics, like the temporal nature of context.

In [11], Hoenle et al. highlight the benefits of integrating meta-data into the context model. They argue, that meta-data facilitate important aspects like the assessment of the quality of context information, sensor fusion and data cleansing and provide more flexibility when dealing with context information. In their approach meta-data are associated to context information at object level as well as at attribute level.

3.2   Why Another Context Model?

If we look at our requirements and at the approaches described above, the first impression is that it should not be a difficult task to find an existing context model that is suitable for our purposes. However, none of the examined approaches supports all of our requirements to a sufficient extent. Ease of development using MDA, as one of our key requirements, is only addressed sufficiently by Henricksen and Indulska, but their model is not based on ontologies as the primary modeling concept. Similar to many related works, we consider the concepts of ontologies necessary to establish a common vocabulary in a heterogeneous pervasive computing environment. Such an environment also implies heterogeneous representations of context information. This is also not explicitly addressed by CML but by the ASC model from Strang *et al.* However, their approach does not provide such an elaborate development support based on MDA as the CML project.

As we could not find an approach, that fulfilled all of our requirements, our next step was to figure out, if one approach can easily be extended to cover all the aspects. Having in mind that CML already utilizes ontologies for issues like privacy we investigated the feasibility of incorporating ontologies as primary modeling concept in CML. But we quickly came to the conclusion, that this would require too much effort, as it would mean to completely replace the ORM and its extensions or to establish a mapping from an ontology based approach to the ORM. Furthermore, even if we had established such a mapping, the problem of heterogeneous representations would still remain unsolved.

The idea to complement the ASC model with MDD support appeared to be quite promising, in particular when considering, that CoOl was also designed to facilitate the mapping to other context models. Problems with the ASC model were found in small details. In our view context information should characterize an entity of the world (e.g. laptop, device, user, *etc*) with a certain type or scope of information (e. g. location, current situation, battery status, *etc*) in a certain representation (e.g. GPS coordinates in the case of location). In our terminology a context scope is a kind of context information type. Therefore, the three concepts entity, type and representation should be clearly separated. In the ASC model, the type of information (called aspect) is only referred indirectly through the scales, which correspond to a certain representation in our terminology. We faced problems with this indirection when building taxonomies of context information types and corresponding taxonomies of representations. Clearly separated concepts not only facilitate building taxonomies, they also ease the automatic model-based generation of context interpreters that are responsible for one context information type and can deal with several representations.

Based on this analysis, we saw the need to design a new context modeling approach that utilizes the advantages and most promising features of the existing works in order to develop a comprehensive integrated approach. As can also be seen from the considerations above, combining the different concepts is not at all a trivial task.

4   The MUSIC Context Model

This section describes the context model of the MUSIC project. In the first subsection we describe the general structure of the new context model. Then we introduce the different layers and show in the last subsection how to use our approach in the Model Driven Development.

4.1   Three Layers of Abstraction

We identify three basic layers of abstraction that correspond to the three main phases of context management: the conceptual layer, the exchange layer and the functional layer. The conceptual layer aims to be leveraged by the developers and to be exploited in the model-driven development approach. This layer enables the definition of context artifacts such as elements, scopes, entities and representations based on standard specification languages like UML and OWL [10]. The exchange layer aims to be utilized for interoperability between devices. At this layer, the context information can be expressed in any adequate representation, such as XML, JSON (JavaScript Object Notation) [9] or simply CSV (Comma Separated Values). Finally, the functional layer refers to the actual implementation of the context model representation and the internal mechanisms used in the different nodes. This model can be object-based, but it does not necessarily need to be interoperable as it is platform-specific and as different devices might use different implementations of it, using for example Java and .NET. The main objective of this layer is efficiency, both in terms of processing speed and resource consumption. This paper focuses on the conceptual and the exchange layers of the proposed hierarchy. Figure 1 illustrates how these concepts fit into these three layers.

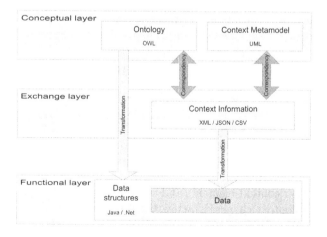

Fig. 1. The three layers of the MUSIC context model

For our context model, we decided to incorporate the concept of ontologies in the conceptual layer of the context model for several reasons. (1) Ontologies facilitate the establishment of a common understanding of the semantics of context elements and their associated metadata and therefore boost interoperability. (2) Similar to the ASC model proposed by Strang *et al.* [15], ontologies can also be used to define the internal structure of context data, thus allowing several representations, their interpretation and automatic conversions between them. (3) By incorporating ontologies, it is possible to model a wide range of relationships between context elements, which is essential for a flexible context reasoning approach. Also, a context meta-model is defined to facilitate automatic transformation between the different layers of the context modeling approach and to define basic guidelines for modeling the ontology.

The ontology is described in OWL and the context meta-model is specified in UML. Together they form the conceptual layer of the MUSIC context modeling approach. The context meta-model defines the general structure of context information and shows how concepts and/or individuals/entities specified in the ontology are referenced. In turn, as the context meta-model defines a general representation of context information it can also be considered as a kind of schema for defining the concrete representations of context elements in the ontology.

At the exchange layer, an instance of the conceptual model is represented in XML (or alternatively in JSON or CSV). The representation in XML is quite straightforward, as it is the common way to represent individuals of the ontology (which can be seen as context information).

The functional layer also defines a set of data structures for storing the context information. As the internal structure of context elements is specified in the ontology, it is possible to automatically generate the corresponding data structures for specific platforms along with appropriate serialization and de-serialization methods. Thus, the data structures can easily be filled with the information represented at the exchange layer without much overhead spent for interpretation. It is also worth noting here, that the information concerning the ontology is only transferred once or on demand. All these features take into account the quite limited resources of mobile devices in pervasive computing environments.

4.2   The Conceptual Layer of the MUSIC Context Model

As depicted in Figure 1 the MUSIC context model is composed of an ontology and a metamodel at the conceptual layer, which is described in the following.

The MUSIC Context Meta-Model. Figure 2 illustrates the proposed Context Meta-model. Context information is abstracted by *context elements* which provide information about *context entities* and *context scopes* and that can be composed of other context elements and can contain a number of *context values*. For example, a context element's *network connections* in a *device's* context can contain the elements *Wi-Fi* and *Bluetooth*, and both elements can have the values *Cost* and *Bandwidth*. *Context elements* are associated to *context scopes* that group context values belonging to the same context domain. For example, the scope *Position* groups context values like: *Longitude*, *Latitude* and *Accuracy*. The *context entities* refer to concrete entities in the world, for example *User*, *Device*, etc.

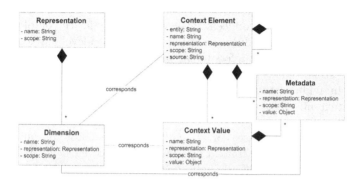

Fig. 2. The MUSIC Context Meta-Model

Metadata can be associated with context elements and context values. Here we distinguish between *predefined* (or suggested) *metadata* and *user-specific metadata*. The proposed model includes the *predefined metadata*: name, entity, scope, representation, source and sourceType. The *name* serves as an identifier. *Scope*, *entity* and *representation* refer to the MUSIC context ontology; *scope* refers to the semantic concept that groups context values belonging to the same context domain and characterizes the context information, e.g. *deviceStatus*; *entity* refers to the concrete individual to which the context information is associated, e.g. "My Windows XP Laptop". The *representation* refers to the internal representation of the context information which is also specified in the ontology. With these types of metadata, it is specified that a context element characterizes the semantic concept *scope* for the individual *entity* and its internal structure corresponds to *representation*. The *source* is a unique identifier of the component that provides the context information (e.g. a context sensor or reasoner). For *context values* the suggested types of meta-data are *name*, *scope* and *representation* that have the same meaning as the corresponding metadata types of the context element. In addition, it is allowed to associate *user-specific metadata* to context elements and context values. In a way, these metadata can be seen as additional *context values* and they are also represented in the same way. However, in contrast to *context values*, metadata can be associated to *context elements* and *context values*. Each *context element*, *context value* and *metadata* has a *representation*. According to aspects in the ASC model described in Strang *et al.* [15], each *representation* (in the ASC model called aspect) aggregates one or more *dimensions* (scales in ASC). Each *dimension* corresponds to a certain *context element*, *context value* or *metadata element*. A *dimension* itself has a *representation*, which again can consist of several *dimensions*. With these concepts, the internal structure of the context information is defined through the context element.

The MUSIC Context Ontology. This section introduces the MUSIC context ontology through an example. This example does not claim completeness but rather aims at showing the general modeling concepts and illustrating how the conceptual layer, which contains the context meta-model, is complemented by an ontology. In order to provide an extensible ontology that is well-structured and easy to understand, we introduce a two-level hierarchy for the ontology, similar to SOCAM. Here, we introduce the structure of the top-level ontology.

The context meta-model refers to the ontology with regard to three aspects: the *context scope* that is characterized by the context element, the *type* of the particular individual/entity of the characterized *scope* and the *representation* of the context information. These different aspects have to be covered while modeling the ontology.

Figure 3 presents the classes corresponding to the semantic concepts we would like to characterize through context information/context elements in our context management system. This figure only includes a small number of classes, such as for example the concept *DateTime* which is a subclass of *BasicConcepts*. As depicted in the figure, the most important relation is that each *Concept* has a *Representation*. The class *Concept* is not only used to classify *EntityTypes*, *ContextScopes* and *BasicConcepts*. Additionally, some further relations between these classes and its subclasses can be defined (e.g. *isLocatedIn*). These relations can be used for ontology reasoning.

As a second part of the ontology, the *representations* for the *concepts* must also be specified. As depicted in Figure 3 a *concept* can have one ore more *representations*. By allowing representing certain context information in several ways, we do not only face the challenge of heterogeneous context sensors for a certain semantic concept, but we also ease the merging of ontologies, at least to a certain extent. If an ontology matches a second one with regards to the classes for the concepts and their relation, and only differ in the representation of context information, the second ontology can be integrated in the first one in a straight forward manner.

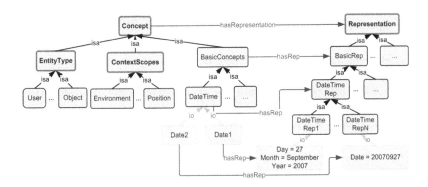

Fig. 3. The main structure of the MUSIC Context Ontology

As we envisage explicit support for heterogeneous representations of context scopes, we also allow the definition of Inter-Representation-Operations (IRO) as in the ASC model [15]. This concept is a further step in supporting context providers and consumers in a heterogeneous environment. It allows to ask for context data by a context consumer by describing a certain *scope*, characterizing a certain *entity* of this *concept* and having a certain *representation*. If this does not match the representation provided by the context sensor, an appropriate one can be computed with the corresponding IRO.

4.3 Model-Driven Development

As already discussed in the previous section, we do not want to provide only a new context model, but rather an integrated approach for context modeling, reasoning and querying together with support for application development. Thus, we use our context model also as a key ingredient in the model-driven application development. In general, context-aware software is developed using traditional programming methods and models, and the use of context information is implemented directly into the source code. Even if the logic used to access and process context information and to react to context changes is isolated within special components, the applications are still difficult to maintain, as source code must be modified to support additional classes of behavior and context. To facilitate the application development process, we use the context ontology also at design-time to support the MDD of context-aware applications. The MDD methodology exploits mainly the conceptual layer, where the context artifacts (elements, sensors, *etc*) are defined based on standard specification languages, like UML and OWL. From the high-level specifications provided at this layer, appropriate data representations and data structures for the other layers can be automatically generated. It is even possible to automatically provide serialization and de-serialization methods to be leveraged at the exchange layer and to incorporate IROs for converting between different representations. Additionally, we provide a software development methodology for adaptive context-aware applications in ubiquitous computing environments. Further information about this methodology can be found in [3]. As depicted in the example in Figure 3, the representation of a concept embodies also the main structure of the context information. This structure can be used to automatically generate the corresponding data-structure. For *data1* in the example in Figure 3, the data-structure in Java would be generated as following:

```
Class DateTimeRep1 implements Serializable{
   private int day = null;
   private string month = null;
   private int year = null;
...   }
Date1 = new DateTimeRep1(27, "September", 2007);
```

Furthermore, both the constructors and the getter/setter methods can be automatically generated.

```
DateTimeRep1(){...}
...
DateTimeRep(int d, String m, int y){
   this.day = d;
   this.month = m;
   this.year = y;}
```

As aforementioned we use the concept of IRO to transfer context information from one representation to another (in our example from DateTimeRep1 to DateTimeRep2). The skeletons of the IROs can also be generated automatically:

```
static DateTimeRep1 IRO_DTRep2_To_DTp1(DateTimeRep2 date2){
   DateTimeRep1 date1 = new DateTomeRep1();
   //TODO for Developer: Fill out the missing calculations and
   check the variables defined and assigned above
   return date1;}
```

Additionally, it is even possible to automatically provide serialization and de-serialization methods to be leveraged at the exchange layer. This means that we can automatically generate the necessary methods to send or receive the data via the exchange layer in the different formats (i.e. XML). Here we use also the IRO. A context sensor which provides the context information in a certain representation, uses its serialization method to submit this data via the exchange layer. Then the context consumer uses the de-serialization method to insert this data into his data structure. In this method, we check if the information corresponds to the requested representation, if not then automatically a corresponding IRO is called. Here we have to highlight, that the application developer does not need to worry about this process of serialization/de-serialization and conversion. The application developer just uses the generated getter-/setter-methods to access to data in the data structure. As part of our comprehensive approach for context modeling, reasoning and querying, we provide also an appropriate Context Query Language (CQL), which is described in Reichle *et al.* [14] in more details. This CQL will also be used for the MDD as we can automatically generate the code corresponding to a static query.

5   Discussion

In this paper, apart from other important requirements we emphasize the need of using ontologies to establish a common vocabulary of concepts and to explicitly address heterogeneous representations of context information in pervasive computing environments. At the same time, we highlight the need for software development support that allows developers to easily construct context-aware and self-adaptive systems. A representative set of related context modeling approaches is described in Section 3. We have argued that none of these approaches fulfills all of our requirements to a sufficient extent at the same time. Therefore, our proposal extends the state of the art, by combining the most promising features of existing approaches to a context model that is comprehensive and fulfills important requirements arising in pervasive computing environments. As it is already shown in Section 3, the task of integrating the different ideas was challenging, as some problems were obvious, while others were visible only when focusing on specific details.

We have introduced a two-level hierarchy for the ontology. Similar to SO-CAM, we distinguish between a top-level ontology capturing global knowledge and general concepts, and the domain-specific extensions. By allowing to integrate domain- or application-specific extensions our context modeling approach is not monolithic but evolvable for new applications entering the system. In order to cope with heterogeneous representations we define the internal structure of context information along with Inter-Representation-Operations in the ontology, similar to the ASC model [15]. In addition to establishing a common vocabulary for context information through an ontology, the concept of Inter-Representation-Operations further boosts interoperability. Therefore, our approach explicitly addresses the requirements arising from a heterogeneous computing environment. Metadata can be associated to context elements and also to context values similar to what is proposed by Hoenle *et al.* [11], which comes as an appropriate mean to deal with the special properties of context information and also facilitates merging of context information when nodes have been partitioned. Last but not least, we incorporate some ideas from Henricksen and Indulska [6] [7] in order to ease the development task by employing an MDD approach. In summary, our new context model provides:

- Support of all three context management layers (conceptual, exchange and functional layer). The exchange layer and the corresponding links to the conceptual and functional layers are introduced to face the challenges that arise from a distributed context sharing scenario in heterogeneous computing environments.
- Explicitly addressing MDD by using the ontology, not only to introduce a general vocabulary and relationships between context elements, but also to define different representations which comprise information about the used data structures.
- An ontology that is divided into two corresponding hierarchies: concepts and representations. The hierarchy of concepts contains the general vocabulary and the relations between the elements, whereas the hierarchy of representations is used to define the internal structure of context elements. With this division, it is possible to use only the light-weight concepts hierarchy for context reasoning while omitting large parts of the ontology that only contain the representations.

Our new context model is based on concepts that have already been proved viable. However, only a simplified version of the context model has been prototyped so far. It is currently used by the pilot service developers in the MUSIC project [3]. They will provide feedback from the implementation phase of the pilot applications. This feedback will then be leveraged to improve and fine-tune our approach. Although we have not yet implemented the complete context management system, we are very confident that it can be done. The first experiences with the new approach are quite promising and it seems to be applicable and sufficient for all our case studies.

However, we are aware that some issues deserve further attention. One issue for example might be the resource limitations of mobile devices that are currently available. Although we keep the ontology as small as possible, utilizing the two-level approach, ontology reasoning at run-time remains a resource consuming task, but is unavoidable to some extent. Furthermore, the classes and data-structures that are generated at design-time can be loaded at run-time, and furthermore, they provide serialization and de-serialization methods. Additionally, they allow interpretation of context information and the conversion between different representations. Thus, we provide a convenient and efficient method for dealing with heterogeneous context information, although these advantages incur additional memory requirements, which could be a serious problem on devices with limited resources. Furthermore, some problems could also arise from the plugging mechanisms used for the ontology. In many cases, extending ontologies through other ontologies also implies ontology merging to some extent, which is a really challenging task.

6   Conclusions and Future Work

In this paper, we have introduced a comprehensive context modeling framework for pervasive computing. We have adopted a three-layer architecture, featuring a conceptual, an exchange and a functional layer. In the conceptual layer, an ontology-based model is used, mainly at design-time, to enable model-driven development of context aware applications. The same context model is also used at run-time for the representation and the exchange of context information in the functional and exchange layers. We have also shown how we extend the state of the art by overcoming some of the limitations of existing approaches and by working towards a comprehensive solution which meets a set of preset requirements. In our on-going and future work, we endeavor to strengthen these results, first by evaluating the potential drawbacks as discussed in Section 5. Furthermore, we will extend our prototype implementation to completely support our approach. The prototype implementation will be used by the pilot application developers in the MUSIC project. Their feedback will then be leveraged to further improve and fine-tune our approach.

Acknowledgments. The authors of this paper would like to thank their partners in the MUSIC-IST project and acknowledge the partial financial support given to this research by the European Union (6th Framework Programme, contract number 35166).

References

1. Chen, H., Finin, T.: An Ontology for a Context Aware Pervasive Computing Environment. In: IJCAI workshop on ontologies and distributed systems, Acapulco MX (August 2003)

2. European EC-FP6 project MADAM (Mobility and ADaptation enAbling Middleware), http://www.intermedia.uio.no/confluence/display/madam
3. European IST-FP6 project MUSIC (Self-adapting applications for Mobile User. In: ubiquitous Computing environments), http://ist-music.eu
4. Gu, T., Wang, X.H., Pung, H.K., Zhang, D.Q.: An Ontology-based Context Model in Intelligent Environments. In: Proceedings of communication Networks and Distributed Systems Modeling and Simulation Conference, San Diego, California, USA, pp. 270–275 (2004)
5. Held, A., Buchholz, S., Schill, A.: Modeling of Context Information for Pervasive Computing Applications. In: Proceedings of the 6th World Multiconference on Systemics, Cybernetics and Informatics (SCI), Orlando (July 2002)
6. Henricksen, K., Indulska, J.: A Software Engineering Framework for Context-Aware Pervasive Computing. In: Second IEEE International Conference on Pervasive Computing and Communications, pp. 77–86. IEEE Computer Society, Los Alamitos (2004)
7. Henricksen, K., Indulska, J.: Developing context-aware pervasive computing applications: Models and approach. Journal of Pervasive and Mobile Computing 2(1), 37–64 (2006)
8. Horrocks, I.: DAML+OIL: a Reason-able Web Ontology Language. In: Chaudhri, A.B., Unland, R., Djeraba, C., Lindner, W. (eds.) EDBT 2002. LNCS, vol. 2490, Springer, Heidelberg (2002)
9. JSON (JavaScript Object Notation), http://www.json.org/
10. OWL Web Ontology Language, http://www.w3.org/TR/owl-features/
11. Hoenle, N., Kaeppeler, U., Nicklas, D., Schwarz, T.: Benefits Of Integrating Meta Data Into A Context Model. In: Proceedings of 2nd IEEE PerCom Workshop on Context Modeling and Reasoning (CoMoRea), Hawaii, March 12 (2005)
12. Preuveneers, D., Van den Bergh, J., Wagelaar, D., Georges, A., Rigole, P., Clerckx, T., Berbers, Y., Coninx, K., Jonckers, V., De Bosschere, K.: Towards an extensible context ontology for ambient intelligence. In: Markopoulos, P., Eggen, B., Aarts, E., Crowley, J.L. (eds.) EUSAI 2004. LNCS, vol. 3295, pp. 148–159. Springer, Heidelberg (2004)
13. Ranganathan, A., Campbell, R.H.: A Middleware for Context-Aware Agents in Ubiquitous Computing Environments. In: Endler, M., Schmidt, D.C. (eds.) Middleware 2003. LNCS, vol. 2672, pp. 143–161. Springer, Heidelberg (2003)
14. Reichle, R., Wagner, M., Khan, M.U., Geihs, K., Valla, M., Fra, C., Paspallis, N., Papadopoulos, G.A.: A Context Query Language for Pervasive Computing Environments. In: Proceedings of 5th IEEE Workshop on Context Modeling and Reasoning (CoMoRea 2008) in conjunction with the 6th IEEE International Conference on Pervasive Computing and Communication (PerCom), pp. 434–440 (2008)
15. Strang, T., Linnhoff-Popien, C., Frank, K.: CoOL - A Context Ontology Language to enable Contextual Interoperability. In: Stefani, J.-B., Demeure, I., Hagimont, D. (eds.) DAIS 2003. LNCS, vol. 2893, pp. 236–247. Springer, Heidelberg (2003)
16. Strang, T., Linnhoff-Popien, C.: A Context Modeling Survey. In: 1st International Workshop on Advanced Context Modeling, Reasoning And Management during UbiComp 2004 (2004)
17. Wang, X.H., Gu, T., Zhang, D.Q., Pung, H.K.: Ontology Based Context Modeling and Reasoning using OWL. In: Proceedings of Workshop on Context Modeling and Reasoning (CoMoRea 2004), Orlando, Florida, USA (March 2004)

Rapid Prototyping of Routing Protocols
with Evolving Tuples

Drew Stovall and Christine Julien

Mobile and Pervasive Computing Group
University of Texas at Austin, Austin TX 78712, USA
{dstovall,c.julien}@mail.utexas.edu

Abstract. Developing software for dynamic pervasive computing networks can be an intimidating prospect. While much research has focused on developing and describing algorithms and protocols for these environments, the process of deploying these technologies is far from mature or streamlined. Furthermore, the heterogeneity of pervasive computing platforms can make the deployment task unapproachable. In this paper, we describe the evolving tuples model and demonstrate how a simple protocol can be quickly and easily developed. Since the evolving tuples infrastructure serves as a unifying base across heterogeneous platforms, the resulting implementation inherently supports cross-platform deployment, a common scenario for pervasive computing.

1   Introduction

Since the introduction of ubiquitous computing [14], much research has studied the coordination and collaboration of devices embedded in environments. As predicted, sensing and computing devices are been developed and deployed, and we are continually developing smaller, better, and longer lasting versions. Our rooms, halls, cars, and even parks will eventually be augmented with a plethora of devices to provide and consume all sorts of information.

However, the heterogeneity of devices can impede the creation and maintenance of applications. The variety of platforms to be supported requires an enormous number of protocol and application implementations. This inevitably leads to environments of incompatible, incomplete, and proprietary systems. Additionally, physical access to the devices to update hardware and software leads to massive efforts, making them impractical if not impossible.

Once deployed, this variety of hardware and software is a stumbling block to successful application maintenance. Small alterations to network protocols or node behaviors can cascade into significant code changes. The work required to recompile and redeploy new features can slow development. To address these issues, we introduce the *evolving tuples model* through which developers can make changes to protocols and applications, run different versions side-by-side, and add features without the cost of traditional redeployment.

In this paper we present the evolving tuples model and examine its use in prototyping behavior for pervasive computing environments. A simple route discovery

R. Meier and S. Terzis (Eds.): DAIS 2008, LNCS 5053, pp. 296–301, 2008.

protocol is described in detail to give a practical example of the work, showing the simplicity of prototyping applications using the evolving tuples model.

2 Background

Originally introduced as part of the Linda [6] system, a *tuple* is simply an ordered list of typed data fields. Tuples are collected in a bag-like data-structure called a *tuple space*. The addition and removal of a tuple from a tuple space is atomic, making it a natural mechanism for buffered communication between parallel processes.

In Linda, a process removing a tuple from the tuple space provides a pattern to which candidate tuples are compared. These patterns take the form of an ordered sequence of *actual* or *formal* values. A tuple that matches a pattern has the same number of fields as the pattern, equal values for any actuals, and the same type as any formals.

While forming a simple mechanism for passing data between processes, this design requires that data producers and consumers are maintained together. Any change in tuple format will require a similar change in the patterns used by existing processes. Since a pervasive computing environment typically consists of devices that are not under the control of a single entity, we must assume that tuple formats and tuple patterns will change independently. In our evolving tuples, as in LighTS [1] and ELights [9], fields are tagged with names, enabling us to decouple the tuple and pattern definitions.

Using tuple space systems, data can be effectively communicated between processes administrated by different organizations. However, behavior must still be specified *a priori* so that an application generating tuples can provide the right data to the consumers. Evolving tuples reduce this level of coupling by directly embedding some of the behavior we expect from nodes into the tuple itself. Specifically, rather then pre-defining the data manipulation recipe to nodes, evolving tuples allow tuple creators to stipulate this behavior at runtime.

3 The Evolving Tuples Model

In this section, we describe the evolving tuples model, consisting of three major components: the tuple format, the evolution process, and the standard deployment. A formal specification of many aspects of this model can be found in [12].

3.1 Evolving Tuple Format

In addition to the name element described in the previous section, the evolving tuples model adds a *formula* element to each tuple field. A field's formula specifies how the value is automatically updated or *evolved*. An evolving tuple is thus a set of tuple fields which comprise a *name*, a *type*, a *value*, and a *formula*.

A field's formula imparts behavior to the tuple as it passes through the network. Previous to the evolving tuples framework, tuple values were either immutable or altered only according to protocols already deployed to network nodes. Though it can be empty or null (⊘), a field's formula is nominally an arithmetic expression. A few simple logical functions are also provided [12].

These formulas can reference the values of peer fields by name. We also allow expressions to access values of a dictionary-like construct called the *evolution context*. The evolution context serves as a lookup table for sensor readings, configuration information, and other context related to the tuple's current location. To access values provided by the evolution context, formulas prefix the value's name with "EC." to differentiate them from references to peer fields.

3.2 Evolution

When a tuple is *evolved*, each of its field's formulas are evaluated, and the existing value is replaced with the result. Since formulas combine both the previous value and the values provided in the evolution context, the new value is viewed as an evolution of the field's value. If a field `count` has a formula of `count + 1`, the current value of the field would be incremented during an evolution.

3.3 Standard Deployment Model

The Evolving Tuples Model includes a reference design that represents the conceptual flow of tuples through each node. While the details of any particular implementation may differ, the externally observable behaviors of each should match those of this reference design. This model contains four components: the *receive* process and three tuple spaces: *inbound*, *outbound*, and *application*. The model is depicted in Fig. 1.

Basic Tuple Exchange. Applications create, initialize, and deposit tuples into the *outbound* tuple space. Since messages require a destination, the reference model requires, at a minimum, a *destination* field. The field's value should be initialized to the address of a neighboring node or to the broadcast address. A system

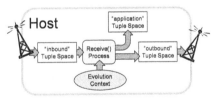

Fig. 1. Flow chart of receive process

process monitors the *outbound* tuple space, removing tuples and transmitting them to their *destinations*. If a transmission fails, the tuple is redeposited into the *outbound* tuple space where it can be selected at a later time for another attempt.

When a host receives a tuple, it is placed in the *inbound* tuple space. The *Receive* process removes and evolves each tuple. If, after evolution, the tuple is destined for this node (via the *destination* field), a copy of the tuple is deposited in the *application* tuple space. If the tuple needs to be forwarded, the *Receive* process deposits a copy of the tuple in the *outbound* tuple space.

Broadcast and Duplicate Elimination. The use of the reserved broadcast address (typically -1) in a tuple's *destination* field designates that the tuple should be sent to every neighboring node. When using this address, the evolving tuples deployment model requires the use of a unique *id* field in the tuple to prevent the host from reprocessing tuples it has seen before. Because the tuple *id* is simply another field in the tuple, it is possible to alter the value of this id using the field's formula. When a tuple's *id* field is changed, it becomes a "new" tuple which will be processed by nodes that have already processed a previous incarnation.

4   A Routing Protocol

In this section we demonstrate how route discovery can be performed using the evolving tuples model. In a network of interconnected nodes, a route from one node to another can be found by flooding the network with a "route discovery message". If each node attaches its own address to a list of addresses in the message, a complete hop-by-hop route will be created. When the target node receives the message, a reply message is broadcast across the network to discover a route back to the source. A more complete discussion of route discovery for pervasive networks can be found in [8].

To build a route discovery tuple, we start with the *source* and *target* fields to hold the addresses of the source node and the target node respectively. No formula is specified since these are constants throughout

Table 1. Route Discovery Tuple

Name	Value	Formula
source	0	∅
target	2	∅
route	0	append(*route*, EC.node)
destination	-1	if (*source* == EC.node, EC.node, -1)
id	0.0	if (EC.node == *target*, newUuid(), *id*)

the process. The *route* field carries the accumulated route to which each intermediate node appends its own address (EC.node). The tuple's *destination* field is used to propagate the tuple to the next node. With one exception, the tuple is always broadcasted and thus the value is usually assigned to the reserved broadcast address -1. When the tuple is being evolved on the source node, we assign the destination to the source's address (*source*) to prevent it from further propagation.

Since nodes discard tuples that contain *id*'s that have already been processed (to avoid duplicates), we must change the tuple's *id* when it arrives at the target before it is re-flooded back to the source. We accomplish this using a simple **if** statement. When the *id* formula is evaluated on the target node, the value is replaced with a new id generated by the **newUuid()** function.

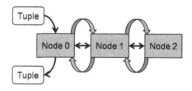

Fig. 2. Example network

The original tuple deposited by the application is shown in Table 1 (field types have been removed for brevity). In this example, the initiating application resides on a node with address 0 and is attempting to discover a route to a node with address 2. If nodes 0, 1, and 2 are interconnected as shown in Fig. 2, the evolution of the tuple's values are shown in Table 2.

When the tuple in Table 1 is deposited into node 0's *outbound* tuple space, it is broadcasted to neighboring nodes (i.e., Node 1). As the tuple moves through this simple network and is evolved, its fields' values change.

When the tuple is evolved on node 1, only the `route` field is changed, and the tuple is broadcasted again. When the tuple is evolved in node 2, both the `route` and `id` fields are updated. By changing the `id` field, we allow the tuple to be re-

Table 2. Tuple Values (after evolution on the node heading the column)

Tuple Field	Node 0	Node 1	Node 2	Node 1	Node 0
id	0.0	0.0	2.0	2.0	2.0
source	0	0	0	0	0
target	2	2	2	2	2
route	0	01	012	0121	01210
destination	-1	-1	-1	-1	0

ceived again by node 1 when node 2 broadcasts it again. Node 1 again updates only the `route` field, and the tuple is passed on to node 0. Here the `destination` field is set to 0 to prevent any further flooding of the tuple.

5   Related Work

Early tuple space designs [6] and implementations [2] for Linda targeted parallel processing environments. Specifically, the atomic insertion and removal operations on tuple spaces relied on locks provided by shared memory. LIME [11] introduced distributed tuple spaces that provided the same atomicity guarantees across a truly global tuple space spanning many devices in mobile ad hoc networks. This adaptation of tuple spaces allows for an abstract representation of the network underlying a pervasive application but requires that tuples be delivered to consumers without interacting with the "lower levels" of the network. We believe that exposing cross-layer information to tuples in our approach allows for more powerful applications at the cost of a more complex representation.

Mobile agent systems also combine behavior with the data that traverses the network. In an effort to provide a wide range of functionality, undue burden is placed on either the developer or the hosts. Systems like Agilla [5] require the developer to understand very low-level programming languages, while systems like TOTA [10] and MARS [3] require hosts to support high-level languages (i.e., Java). We feel that the evolving tuples model strikes a balance between the skills required to use the system and the capabilities required of the network hosts.

While rooted in different technologies, there are a number of efforts to ease development for pervasive computing applications. Visual programming techniques [13] reduce the learning curve for new developers. Other approaches [7] provide abstraction to manage complexities. Still others address recompilation and redeployment head on through more complex hardware [4].

6 Conclusions and Future Work

We have presented the evolving tuples model and shown how it can be used to implement a simple route discovery protocol. As we continue to evaluate the model, we anticipate exposing a variety of other domains to which the evolving tuples model is well suited. We feel that our model has the potential to make developing pervasive computing applications more approachable and fruitful.

Acknowledgments

The authors would like to thank the Center for Excellence in Distributed Global Environments for providing research facilities and the collaborative environment. This research was funded in part by NSF Grant #CNS-0626777 and AFOSR Grant #FA9550-07-1-0157. The views and conclusions herein are those of the authors and do not necessarily reflect the views of the sponsoring agencies.

References

1. Balzarotti, D., Costa, P., Picco, G.P.: The LighTS tuple space framework and its customization for context-aware applications. Int'l Journal on Web Intelligence and Agent Systems (WAIS) 5(2) (2007)
2. Butcher, P.: A behavioural semantics for Linda-2. Software Engineering Journal 6(4), 196–204 (1991)
3. Cabri, G., Leonardi, L., Zambonelli, F.: MARS: A programmable coordination architecture for mobile agents. IEEE Internet Computing 4(4), 26–35 (2000)
4. Dyer, M., Beutel, J., Kalt, T., et al.: Deployment support network - a toolkit for the development of WSNs. In: Langendoen, K.G., Voigt, T. (eds.) EWSN 2007. LNCS, vol. 4373, pp. 195–211. Springer, Heidelberg (2007)
5. Fok, C.-L., Roman, G.-C., Lu, C.: Rapid development and flexible deployment of adaptive wireless sensor network applications. In: Proc. of ICDCS, June 2005, pp. 653–662 (2005)
6. Gelernter, D., Bernstein, A.J.: Distributed communication via global buffer. In: Proc. of PODC, pp. 10–18 (1982)
7. Handorean, R., Payton, J., Julien, C., Roman, G.-C.: Coordination middleware supporting rapid deployment of ad hoc mobile systems. In: Proc. of ICDCS Workshops, May 2003, pp. 362–368 (2003)
8. Johnson, D.B., Maltz, D.A.: Dynamic source routing in ad hoc wireless networks. In: Mobile Computing, vol. 353, Kluwer Academic Publishers, Dordrecht (1996)
9. Julien, C., Roman, G.-C.: EgoSpaces: Facilitating rapid development of context-aware mobile applications. IEEE Trans. on Soft. Eng. 32(5), 281–298 (2006)
10. Mamei, M., Zambonelli, F.: Programming pervasive and mobile computing applications with the TOTA middleware. In: Proc. of PerCom., pp. 263–273 (2004)
11. Murphy, A.L., Picco, G.P., Roman, G.-C.: LIME: A coordination middleware supporting mobility of hosts and agents. ACM TOSEM 15(3), 279–328 (2006)
12. Stovall, D., Julien, C.: Resource discovery with evolving tuples. In: Proc. of ESSPE, September 2007, pp. 1–10 (2007)
13. Weis, T., Knoll, M., Ulbrich, A., Muhl, G., Brandle, A.: Rapid prototyping for pervasive applications. IEEE Pervasive Computing 6(2), 76–84 (2007)
14. Weiser, M.: The computer for the 21st century. Scientific American (September 1991)

Author Index

Lecture Notes in Computer Science

Sublibrary 3: Information Systems and Application, incl. Internet/Web and HCI

For information about Vols. 1– 4606
please contact your bookseller or Springer

Vol. 4813: I. Oakley, S.A. Brewster (Eds.), Haptic and Audio Interaction Design. XIV, 145 pages. 2007.

Vol. 4810: H.H.-S. Ip, O.C. Au, H. Leung, M.-T. Sun, W.-Y. Ma, S.-M. Hu (Eds.), Advances in Multimedia Information Processing – PCM 2007. XXI, 834 pages. 2007.

Vol. 4809: M.K. Denko, C.-s. Shih, K.-C. Li, S.-L. Tsao, Q.-A. Zeng, S.H. Park, Y.-B. Ko, S.-H. Hung, J.-H. Park (Eds.), Emerging Directions in Embedded and Ubiquitous Computing. XXXV, 823 pages. 2007.

Vol. 4808: T.-W. Kuo, E. Sha, M. Guo, L.T. Yang, Z. Shao (Eds.), Embedded and Ubiquitous Computing. XXI, 769 pages. 2007.

Vol. 4806: R. Meersman, Z. Tari, P. Herrero (Eds.), On the Move to Meaningful Internet Systems 2007: OTM 2007 Workshops, Part II. XXXIV, 611 pages. 2007.

Vol. 4805: R. Meersman, Z. Tari, P. Herrero (Eds.), On the Move to Meaningful Internet Systems 2007: OTM 2007 Workshops, Part I. XXXIV, 757 pages. 2007.

Vol. 4804: R. Meersman, Z. Tari (Eds.), On the Move to Meaningful Internet Systems 2007: CoopIS, DOA, ODBASE, GADA, and IS, Part II. XXIX, 683 pages. 2007.

Vol. 4803: R. Meersman, Z. Tari (Eds.), On the Move to Meaningful Internet Systems 2007: CoopIS, DOA, ODBASE, GADA, and IS, Part I. XXIX, 1173 pages. 2007.

Vol. 4802: J.-L. Hainaut, E.A. Rundensteiner, M. Kirchberg, M. Bertolotto, M. Brochhausen, Y.-P.P. Chen, S.S.-S. Cherfi, M. Doerr, H. Han, S. Hartmann, J. Parsons, G. Poels, C. Rolland, J. Trujillo, E. Yu, E. Zimányie (Eds.), Advances in Conceptual Modeling – Foundations and Applications. XIX, 420 pages. 2007.

Vol. 4801: C. Parent, K.-D. Schewe, V.C. Storey, B. Thalheim (Eds.), Conceptual Modeling - ER 2007. XVI, 616 pages. 2007.

Vol. 4797: M. Arenas, M.I. Schwartzbach (Eds.), Database Programming Languages. VIII, 261 pages. 2007.

Vol. 4796: M. Lew, N. Sebe, T.S. Huang, E.M. Bakker (Eds.), Human–Computer Interaction. X, 157 pages. 2007.

Vol. 4794: B. Schiele, A.K. Dey, H. Gellersen, B. de Ruyter, M. Tscheligi, R. Wichert, E. Aarts, A. Buchmann (Eds.), Ambient Intelligence. XV, 375 pages. 2007.

Vol. 4777: S. Bhalla (Ed.), Databases in Networked Information Systems. X, 329 pages. 2007.

Vol. 4761: R. Obermaisser, Y. Nah, P. Puschner, F.J. Rammig (Eds.), Software Technologies for Embedded and Ubiquitous Systems. XIV, 563 pages. 2007.

Vol. 4747: S. Džeroski, J. Struyf (Eds.), Knowledge Discovery in Inductive Databases. X, 301 pages. 2007.

Vol. 4744: Y. de Kort, W. IJsselsteijn, C. Midden, B. Eggen, B.J. Fogg (Eds.), Persuasive Technology. XIV, 316 pages. 2007.

Vol. 4740: L. Ma, M. Rauterberg, R. Nakatsu (Eds.), Entertainment Computing – ICEC 2007. XXX, 480 pages. 2007.

Vol. 4730: C. Peters, P. Clough, F.C. Gey, J. Karlgren, B. Magnini, D.W. Oard, M. de Rijke, M. Stempfhuber (Eds.), Evaluation of Multilingual and Multi-modal Information Retrieval. XXIV, 998 pages. 2007.

Vol. 4723: M. R. Berthold, J. Shawe-Taylor, N. Lavrač (Eds.), Advances in Intelligent Data Analysis VII. XIV, 380 pages. 2007.

Vol. 4721: W. Jonker, M. Petković (Eds.), Secure Data Management. X, 213 pages. 2007.

Vol. 4718: J. Hightower, B. Schiele, T. Strang (Eds.), Location- and Context-Awareness. X, 297 pages. 2007.

Vol. 4717: J. Krumm, G.D. Abowd, A. Seneviratne, T. Strang (Eds.), UbiComp 2007: Ubiquitous Computing. XIX, 520 pages. 2007.

Vol. 4715: J.M. Haake, S.F. Ochoa, A. Cechich (Eds.), Groupware: Design, Implementation, and Use. XIII, 355 pages. 2007.

Vol. 4714: G. Alonso, P. Dadam, M. Rosemann (Eds.), Business Process Management. XIII, 418 pages. 2007.

Vol. 4704: D. Barbosa, A. Bonifati, Z. Bellahsène, E. Hunt, R. Unland (Eds.), Database and XML Technologies. X, 141 pages. 2007.

Vol. 4690: Y. Ioannidis, B. Novikov, B. Rachev (Eds.), Advances in Databases and Information Systems. XIII, 377 pages. 2007.

Vol. 4675: L. Kovács, N. Fuhr, C. Meghini (Eds.), Research and Advanced Technology for Digital Libraries. XVII, 585 pages. 2007.

Vol. 4674: Y. Luo (Ed.), Cooperative Design, Visualization, and Engineering. XIII, 431 pages. 2007.

Vol. 4663: C. Baranauskas, P. Palanque, J. Abascal, S.D.J. Barbosa (Eds.), Human-Computer Interaction – INTERACT 2007, Part II. XXXIII, 735 pages. 2007.

Vol. 4662: C. Baranauskas, P. Palanque, J. Abascal, S.D.J. Barbosa (Eds.), Human-Computer Interaction – INTERACT 2007, Part I. XXXIII, 637 pages. 2007.

Vol. 4658: T. Enokido, L. Barolli, M. Takizawa (Eds.), Network-Based Information Systems. XIII, 544 pages. 2007.

Vol. 4656: M.A. Wimmer, J. Scholl, Å. Grönlund (Eds.), Electronic Government. XIV, 450 pages. 2007.

Vol. 4655: G. Psaila, R. Wagner (Eds.), E-Commerce and Web Technologies. VII, 229 pages. 2007.

Vol. 4654: I.-Y. Song, J. Eder, T.M. Nguyen (Eds.), Data Warehousing and Knowledge Discovery. XVI, 482 pages. 2007.

Vol. 4653: R. Wagner, N. Revell, G. Pernul (Eds.), Database and Expert Systems Applications. XXII, 907 pages. 2007.

Vol. 4636: G. Antoniou, U. Aßmann, C. Baroglio, S. Decker, N. Henze, P.-L. Patranjan, R. Tolksdorf (Eds.), Reasoning Web. IX, 345 pages. 2007.

Vol. 4611: J. Indulska, J. Ma, L.T. Yang, T. Ungerer, J. Cao (Eds.), Ubiquitous Intelligence and Computing. XXIII, 1257 pages. 2007.

Vol. 4607: L. Baresi, P. Fraternali, G.-J. Houben (Eds.), Web Engineering. XVI, 576 pages. 2007.